The BOOK of GAMES

The BOOK of GAMES

STRATEGY, TACTICS & HISTORY

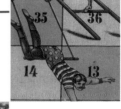

JACK BOTERMANS

STERLING

New York / London
www.sterlingpublishing.com

Translated from the Spanish by Edgar Loy Fankbonner

STERLING and the distinctive Sterling logo are registered trademarks of
Sterling Publishing Co., Inc.

Library of Congress Cataloging-in-Publication Data

Botermans, Jack.
    The book of games : strategy, tactics & history / Jack Botermans ;
[translated from the Spanish by Edgar Loy Fankbonner].
        p. cm.
    Includes index.
    ISBN-13: 978-1-4027-4221-7
    ISBN-10: 1-4027-4221-5
  1. Indoor games. 2. Board games. I. Title.

GV1229.B53 2007
794—dc22

                                                            2007010173

            10 9 8 7 6 5 4 3 2 1

        Published in 2008 by Sterling Publishing Co., Inc.
            387 Park Avenue South, New York, NY 10016
        Copyright © 2006 by Bookman International B.V., Bussum,
    The Netherlands and Jack Botermans, Amsterdam, The Netherlands
English translation and compilation copyright: © 2007 by Sterling Publishing Co., Inc.
        Distributed in Canada by Sterling Publishing Co., Inc.
            c/o Canadian Manda Group, 165 Dufferin Street
                Toronto, Ontario, Canada M6K 3H6
        Distributed in the United Kingdom by GMC Distribution Services,
    Castle Place, 166 High Street, Lewes, East Sussex, England BN7 1XU
        Distributed in Australia by Capricorn Link (Australia) Pty. Ltd.
            P.O. Box 704, Windsor, NSW 2756, Australia

            Book design and layout by Alexis Siroc

                    Printed in China
                  All rights reserved

        Sterling ISBN-13: 978-1-4027-4221-7
            ISBN-10: 1-4027-4221-5

        For information about custom editions, special sales, premium
        and corporate purchases, please contact Sterling Special Sales
    Department at 800-805-5489 or specialsales@sterlingpublishing.com.

Contents

◆ ◆ ◆

BACKGAMMON 7

SNAKES AND LADDERS 19
Ups and Downs 31

SALTA 33

WHITE HORSE 45

WINDMILL 55

DOMINOES 69
Bergen 77
Fools 79
Forty-Two 81
Solo Dominoes 95
Tien Gow 99
Chinese Dominoes 105

SHOGI 107
Shogi: Part 2 117
Shogi: Part 3 129

GOOSE 141

ENGLISH CHECKERS 153

SENAT 163

POKER 173
Dice Poker 175

PACHISI 187

ALQUERQUE 199

CHINESE CHESS 211
Chinese Chess: Part 2 225

ASSAULT 235

HORSE RACES 251

JUNGLE 265

AGON 277

DUODECIM SCRIPTA 287

GO 299
Go: Part 2 315
Go: Part 3 325

DICE GAMES 335
Bidou 337

MANCALA 349
Wari 351

SIEGE OF PARIS 365

POLISH CHECKERS 379

THE CHIMERA OF GOLD 393

MIKADO 403

RENJU 415

JINX 425

SUN AND ANCHOR 435

HEX 449

SHUT THE BOX 461

CHINESE CHECKERS 475

SAXON HNEFATAFL 485

PLANKS 497
 Planks: Part 2 505

HASAMI SHOGI 513
 Hasami Shogi: Version 2 523

OTHELLO® 527

CRAPS 541

TABULA 557

SHASHKI AND BASHNE:
CHECKERS IN RUSSIA 569
 Bashne 571

RITHMOMACHIA 585
 Rithmomachia: Part 2 601
 Rithmomachia: Part 3 609

MING MANG 619

TANGRAM 627

YUT 641

DABLOT PREJJESNE 655

TSUNG SHAP 667

COAN KI 677

NARDSHIR 689

MASTERMIND® 699

THE ROYAL GAME
OF UR 711

THAAYAM 723

INDEX 733

◆ ◆ ◆

Backgammon
History of the Game

◆ ◆ ◆

For some experts in the history of games, the earliest precedent for this exciting game of strategy can be found in Egypt, some 5,000 years ago. Backgammon apparently evolved from Senat (see page 163). An ancient game board very closely resembling a backgammon board was found in the tomb of the pharaoh Tutankhamen (fourteenth century B.C.E.). Backgammon is thought to be a direct descendant from Tabula, (see page 557) an ancient Roman game, and is similar to *Nardshir* or "nard," a game that was played with much fervor in the Arab world during the Middle Ages (see page 689).

Tric-Trac Players at an Inn by Adriaan van Ostade *(Teylers Museum, Haarlem).*

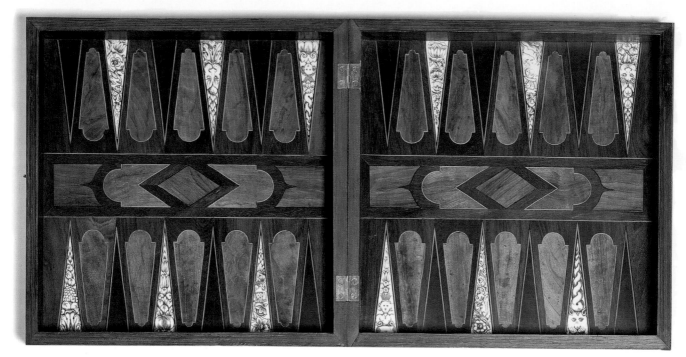

A *Tric-Trac* board made in Germany at the end of eighteenth century *(Reynaud Collection, Limoges)*.

There is also evidence of backgammon's possible Chinese origin. The *Hun Tsun Sii*, written during the Sung dynasty (960 to 1279 C.E.), claims that the game was invented in western India. According to this text, backgammon arrived in China during the Wei dynasty (220 to 265 C.E.), and was very popular between 479 and 1000 C.E. In Japan the game was given the name *sunokoro*. There it was played in secret because Emperor Jito (690 to 697 C.E.) had banned the game.

Its Meaning and Evolution

Setting aside the debate about its origins, it is clear that the invention of backgammon was profoundly influenced by the yearly cycle and the calendar. The twenty-four dots on the game board correspond to the hours of the day, while the twelve months of the year are represented by a dozen dots on each side of the board; the thirty chips symbolize the days of the month.

Assuming that the evolution of backgammon began with nard, the arrival of this game in Europe must be attributed to the Arabs, during the occupa-tion of Sicily by Muslim forces. From Sicily it traveled to Italy and Spain. As with the modern-day version, early backgammon used a board with twenty-four dots and conferred fifteen chips to each player. Two dice were used for scoring.

At the start of the seventeenth century, a new and more attractive version of the game appeared. The artistic quality and the detail of the board and the shakers for the dice improved, to suit the tastes of the upper classes. The game enjoyed great popularity and quickly spread throughout Europe, where it was given different names. In England it was given the name *backgammon*; in Scotland it was shortened to *gammon*; in France it was called *tric-trac*; and in Germany it was given the name *Puff*. In Spain it was known as *tables reales*, and in Italy as *tavole reale*, or "royal boards."

In 1743, the English games expert Edmund Hoyle authored the modern-day rules for backgammon. Its popularity has grown since the start of the twentieth century to become one of the most well-loved board games in the world.

Playing Backgammon

Backgammon is one of the most widespread board games played in the world. It owes its popularity not only to its entertainment value but to the multiple strategic options it has to offer. The object of backgammon is to be first to get all one's pieces off the board. The rules and techniques for playing backgammon are not particularly complicated, and anyone can easily attain a level of skill in the game. However, unlike other games in which chance or skill plays a greater role, backgammon requires a great deal of planning and analysis. Constant practice and the experience it yields are what make a genuine expert player.

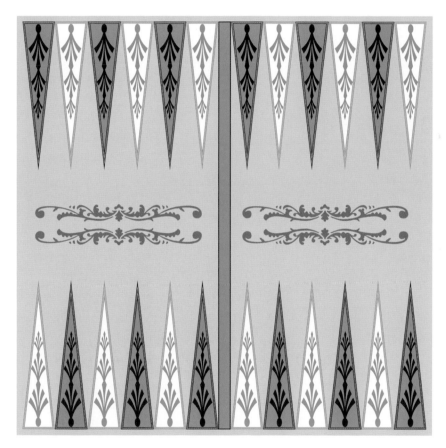

The game of backgammon requires fifteen black chips and fifteen white chips.
The movement of the chips on the board is determined by a throw of the dice.

Players	Special materials
2	game board
	30 chips
Average duration	2 or 4 dice
45 minutes	1 doubling cube
Category	
strategy	

Rules of the Game:
Preliminaries

The backgammon board usually takes the form of the inside of a hinged box, which opens at the middle. The vertical bar divides the board in two, separating the two inner fields from the two outer fields. The board is made up of twenty-four elongated triangles of two alternating colors, six for each of the four fields of the board. The triangles are called *points* or *pips*. Each player has an outer field and an inner field or "home" field. The six points in the inner field are numbered 1 through 6, and the points in the outer field are numbered 7 through 12. Two of the twenty-four points (those numbered 7) are called *bar points*. The game pieces on points numbered 1 (which have two pieces each) are called *runners*. White's inner field is on the right-hand side of the board, and his outer field is on the left. Black's two game fields face one another in the top half of the board.

To begin a game, each player places fifteen pieces on his or her points, as shown in Diagram A. Players roll the dice to determine who will make the first move, the player with the higher roll opens. The opening player does not roll again but must use the number already rolled. At each subsequent turn, each player must roll the dice again.

Rolling the Dice

When rolling the dice, it is important to remember that they should always be rolled on the right-hand side of the board and that one side of each die must always be touching the board. If, for example, one of the dice falls on the left-hand side of the board, on top of a game piece, or on the center bar, the player must roll both dice again and the previous roll does not count.

Once the player has finished moving his pieces according to the points on the dice, he must remove the dice from the board. After doing so, it becomes

DIAGRAM A:
Backgammon board with game pieces in the opening position.

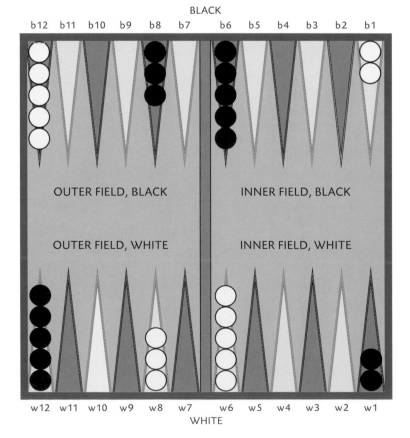

the other player's turn, and the first player may not take back the previous move.

If a player rolls the dice before his opponent has finished his turn, this throw will not be valid and will have to be repeated.

Blocking

You can block a point, to keep your opponent from using it, by placing two or more pieces on it (Diagram B).

A player cannot put any pieces on a point blocked by his opponent. If a player manages to block a series of six contiguous points, it's called a *prime* or *series of points*. It is impossible to move any of the pieces behind a prime an opponent has set up, because the points on the dice are counted separately, and a single die cannot yield more than six points. Only when a player breaks his own prime can his opponent once again move his blocked pieces.

DIAGRAM B:
To block a point, place two or more pieces on it.

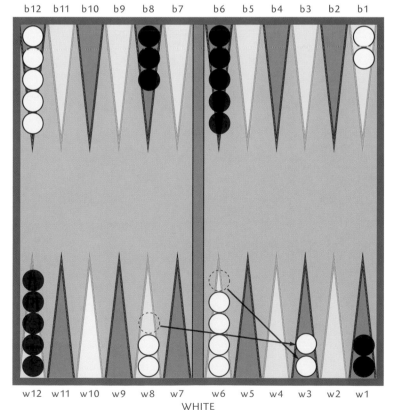

Moving the Pieces

In backgammon, each color moves in a different direction. The black pieces move clockwise, while the white pieces move counterclockwise. The pieces move in the following sequence: enemy's inner field, enemy's outer field, one's own outer field, and one's own inner field. Pieces may never move backward. The pieces constantly intermingle and are hit and sent to the bar frequently. The roll of the dice decides how many points a piece will move. Each player can move two pieces at a time, one per die. Although it does not matter which piece he moves first, each move should end either:

- on an empty point,
- on a point where there are only pieces of the same player's color,
- or on a point where there is at most one enemy piece.

Instead of moving two pieces, a player can also opt to move a single piece, adding up the points on the two dice. In this case, the points on each die count as a single move. For instance, if a player rolls a two and a four, he can make one two-point move and then a four-point move, or first a four-point and then a two-point move. But the dice never count as a six roll. This becomes important when you encounter a block, which is off-limits (Diagram C).

Rolling a Double

When a player rolls a double, it is as though he had rolled four times that number of points. In this case, every combination is valid. For example, if White rolls double-threes, he has the following options:

- Move one piece three points (Diagram D1)
- Move two pieces six points each (Diagram D2)
- Move four pieces three points each (Diagram E1)
- Move one piece nine points and another piece three points (Diagram E2)

Sometimes it is impossible to use quadruple the value rolled. If so, you should use as many of the points as you can. In any event, after rolling doubles, you do not get to roll again.

DIAGRAM C:
Black rolls the dice and gets a two and a four. He first moves his runner four points and then two, putting the piece on point number w7. He wouldn't be able to move the two and then the four, because then it would land in a block, which is not allowed. If point w5 had also been blocked by the opponent, Black would not have been able to move his runner with the points he rolled.

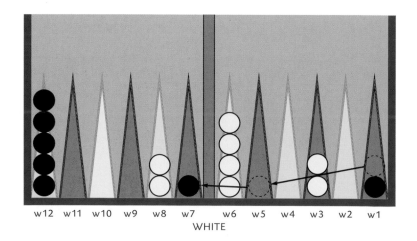

w12 w11 w10 w9 w8 w7 w6 w5 w4 w3 w2 w1
WHITE

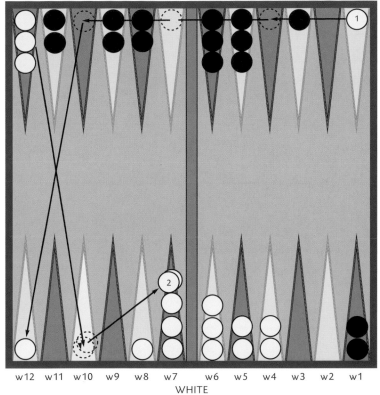

DIAGRAM D1–D2

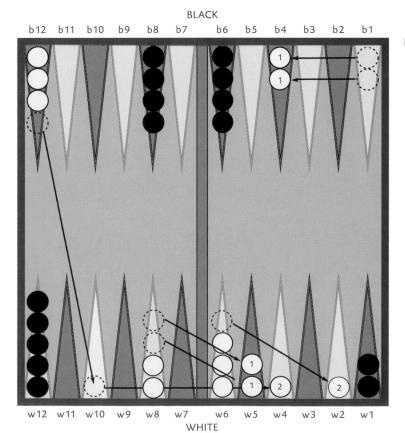

DIAGRAM E1–E2

In the early twentieth century, you could usually find game boxes with a checkerboard and chessboard on the outside and a backgammon board on the inside.

Tric-Trac Players, sketch by Adriaan van Ostade (1640).

Capturing Pieces

A piece that sits by itself in a point is called a *blot*, and is considered "uncovered" and quite vulnerable. If a player moves a piece onto a point where there is an opponent's blot, or touches that piece as he moves his own, the blot is considered hit and must be placed on the center bar. Hitting enemy pieces isn't mandatory except when there is no other possible move. Hit pieces must be returned to the game in the inner field of the player who loses them before the player can move other pieces. In theory, the piece can be placed on any of the six points of the inner field, but in practice, the player's options are usually limited, because the piece must be placed on an open point that has not been blocked by the opponent. In compensation, a new piece being added to the board can land on a point on which the enemy has a blot and capture it.

For example, if Black has blocked points 4 and 5, White will have to roll a one, a two, a three, or a six in order to put his piece back on the board. Let's say he rolls a one and a four. He places the piece on point 1 and moves the other piece four points over. If instead he rolls a four and a five, he would not be able to put his piece on the board and would have to pass, since every piece on the bar must be returned to the board before the player can move any other pieces (Diagram F).

DIAGRAM F:
The hit piece on the bar can be entered at any unblocked point in the opponent's inner field.

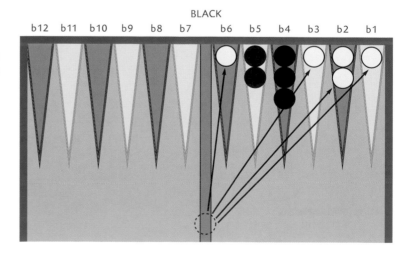

Bearing Off

Once all a player's pieces reach the inner field or "home," the player can take them off the board one by one, called *bearing off*. As explained, the points in the inner field are numbered one through six, and pieces are removed from the board according to the points the player rolls. If, for instance, a player rolls a one and a four, he removes a piece from point 1 and a piece from point 4. If there is no piece on point 1, he removes the piece from point 4 and moves another piece in the inner field one point over, if possible. When bearing off, double rolls also count twice. Thus, if a player rolls double-twos and there are four pieces on point 2, he can remove them all at once.

It is not mandatory to bear off pieces—in fact, sometimes it is not even advisable. For example, removing one piece may leave another piece uncovered, and if your opponent captures the uncovered piece, it will be taken off the board but will stay on the bar and have to be re-entered into play before you can move any other pieces. This is especially complicated if your opponent has had the opportunity to block all the points in his inner field. If no open point is left in that field, there is no choice but to wait until one opens up. Thus, it is more sensible to move a piece in the inner field than to leave a piece uncovered (Diagram G).

Pieces can be removed from the board even if their position does not match the number rolled, as long as the number on the dice is higher. For example, if you roll a six and there are no pieces on points 6 or 5, you can remove a piece from point 4.

Backgammon player in a Dutch etching from 1845.

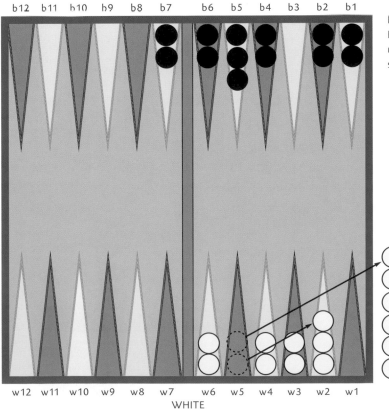

BLACK

b12 b11 b10 b9 b8 b7 b6 b5 b4 b3 b2 b1

w12 w11 w10 w9 w8 w7 w6 w5 w4 w3 w2 w1

WHITE

DIAGRAM G:
How to avoid having an uncovered piece in the final stage of the game.

The Doubling Cube

The die for doubling wagers is used to increase the suspense of the game because it doubles all point values. The doubling cube is usually larger than the others. Instead of black dots, it has numerals on each of its six sides—2, 4, 8, 16, 32, and 64. At the start of the game, the cube is placed on the center of the board with the number 64 faceup (the 64 is worth either 64 or 0 points). After the first roll, and for the rest of the game (even in the final play), each player can double the bet. Of course, if a player feels that he has sufficient advantage, he may propose doubling the wager by placing the betting die on the table with the number 2 on top. However, he must do this before rolling the dice.

When a player proposes to double the wager, his opponent can exercise his right of refusal. If he does, however, he concedes the game, though he loses only his original bet. However, if he decides to accept the offer, he puts the betting die by his die on the table. Now this player is the only one who can raise the bet—from 2 to 4. The other player then has the right to refuse the double.

If a player, for example, raises the bet to twice the original wager and the other player accepts (but without raising again from 2 to 4), the first player will get twice the original wager if he wins. If he wins with a gammon, he will receive four times the original bet, since gammon always doubles

STRATEGY

Players should avoid overloading their points, especially in their inner fields. There is no need to have more than three pieces in any given point. The player will likely benefit from distributing his or her pieces throughout several other points.

DIAGRAM H:
White has scored a backgammon, since he was able to remove all his pieces from the board while his opponent still had one in White's inner field.

The cube for doubling wagers has numerals on its side instead of dots.

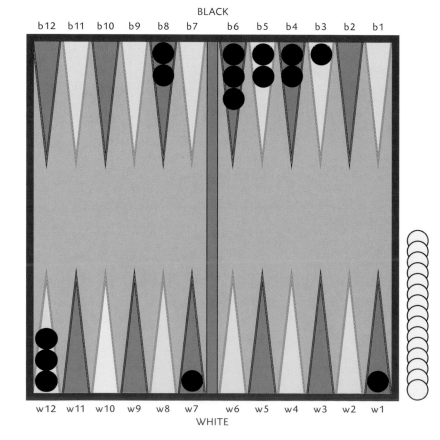

Interior of an Inn by David Teniers. His paintings originally had a moralistic overtone, but they have since come to be valued for the realism with which they immortalized everyday life in the seventeenth century.

the wager. If he wins with a backgammon, the other player will have to pay six times the original wager, because a backgammon entitles the player to three times the number on the betting die. As you can see, the wagers increase considerably if the players raise the bet several times and then one of them wins with a backgammon.

Automatic Raising

The dice are rolled for the first time to determine which player makes the first move. If, at this point, the two players get the same results, the bet is automatically raised. The betting die is placed on the board with the number 2 faceup, and the players roll the dice again to decide which player will open. The first player to raise should do so with the number 4.

The Winner

The first player to take all his or her chips off the board wins—this is called a *single-point game*. If, however, the player is able to get all the pieces off the board before the opponent has removed even one of his, one of two things can happen:

- A *gammon*: when there are no pieces in the opponent's inner field, the final bet is doubled.
- A *backgammon*: when one or more pieces remain in the opponent's inner field or on the center bar.

A game of backgammon in the eighteenth century *(Engraving by Nicolas Lancret).*

Snakes and Ladders
History of the Game

◆ ◆ ◆

Snakes and ladders is an ancient game whose source appears to be *moksha patamu*, the mystical race game from India used to complement religious instruction. (In the United States, it is more commonly known as Chutes and Ladders®, and is produced by Milton Bradley®, a division of Hasbro, Inc.) However, as is the case with many other board games, its origins could go back to an even more remote point in history, as evidence from ancient civilizations, Egypt for example, seems to show.

Snakes and ladders depicts the eternal struggle between good and evil. Good acts are rewarded with success, while bad acts lead inexorably to misfortune.

The oldest snakes and ladders game boards in existence are circular in shape.

Reincarnation

In the Hindu religion, good and evil (*pap and punya*) exist side by side in all human beings. The soul must make a long journey to reach heaven through a series of reincarnations. The more good acts a person undertakes, the shorter the journey; bad acts, on the other hand, always make the journey longer. It is even possible for a human being to be reincarnated as a lower life form such as an animal. The ladders that appear in snakes and ladders symbolize good acts; harmful acts are represented by serpents (or chutes). The serpent was chosen deliberately for its symbolism of life after death. The serpent changes its skin every year, and therefore appears to be reborn over and over again.

The object of the game is to reach the last box on the board. The first player to reach it wins the game. In a metaphorical sense, that player has attained *nirvana*.

The Board

The first snakes and ladders boards were circular. This shape imbues the game with mythical significance ascribed to the spiral by many cultures. In many civilizations, the circle symbolizes time and eternity, and similarly, the spiral represents immortality. Some researchers believe that the Greek spiral known as the *paestum* also bears a relationship to spiral-shaped games.

The spiral-shaped serpent appears often in the game board, perhaps because the serpent is the most ancient symbol of the cosmic life force. It shows up in images and legends from the most diverse cultures, as we know from the popular traditions from India and various central European countries. In ancient Egypt, these same philosophical and spiritual themes were found in games similar in form to that of snakes and ladders. The game boards for playing dogs and jackals, found in tombs of the ninth and thirtieth dynasties, are a prime example.

It is possible to find round playing boards for snakes and ladders at some of the most important museums throughout the world, such as the Victoria and Albert Museum in London or the British Museum, which houses one of the most ancient examples known. This specimen originated in Egypt and dates from the year 2800 B.C.E. It comprises a limestone board with a serpent in the form of a spiral.

In the modern-day game, the religious significance has almost completely disappeared, and the ancient Hindu rules have been adapted to current beliefs. In 1893, the Englishman R.H. Harte introduced a square board, and henceforth, this format has not changed, and neither have the number of squares, which are always 100. With the shift away from the original symbolism of the game, the images that appear on the board are varied and display a spirit of creativity more in keeping with game play.

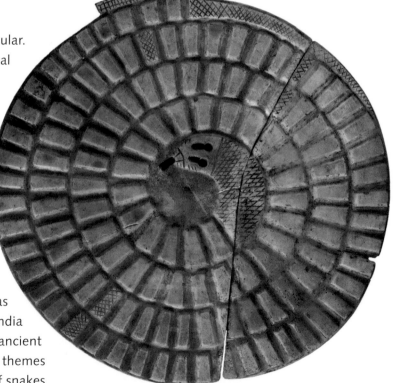

A curious example of a board in the form of a serpent. The board's surface has lost the colors and symbols of the original.

Playing Snakes and Ladders

Snakes and ladders is an entertaining game with a mystical and spiritual basis. Further, it is an ideal social game, since it can be played with as many people as you wish, regardless of age. Chance determines the winner. This is probably the reason the game is so popular among children. The objective is to reach *nirvana*, that is, heaven. But before arriving there, it is necessary to carry out a sufficient number of noble actions and to pass through several lives (incarnations). Noble actions are symbolized on the board by means of ladders. If a player takes the "wrong path," the snake forces him to retrace his steps. For him, the path to heaven becomes harder and longer as he is reincarnated as a being more distant from nirvana, possibly as an animal.

Board and pawns for the game snakes and ladders. Each player uses a pawn of a different color.

Players	**Special materials**
indeterminate	a special game board
	1 game piece or pawn per player
Average duration	1 die
45 minutes	
Category	
classic; racing	

Rules:
Preliminaries

Each player chooses a piece or a pawn (both are valid for this game) of his or her preferred color. It is important that everyone choose a piece of a different color. Players throw the die by turns clockwise. The one who gets the highest roll starts the game.

Movement of the Pieces

Before being able to introduce a piece on the board, a player must roll a six. Once this occurs, the die is thrown again. Only then can the player put the piece in play on the square that corresponds to the value of the throw. Each piece moves in accordance with the number thrown on the die, and in the order indicated by the board, which goes from 1 to 100 (Diagram A).

The Squares

When a player puts his piece on a square with a snakehead, he has to slide the piece downward along the length of the snake's body, to the square where the snake's tail is resting. Snakes always force the pieces to go backwards.

DIAGRAM A:

In this game, three players take part: Orange, Green, and Blue. The player with the pink piece throws the die, but does not roll a six. The turn goes to the player with the blue piece. He is more fortunate and throws a six. He throws again, and this time gets a five. The blue player places his piece on square 5. The next turn goes to Green, who gets a three, and therefore cannot put his piece in play. Pink does not get a six on his second turn either. But Blue gets a four and goes forward, his piece advancing to square 9. For the time being, he is the only player with pieces in play on the board.

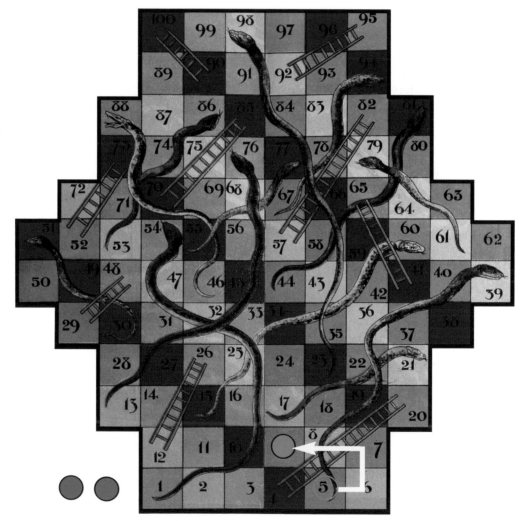

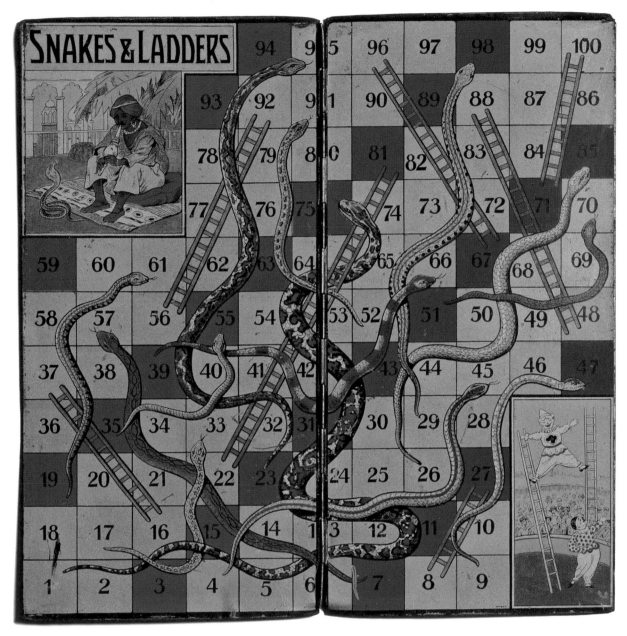

At the beginning of the nineteenth century, snakes and ladders was as popular in Europe as it was in parts of the East. This board was made in England circa 1920.

In contrast, the ladders allow for one to advance a great deal. If a piece reaches a square where the first rung of a ladder is seen, he will be able to "climb" the ladder into the square whose image had the last rung (Diagram B).

Throwing the Die

If, during his turn, a player rolls a six, he has to move the piece as though he had obtained any other result, even climbing a ladder or descending a snake if the play requires it. Immediately after, the player must throw the die a second time.

Capturing the Pieces

When a piece is placed on a square occupied by another player's piece, it captures that piece, which must then be removed from the board. The player to whom the piece belongs must roll a six before being allowed to place it back on the board (Diagram C).

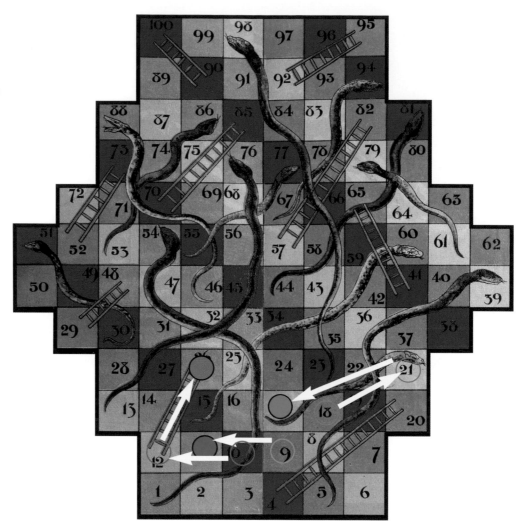

The Goal

To proclaim yourself the winner, you must reach square 100. But it is also necessary to determine who is in second, third, or last place. Therefore, play does not finish when the winner reaches square 100 but continues until the last player reaches the final series of squares.

The Winner

The player who first reaches square 100 wins. But the piece can enter this square only by an exact throw of the die. If the value of the die exceeds the number of existing squares, the remaining steps have to be taken backwards. This forward and backward movement continues until the die allows an exact move into square 100 (Diagram D).

Sins and Virtues

In snakes and ladders, each square with a snakehead symbolizes a sin, or misdeed, and each square where a ladder begins symbolizes a virtue. Stated more concretely, they are as follows:

- Sins: disobedience, impurity, vanity, theft, lying, drunkenness, usury, homicide, wrath, rebellion, greed, and desire
- Virtues: trust, kindness, self-confidence, goodness, love, knowledge, mercy, and asceticism

It is easier to travel the path of evil than that of good. In this version, there are 12 sins, as opposed to only 8 virtues.

Moksha Patamu

Moksha Patamu was an ancient ritual game practiced in India from which was born (most likely in England) the game snakes and ladders. Moksha Patamu was used as a tool for enhancing meditation. The aim was to reach *nirvana*, after advancing by means of the ladders that symbolize virtue, or else to go backwards on account of sin, represented by the form of a serpent. The Hindu religion teaches that during his entire existence, humanity is accompanied by and confronted with good and evil. Which path each individual chooses is of supreme importance. But that decision depends not only on his own criterion, but also on fate (the luck of the draw). Virtue shortens the path to infinite perfection, while sin makes the path more arduous.

VARIATION

Snakes and ladders can also be played as a series of rounds. Players must agree in advance on the number of rounds to be played. After the game, it is noted how long the first player required to reach number 100. It is also necessary to note the arrival time of the other players. After the first round, the winner has a time of zero minutes. Number 2 in line would have two minutes (if he reached the end two minutes after the first player) and number 3 has five minutes. After the second round, the times are added up. Once the agreed-upon number of games have been played, the definitive winner is calculated. Victory goes to the player with the least amount of time.

DIAGRAM C:
Blue moves his piece to square 80. He rolls a five and proceeds to square 85. Green moves his piece four squares, from 74 to 78. Now it is Orange's turn: he throws a two and places his piece on square 70, where a ladder begins. Ascending the ladder, he reaches square 85 and captures Blue from his opponent. Blue must roll a six before being able to recommence play.

DIAGRAM D:
The last phase of the game. Blue occupies square 97, Orange is on square 95, and Green is on square 93. It is Blue's turn. He needs a three to win but rolls a four; thus, he can only "graze" square 100 because he is forced to go back to square 99. Now it is Green's turn. He rolls a three and places his piece on a square where a ladder begins: this ladder takes him directly to square 100, where green proclaims himself victorious. Orange gets a three and places his piece on a square with a snakehead. His piece must go back to square 23.

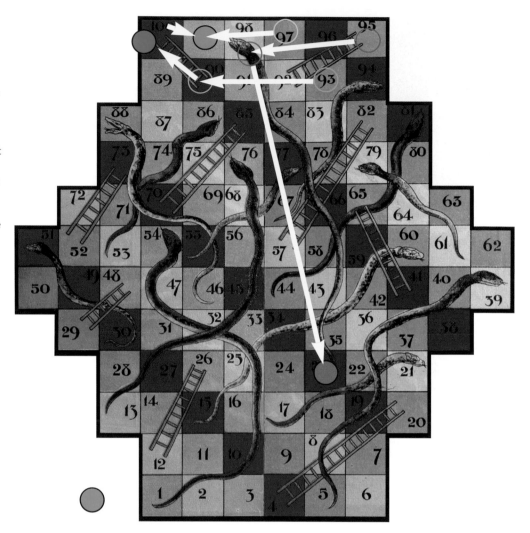

Ups and Downs

"Ups and downs" is a variation on snakes and ladders (see page 31). Similar to the way a person has a good side and a bad side, so too does he live through better and worse moments. Ups and downs originated at the beginning of the twentieth century. On the board is depicted a fantastical circus in which are found an acrobat, a trapeze artist, a clown, and many performing animals. The board is divided into 120 squares, and the object is to reach square 120. In addition to the board, you need one piece for each player and two dice. As in snakes and ladders, as many people can play as desired.

Each player moves his piece according to the number rolled on the dice. The pieces move in the numerical order of the boxes. Both dice are used until a player reaches box 108. From that point on, players may roll only one die at a time. If a player moves backward to a box lower than 108, he can

---

VARIATION

To speed up play, one can utilize two dice instead of one. If so, it is necessary to obtain doubles—the same points from the two dice— to be able to introduce a piece into play.

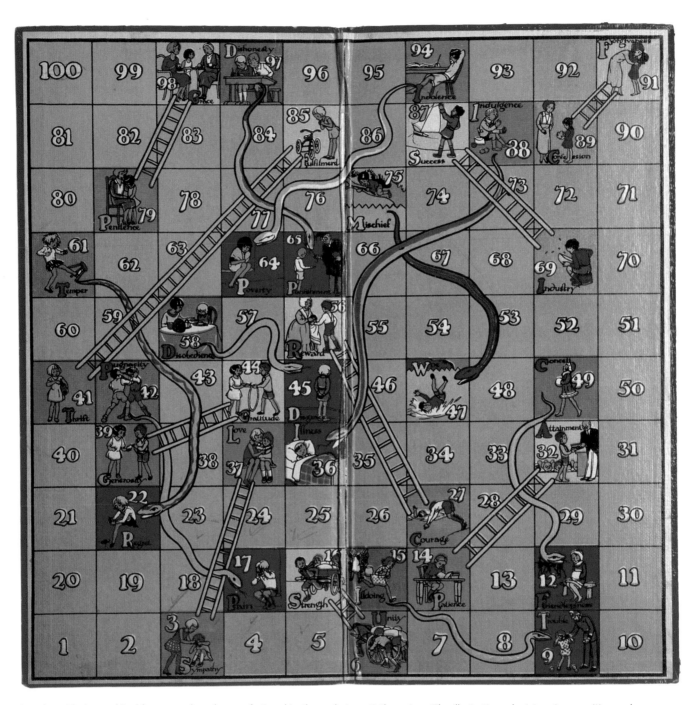

American Chutes and Ladders game board, manufactured in the early twentieth century. The illustrations depict various positive and negative acts, whose function in the game is to allow the players to move forward or backward.

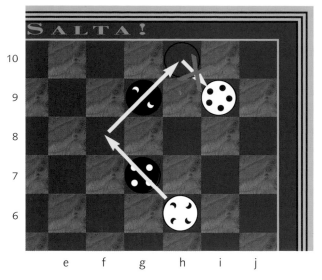

DIAGRAM C:
From h6, White has to jump over his opponent's piece at g7. He jumps into f8 and has to make another jump into h10. He cannot jump backward over the piece on i9, so the turn passes to Black.

Object

The object of the game is to take the opponent's opening positions with the matching pieces from your own side. For example, the piece with a single white star from a1 is placed in j10, which was the starting position of the piece with the single black star. The final goal of the piece with two white moons that begins the game in square d2 is g9 (where the piece with two black moons was originally placed). When the two players have met their goals, the final position of the pieces will be the same as their opening positions, only black and white will have traded places.

A Salta board from around 1930. Note that the placement of the pieces is incorrect—the pieces are on the light squares instead of the dark.

The Winner

The winner is the first player to occupy his opponent's starting position. As soon as one of the players achieves this, the other player may not move any more pieces. Players count the number of moves separating the other player from his final goal. For example, if he has ten moves to go, he gets negative ten points and the winner gets positive ten points. Once the games have been played, the players add up their negative and positive points to determine the final winner (Diagram D).

Sarah Bernhardt, the celebrated French stage actress, plays a Salta match against the German Konrad Büttgenbach, 1901.

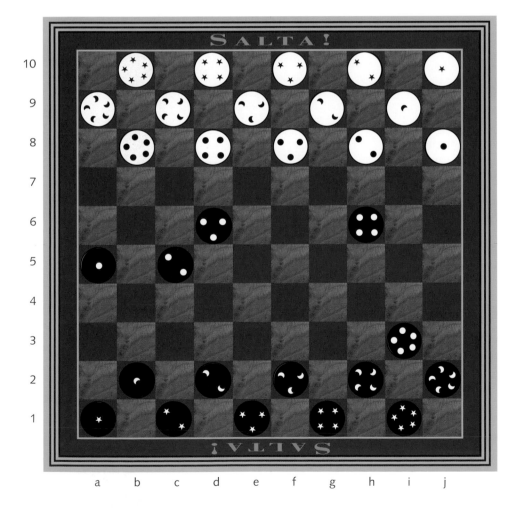

DIAGRAM D:
White wins. Black still needs ten more moves to finish, so Black gets ten points taken off, while White earns ten points.

The First Match

The rules of the game have now been explained, and now it's time to start playing. To help orient new players, herein are presented some interesting game scenarios the beginner will undoubtedly face during his or her first match. Being a good Salta player requires a lot of experience, which comes only through practice. The more experience you gain, the quicker and more exciting the game will be.

Opening Moves

1 As mentioned, Black makes the first move. He moves his piece from h8 to g7. White decides to make the same opening move, and takes his piece from c3 to d4. With these two opening moves, the players open up the space they need to move their star pieces forward (Diagram 1).

2 The first moves having been made, Black must make his next move, for which he jumps from j10 to d4, passing through h8 and f6. An excellent move! The star pieces not only have to cross the longest distance but must also move before any of the other pieces. It is therefore a good idea for them to cross the board first. With the move he has just made, Black has jumped over two of his own pieces and one of White's. The star piece becomes the first to reach the other half of the board, which brings it close to its final position. The white pieces have a *salta*, which means they are required to jump over the piece that has just arrived at d4. This must be done with the piece on square e3, which jumps to c5 (Diagram 2).

3 After a few more moves, it is Black's turn, and now he has a Salta. He has two options: a single jump from e7 to g5, or a multiple jump from g7 to c3, passing through e5. Black chooses the latter option, which puts his two-sun piece in its final position. Further, this move considerably limits the white pieces' mobility.

It is now White's turn, and he moves his piece from g3 to f4.

Black would prefer to move more of his star pieces, but the piece at e7 has a *salta*, so it must jump to e3, passing through g5. White still has not moved any star pieces, so he decides to focus his efforts on this goal, moving the piece from b2 into a3 (Diagram 3).

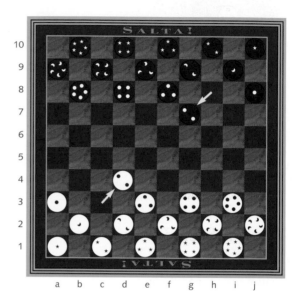

DIAGRAM 1:
Opening moves.

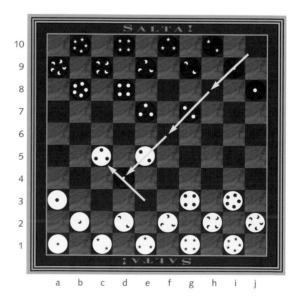

DIAGRAM 2:
Black jumps over his own pieces as well as his opponent's, forcing White to make a *Salta*.

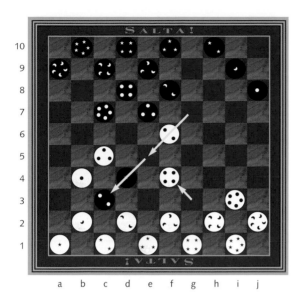

DIAGRAM 3:
Black jumps with his piece from g7 into c3, passing through e5, to land in its final position.

Taking a Step Back

4 At this stage of play, Black takes a step back, from h4 to g5. This move is a strategic one. With it, in his next turn Black hopes to make a multiple jump with the two-star piece, taking this piece to its final position in a single move. Lucky for Black, White has not caught on to his strategy, busy as he is moving his own two-star piece to its final position, from g9 to h10. Black can carry out his

plan and jump with his two-star piece from g5 to c1, passing through e3 (Diagram 4). White decides to move his three-star piece and accelerates the game by jumping over his own pieces, from e1 to e5, passing through g3. The danger of jumping over other pieces to get to the other side quickly is that the jumping piece can be detoured from its path. In his next few moves, Black tries to use the same bridge he has before, moving his piece from f6 to g5, hoping to arrive at e3 in his next move.

Getting the Opponent Out of a Corner

5 White would like to free up the corners where he has to put his star, sun, or moon pieces. Moving the piece from g7 to f8, he tries to force Black to move his piece out of square i9 (Diagram 5). It is a clever idea, but Black has several options and instead decides to move the piece from g5 into e3. White keeps trying.

White insists on forcing the two-star piece out of its corner. Realizing that Black still has several options (he can also jump with the piece on e9), White moves the three-moon piece from f8 to g9.

Thus, Black has only one *salta* left and must do what White wants him to do: move his piece from i9 to g7.

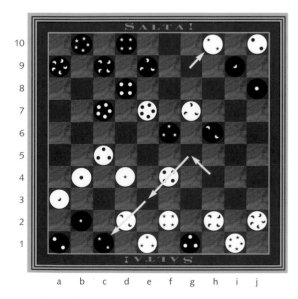

DIAGRAM 4:
What is gained by taking a step backward.

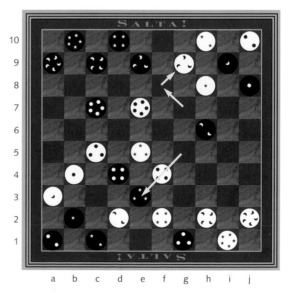

DIAGRAM 5:
How to get the opponent out of a corner.

If a Player Forgets to Make a Salta

The game continues on its course. The two players are busy trying to take their respective pieces to the opposite side of the board until Black realizes that he has a *salta*, and more importantly, that he already had the *salta* in his previous turn. What's done is done, and in any event, White hasn't noticed. This is not deceit or trickery, for it is typical at the start for one of the players to forget to make a *salta* and for the other player not to notice. Black now moves the piece that has the *salta*.

„SALTA ist ein äusserst ingeniöses Spiel, aus dem man mit Leichtigkeit Taktik und Strategie erlernen kann.'' (Worte Sr. M des Deutschen Kaisers am 8. April 1900.)

Schachmeister WALBRODT.

Saltameister BARTMANN.

Wettschachmeister Dr. EMANUEL LASKER.

Dr. HAUSER Präsident d. Berliner Salta-Gesellschaft

Das erste Salta-Turnier wurde um den Preis von 1000 Mark auf einem Salta-Prunkspiel gespielt, welches aus massivem Gold und 5500 Brillanten im Werthe von 120 000 Mark von den Hofjuwelieren Sr. M. des Kaisers hergestellt und diesen auf der Welt-Ausstellung in Paris mit der goldenen Medaille prämiirt wurde.

In the image at left is the chess champion Carl Walbrodt, the Salta champion Bartmann, and at right, then-world chess champion Dr. Emanuel Lasker. The man at the center of the table is the president of the Players' Association in Berlin, a Dr. Hauser. The headboard reproduces a phrase by the German Kaiser, who stated, "Salta is a very clever game which allows one to learn strategies and tactics very easily."

Star Pieces, Final Positions

Because the star pieces must be taken to the final row on the board, it is wise to try to place them in their final positions as early as possible. If you wait too long, this can pose complications later on, because the more pieces that near the final position, the more they obstruct one another. Therefore, it is advisable to take the star pieces to the other side of the board as soon as possible, followed by the moons, and finally the suns.

Final Steps

The game is nearing its end. The Black star pieces have reached their final positions, and most other pieces have reached the opposite side of the board. Because the black pieces moved more effectively at the start of the game, they have a slight advantage over White's. Now the decisive factor is to place all the pieces in their corresponding positions. White and Black both try to do this as efficiently as possible. At this stage, it makes for interesting strategy to force out of their squares the pieces that have already made it to the other side.

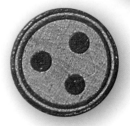

Quick Moves

6 White must take his five-star piece two squares' distance, from square d8 to the final position, b10 (Diagram 6). In b8 is a white three-sun piece, four spaces away from its final position. These plays can be made in six moves. But there is a quicker way: first, White must move the piece from b8 to c9. Black responds by moving a piece from i3 to j2. Now White can jump over the three-sun piece and put his five-star piece in the corresponding position (from d8 to b10), and the star piece is now three squares away from its final position. This saves White one move, which can be decisive for a victory.

The Resolution

7 Black has already been able to place all his star and moon pieces in their final position, White is still busy trying to put his star pieces in their corresponding positions. Everything here suggests that

White is going to lose. The mistake White made was that, although he already moved out his star pieces before the stars and suns, he did not make sure that they crossed the board diagonally. Thus, White ended up in a situation where the pieces with the most stars are in the place of the pieces with the fewest stars, and vice versa. Since his pieces are now on the opposite side of the board from where they should be, the moon pieces obstruct one another considerably, and even the suns must be moved back. This is a common error that can seriously complicate the final stage of a first game. It seems clear that Black is going to win. By the time the black pieces reach their final places, White will still need to make another three moves. Thus, White loses three points and Black wins three (Diagram 7).

The Players Run Out of Salta

The closer the end of the game approaches, the lower are the odds of getting a *salta*. The two players are busy putting all their pieces into their final positions in as little time as they can.

Often, a good number of moves are still needed to reach the final goal. In fact, at this stage, one needn't worry about the opponent so much, so moves are made more fluidly and more quickly.

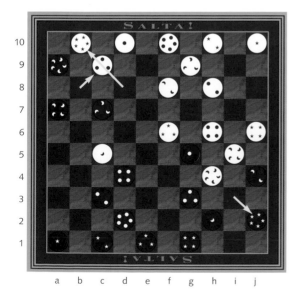

DIAGRAM 6:
White has figured out a way to put his pieces in their places and to save himself a move.

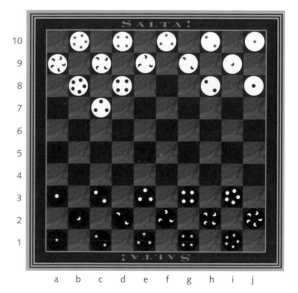

DIAGRAM 7:
Final position: Black has won, being the first to reach the final position.

Solo Salta

There is an entertaining variation on Salta for people who want to play solo. In Germany, Salta became so popular that there was even a magazine dedicated to its play, which in 1902 published a problem for solo Salta and offered substantial cash prizes for those who could solve it. The object was to move the pieces to their final positions in the fewest moves possible. The grand prize was 500 marks, second place was 200 marks, and an additional 300 marks were to be divided among the first twenty-five readers to submit their solo Salta game to the magazine, which published the games alongside with the winners' names.

I. Preisaufgabe
über
1000 Mark
auf dem
Salta-Solo-Spiel.

Die Redaction der Deutschen Salta-Zeitung Hamburg setzt für die 27 zuerst eintreffenden kürzesten Lösungen des nachstehenden Salta-Solo-Problems 1000 Mark als Preise aus:

SALTA-SOLO.

Bedingungen: Das vorstehende Problem soll gelöst und mit Buchstaben-Angabe der einzelnen Züge (laut Spielregel) der Redaction der Deutschen Salta-Zeitung bis spätestens 31. December 1901 zugesandt werden.

Die genaue Adresse des Absenders ist erforderlich.

Diejenigen 27 ersten Einsender, welche das obige Problem mit den wenigsten Zügen lösen, erhalten folgende Preise:

1. Preis dem 1. Einsender der kürzesten Lösung						**Mark**	500
2. " " 2. " " " "						"	200
3. " " 3. " " " "						"	100
4. " " 4. " " " "						"	50
5. " " 5. " " " "						"	25
6. " " 6. " " " "						"	15
7. " " 7. " " " "						"	10
8.—27. " den 20 folgend. Einsendern der kürzesten Lösung						"	100
27 Preise.						Summa **Mark**	1000

The prizes for the 1902 solo Salta competition, as published in a German specialty magazine devoted to the game. The great number of people who submitted their entries is a testament to the game's popularity in the early twentieth century.

White Horse
History of the Game

◆ ◆ ◆

The game of White Horse was designed around 1800 by the Viennese art merchant H.F. Müller. It spread throughout Europe in the early nineteenth century. It became especially popular in Germany, where it was known as *Schimmel*. In Holland it was widely known as *Klok en Hamerspel*, and in Britain there were many groups devoted to playing the version *Clock and Hammer*. Games of chance enjoyed great popularity at this time, and Clock and Hammer was occasionally played as a betting game, which may have helped its spread. Today it is played at family gatherings, a setting in which the betting is confined to chips or other small objects.

A Dutch game of White Horse from 1920. The cards are lithographs with magnificent illustrations.

Early nineteenth-century scene with games played at a British inn.

A Popular Family Game

When the game became popular at family gatherings, beautiful game boxes began to appear on the market. The cards depicting various subjects are the most important part of the game and were carefully and colorfully designed.

Besides the eight dice, the game box often included a dice cup, a small bag filled with coins, a betting can, and a small gavel for the auctioneer. The box was divided into compartments so each element of the game was kept in a special place. In the nineteenth century, it must have been quite an event when, in a bourgeois family, the mother or father pulled the white horse out of its box and the whole family sat down to spend an afternoon playing the game. Families at the time tended to be large, which was fortunate because White Horse is a social game in the true sense of the word, requiring six or more people to play. It is a highly varied game and features different stages, each of which has its own rules. The concentration and ingenuity of the players are put to the test at each stage. Of course, chance also plays an important role. This is one reason the game was so well liked by aficionados of games of chance. Originally the game was not played at home, but at inns or pubs in towns and cities. As you can imagine, at such locations you would have found a much simpler version of the game than the luxurious boxed sets people used to play at home.

Playing White Horse

White Horse is a highly varied game of dice requiring a great deal of concentration, which makes for a very engrossing game. It is an ideal game for social gatherings, given that it requires six to ten players. The game unfolds in three phases. Each phase tests the ability of the play-ers, and each has its own rules. Once you learn White Horse's myriad rules, it becomes easier than it at first seems, and even a child can take part in a game with little trouble. The winner is the player who ends up with all the pieces.

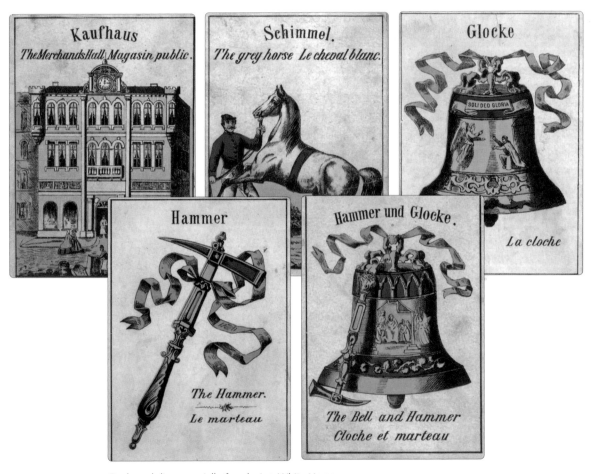

Cards and dice especially for playing White Horse.

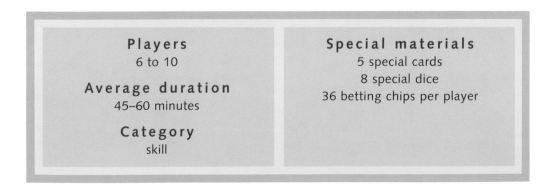

Players	Special materials
6 to 10	5 special cards
	8 special dice
Average duration	36 betting chips per player
45–60 minutes	
Category	
skill	

Rules:
Preliminaries

White Horse is played with five cards on which are pictured a white horse, an inn, a hammer, a bell, and a bell and hammer. There are eight dice, with five blank sides each. On the sixth side, six of the dice have a different number of dots, from one to six; the two remaining dice have a hammer and a bell, respectively. Each player receives thirty-six betting chips. The player who rolls the highest number becomes the auctioneer and banker. He places four of his chips in the bank and invites the other players to do the same.

Phase One

This phase involves an auction for the five cards. After agreeing on the value of each card, the banker sells them to the highest bidder. When all the cards have been auctioned off, the chips collected from the players are deposited in the bank. The auctioneer strikes the table to indicate that phase one, the auction, has ended.

Phase Two

This phase calls for the dice. Players take turns rolling them all at once. The player with the white horse card begins. The value of the roll depends not only on the number of points rolled, but also on the card the roller is holding. Each player can win or lose chips according to the following rules:

- If a player rolls the dice and gets only points (remember, he might also roll blanks) and therefore rolls neither the hammer nor the bell, the banker must give him as many chips as the number he rolled. If, besides the points (and any blanks), the player rolls a bell or hammer, the banker gives to the player who holds that picture card the number of chips corresponding to the value of the dice.

- If a player rolls points, a bell, and a hammer, players who hold those picture cards receive chips from the bank. A roll in which all the dice are blank is called a "white horse." If the player with the white horse card rolls all blanks, all the other players must give him one chip apiece. If a player other than the one holding the white horse card rolls all blanks, he must pay one chip to the player with the white horse card.

The cards in White Horse are often decorated with wonderful illustrations, but there are also simpler versions.

- If a player rolls a bell or a hammer and all the other dice are blank, the owner of the matching card must pay one chip to the player with the white horse card. If a player rolls blanks, a bell, and a hammer, players who hold those picture cards must pay a chip to the player with the white horse card.

Phase two ends when the banker must pay out more chips than are left in the bank.

Phase Three

In this stage, the inn opens its doors. These are the rules:

- If a player rolls only points, he must pay the innkeeper the difference between the number of points he rolled and the number of blanks, if the number of points is greater than the number of blanks. If he rolls fewer points than there are chips in the bank, the difference in chips comes from the bank.

Example 1

There are seven chips left in the bank. The player whose turn it is rolls ten points, so he pays the innkeeper three chips.

Example 2

There are seven chips left in the bank. This time the player rolls four points, so he gets three chips from the bank. The game continues with the four remaining chips.

If a player rolls points and a hammer or bell, the player with the matching picture card must pay the innkeeper the difference between the number of points and the reserve in the bank.

If the player rolls points as well as a hammer or a bell, then the players holding the bell, the hammer, and the hammer and bell cards must pay the innkeeper.

The End of the Game

There are three chips left in the bank. The player whose turn it is rolls six points and a bell, so the player with the bell card must pay the innkeeper the difference. If someone rolls a white horse, then the player with that card pays the innkeeper one chip.

The round ends when a player has as many points as there are chips in the bank, or when he rolls a combination of one, two, three, four, five, six, and two blanks. In either case he gets all the chips in the bank. The winner of this round becomes the auctioneer and will play the banker in the next round.

The Winner

The winner is the player who ends up with all the chips.

The game of White Horse was presented in beautiful boxes. Depending on the price, it often came with a bag of betting chips, a little gavel, and betting cups.

The First Match

The following pages reproduce a typical game of White Horse. Among other things, it will show the first rounds of phases one and two, where the players roll the dice. Every game is different, but the following examples can be very helpful to a player tackling this multifaceted game for the first time.

Preliminaries

1 The game described here features eight players. Each player rolls the dice, and the player who rolls the most points becomes the auctioneer and banker. Every player receives thirty-six chips (or thirty-six of whatever object is used for betting—beans, matches, pennies, etc.) and places four of these in the bank. The bank's total initial balance is therefore thirty-two chips. The auctioneer places the cards in front of him on the table. The minimum value of each card is five chips. The game may now begin (Diagram 1).

The Auction

2 The auctioneer picks up the bell card and shouts, "Who will be the highest bidder?" The Player 1 shouts, "Five chips!" The Player 4 also appears interested and shouts, "Six chips!" No other player wishes to bid, so the auctioneer calls out, "Do I hear more than six chips? Going once, going twice, sold!" Each card is sold in this fashion, one by one, to the highest bidder. When the auction is over, the five players have each acquired one card and reveal the balance of their accounts to the others (Diagram 2).

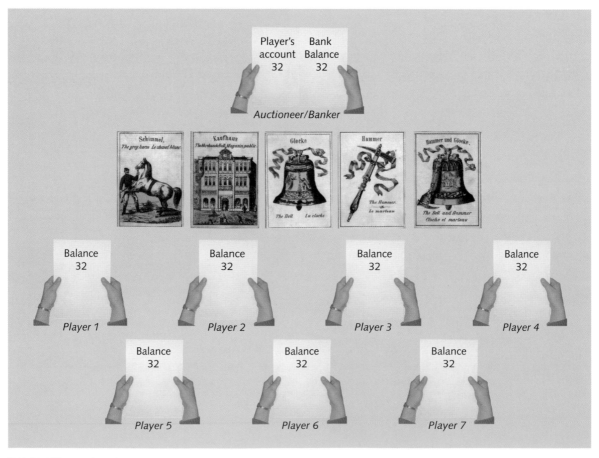

DIAGRAM 1: Before the auction

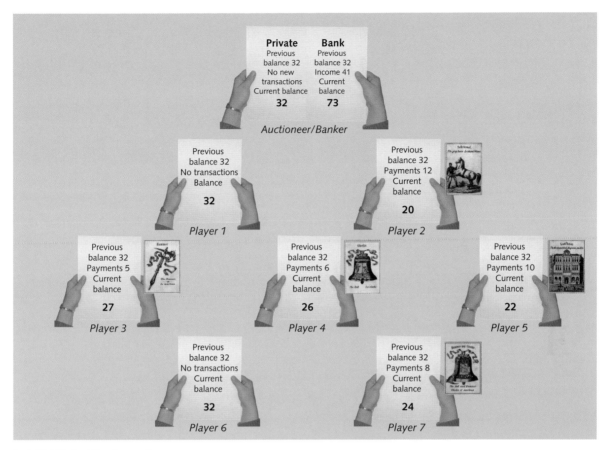

DIAGRAM 2: After the auction.

Phase Two

3 Players now move from the auction hall to the salon. The Player 2 begins because he has the white horse card. He rolls all the dice at once, and besides getting six blank dice, gets six points. The banker pays out six chips. Now it is Player 3's turn, and he rolls a bell, a hammer, and four points. Because he already holds the hammer card, the bank pays him four chips. Players holding the bell card (Player 4) and the hammer and bell card (Player 7) are also paid four chips each by the bank. Player 4 rolls a white horse and therefore must pay a chip to Player 2, who holds the white horse card. Player 5 rolls a hammer and all-blank dice and therefore pays a chip to Player 3, who holds the hammer card. Player 6 rolls no points—only blanks, a hammer, and a bell. Player 2 (who holds the white horse card) is grateful because, thanks to Player 6, the players holding the hammer card, the bell card, and the hammer and bell card must each pay him one chip.

Player 7 rolls many points—fifteen altogether. This means the bank must pay him fifteen chips (Diagram 3). The banker, too, rolls high: he gets twelve points and therefore twelve chips from the bank. Player 1 rolls blank dice and a hammer. Player 3, who holds the hammer card, must surrender one of his chips to the player holding the white horse card.

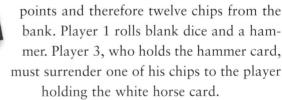

The eight dice for White Horse are more easily thrown with a tumbler.

	Player 2	Player 3	Player 4	Player 5	Player 6	Player 7	Banker	Player 1	Bank
Initial balance	20	27	26	22	32	24	32	32	73
After 1st roll	+6								−6
Current balance	26								67
After 2nd roll		+4	+4			+4			−12
Current balance		31	30			28			55
After 3rd roll	+1		−1						
Current balance	27		29						
After 4th roll		+1		−1					
Current balance		32		21					
After 5th roll	+3	−1				−1			
Current balance	30	31				27			
After 6th roll						+15			−15
Current balance						42			40
After 7th roll							+12		−12
Current balance							44		28
After 8th roll	+1	−1							
Current balance	31	30							
Total score	**31**	**30**	**29**	**21**	**32**	**42**	**44**	**32**	**28**

DIAGRAM 3:
First round of dice in phase two.

After the first round of phase two, the bank's balance has dropped forty-five chips—from seventy-three to twenty-eight. The banker has the most chips of any player, and now it is time to clear up any doubts as to whether his success is the result of financial skills or simply luck. Player 7 is hot on the banker's heels. Player 5 has the fewest chips but holds a card that can earn him many more during phase three. It is worth noting that Players 1 and 6, who hold no cards, have made little progress during this phase. The player holding the white horse, however, has managed to increase his balance considerably. Player 7 had the good fortune of earning fifteen points in a single roll of the dice, which doesn't happen very often.

Cassell's Book of Sports and Pastimes, published in 1911, is among the first to describe the game White Horse. It is illustrated with the etching above.

End of Phase Two

The length of this round depends largely on the number of points each player rolls. The bank will undoubtedly go broke sooner or later. In the example below, that moment comes when Player 7 wins eight chips and the bank has only seven. Once this happens, it is time to exit phase two and count up the balances for phase three.

Phase Three

4 It is time to continue the game with Player 7's roll at the inn. Player 7 rolled eight points as well as some blank dice. The bank does not have enough chips to pay out. Player 7 must therefore surrender the difference (one chip) to the innkeeper, Player 5. Now it's the banker's turn. He rolls 10 points and some blanks. This makes the innkeeper happy, because without any effort on his part, he has earned three chips from the banker's private balance (the difference between ten and seven). Player 1 rolls two points and a hammer. That number is lower than the balance remaining in the bank. If he had rolled higher, then Player 3, who holds the hammer card, would have had to pay the innkeeper the difference between Player 2's points and the number of chips in the bank. In this case, however, the bank must pay two chips to Player 1. The round continues with only five chips in the bank. Player 2 rolls a white horse and must turn over one of his chips to the innkeeper, Player 5. Player 3 is next, and he too rolls a white horse. The innkeeper gets another chip. Player 4 gets six points, a bell, and a hammer. He has earned more points than there are chips in the bank, so the players holding the bell, hammer and bell, and hammer cards must each turn over one of their chips (six minus five) to the innkeeper. Player 5 rolls eight points. Once again, the number on the dice is greater than the number of chips in the bank. Eight minus five is three, and Player 5 (the innkeeper) may not turn over three chips to himself, so he must give them to the bank. Player 6 rolls a white horse, forcing the player with the white horse card (Player 2) to hand over one of his chips to the innkeeper (Diagram 4).

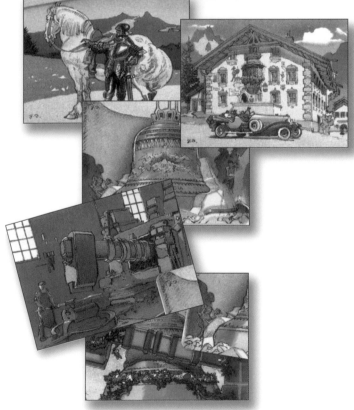

German game of White Horse, circa 1920.

	Player 2	Player 3	Player 4	Player 5	Player 6	Player 7	Banker	Player 1	Bank
Initial balance	31	36	41	21	34	42	44	32	7
After 1st roll				+1		−1			
Current balance				22		41			
After 2nd roll				+3			−3		
Current balance				25			41		
After 3rd roll								+2	−2
Current balance								34	5
After 4th roll	−1			+1					
Current balance	30			26					
After 5th roll		−1		+1					
Current balance		35		27					
After 6th roll		−1	−1	+3		−1			
Current balance		34	40	30		40			
After 7th roll				−3					+3
Current balance				27					8
After 8th roll		−1		+1					
Current balance		33		28					
Total score	**30**	**33**	**40**	**28**	**34**	**40**	**41**	**34**	**8**

DIAGRAM 4:
The first round of dice in phase three.

STRATEGY

A player's chances improve if he holds a card. In phase two, the most important card is the white horse, whereas in phase three the inn card can be very advantageous, all of which underscores the importance of the opening auction. Bidding for the white horse or inn cards makes for more interesting play.

After the first round of dice in phase three, Players 1 and 6, who hold no cards, have seen little change in their positions. The innkeeper (Player 5) has played an important role in this phase, and has managed to increase his winnings significantly thanks to the other players' contributions.

The End of the Round

The first round is over when one of the players gets exactly eight points. The unlikely roll of 1, 2, 3, 4, 5, and 6 points, and two blank dice, can also bring this round to an end.

A real auctioneer's hammer makes the game complete.

Windmill
History of the Game

◆ ◆ ◆

The arms of this windmill have been spinning...since the year 2000 B.C.E., the earliest known time when the windmill game is known to have existed. An engraved stone board was discovered in the cemetery of a small Irish village, revealing that this is one of the oldest games known to man.

Another trace of the game was found in Egypt on one of the slates in the ceiling of the temple of Kurna. Engraved on it were seven game boards, among them the windmill game. The games were probably engraved by the workers who built the temple in around 1400 B.C.E. The evidence of this game's ancient history is extensive. Many countries have discovered traces of the game, which predates the Common Era. It remains a very popular game in many parts of the world.

The image above depicts a game played in the court of the Spanish king, Alfonso X, who ruled in the thirteenth century C.E. This illustration is taken from Alfonso X's *Book of Chess, Dice, and Slates* (1283). The original is in the library of El Escorial (Madrid).

Rules

Most game boards consist of concentric squares subdivided by lines through the middle. Some variations also have diagonal lines running from the corners of these squares. It doesn't matter what the board looks like. Its purpose is to allow two players to face one another for a quarter of an hour. Players agree ahead of time on how many matches will be played. The following pages describe the most well-known variations on windmill: Three Men's Morris, Six Men's Morris, and Nine Men's Morris. The "men" refer to the game pieces, not the number of players. In each of these games the goal is to form a windmill—always in a straight line up and down or across the board, but never diagonally.

Three Men's Morris

The name Three Men's Morris derives from the Old English word *merels*, whose Latin root is the word *merellus*, meaning game piece or playing chip. Its French name, *Jeu de Marelle*, also shares this etymology. The ancient Egyptians enjoyed playing this game, and it was also known in China around 500 B.C.E. In Spain, the game is known as *tres en raya*, or "Three in a Row." The board comprises a grid of nine squares created by the intersection of the two lines that traverse the squares. One of the players has white pieces and the other has black. They take turns placing one of their chips on the game board. The winner is the first to get a "windmill" (Diagram A).

A Variation on Three Men's Morris

The board that was found engraved in the temple of Kurna in Egypt is somewhat more complicated. It, too, has nine boxes, but with the addition of diagonal lines (Diagram B).

The rules are different as well. In this variation of classic Three Men's Morris, each player gets three pieces. These are placed on the board one by one. Then the players take turns moving one of their pieces to a new, empty square on the board. The game is over when one of them gets three pieces in a row, winning the game. The player who makes the first move has a better chance of winning, if he plays skillfully. Players roll the dice before beginning the game to determine who will go first.

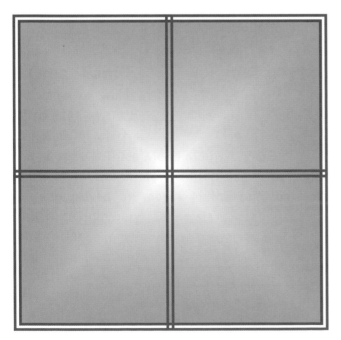

DIAGRAM A:
A Three Men's Morris game board.

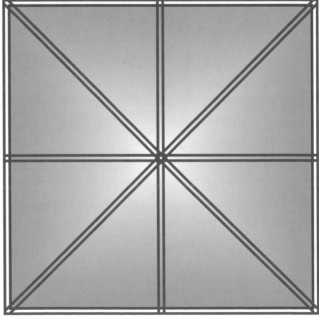

DIAGRAM B:
Kurna game board.

Six Men's Morris

This game was very popular during the Middle Ages, but in Europe it was seldom played after the sixteenth century. In West Africa a variation on this game still exists, the only difference being that it adds a new way of defeating one's adversary. In Six Men's Morris, one player gets six white pieces and the other gets six black pieces. The board has more squares than a Three Men's Morris board (Diagram C).

Six Men's Morris also has more rules. Players take turns placing their chips in empty squares on the board. They try to form a windmill on the sides of the inner and outer square. As soon as one player forms a windmill with his pieces, he can remove one of his opponent's pieces from the board. When all the pieces are on the board, players take turns moving one of their pieces to an adjacent, empty square. The game is over when one player has only two pieces left.

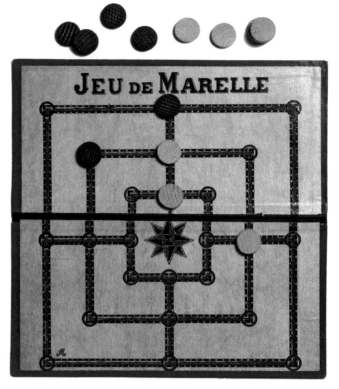

Jeu de Marelle, a French variation on windmill, played with nine pieces (early twentieth century).

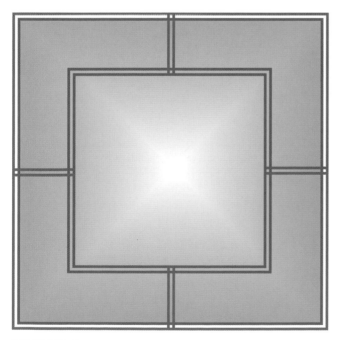

DIAGRAM C:
A Six Men's Morris board.

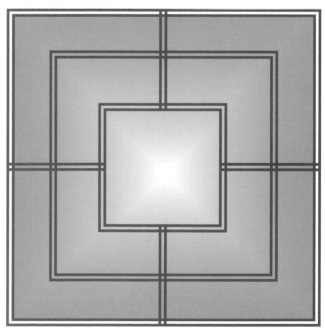

DIAGRAM D:
A Nine Men's Morris board.

Nine Men's Morris

This is the most well-known variation on windmill. As the name indicates, each player gets nine pieces, and the board has a few more squares (Diagram D).

How the Pieces Move

The players take turns, each of them placing one of their pieces in an empty square to try to form a windmill. The pieces can move up, down, left, and right, but never diagonally. Once all the pieces are on the board, players keep taking turns to move each of their pieces to an adjacent square. The objective remains to place three of one's pieces in a straight line.

Capturing Pieces

In Nine Men's Morris, players do not "capture" their opponents' pieces as they might in most other games. To capture an opponent's piece, a player does not even have to have one of his pieces near an opponent's. Each time a player places three pieces in a row, he can eliminate any one of his opponent's pieces from the board—unless that piece is already part of a windmill. Once a piece is captured, it cannot be returned to the board.

Other Situations

A player can form many windmills in a single game, and in the process eliminate the opponent's pieces. A player may have only three pieces left, and those may be part of a windmill. Come that player's turn, he will have to break his own windmill by moving one of the pieces, even if it means later losing one of the pieces—and in fact losing the game—when his opponent takes another turn.

Winning

There are two ways of winning this game:

- A player is able to block all his opponent's pieces that are still on the board so the opponent can no longer move any of them.
- A player eliminates enough of his opponent's pieces that the latter is left with only two.

CURIOUS FACT

A.S. White calculated that a player who begins a game of windmill has three possible opening moves. He can place his piece either in the center of the board, along one of the sides, or in a corner. When the other player makes his first move, twelve possible moves remain. In seven of these, the first player will win; in the other five, the second player will win. In theory, the player who goes second can win the game only if his opponent makes a mistake.

The First Match

Three Men's Morris and Six Men's Morris can be mastered quickly and easily. Nine Men's Morris is somewhat more difficult, so the following pages show some possible situations that can arise at the opening of such a match. These may be useful if you wish to begin playing on your own. To make the descriptions easier to follow, the squares on the board are numbered from 1 to 24.

Phase One

1 Black makes the first move by placing his piece on square 18. White puts his first piece on square 3. The second black piece is placed on square 13. White immediately senses the danger of Black forming a windmill and so places one of his pieces on square 9. After much reflection, players put each of their pieces on the board. After eighteen moves, phase one of the game comes to a close (Diagram 1).

Forming a Windmill

2 Both players have now placed all their pieces on the board, but they are less fortunate when it comes time to form a windmill. Unable to form one, neither player can eliminate his opponent's pieces. At the start of phase two, it is time to unravel this problem. Each player moves a piece to an empty square. Black goes first, moving a piece from square

This image of a couple playing windmill is from a medieval French manuscript *(Bodleian Library, Oxford)*.

1 to square 2. This is an intelligent, well-considered move. With it he is sure to form a windmill with his next move, by moving this piece from square 6 to square 5. The first windmill of this game is thus formed across squares 2, 5, and 8. White has already figured out this strategy, but there is nothing he can do to avoid it. To keep his opponent from forming a windmill, he would have to put one of his pieces on square 5, but he cannot reach this position with any of his pieces. Consequently, he tries to begin forming a windmill by moving his piece from square 22 to square 10. Black doesn't miss the opportunity to remove one of White's pieces from the board, and chooses the piece on square 9 (Diagram 2).

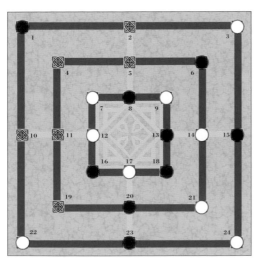

DIAGRAM 1:
Situation after phase one. Both players have placed all their pieces; for the moment, neither of them has been able to form a windmill.

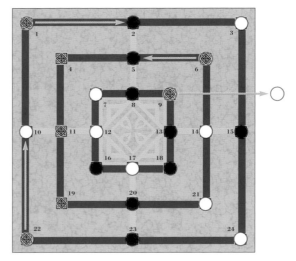

DIAGRAM 2:
Black moves one of his pieces from square 1 to square 2, and in his next turn, from square 6 to square 5. Black's first windmill is now made, and White loses the piece on square 9.

An Ideal Situation

3 Apparently Black has a pretty good feel for this game. Maybe he is a seasoned Nine Men's Morris player, or maybe he is just lucky. Soon he forms a second windmill, across squares 9, 13, and 18, by moving his piece from square 8 to square 9. White loses another piece. Black chooses to remove the piece on 7, another well-considered decision, because by doing so he can move the piece just transferred from square 9 to square 8, in his next turn. Returning to his previous position, he forms yet another windmill using the same squares as the first. The only piece White could have used to stop Black is the piece on square 7, and that one has just been eliminated (Diagram 3).

If you want to play a first match, you can follow this example move by move:

1. **B: 18**, 2. **W: 3**, 3. **B: 13**, 4. **W: 9**,

5. **B: 16**, 6. **W: 17**, 7. **B: 1**, 8. **W: 7**, 9. **B: 8**,

10. **W: 24**, 11. **B: 15**, 12. **W: 14**, 13. **B: 23**,

14. **W: 21**, 15. **B: 6**, 16. **W: 12**, 17. **B: 20**,

18. **W: 22**, 19. **B: 1-2**, 20. **W: 22-10**,

21. **B: 6-5**, 22. **W: 12-11**, 23. **B: 8-9**,

24. **W: 14-6**, 25. **B: 9-8 and captures 11**,

26. **W: 21-14**, 27. **B: 8-9 and captures 10**,

28. **W: 4-21**, 29. **B: 13-14**.

Some Good Advice

To avoid losing one piece each time his opponent makes a windmill, White has to try to break the double windmill. But before doing so, he watches Black eliminate another one of his pieces. Another possibility is for White to try making his own windmill, in order to eliminate at least one of Black's pieces. This will not solve White's problem, either, because one cannot eliminate a piece that is already part of a windmill. To make matters worse, four of White's remaining seven pieces are blocked, and Black has no need to eliminate one of the blocked pieces from the board.

What can White do, then? Try to break one or more of the blocks? Luck is not on his side in this match.

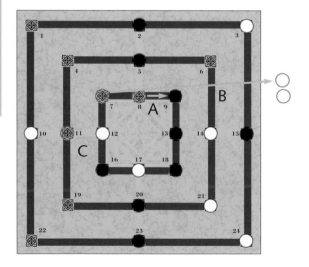

DIAGRAM 3:
An ideal situation. Black's pieces form a new windmill with each turn. Black accomplishes this by moving his piece from square 8 to square 9, and then moving it back to square 8 in the next turn. White can do nothing to stop it, because Black already eliminated the piece on square 7 in his first move.

A Tricky Problem

Meanwhile, White has seen his pieces dwindle to five. Only two of these—the pieces on squares 6 and 21—are not blocked. But he can move only one or the other, because the sole opening for each of them is square 14. Black still has all his pieces and is clearly going to win. But will Black win because White has only two pieces left, or because he has managed to block all White's pieces? Which is the quickest way to win?

How Does Black Win?

4 In the final phase of the game, Black continues to reflect on his moves carefully and calmly, knowing he is certain to win. As one might expect, he makes yet another windmill, moving a piece from square 8 to square 9. This move is already quite familiar and will allow him to take another one of White's pieces. When Black moves the piece back to square 8 in his next move, he can take yet another

of White's pieces. How long will this go on? Black considers his next possible moves. If he moves his favorite piece from one square to another, he can eliminate White's pieces on squares 6 and 21. He chooses these two because they are the only white pieces that aren't blocked. What then? The three remaining white pieces are now blocked. Even though Black's immediate goal was to capture his opponent's pieces, Black will in fact win because he managed to block all of White's moves (Diagram 4).

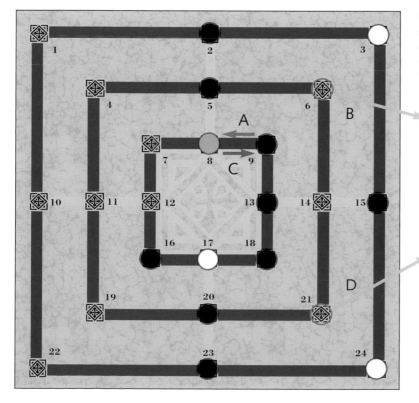

DIAGRAM 4:
A possible finale. Black makes two windmills in a row and eliminates two of his opponent's pieces. The rest of White's pieces are blocked and cannot move, so Black wins.

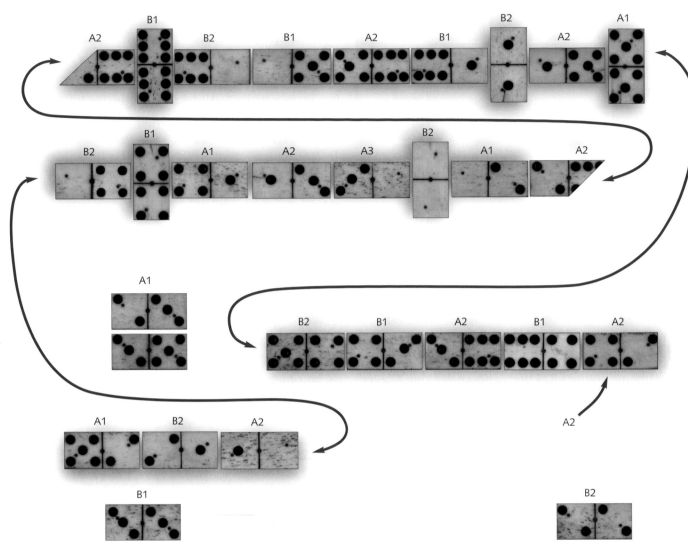

DIAGRAM 4:
Domino. Team A wins with twenty-three points.

Ending

This first round has run its course without any problems: the players were not blocked and were able to play to the end. This isn't always the case, as you will find out when starting to play for real. The game of dominoes is full of surprises, which is what makes it so entertaining.

Other Variations

After the first round, the novice player will undoubtedly want to learn the many other forms of play dominoes has to offer. Below are explained the rules of some of the most popular variations. All the following games are played with twenty-eight pieces.

Below is a move-by-move breakdown of the match, for those who wish to play a first match by following this example. The first number represents the dots on the side of the tile the player puts down on the free end of a tile already on the table.

B1: **6-6**, A2: **6-2**, B2: **6-0**, A1: **2-0**,

B1: **0-5**, A2: **5-6**, B2: **0-0**, A1: **0-3**, B1: **6-1**,

A2: **3-1**, B2: **1-1**, A1: **1-4**, B1: **4-4**,

A2: **1-5**, B2: **4-0**, A1: **5-5**, B1: **pass**, A2: **0-1**,

B2: **5-4**, A1: **pass**, B1: **4-3**, A2: **3-6**, B2: **1-2**,

A1: **2-5**, B1: **6-4**, A2: **4-2**.

Bergen

An interesting variation on draw dominoes is Bergen. It is said to have been invented by English sailors whose ship was stranded at the Norwegian port of the same name. The most entertaining aspect of the game is that it is played with points. The goal is to gain as many points as possible. Bergen is a game for two to four players. When there are one to three players, each of them takes six tiles. When four people are playing, each of them takes five tiles. The rest of the tiles stay on the table.

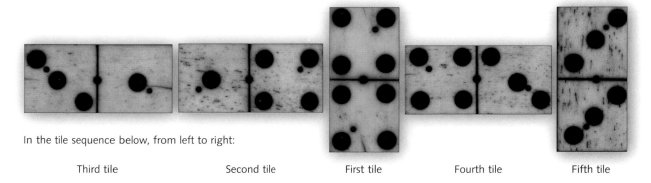

In the tile sequence below, from left to right:

| Third tile | Second tile | First tile | Fourth tile | Fifth tile |

DIAGRAM B:
An example of Bergen. The player who put down the fourth tile gets two points because the open end of this tile is the same as that of the third. The player who put down the fifth tile gets three points because the tile is a double, and it matches the tile at the other end.

The Rules

Bergen follows the same general rules as dominoes. Tiles can be joined when one of their sides share the same number of dots. The player with the highest-numbered double tile makes the first move. Double tiles are always placed lengthwise on the table, as is the first tile at the start of the game. After putting down the first tile lengthwise, the rest are placed perpendicular to it. Players take turns putting down a tile on one of the two free ends. When a player cannot or will not play one of his tiles, he must take a tile from the table.

Counting Points

A player gets two points when he puts down a tile in such a way that both open ends on the table have the same number of points (Diagram B).

Diagram B shows how the player who put down the fourth tile receives two points: the open, outer end of his tile has the same number of dots as the tile on the other end of the table. In this example, the player who put down the fifth tile, a double-three, also receives three points because his tile has the same number of dots as the open end of the tile on the other side of the table.

If a player uses all his tiles, he gets an additional two points. As a general rule, players score between ten and fifteen points per round.

The Fourth Trick

5 This time Player C starts. He decides to use his last trump and win this trick as well. The other players discard tiles of little value. Player C wins the fourth trick, but since no special tiles are on the table, he earns only one point (Diagram 5).

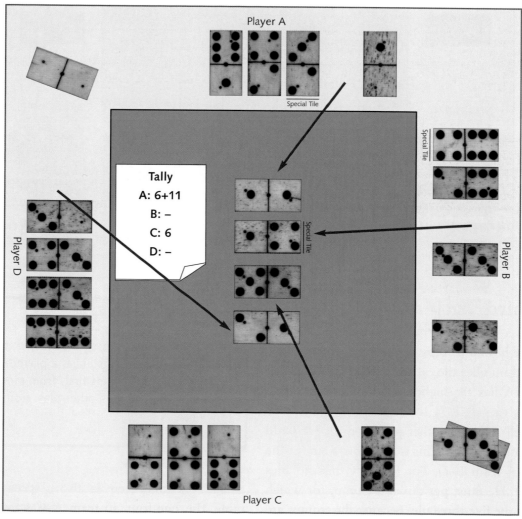

DIAGRAM 4:
The third trick. Player A has no more trumps. The wild number is one. A's partner plays a trump and wins the trick with six points.

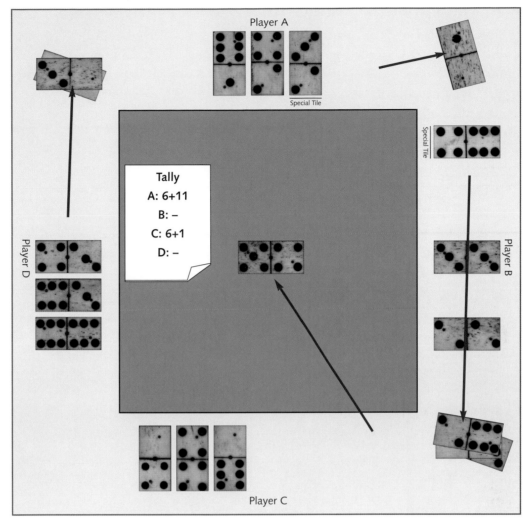

DIAGRAM 5:
The fourth trick. Player C plays his last trump and wins this hand with one point.

The Fifth and Sixth Tricks

Player C also starts the fifth trick. He holds the double-four tile; if he puts it on the table, he will win this trick, too.

The fifth trick unfolds as follows:

Player C:	double-four
Player D:	four-three
Player A:	four-two
Player B:	four-six

Player B is forced to use the special six-four tile, worth ten additional points. With this, the opposing team earns eleven points in this trick. For the third consecutive time, Player C can begin a trick. Players put down the following tiles:

> **VARIATION**
>
> For variety's sake, players sometimes decide that the highest bidder must also call a trump.

Player C:	six-zero
Player D:	double-six
Player A:	six-one
Player B:	discards the double-two

For the first time, a member of team B–D wins a trick. Player D has used the double-six, earning one point.

The End of the Game

6 In the seventh and final trick, each player puts his final tile on the table. Player D begins, turning his six into the wild number. The other players discard their tiles, because none has a tile with the number six. Player A has the last special tile, the three-two. Although the tile was discarded, the winner of the trick will receive an additional five points. Player D wins this trick with six points.

After the seventh trick the points are tallied. Team A–C has thirty-five points, while team B–D has only seven. Player A bid thirty-seven points at the start of the game, but unfortunately, that bid was too high. The thirty-seven points he bid go to Players B and D. Adding these to the seven points they earned, they receive a total of forty-four points. Players A and C receive only the thirty-five points they earned (Diagram 6).

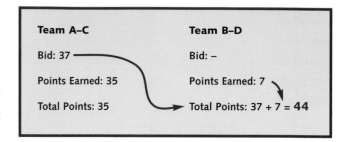

Team A–C	Team B–D
Bid: 37	Bid: –
Points Earned: 35	Points Earned: 7
Total Points: 35	Total Points: 37 + 7 = **44**

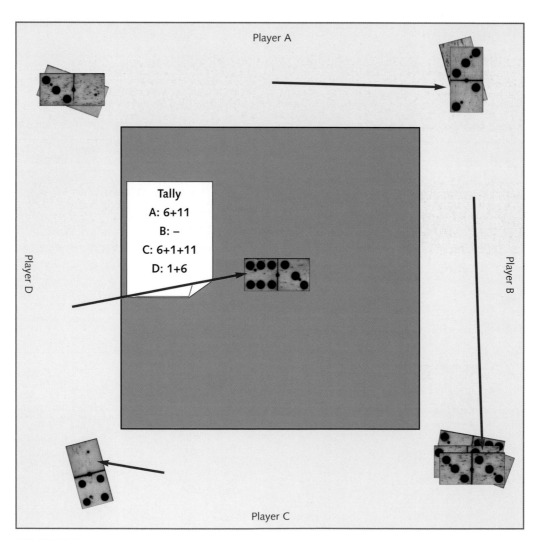

Player A

Tally
A: 6+11
B: –
C: 6+1+11
D: 1+6

Player D

Player B

Player C

DIAGRAM 6:
The end of the game. Player D wins the seventh trick with six points. During the final tally it is determined that team A-C has earned thirty-five points. Player A had bid thirty-seven; this bid goes to players B and D, who win the game.

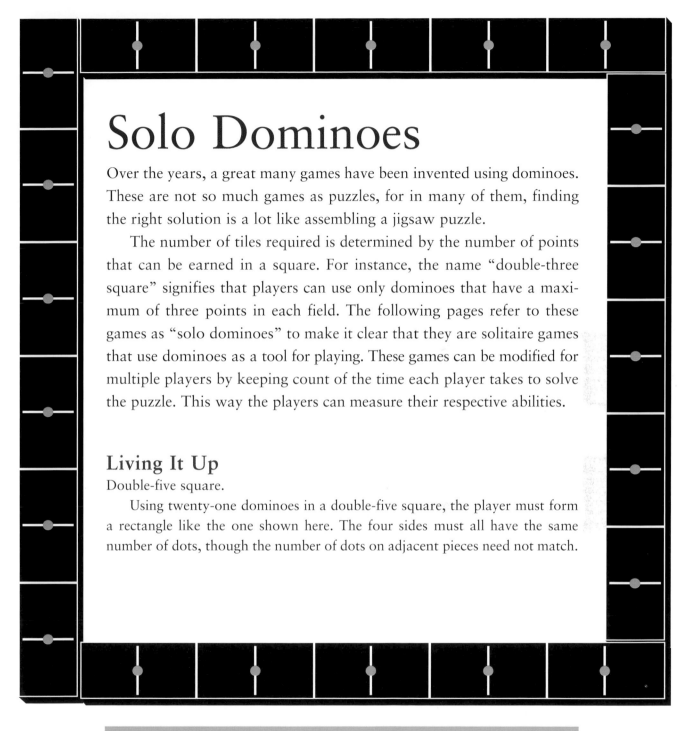

Solo Dominoes

Over the years, a great many games have been invented using dominoes. These are not so much games as puzzles, for in many of them, finding the right solution is a lot like assembling a jigsaw puzzle.

The number of tiles required is determined by the number of points that can be earned in a square. For instance, the name "double-three square" signifies that players can use only dominoes that have a maximum of three points in each field. The following pages refer to these games as "solo dominoes" to make it clear that they are solitaire games that use dominoes as a tool for playing. These games can be modified for multiple players by keeping count of the time each player takes to solve the puzzle. This way the players can measure their respective abilities.

Living It Up
Double-five square.

Using twenty-one dominoes in a double-five square, the player must form a rectangle like the one shown here. The four sides must all have the same number of dots, though the number of dots on adjacent pieces need not match.

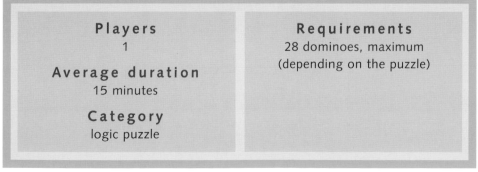

Players	Requirements
1	28 dominoes, maximum (depending on the puzzle)
Average duration	
15 minutes	
Category	
logic puzzle	

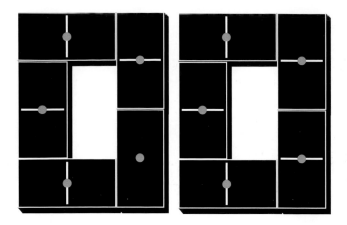

Twins

Double-three square.

The player must form two rectangles, as in the diagram at left. This may look simple, but looks can be deceiving. The total number of each side must be the same in both rectangles. Luckily, though, the sides of adjacent tiles need not match.

Crosses

Double-six square.

To help solve this puzzle, this diagram shows how the dominoes must be placed to form two crosses. The total number of points at each end of each cross must match. One point is made up of eight dominoes, and the dots of the center piece count double.

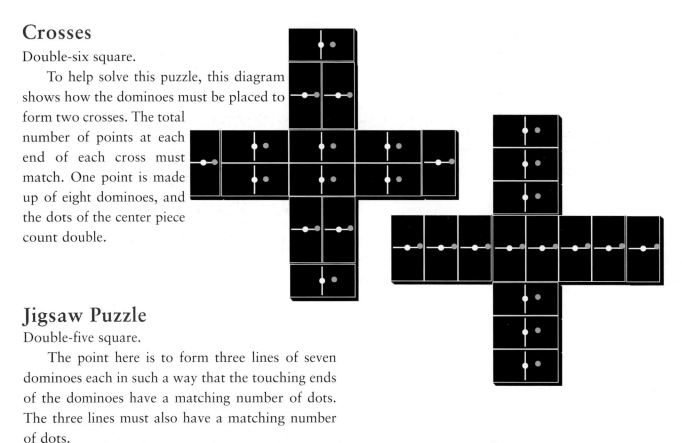

Jigsaw Puzzle

Double-five square.

The point here is to form three lines of seven dominoes each in such a way that the touching ends of the dominoes have a matching number of dots. The three lines must also have a matching number of dots.

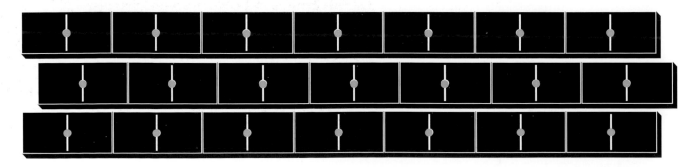

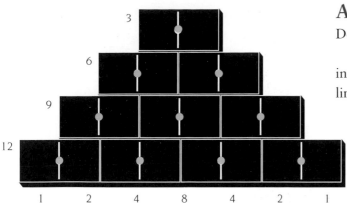

A Little Wall

Double-three square.

The dominoes are placed on the table, as shown in the illustration, so the horizontal and vertical lines have the right number of dots (as indicated).

Vertical Sum

Double-three square.

The dominoes are placed as shown in the illustration. This must be done in such a way that the sum of the dots in each vertical line matches that of the others.

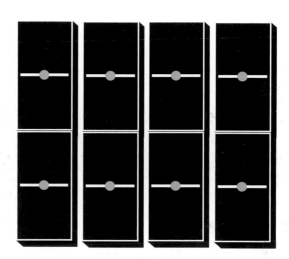

Waves

Double-six square.

If you are using four dominoes per wave, you can form a total of seven waves. As in the official rules for dominoes, the touching ends of pieces must have equal numbers of dots. The total number of dots in the short lines must match that of the long lines, in the middle.

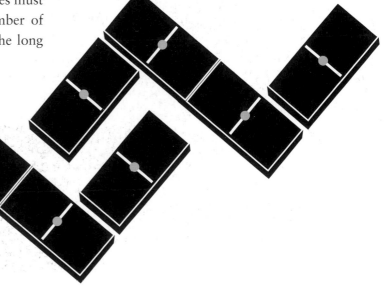

Domino Quartets

Double-six square.

Since before 1900, solving domino quartets was a popular pastime. One such indication is its inclusion in Gaston Bonnefont's book *Games and Recreations for Young People* (*Les Jeux et les Récréations de la Jeunesse*), published in 1880, which made this diverting puzzle a real classic.

Each time it is a matter of forming fourteen quartets of dominoes with four series of pieces so that each quartet is a double. (This illustration shows one of the 342,720 solutions possible.) To make the puzzle even more complex, you can add the condition that the fourteen quartets must be placed in a pre-established order. For example, above and to the left, the blank quartet, after which follows the quartet of ones, until you reach the six-pointed domino quartet. From there it is a matter of going back and reducing the number of each quartet's points until you are left with only blanks.

In this imaginative work of Jerzey Skarzyski (1943) are seen games such as dominoes, dice, roulette, and a game board.

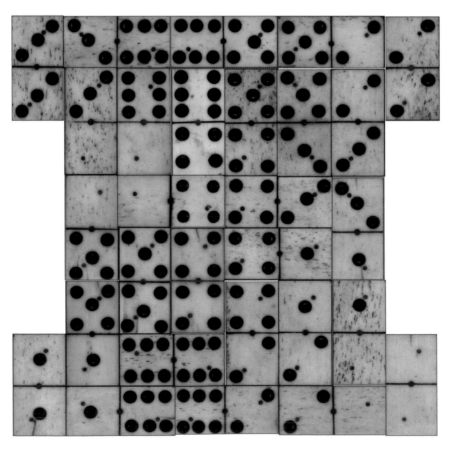

Arrangement with double-sixes.

Tien Gow

Tien Gow is an extraordinarily fun and captivating domino game for four players. The game originated in China and is especially popular among the Hokkien people of the Fujian province, but deserves to be known throughout the world. Tien Gow requires a complete set of Chinese dominoes. Players use the pieces individually or form "words" with the tiles such as "sky," "earth," and "plum blossom." One of the players also takes the role of banker, which is highly coveted: *everyone* wants to be the banker, for as long as possible. Players have no part in choosing the tiles they are assigned, thereby introducing the element of chance. What is certain is that each player can affect his or her chances of winning through skill in playing. The best opportunities are reserved for those players who are able to think ahead and foresee an entire round. Players must therefore plan their strategy in this game.

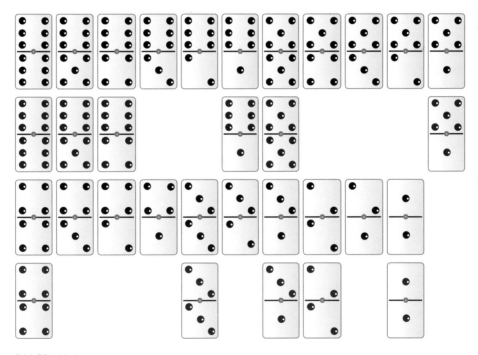

DIAGRAM A:
A complete set of Chinese dominoes.

Players	Requirements
4	set of Chinese dominoes
Average duration	pen and paper
30 minutes	
Category	
skill	

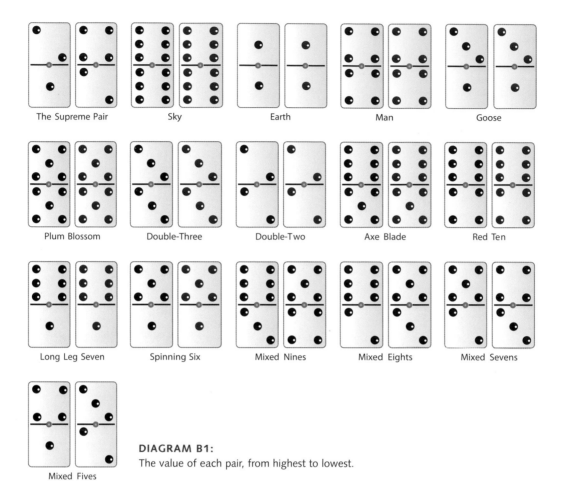

DIAGRAM B1:
The value of each pair, from highest to lowest.

The Supreme Pair · Sky · Earth · Man · Goose

Plum Blossom · Double-Three · Double-Two · Axe Blade · Red Ten

Long Leg Seven · Spinning Six · Mixed Nines · Mixed Eights · Mixed Sevens

Mixed Fives

Preliminaries

Chinese dominoes are different from their European counterpart in several ways. First of all, Chinese dominoes include tiles with red dots as well as black (Diagram A). When you remove all the blank tiles from a European set, you are left with twenty-one tiles; if you add the eleven red tiles, you get a set of thirty-two tiles, a full set of Chinese dominoes. Eleven of the thirty-two tiles are duplicates. Twenty-two pieces are known as "civilians," and the ten remaining pieces are "soldiers."

The game can last as long as the players wish. It is a good idea to decide ahead of time how long a game will be—say, thirty minutes. Before starting a game, players roll a die to see who will be the banker in the first round (the highest roller wins). It is advisable to assign a player the task of writing down the total number of points for each player at the end of each round.

Pairings and Their Value

The value of the tiles is determined by the number of dots on each one. Double-six is the most valuable, and double-one the least. Players can form twenty-four different pairs with the dominoes. The highest are made up of soldiers two-one and four-two. These are called, appropriately enough, "the supreme pair." The lowest combinations are three-one and four-one, or three-one and three-two, which do not have a special name. Double tiles together form a pair of civilians; military tiles form pairs whose numerical value comprises the dots on all the tiles. The "supreme pair" is an exception to this rule because it consists of a tile with three points and another with six (Diagrams B1 and B2).

A Round

At the start of a round, all the tiles are placed facedown in the middle of the table and shuffled. Then the banker makes a "woodpile" out of them, placing eight piles of four dominoes on the table. He gives two of these piles to each player so everyone has eight tiles. The banker begins by putting down one of his tiles facedown on the table. Next, the player to his left adds one of his tiles, and the other players take turns doing the same. When there are four tiles on the table, the player who put down the tile of greatest value wins the trick. He forms a pile with the corresponding tiles and puts it on the table in front of him. The winner of the trick then puts a tile down on the table, and the other players add one new tile each.

There is a difference, however, between the first and second tricks in a round: the first player in the first trick can put down only one tile on the table. In subsequent tricks, players may put down one or more pairs instead of a single tile. The first must always be followed by the other players. If the first player puts down a pair, the other players must put down two dominoes; if the first player chooses a single tile, the others must add one tile. The round concludes when the players have put down all their dominoes on the table. The winner of the final trick becomes the banker in the next round. Naturally, it can be the same person as before.

A sample game:

Player B puts down the five-five tile, and Players C, D, and A follow this move with the three-one, double-four, and six-five tiles, respectively. The winner of the trick is Player A (Diagram C).

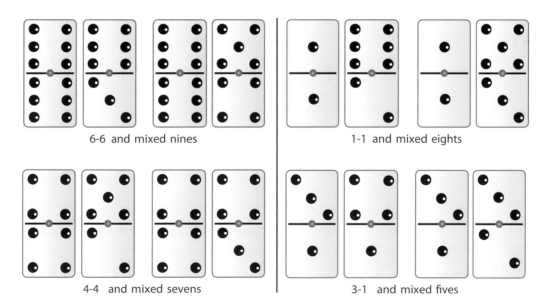

6-6 and mixed nines

1-1 and mixed eights

4-4 and mixed sevens

3-1 and mixed fives

DIAGRAM B2:
The value of the pairings from highest (top left) to lowest (bottom right).

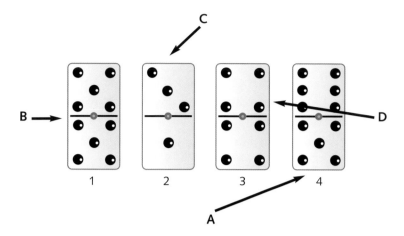

DIAGRAM C:
An example of play. Player B begins by putting a
domino tile on the table. The other players must add
a tile. Player A puts down the highest-value tile and
takes a trick.

STRATEGY

It is sound strategy to keep the pieces of higher
value for use later on, in the deciding round.
The winner of this round generally receives
points from the other players and continues as
banker during the next round.

A Trick

As already noted, the first player decides how many
tiles each player will put on the table. In the event he
puts down a single tile, his choice also decides what
kind of tile the others must put down. If he puts
down a civilian tile, the others must do the same; likewise, they must put down a military tile if the first
player does so. If a player is unable to put down the
right kind of tile, he must put another tile aside. It is
important that this player win the trick in question.

Pairs may consist of two civilians or two soldiers. If the first player opens with a pair, the player
who adds the most valuable pair will win the trick.
In this case, the type of tile (civilian or military) is of
no importance. If one of the players is unable to follow, he must put down two of his tiles. The type of
tile becomes important again when the first player
puts down two pairs. Regardless of the type(s) of tiles
on the table, the remaining players must add two
pairs of the same type. Thus, each must put down
two pairs of either type. The trick goes to the player
who puts down the most valuable pair, regardless of
the value of his second pair (Diagram D).

To Finish

In Tien Gow, the supreme pair has the highest value
only if the first player has put it on the table. If any
of the other players does so, this combination has
the lowest value of all the pairs. By themselves, the
tiles that form the supreme pair have a low value.
The two-one is the single lowest tile, and the four-
two is in twenty-ninth place among the thirty-two.

TIP

One player writes down the name of the player
who becomes the banker. If this person continues to be the banker in the following round(s),
this too is written down, making it easier to tally
the points.

Tallying Points

The points are tallied at the end of each round. A player who has not taken any tricks "pays" four points to the person who won the last trick, who becomes the banker in the next round. Players who have won one, two, or three tricks subtract this number from the number four and pay the difference to the winner of the last trick. Thus, the player who won two tricks loses four minus two points, which he pays to the banker in the next round.

If a player has won exactly four tricks, he neither wins nor loses any points. Lastly, the player with more than four tricks subtracts four from this quantity and receives the difference from the winner of the previous round.

When the banker in one round is also the banker in the next, the method of tallying points changes. After the second of these rounds is over, the four from the previous round becomes the number eight. So, for instance, if a player has three tricks after this round, he subtracts this number from eight and pays the difference to the winner of the final trick. If the same person is still the banker in the third round, the eight becomes a twelve. As long as the banker remains the same, this number increases by four points after each round. There is no limit to the number of times the same person can play the banker.

Here is an example of play:

At the end of a round in which Player C is banker for the first time, Player D wins the final trick,

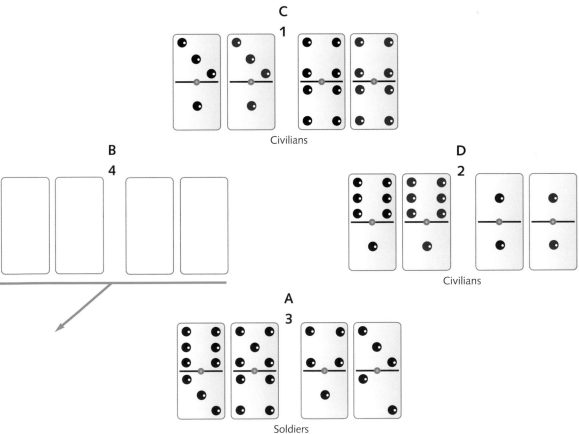

DIAGRAM D:
A trick. Player C opens with two pairs, and the other players are obliged to add two pairs each of the same type. Player B cannot do so and must therefore discard four of his dominoes. The highest pair on the table is "earth," which belongs to Player D. He wins the trick.

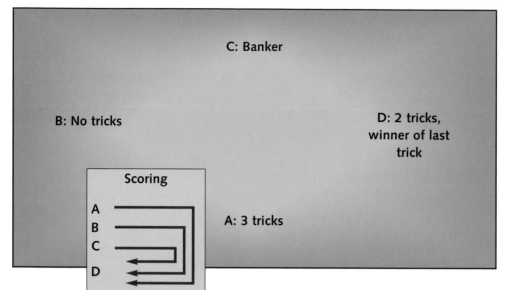

C: Banker

B: No tricks

D: 2 tricks, winner of last trick

Scoring

A
B
C
D

A: 3 tricks

DIAGRAM E:
Tallying points. The winner of the last trick loses points only if one of his partners has taken more than four tricks. After six tricks, Player D receives a total of eight points and will become the banker in the next round.

becoming the banker in the next round. Player C has a trick and must therefore pay three points (four minus one). Player D also receives one point from A, who had three tricks, and four points from B, who has won no tricks in this round (Diagram E).

Additional Points

With some combinations, players can score additional points, as is true of the supreme pair. When the banker opens with this combination, the other players must give him four points. If another player puts this combination down on the table, the banker must pay *him* four points, and he also receives two points from the other players. You can also score additional points with the following pairs:

Six-six and a mixed nine

One-one and a mixed eight

Four-four and a mixed six

Three-one and a mixed five

If the banker, as the first player, puts one of these combinations on the table, he gets eight points from each player. If one of the other players opens with one of these combinations, he gets eight points from the banker and four points from the other two players.

STRATEGY

Suppose the first player has already won three tricks and everyone still has two dominoes left. If so, the first player must carefully evaluate whether he can still win two tricks with each individual tile he has left. If possible, he is better off earning one point and not putting a pair down on the table.

VARIATION

Tien Gow is often played as a betting game, where players win money or other items instead of points. When doing so, make sure you have plenty of the commodity you are betting.

Chinese Dominoes

Most sources indicate that dominoes were invented by the Chinese in the seventeenth century. Like the Koreans, the Chinese, it appears, originally used the tiles in divination. American scholar R. C. Bell acknowledged the Chinese ancestry of dominoes but believed dominoes to be much older. In Bell's view, the designers of the first domino tiles were inspired by the design of dice, which were introduced in China via India. Later on, dice would also serve as the basis for the tiles in mah-jong and European dominoes. Other historians share Bell's hypothesis.

Some believe that Marco Polo (1254–1323) was responsible for introducing the Europeans to dominoes, which he brought back from China.

The tiles in Chinese dominoes, "little bricks that symbolize a roll of the dice," have the same names as the corresponding rolls in a game of dice. A game consists of thirty-two tiles with no blanks. Twenty-one tiles represent all the possible combinations from rolling two dice. The tiles in this group are called "soldiers"; the eleven additional tiles are replicas of eleven soldiers and are called "civilians."

In the Eastern world, domino cards were also used in divination. Later on these cards would acquire their own unique design.

Korean dominoes. An image from Stewart Culin's *Chess and Playing Cards*, 1886.

Differences

One can assume that, although the game was played with cards, dominoes existed in China as early as the Tang dynasty in the seventh and eighth centuries. Both the cards and the tiles in Chinese dominoes are quite different in design from their Western descendants. Chinese dominoes often display fine craftsmanship. The tiles were carved from bone, which is probably why they were given the name *kwat p'ai*, meaning "bone tablet." They are usually longer and narrower than European tiles and have no line through the middle. The dots on the one and four tiles are red, and the double-sixes are half red, half white; the dots on the other pieces are white. In different parts of China, dominoes was played with smaller pieces made of bamboo, wood, or a combination of wood and bone. Chinese domino pieces engraved with the characters from chess have also been found. The critical difference in terms of play is that the tiles in Chinese dominoes are generally joined lengthwise, not end to end.

Extra Pieces

A great deal of historical evidence supports the idea that dominoes were descended from dice. The question remains as to why the Chinese added eleven more tiles to the original set of dominoes. The explanation relates in part to the fact that the Chinese initially used dominoes solely for the purpose of divination. A plausible explanation is that the thirty-two dots are meant to symbolize the four cardinal compass points and the corresponding division of the world. It is highly likely that the tiles were originally seen as magical tools for fortune-telling. The same is true of the domino cards, which are the same as the domino pieces in all but their shape and size.

Today

Today dominoes is played practically everywhere in the world. In the Far East are found some forty-seven variations on the game, which have been given imaginative names such as "In the Temple," "Leaping Antelope," or "Little Serpents." A favorite domino game among the Chinese is Tsung Shap, which translates as "*disputing tens*." (See page 667 for a full presentation of the Tsung Shap version of dominoes.)

Shogi
History of the Game

◆　◆　◆

In no other place is a more accurate reference made to the origins of this mysterious Japanese version of chess than in Rimsky-Korsakov's opera *Sadko*. In the opera, an Indian merchant sings, in reference to this game, "from the land of wonders to the shores of the Ganges." Claims about the origins of chess abound, yet it is generally acknowledged that the Indian game of *shaturanga* is the prototype from which other versions have developed. A variation on *shaturanga* in Japan would later become the basis of shogi.

One of the many legends of the origin of *shaturanga* dates from 2000 to 3000 B.C.E. According to this legend, it was invented by the wife of the king of Ceylon when the capital, Lanka, was besieged by Rama, the legendary hero of the Ramayana. In the fifth century A.D., a new version of *shaturanga* appeared that was played on an eight-by-eight board. The first references to this version of the game in Indian literature are from the seventh century. In a romantic prose work, the poet Subandhu describes the relationship between an Indian princess, Vasavadatta, and her king. In the margins he mentions that in the "time of rain" the game was played using green and yellow frogs instead of ordinary game pieces. It remains unclear whether the poet was referring to chess. Nonetheless, there is little doubt with respect to the biography of the famous pacifist king Shri Harsha (606–647), under whose reign there were no wars other than fighting among the bees collecting honey and no armies other than those on the chessboard made up of eight-by-eight squares.

An illustration by Hokosai Manga. This image is part of a series of twelve that captured everyday life in Japan circa 1820.

number of squares on the board. *Chu-shogi*, which appeared around 1350, was played on a twelve-by-twelve board. There were three different versions as late as the sixteenth century: *sho-shogi* (little shogi, with a nine-by-nine board), *chu-shogi* (middle shogi), and *dai-shogi* (great shogi, played on a fifteen-by-fifteen board). Later on there appeared all kinds of larger versions, such as *maka dai-dai shogi* (ultra great-great shogi, played on a nineteen-by-nineteen board). A newer version, developed around 1570, allowed players to reintroduce pieces that had been lost to an opponent.

In general, players found newer versions more attractive. This is why many variations disappeared. Today, only modern shogi (played on a nine-by-nine board) and "middle shogi" survive.

Shogi Culture

In the Tokugawa period (1600–1868), when Japan was isolated from the rest of the world, shogi, like go, was a well-protected game. There were shogi houses frequented by the Shogun, who competed among themselves. In 1868 the Shogun lost power, and as a result, go and shogi houses lost their financial backing. After this time of neglect, the first decade of the twentieth century saw organized tournaments sponsored by national newspapers. Since then, shogi has grown to the level of being the most important game of strategy in Japan.

The extensive literature on shogi can be studied in Japan's many specialized urban schools, among other places. Japan has some ten million shogi players. Once a year, players compete for the national title in the Tournament of Meijin-sen.

Origins

Many theories indicate that shogi originated in Southeast Asia as a variation on chess. The fact that the pawns in Thai chess are also placed on the third line, and that the elephant moves the same way as the silver general in shogi, supports this thesis. Masukawa Kiochi, the Japanese games historian, states that "people from the sea brought the game through the *black current* (the cold current in the Southeast Asian gulf) to Japan." The oldest known pieces were found in an empty well in the most ancient temple in Japan—Horyuji, built in the seventh century.

Variations on Shogi

Many variations on shogi have developed since its inception. The name of the game refers to the

Playing Shogi

Shogi is the Japanese equivalent of chess. Although it has some things in common with its Western counterpart, the rules are very different. As in Western chess, the object of the game is to checkmate the enemy king. Three of the chessmen are especially important: the king, the rook, and the bishop, all of which move the same way. The resemblance ends there, because shogi uses many, quite different rules from chess that make it a dynamic, ever-surprising game. For example, when a player takes an enemy piece, he can add it to his own army and put in on any space on the board he likes. Shogi is the game of "reversal of fortune" *par excellence* in which your own pieces end up counting against you when they are captured by the enemy. You can never be sure you are actually winning until you capture the enemy king.

Shogi is played on a board with nine-by-nine rows of squares. In the fourth and seventh rows are two dotted crosses that divide the board into three equal sections.

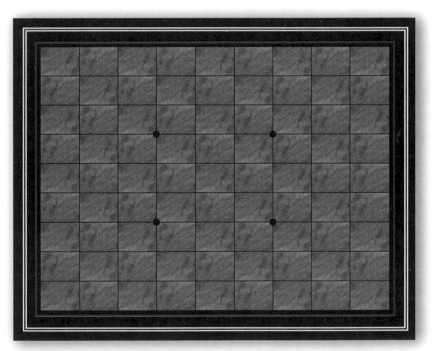

Shogi is an exciting and pleasant pastime.

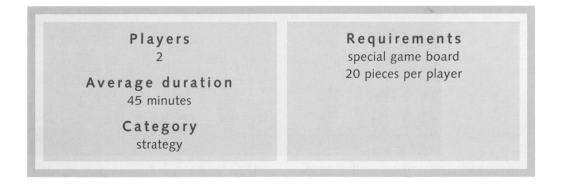

Players	Requirements
2	special game board
	20 pieces per player
Average duration	
45 minutes	
Category	
strategy	

Freedom of Movement After Promotion

Some pieces are already so powerful that they cannot be promoted any further—like the king or the gold general. Others, such as the silver general, the knight, and the lance, become gold and lose their original freedom of movement. A promoted rook becomes a "crowned" rook; it preserves its freedom of movement and can now also move like a king. The bishop, once promoted, is called a "crowned bishop." Like the rook, it preserves its freedom of movement but can now also move like a king.

The Goal of Promotion

Clearly the rook, bishop, and pawn all gain an advantage when they are promoted, so an astute player will promote these pieces as soon as possible. On the other hand, it is preferable for the knight and the lance to retain their initial mobility. A piece's original movements also may be more useful than its movements after promotion to silver. This is not a problem, because players are not obliged to promote their pieces at the first opportunity. Promotion becomes obligatory only once a piece reaches the final row: if the player does not promote a piece at this point, the piece "dies" on the board. The knight

must also be promoted as soon as it reaches the second-to-last row (the second or eighth, depending on the side).

Aerial Attacks

Shogi owes much of its intrigue to the rule allowing the owner of a piece to reintroduce the piece after it has been captured, if and when he chooses. This rule is also responsible in large part for the anxiety and excitement that can overcome players when they lose a piece only to see it return "from the air" to turn against them.

For each turn, a player can reintroduce one of the pieces he has captured, on whatever square he pleases. The piece must point in the same direction as his other pieces. When a player reintroduces a piece, he may make no other move in the same turn.

Illustration from Stewart Cullin's *Chess and Other Board Games*, 1898.

Conditions

There are two conditions for reintroducing a piece to the board:

The square onto which the piece is reintroduced must be empty; and a piece cannot be placed on a square where the piece cannot move. For example, a pawn or a lance cannot be reintroduced on the first or second row.

Further, a player cannot place two pawns in the same row. In other words, a pawn cannot be placed on a straight line with another pawn of the same color. When the other pawn has been promoted, however, this is no longer forbidden. Finally, a player cannot checkmate with a pawn. If he does, he automatically loses the game.

The Most Powerful Pieces

Without a doubt, the bishop and the rook are the two strongest pieces. Which is the more powerful of the two? Probably the rook. Some experts maintain that the rook is equal to three generals; others say it equals two generals and a knight or lance. The lance is at least as important as two generals and is the most effective piece at the start of the game. Of course, players will try to develop strategies for the bishop and rook that will open up as many straight and diagonal lines as possible. One should keep in mind that a bishop "fallen from the sky" can be a dangerous weapon indeed.

Gold generals usually do not advance the game much because they are likely to be trapped if they cannot move backward. However, their services may become highly valuable when it comes time to protect the most important piece of all: the king.

O-sho = king

Hisha = chariot

Kakko = bishop

Kin-sho = gold general

Gin-shō = silver general

Kei-ma = knight

Yari = lance

Fu-hyo = pawn

Shogi pieces arranged in a row. The pieces showing red calligraphy on their reverse side have been promoted.

White has yet to make his twelfth move. He decides to move his gold general from D9 to E8.

In his thirteenth move, Black responds by moving his pawn from C3 to C4. White moves his pawn from F7 to F6 (Diagram D).

Not Too Fast!

The thirteenth move allows us to delve deeper into the theory of openings. White has fended off the quick and ingenious attack by Black. By moving his pawn from C3 to C4, Black has opened up his bishop's line and created the expectation of sacrificing it later on in exchange for White's silver general. Thanks to his F7–F6 move, White has destroyed any of Black's hopes of capturing his silver general. It is now clear that either player can capture his opponent's silver general by moving a pawn to H6. But an attentive player will realize that there is not yet a single square into which he can successfully move his silver general. To launch a victorious attack, the player must first open up the game by moving some pawns forward and sending the H1 knight into battle.

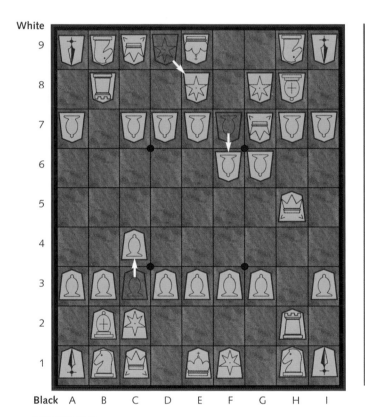

White

9 8 7 6 5 4 3 2 1

Black A B C D E F G H I

DIAGRAM D:
Layout of the board after the thirteenth move. The static rook opening has reached its end.

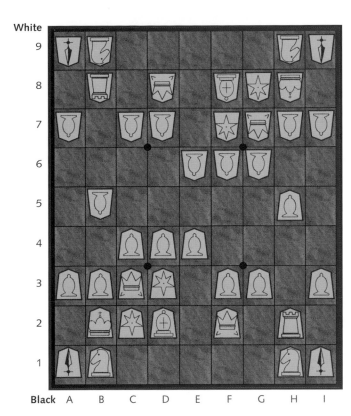

White

9 8 7 6 5 4 3 2 1

Black A B C D E F G H I

DIAGRAM E:
Yagura opening.

Not surprisingly, an impatient player would want to try these strategies right away, but it is better to wait. To execute this offensive effectively, a player would require the experience of the great shogi grand masters. The grand masters maintain that a great attack from both sides leads immediately to a weakening in the position of the pieces on the board; a player, therefore, should never attack except to rescue the king. If a player disregards this advice and launches an attack, he is doomed to fail. Upon studying Diagram D, an inexperienced player would probably say that Black's king is sufficiently protected—he has a golden general to one side and another not far to his left. But this is not enough, because there are still too many open squares surrounding him—for instance, the two unprotected pawns if front of the king. Later on he will have no time to defend them. This is something that is repeated to every new shogi player, though nearly everyone ignores it. Those novice players will have

to learn the hard way before they understand the importance of keeping the king safe in a "fort" while opening the game.

Yagura Opening

One of the most effective and safest shogi openings from the static rook setup is called the *yagura*. The only disadvantage to this opening is that the adversary may choose the same one, making it that much more difficult to gain any advantage (Diagram E).

Both sides have entrenched themselves and mobilized their forces. One of the players will now have to begin an attack, which will weaken his opening position. The moves following an attack leave openings where the attacker's opponent can move his own pieces. Thus, a failed attack will often lead to a swift defeat. Therefore, the importance of having a well-prepared attack should be reiterated.

In this situation, Black will probably carefully move his silver general forward and position it behind the pawn in the third column, which will likely be sacrificed.

Moves following the yagura opening

1. B: C3-C4, 2. W: B7-B6, 3. B: C1-D2,

4. W: G7-G6, 5. B: D2-C3, 6. W: B6-B5,

7. B: H3-H4, 8. W: F9-G8, 9. B: D1-C2,

10. W: G9-F8, 11. B: G1-F2, 12. W: C9-D8,

13. B: H6-H5, 14. W: F8-G7, 15. B: E3-E4,

16. W: E7-E6, 17. B: F1-F2, 18: W: D9-E8,

19. B: D5-D4, 20. W: F7-F6, 21. B: E2-E3,

22. W: E8-F2, 23. B: B2-C1, 24. W: H8-G9,

25. B: C1-D2, 26. W: G9-F8, 27. B: E1-D1,

28: W: E9-F9, 29. B: D1-C1, 30. W: F9-G9,

31. B: C1-B2, 32. W: G9-H8.

For example, if Black moves his silver general to G4, he can move his knight directly behind it and then move the pawn to F5. If he plays this well, he may force White to capture his piece so the knight will then have to enter into battle. Before advancing a knight in this manner, all the pieces must be perfectly positioned to break file. Later on, there will be no time to do so, because Black can lose his knight immediately if White gets the chance to move a pawn in front of it.

Dynamic Rook Openings

In this series of openings, which are generally mixed and matched, the king is kept safely on the right-hand side of the board after the rook abandons its opening position.

1. The center column, or *naka-bis-ha* (the central position of the rook), often provokes a violent attack by the opponent's rook. If the attack is made too quickly and is unsuccessful, the formation of the pieces is usually ruined.

The shogi struggle for the throne, thirtieth session. The player at right is Koji Tanigawa, a very well-known player in Japan.

2. A position from which one rook faces another, producing a *mukai-bisha* (a challenge among rooks). This is a strong defensive position, recommended when there is a chance of a counterattack.

3. One of the two columns between the center of the board and the rook. The rook is not meant to stay in a single column for the rest of the game. In dynamic rook openings, the rook moves from one side to another depending on the layout of the board. The rook should be very flexible. Compare this with static rook openings, in which the rook sometimes remains in its opening position for the duration of the game, making its influence felt without ever moving a single space.

A Typical Static Rook Opening

A typical static rook opening can begin perfectly with the following moves:

1. Black moves his pawn from C3 to C5. White makes the same move, moving his pawn from G7 to G6.

2. The black pawn on D3 moves to D4. Black chooses this simple move because he wants to block the line between the bishops. His goal is to attain the desired formation without feeling constantly threatened by the bishop taken by his opponent. White moves his pawn from B7 to B6: a static rook move.

3. Black moves his golden general from D1 to C2, and White immediately reacts with an equivalent move: G9–F8.

4. Black's golden general moves from C2 to D3. White then moves his pawn from B6 to B5.

5. Now it is Black's turn: he moves his bishop from B2 to C3. This move is of vital importance when the white pawn threatens B4. From now on, the bishop controls its advance (Diagram F).

The black bishop will move to B2, C2, D2, or E2, and the king will be safe at H2, where it is protected by at least two guardians.

Fourth "Ladies' Open." This women's tournament was held at the Park Hotel in Sapporo, Japan. At right, the player Nakai.

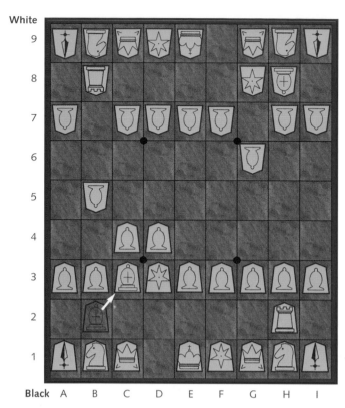

White

(Board diagram with rows numbered 9 through 1, and columns labeled A through I)

Black A   B   C   D   E   F   G   H   I

DIAGRAM F:
An example of a dynamic rook opening.

Many caricatures depict the shogi phenomenon. Because it once was a game played by the elites, many Shogun and Samurai appear in these illustrations. This engraving shows a Samurai sweeping the floor with shogi pieces.

STRATEGY

There is no better way to surprise one's opponent than to invent a few opening moves of one's own.

Additional Moves

White seeks a secure position and moves his pieces from G9 to F8. Black moves the rook from H2 to C2. The white pawn moves from F7 to F6.

Black's king moves from E1 to F2, and White moves his gold general from D9 to E8.

Black keeps advancing his king, from F2 to G2. Now White also moves his king, from E9 to F9.

Black takes his king from F9 to his rook's opening position at H2. White moves his silver general from F8 to G7.

Black moves his silver general from G1 alongside his king, at G2. This is a very important move, typical of the moves in a dynamic rook opening. The gold and silver generals mutually protect one another. Later on, once the rooks have been taken (which often happens in a dynamic rook opening), White will reintroduce a rook, perhaps on D1. He knows from experience that this position is difficult to defeat. White moves his gold general from E8 to F7.

Black moves his silver general from C1 to D2. White then attacks with his bishop, advancing it from H8 to G9.

The black pawn moves from E4 to E3, and White's pawn moves from E7 to E6. The black bishop moves from C2 to B2. White threatens to break through his adversary's ranks and positions himself at B4. B4 is now controlled by both the rook and the bishop at G9. The threat has now been neutralized. This is an example of how to use the rook in this type of opening. The white bishop at G7 moves to E9.

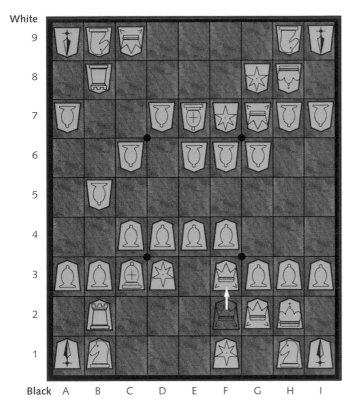

White

Black A B C D E F G H I

DIAGRAM G:
This move for the silver general was developed by the shogi master Ohno. It marks the end of the dynamic rook opening.

Black's silver general at D2 moves to E3, and the White king moves from F9 to G9.

Black moves his pawn from F3 to F4, while White advances his king from G9 to H9.

Black's silver general moves from E3 to F2. This move was developed by the shogi master Ohno, an authority in the field of openings. His intention is to move to F3, but first comes White's turn: he moves his pawn from C7 to C6.

Just as expected, Black succeeds in moving his silver general to F3 (Diagram G).

Black will end up thrusting his knight into battle when he moves his pawn from G3 to G4. If he later moves another pawn from F4 to F5, he can more effectively threaten his opponent. White will be able to block him if he moves his bishop to C7.

A shogi championship, fifteenth session. Grand master Ooyama, age sixty-six, wins with a straight score.

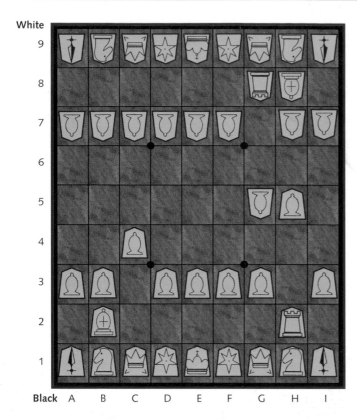

White

9 8 7 6 5 4 3 2 1

Black   A B C D E F G H I

DIAGRAM H:
The Ishida variation.

The Ishida Variation

The Ishida variation is a well-known dynamic rook opening that can throw an opponent off his game completely in just a couple of moves—especially if he is unfamiliar with it. This variation was developed more than a century ago by a blind chess player named Ishida. The diagram shows the moves leading up to an Ishida formation from the perspective of the White player:

Black moves his pawn from C3 to C4, and White reacts by moving his pawn from G7 to G6.

The pawn game continues: the black pawn moves from H3 to H4, and White moves from G6 to G5.

The black pawn moves from H4 to H5. White moves his rook from B8 to G8 (Diagram H).

Now, if White makes the mistake of moving his pawn unthinkingly from H7 to H6, Black will take it. Predictably, White will then take the black piece with his rook. Black, consequently, will move a pawn from G3 to G4—quite an effective tactic!

Wrapping Up

For now, the reader has enough information with which to become familiar with shogi. He can have a good time playing, testing his ingenuity and strategic gifts as he makes his first moves on the board.

The cat (the master) plays with his mice—the shogi pieces.

TIP
If you put yourself in the position of the White player, you will quickly realize that it is a challenge not to lose this game immediately.

Shogi: Part 3

Shogi has a completely Japanese feel to it, even as it spreads throughout the world. This should come as no surprise, for this fascinating game—played avidly by more than twenty million Japanese—has a history that is as intimately connected to Japanese culture as any other tradition. In present-day Japan, there are about 150 professional shogi players, of whom only about five are women. An official competition usually lasts an entire day. The system of *dans* and *kyus* is complemented by a whole system of handicaps. The stronger player uses two pieces fewer than the weaker player to compensate for the difference in their skill. These two pieces are removed from the board before the game begins and are never used. In the great tournaments, the handicap is seldom used; rather, this system is used in schools where professionals play against amateurs, or in the many shogi clubs scattered throughout the country. To compensate for a player's relative lack of skill, a more experienced player may remove as many as six of his pieces from the board, which equals eleven degrees of difference in terms of strength. The stronger player in this case must play without a rook, bishop, knights, or lances. Thanks to this system, a beginning player can challenge a stronger opponent from a position of relative equality.

Engraving from a shogi manual from 1878. A samurai plays a priest while the fox-headed judge observes the match.

Variations on Goose

The rules of the game on the preceding pages pertain to a relatively modern version of Goose and differ somewhat from the original rules. The following pages describe this history and explain the rules of one very interesting variation.

Brepols' Goose

Brepols' Goose board (pictured on the preceding page) has 63 spaces. The game's accessories are the same as in the modern version, and the number of players is also unlimited. Before beginning, the player decides how many chips to use in order to start the game.

TIP

After the winner reaches his goal, the other players can keep playing. The starting position and the chips in the pot are not all that counts in this version of the game!

The rules for the first roll are:

- With a three and a six the pawn is placed on space 26.
- If a player rolls a four and a five, he places his pawn on space 53.

The Geese Are Always Positive

In this game players also add up the points rolled on the two dice and move their pawns that number of spaces. If a pawn lands on a goose, it moves to the next goose and the player rolls again. In the Brepols variation, none of the geese face backward or forward, nor are there any dead geese—landing on a goose is always positive. If a pawn lands on a space occupied by another player, the two pawns must switch places. The player whose pawn is ambushed must pay two chips into the pot.

Around 1930, by which time Goose had become enormously popular, the game pieces underwent some great changes. Manufacturers designed special dice, pawns, and chips. The most surprising feature of the goose pawns pictured above and on the following page is their movable heads.

Special Positions

When a player reaches a bridge (at 6 or 12), he must pay a chip into the pot, but if he pays double he can move directly to space 12 (although usually when a player lands on one of the bridges, he moves his pawn to the other bridge and rolls again after paying a chip into the pot). Likewise, when a player lands on one of the dice spaces (26 or 53), he moves his pawn to the other dice space (forward or back) and rolls again.

When a player arrives at the inn at space 19, he must summon all his patience, for he must wait a turn as well as pay into the pot whatever number of chips each other player paid at the start of the game. If a player lands in the well on 31, he has reason to feel frustrated, for he must remain there until he is rescued by another player—that is, until another player falls into the well. He can then trade places with the new arrival, but only after paying the same number of chips he paid in at the start of the game. This rule also applies to a player who lands in the maze; when this happens, the player must also move back three spaces. If a player lands in jail (space 52), he must pay one chip and wait for another player to liberate him by also landing in jail. If a player lands

on a skull, he must start all over again. The first player to reach space 63 with the exact number of points wins—as a reward, he wins the contents of the pot.

Monkey

The game of Monkey is a fun variation on goose. Any number of people can play, and it is suitable for players of all ages. Each player receives a pawn and twelve chips, six of which he must pay into the pot. After the players roll to determine who will make the first move, the first player rolls the dice and adds his points; he then moves his pawn accordingly.

Squares with Monkeys

If a pawn lands on a square where there is a monkey, it advances again the same number of places and continues to a new square where there is no monkey. If the player draws a three and a four, or a five and a six, he has to go to the bridge on square 6. To leave this square, it is necessary to pay two chips into the pot. If he cannot pay them, he loses his turn.

If a player lands on the same square as another player, the two pawns must trade places. The "bumped" player will have to pay over one chip. But pay attention: he is not paying into the pot but to the other player.

Special Positions

The player that lands on a lodge located on square 19 loses one turn and must pay four chips into the pot. If he cannot pay all of it, he will deposit two pieces and lose two turns. If a player reaches the well (square 32), he will not be able to escape from it until another player falls into it and "rescues" him. The "rescuer" must remain in the well, but receives two chips from the rescued player. To climb the towers at square 51 is also costly. The player must remain on that square until somebody occupies his place, to whom he must pay three chips. If a player has already gone two turns without playing, and no one has rescued him yet, he can continue play after paying out eight chips. In the labyrinth (square 53), the player loses his sense of direction. To reorient himself, he must pay one chip into the plate and go back to square 47. But without a doubt, the worst luck is to land on square 58, decorated with a skull, since that player must go back to the beginning.

If a player rolls a number higher than he needs to reach the final space, he must move back the extra number of spaces. The winner is the first player to roll exactly the right number to reach space 63. That player will do a monkey-dance!

The new game of Monkey is one of many variations on the traditional game of Goose. This color lithograph is from 1920.

CURIOUS FACT

Goethe, the great German writer, understood the symbolic meaning of Goose. In his collection of poems, *West-Eastern Divan*, he writes, "Life is like a game of goose. The more one moves forward, the closer one is to the goal, where no one would like to be. It is said that geese are stupid, but oh, we mustn't believe what people say, for a goose looks back once to force me to retreat. Many and varied are the things of this world, where everything must go forward and in which, when someone stumbles, no one turns back to help him."

Alsa

Alsa is the name of a French brand of leavening used for baking cakes. The manufacturer used the game of Goose to promote its products, and the game could be obtained in exchange for special "Alsa stamps." The board came with a little pouch containing dice and pawns.

Alsa differs from other variations on goose in that players do not pay any chips into the pot at the start of the game.

To win, a player must arrive at number 63 by rolling the exact number. If he rolls too high, he must move back the extra number of spaces.

The players roll one die, and the person who rolls the highest gets to make the first move. He now rolls both dice and places his pawn on the

The pawns in Alsa were large chips advertising various products manufactured by the company.

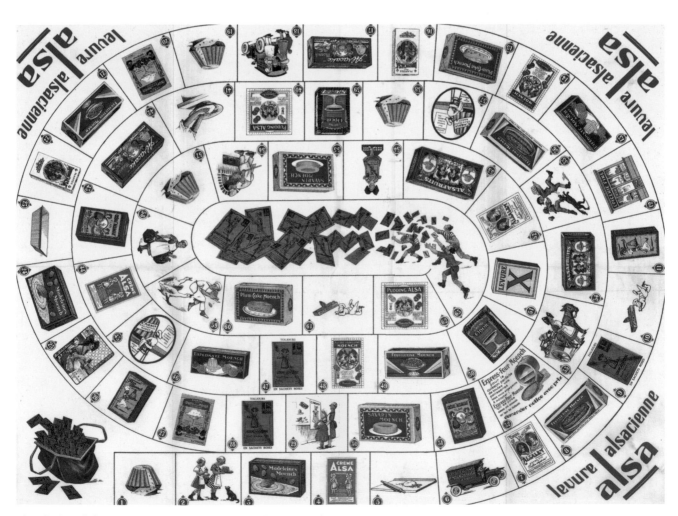

This Alsa board, from around 1930, is based on Brepols' version of Goose.

corresponding space. The other players take turns doing the same.

If in the first round a player rolls a three and a six (for a total of nine), he can move directly to space 19. (The original rules of the game stated: "The player may continue until reaching a space with a delicious cake made with Alsa.")

If the player rolls a four and a five (the sum of which is nine), he may move directly to space 57, which features the last of the cakes.

Special Positions

During a game, each time a player lands on the number 6, which pictures an Alsa delivery man, he moves forward to number 12, where there are packages of Alsa leavening; this space shows a shopkeeper receiving an order from the company.

A player is unlucky if he lands on the number 23. The miller needs help kneading dough, so the player loses two turns.

Space 56 is also unlucky, for there he finds a cake baked *without* Alsa. The player must then retreat to space 12 to buy a package of leavening from the shopkeeper.

Space 51, which shows a package of non-Alsa leavening, is *very* unlucky. If a player lands there, he must remain on that space until rescued by another. The player who "rescues" him must stay there while the rescued player is allowed to continue the game.

The kitchen at space 25 is bad news as well. If a player lands on this space, he must stay there baking cakes until another player relieves him of this task.

If a player lands on space 58, he must start all over again: the woman of the house has gone grocery shopping and forgotten her Alsa, so she sends the player out to get it!

Illustration of a game of Goose from Holland, 1920.

English Checkers
History of the Game

◆ ◆ ◆

There are many different stories about the origin of checkers, as for so many other games. Some maintain that the game was played as early as 1000 B.C.E., while others believe it was not invented until the eighteenth century. Spain and France are commonly named as its birthplace. However, in the tombs of the Pharaohs, game boards with twelve black and twelve white pieces have been found that appear to have been checkers sets. Also, descriptions of this game come down to us from ancient Greece and Rome.

One theory of the game's origins holds that it was invented around 1100 in the south of France, where it was called *Fierges*. This game was played with backgammon pieces and a chessboard. Pieces were captured in the same manner as in the game windmill. Each player received twelve pieces called *ferses*, like the queens in medieval chess.

A cartoon depicting the *goût du jour*, from the late eighteenth century.

Winning by Capturing

2 A game of checkers often ends up being a match of two kings against one. The lone king is forced to retreat to the left-hand corner and is then obliged to move out and capture again.

It is important to keep this classic maneuver in mind. The endgame is decided in the following moves (Diagram 2):

1. White: G8–H7; Black: G6–F7
2. White: H7–G8; Black: F5–E6
3. White: G8–H7; Black: F7–G8
4. White: H7–G6; Black: G8–H7
5. White: G6–H5; Black: E6–D5
6. White: H5–G4; Black: D5–E4
7. White: G4–H5; Black: E4–F3

The result of these moves is that Black captures the white king and wins the game.

Winning by Blocking

3 Starting from the position shown in Diagram 3, Black blocks his opponent's last remaining pieces. He moves a piece from G8 to F7. White moves from H7 to G8. Black moves from F7 to G6, giving White no choice but to capture the black piece at G6 (White moves his piece from F5 to H7). Black moves his king from D7 to E6. The white piece must abandon the right-hand corner and move from G8 to F7. The Black king at E6 captures the white piece and jumps to G8. The white piece that remains on the board has nowhere to move. Black wins by blocking (Diagram 3).

Checkers pieces with cameos from the sixteenth century.

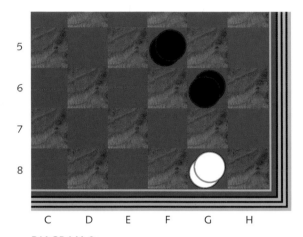

DIAGRAM 2:
A classic endgame in which two kings of the same color play against a single king of the other. After a few simple moves, Black finishes the game and wins.

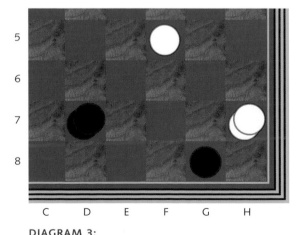

DIAGRAM 3:
Each player has a king and an ordinary piece. Black wins the game by capturing the king and blocking the other white piece.

French advertisement for a numerical version of checkers, 1850.

Variations

In its long history, checkers has had different variations played on the same 8 x 8 board. Cat and Birds, Belgian checkers, and diagonal checkers are three diverse examples.

Cat and Birds

In this entertaining game, the cat wants to capture the birds. Twelve white "birds" are placed on the board, as in English checkers. The black cat is alone and sits on the black square on the bottom left-hand corner opposite the birds. White begins, moving a bird forward diagonally from its square.

The black cat can move backward as well as forward. Unlike the birds, it can capture the other pieces. It does so in the same manner as a king in English checkers—in a single move it can capture several birds by jumping forward and back. The birds can win by trapping the cat so that it has nowhere to move; the cat can win by capturing all the birds.

The birds have more chances of winning, so sometimes the players agree that the cat can make two moves per turn. Sometimes the game is played with two cats. As a general rule, people play several games until the cat wins. If they continue playing, White starts each subsequent game with one piece fewer than before. When the cat wins, players switch sides. The player who gets to play the birds for the greatest number of games is the final winner (Diagram D).

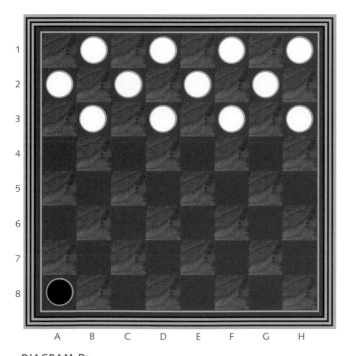

DIAGRAM D:
Starting position in a game of Cat and Birds.

Belgian Checkers

This game is played by exactly the same rules as English checkers, except the goal is completely opposite: the player to lose all his pieces first wins. This means adopting a completely different way of thinking of the game. Belgian checkers (known in Britain as the Losing Game and in France as *Coquimbert*) has its own unique set of strategies and tactics.

As in English checkers, players can and must capture their opponents' pieces, but here, that is exactly what your opponent wants you to do.

Crowning a piece is clearly a losing strategy, so you want to try to force your opponent to do so.

Diagonal Checkers

The rules and objective of this game are essentially the same as for English checkers. The big different lies in the opening position of the pieces. Each player puts twelve pieces in diagonal rows. The pieces move diagonally one space at a time. A piece is crowned when it reaches the opposite end of the board, which is much smaller in this version of the game, consisting of only two squares on each end: A2 and B1, or G8 and H7 (Diagram E).

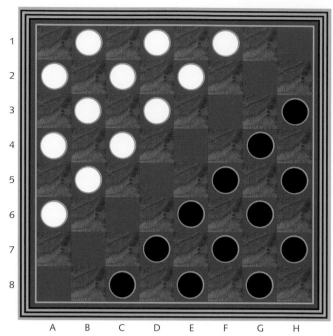

DIAGRAM E:
Opening position in a game of diagonal checkers.

Photo of a checkers championship from a January 1885 edition of *La gazette du Jeu de Dames.*

Senat
History of the Game

◆ ◆ ◆

According to archeological findings, Senat, also known as Senet, was played as early as 3200 B.C.E. The proof is that the game was found in the tomb of Hesy (2686-2613 B.C.E.). The Pharaohs owned magnificent game boards made of highly valuable wood and encrusted with ivory. Four intact boards were found in the tomb of Tutankhamen (circa 1337 B.C.E.), among them an adjustable table with legs shaped to resemble lion's paws.

At the 1986 World's Fair in Vancouver, Canada, the Egyptian pavilion was designed to look like a temple, in which was held an exhibition of objects from the Museum of Cairo from the era of Ramses II (1290–1224 B.C.E.). Among them was a wooden door from the tomb of Sennedjem. In the "temple," one could purchase a poster depicting a section of this door, which bore the image of Sennedjem playing a game of Senat against an invisible adversary, under the watchful eye of his wife Lyneferty. The woman squeezes her husband's shoulder and arm. Sennedjem has a great kerchief in one hand, while the other rests on one of his ten pawns. The catalog for the exhibition read, "Before them we see a table covered in offerings: loaves of bread, baskets of fruit, figs, garden produce, and cucumbers, all of them displayed decoratively on a tablecloth. In the lower part of the image we see a cabbage, a head of lettuce, and two bottles of milk, completing this rather symbolic meal."

Tapestry depicting a game of Senat. Here a lion plays against an antelope.

Mural on the door of Sennedjem's tomb at Deir-el-Medina, west of Thebes.

Symbolic Meaning

The Egyptians apparently found Senat to be a pleasant and relaxing game. The game also had symbolic, mystical significance. The board is divided into thirty squares, known as "houses." Some of them feature hieroglyphics, while the rest are home to gods, with whose help lions and jackals move across the board. This movement symbolizes the drifting of souls through the world of the dead. Sennedjem's invisible opponent, for instance, is none other than Osiris, the guardian of the shadow world. The dead had to plead with Osiris to grant them eternal life. It was therefore believed advantageous to master the game of Senat before one's death.

Murals

The most surprising characteristic of ancient Egyptian murals, which exemplify the artistic vision of this civilization, is that people and objects were always depicted in profile. Ramses III (1182–1151 B.C.E.) likewise enjoyed Senat. The wall of his palace of Medinet Haboe bears a fresco that shows him playing Senat with two women.

Over the years many murals have been found which depict a dead person enjoying a festive banquet.

A Very Popular Game

Senat was not only a game for the pharaohs—it was very popular in all strata of Egyptian society. An ordinary person would not be discouraged by not having the resources of his rulers—he would simply draw the Senat board in the sand and use stones or bits of clay as pawns. Evidence shows that the laborers who built the pyramids made Senat boards out of clay so they could play a quick game during their breaks from work.

Research

Without a doubt, a great deal of information about Senat has been discovered through archeological research, especially in temples and tombs. But none of the Egyptian documents provides clear information about the rules of the game. Therefore, they have been reconstructed by Swiss archeologist Gustave Jéquier. After an exhaustive study, German archeologist Edgar B. Pusch was able to confirm the salient points of the game.

Characteristic Senat pieces have been found throughout Egypt. The pieces in this image are from the collection of the British Museum in London.

Playing Senat

Senat is also known as *senet or s'ent*. In the hieroglyphic writing used during the era when the game originated, its name was written like this:

Regardless of what the game was called or how it was written, the meaning always remained the same: to signal the transition of the human spirit toward a new life beyond death, beyond the underworld. Perhaps because of this symbolism, Senat was the most popular board game in ancient Egypt. In some ways the game is truly immortal, for it survives today in the form of its descendant, backgammon. Taken literally, Senat is primarily an exciting racing game in which lions and jackals try to pass one another. Instead of dice, the game uses four little sticks with two faces on them. One player uses five lions while the other uses five jackals. Players must move across the board with their pawns as quickly as possible in order to finally remove them, one by one. The first to do so is the winner.

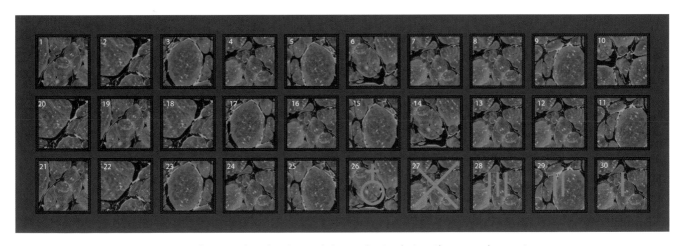

Senat requires this game board and special dice. To begin playing, the game also requires five black pieces (lions) and five white pieces (jackals).

Players	Requirements
2	special board
	5 each, white and black pieces
Average duration	4 special dice
30 minutes	
Category	
ancient, racing	

A Variation on Senat

There are several variations on Senat. This example uses ten lions and ten jackals, which makes the game more complicated and forces the players to pay closer attention. The rules of the game are basically the same as before, except for some changes: the two sides take turns placing their lions or jackals in the first twenty houses. As usual, the lions occupy odd-numbered houses, and jackals occupy even-numbered ones. The player who begins the game plays with the jackals. In his first turn, he moves the jackal from 20 to 21. The lions must make their first move with the lion in house 19.

The Key Difference

In terms of capturing pieces, constructing blocks, and the system of marked houses, this variation is identical to the version played with five lions and five jackals.

Here, too, the two players must remove their lions or jackals from the board as quickly as possible. There is, however, one important difference: a player can begin to remove his pieces from the board only after he has five pieces in the third row. If a lion or jackal is captured, and the number of pieces in the final row falls below five, the player must add more pieces before he can keep removing pieces from the board.

If the number of pieces in the last row falls below five because a lion or jackal has been removed from the board, the player must correct the deficit before any of his other pieces reaches house 30 and can be retired.

This image was found in a 3,000-year-old papyrus. An Egyptian man plays Senat against an invisible opponent while his wife watches the game over his shoulder (British Museum, London).

Poker
History of the Game

◆ ◆ ◆

Poker was originally a game common to the United States. In most every Hollywood Western, after a long day of work cowboys would be seen playing poker in a saloon. Most poker historians agree that the name comes from an eighteenth-century French game called *poque*. There are also those who believe poker to have derived from the German game *Pochspiel*, in which players must lie to one another. Others relate it to the Hindustani game of *pukka*. The poker historian John Scarne dismisses all these theories and claims that the name is derived from the word poke, which in the United States was a colloquial word meaning "sack" or "bag." The term originated in the Middle Ages, when pants did not yet have pockets, and valuables were kept in a bag tied to one's belt. The first pickpockets were known as "cutpurses" because they would steal their victims' money by cutting the string that held the poke. One of the first mentions of poker appeared in 1834, when Jonathan H. Green published the rules of the game. By that time the game already had many fans, especially on Mississippi riverboats. Players were inspired by sailors who played *As-Nas* in New Orleans, an old Persian game whose basic rules are similar to those of poker.

Nowhere was poker more popular than on the riverboats that plied the Mississippi.
In 1835, no fewer than 2,000 professional players worked on 250 steamboats.

A game parlor in Cripple Creek, Colorado, circa 1895. Besides poker, the parlor featured faro, keno, and a wheel of fortune.

The ace in poker almost certainly got its name from *As-Nas*, an ancestor of the Italian game of *primero* and the French *gilet*, which became *brelan* during the reign of Charles IX (1560–1574). Brelan was the basis for later variations known as *bouillotte* and *ambigu*. In American poker (as played by the French), four cards of the same suit are called *brelan* or *berlanga*.

Mississippi Riverboats

Before the arrival of the steam engine, river traffic only flowed in one direction: downstream. Inland pioneers transported animal skins and *tarwe* on rafts. In New Orleans they would purchase many items with their earnings, which they would in turn have to transport by land. As a result, this period was a golden age for gamblers and cardsharps. There came a time when so much gambling and robbery took place along these roads that laws were passed to limit these activities. Clergymen warned they could lead to purgatory and the end of the world. On December 16, 1811, the Mississippi was shaken by an earthquake. Even as houses collapsed and some men fell to their knees in prayer, others simply carried on playing poker. In the town of Paducah, one enthusiastic player who took these events to mean that the end of times was nigh, raised his eyes to the heavens and pled, "Please, God, let me at least finish this hand!"

Professional Players

The year of the earthquake was the year that the first steamboat appeared on the Mississippi. From that point on, goods could travel both upstream and downstream. In 1815 the steamboat *Enterprise* was the first to travel up and down the Mississippi, from New Orleans to Louisville in twenty-five days. Within five years there were seventy steamboats, some of which were strictly passenger boats. Passengers often passed the time by playing poker. By 1835, the Mississippi carried 250 boats, on which there were some 2,000 professional players.

Playing Dice Poker

Dice poker is an enjoyable game known throughout the world. But is the image it evokes truly accurate? Despite appearances, chance plays a very small part in this game. Poker requires several skills, including mathematical judgment, a good memory, and analytical ability. It is also important to keep a straight face when playing, which has come to be known as wearing a "poker face."

In theory, any number of people can play dice poker at one time, but in practice the ideal number appears to be five. The goal of dice poker is to roll the most valuable combination of dice at each hand. To do this, players roll five special dice printed with six different figures, rather than dots. These are, in order of their value: ace, king, queen, jack, red (ten), and black (nine).

The star of the French television movie *Ferdinand the Cowboy*, Ferdinand Raynaud, takes money from a band of gamblers in a game of poker.

The five special dice used to play dice poker.

Players	Requirements
2	5 special poker dice
	dice cup
Average duration	poker chips, their number
30 minutes	determined in advance
Category	
skill	

Rules:
Preliminaries

Each player sits before one of the arms of the cross on the board. If only two people are playing, each one uses the two colors on their side: red and blue versus black and white. Note that each of them will play with his two colors, alternating between them from one turn to the next. At the outset, the sixteen pawns are in the center square or *charkoni*. The player who rolls the highest number with the sticks

Bone throwing sticks, made circa 1800.

or dice starts, moving his first pawn. The other fifteen pawns do not enter the game until the player rolls a double with the sticks or dice (although some players allow the pawns to move according to the first roll, even if it is not a double). The throwing sticks are long and have four sides. One side has a dot, and its opposite has a six. The other two sides have a two and a five. This means that, when playing with ordinary six-sided dice, the four and the three do not count. If a player rolls a three or a four on the dice, he must roll again until he gets a one, two, five, or six.

A modern variation on pachisi. The game of Luisa was published in New York in 1892 by the McLoughlin brothers.

DIAGRAM A:
The course of a pawn. The *charkoni* is both the starting point and the goal.

How the Pawns Move

When it is a player's turn to move, he rolls the three sticks or dice all at once and moves one of his pawns the number of spaces he rolled. If he must roll the dice several times in the same turn, each allows him to move a different pawn. If more than one pawn occupies the same square, these pawns are considered one and the same and can move together the same number of squares. If the two sticks show the same number of points, and two pawns are in the same square, they can move twice that number of spaces together. If any square is occupied by more than one pawn, they move conventionally. The pawns leave the *charkoni* through the center aisle and move counterclockwise along the outer aisle of that arm. When a pawn reaches the door of the cen-

ter square, it moves diagonally from the outer aisle of that arm to the outer aisle of the adjacent arm. Thus, the pawns pass from one arm to another without entering the *charkoni*. When a pawn has run the entire course, it must once again enter the *charkoni* through the center aisle (Diagram A).

Capturing Pawns

When a pawn arrives at a square that is occupied by an adversary's pawn, it captures the opponent pawn, forcing it to return to the center square. Pawns do not capture by jumping over one another, but by taking another's space. The capturing player can roll again and move a second time. The owner of the defeated pawn must later reintroduce the pawn, setting it on its course around the board all over again.

Barriers

Barriers are constructed in order to block an opponent and to help one's own game. They are formed by two or more pawns in a single square. When playing in teams, players can construct a barrier with their own or their partner's pawns. Players may not jump over an opponent's barrier. Barriers may not be erected until at least one of a player's pawns has run half the course of the board; further, a barrier is not always formed when two or more pawns occupy the same space on the board. A barrier can be torn down when the opponent's pawn reaches that square after rolling an exact number of the dice. The pawns that form the barrier must then return to the center square.

An example of play (Diagram B):

There are barriers at positions A and B. They were allowed because in both cases, one of the pawns had already run half the course of the board. Now it is Black's turn, and he rolls a five. He cannot jump over the barrier and so is unable to move his first pawn. Instead he opts for moving the second, and captures Blue's third pawn. After Black's extra move, it is Red's turn. He rolls a four and decides to move his fourth pawn, destroying his opponent's barrier (B).

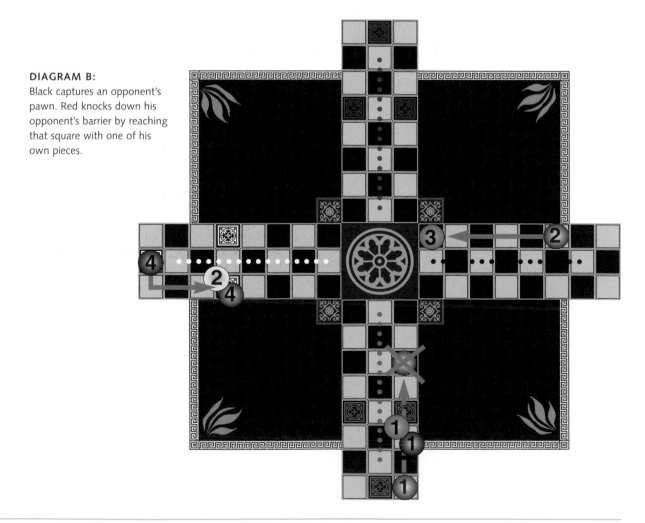

DIAGRAM B:
Black captures an opponent's pawn. Red knocks down his opponent's barrier by reaching that square with one of his own pieces.

Charkoni

The ultimate goal of all pawns, *charkoni*, must always be entered with an exact number of steps. If a player does not roll exactly the right number needed to arrive at *charkoni*, he must move another pawn. If that isn't possible either because the other pawns have already arrived at *charkoni* or because they are blocked, he loses his turn and must pass the dice to the next player. When a pawn enters *charkoni*, it must be laid on its side so it is not mistaken for an eliminated pawn or for a pawn not yet in play.

When the game is between two players, they enter charkoni according to an established order: the fourth red pawn must enter the center square before the last blue pawn may enter. The same is true for the fourth white pawn, which must enter *charkoni* before the fourth black pawn may do so. When four people play and one of them has managed to introduce all his pawns into *charkoni*, he will help out his partner in what remains of the game.

An example of play (Diagram C):

This is an example of play between two people. The player with red and blue pieces has rolled a ten and must play with blue. This seems to be a good move, because with a ten, the fourth blue pawn can enter *charkoni*. Unfortunately, the fourth red pawn must arrive there first. The player cannot move any of his blue pawns unless he decides to have his fourth pawn run another lap around the course. He could do this in order to give the fourth red pawn the chance to reach the final goal and to save it from his opponent's pawns, which are right on his heels.

STRATEGY

The number of pawns forming a barrier equals the number of pawns a player can lose all at once. After all, a barrier can be destroyed in an instant. It is therefore not a good idea to create barriers with more than two pawns.

DIAGRAM C:
The owner of the blue and red pawns rolls a ten. He must move a blue piece, but his last blue pawn cannot enter *charkoni* until his fourth red pawn has done so.

Furthermore...

A player may decide at any time, before or after rolling the dice, to pass his turn and not move any of his pawns. This can sometimes be very convenient, as when the player is waiting for his partner's pawn in order for them to build a barrier together. As mentioned, a pawn can always run another lap around the board, even if it has already reached its goal.

An example of play (Diagram D):

It is White's turn, and he rolls a ten. His first three pawns are safe within charkoni, so he wants to move the fourth. But if he moves that pawn the ten spaces he rolled, he almost misses placing it on his own arm, where it is safe, and puts that pawn dangerously close to three of his opponent's pawns. In a case like this, a player has two options:

- He can pass on his turn, in the hopes of rolling a thirteen or higher in the next round; or
- He can take a risk and move his pawn.

The Winner

The winner is the first team or player to return all pawns to the safety of *charkoni* after each piece has run the course of the board at least once.

DIAGRAM D:
White rolls a ten. If he moves his fourth pawn, he puts it dangerously close to three of his opponent's pawns; it is better to pass and to lose a turn.

The First Game

The following pages highlight interesting positions and options for play. For clarity's sake, the diagrams show only the pawns relevant to the move or position in question. The rules and examples discussed here correspond to the version of the game played with throwing sticks instead of cowrie shells. For the same reason, this game has no safe houses, although they are pictured on the board. Throwing sticks are long and have four sides, the two and the five being on opposite sides and the one and the six on the others.

To Hunt or Be Hunted?

1 It is Red's turn and he rolls thirteen points. If he moves his first or second pawn, they will end up ahead of the opponent's pawns, which will try to capture it. If on the other hand he moves his third pawn, it will stay behind the opponent's pawns and can later try to capture *them*. Red must ask himself whether he prefers to hunt or be hunted (Diagram 1).

The original version of pachisi used cowrie shells as dice.

DIAGRAM 1:
To hunt or be hunted? Red rolls a thirteen. If he moves his third pawn, he stays behind his opponents.

The First Game

The expression "practice makes perfect" is undoubtedly true in Alquerque. Each move should be carefully considered to try to foresee all its possible consequences. In a game between two expert players, even a one-piece lead can be decisive. Thus, a brief moment of distraction can make the difference between winning and losing. The following pages set forth some interesting play situations.

Opening Moves

1 A coin toss determines that White will open the game. He must move a piece to the only empty square, number 13. He can use the pieces on squares 14, 17, 18, or 19. Which one he chooses is unimportant, because that piece will inevitably be lost as soon as Black makes his first move. White decides to move his piece from square 14 to 13, which allows him to keep his back rows closed off. Black must capture the white piece on square 13 but can do so only with the piece at square 12, which he moves to

14. When White has his second turn, he will eliminate this black piece with his piece on square 15. Black's turn is next, and this time he cannot capture any pieces. He can, however, move the pieces in squares 7, 9, and 10. Of the four moves available, only one would prevent White from capturing one of his pieces later: moving from square 9 to 15. Moving the piece from 14 to 13 in his first move, White has opened the game intelligently. He has lost one piece, but he has also captured one, and his other pieces still maintain a closed position on the board (Diagram 1).

DIAGRAM 1:
The layout of the game after two opening moves. White has lost one piece.

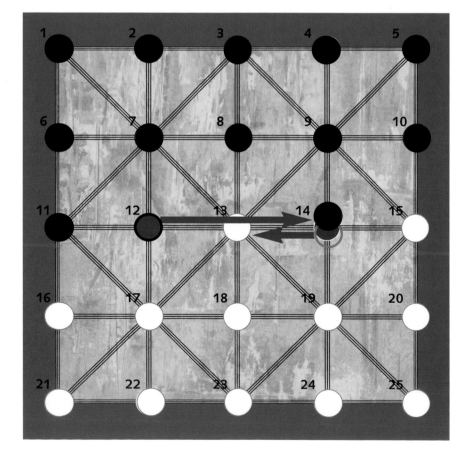

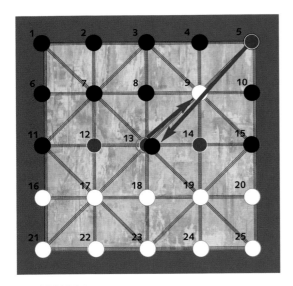

DIAGRAM 2A:
The black piece at square 5 captures the white piece that now occupies square 9.

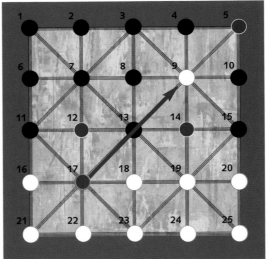

DIAGRAM 2B:
Next, the white piece at square 17 captures Black's piece at 13.

Pursuit

2 White is about to make his third move. As with his first turn, any piece he decides to move will be eliminated by Black's next move. Now, even if White loses a piece, Black will also lose a piece in the next turn. White chooses the piece at square 13 and moves it to 9 (Diagram 2A). Black captures it with the piece on square 5 and moves his piece to the center square, number 13. There he is eliminated by the white piece at 17, which moves to 9 (Diagram 2B). It is Black's turn again. He must capture with his piece at square 4, placing it on 14. The logical result is that in the next turn White captures the piece at 14.

After four moves, Black has captured three of his opponent's pieces, and White has captured two of his, so Black continues to play with ten pieces

while White has nine. If this trend persists, White is sure to lose, for he was the first to move.

Counterattack

After White actually captures the piece at 14, it is Black's turn. He cannot capture any pieces and so moves his piece from square 11 to 12. This is the only piece he can move without being threatened or captured by White in the next move. White tries to build a counterattack and decides to do so from behind. He moves his piece from 24 to 19. Now that Black cannot capture any pieces from his present position, he considers capturing several pieces at a time by moving his piece from square 3 to 4. All signs indicate that White's counterattack will fail and Black will gain even greater control over the game.

Persian miniature from 1489 depicting two men playing Chinese chess.

The Han Dynasty

The Chinese chessboard is divided into two halves, symbolizing the yellow Hwang-ho River. The river divides the warring states of Chu and Han. This is a faithful reflection of the historical situation in China before the consolidation of the Han dynasty in 206 B.C.E. This is probably the reason why the game is commonly known as "The Great Coup at Yellow River." The two emperors have locked themselves in, side by side, in their narrow fortresses, where they cannot be seen. Instead of ordinary chessmen, the game uses pieces that reflect Chinese tradition. Instead of kings there are emperors, who are seconded by two mandarins rather than bishops. There are also elephants and chariots. It should come as no surprise that the men who invented gunpowder also included cannons among the pieces of this game.

Exhibition

In 1987, an exhibition was held at Fu-Hua Gallery in Taipei, Taiwan, which displayed a variety of new Chinese chess pieces. In the exhibition were found wonderful examples of pieces created by some of Taiwan's most distinguished designers, architects, and popular craftsmen. Chiang-Ichu described the exhibition thus in the July 1987 edition of the *Free*

China Review: "This game of Indian origin developed a Chinese variation during the Tang dynasty (618–907). By the time of the Sung dynasty (960–1279), the game had a solid base that was closely related to the philosophy of yin and yang."

Expert writer on games and their history R.C. Bell owns a great collection of chessmen. He possesses, for example, several ball-shaped ivory pieces that contain various sculpted figures. The rank of each piece is indicated by a tiny image on the ball.

The same collection also includes black-and-white pieces, each of which has an erotic significance. Theory suggests that this is a reproduction of a rare, nineteenth-century set cast in ebony and ivory. More recent sets comprise a combination of modern and traditional materials.

Chinese Chessboards

Over the years, this game has been played on different kinds of boards. Relatively poor Chinese workers often played on pocket paper boards, which they could throw away once they started to tear. Wealthier players used marvelous, handcrafted wooden boards that could be opened or used as cases for storing the pieces.

Playing Chinese Chess

Chinese chess is an extraordinary game of strategy that never fails to surprise, thanks to the vast array of possibilities it has to offer. One of the game's characteristics is the curious manner in which some of the pieces enter into play, and the limited freedom of some of the others. For instance, elephants may not cross the river, jump, or make long-distance moves. The emperor and mandarins may not leave the fort, and therefore often obstruct one another. These rules confer upon Chinese chess its unique identity. It also has one point in common with Western chess. The goal of both games is the same, which is to checkmate the opposing emperor or king. In the original *choo-hong-ki* (the Chinese name for this game), each piece bears a calligraphic inscription, but the red and blue armies are somewhat different. The blue emperor is called Tsiang (general), while the red emperor is named Shuai (governor). In the West, players often use pieces with identical symbols for both teams instead of Chinese calligraphy.

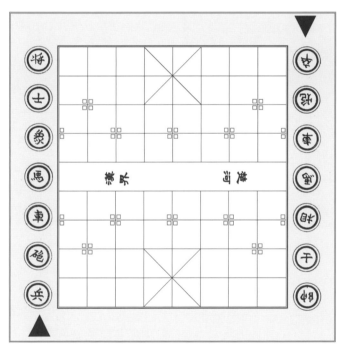

The special board and pieces required for Chinese chess.

Players
2

Average duration
45–60 minutes

Category
strategy

Requirements
special game board
16 special pieces per player

Rules:
Preliminaries

Chinese chess is played on a board with 8 × 9 squares. But because the pieces sit on the points of intersection between these squares, it makes more sense to speak of nine lines by ten. Two fortresses are marked on the board by crosses. The Yellow River, which separates the two armies, is represented by a horizontal bar across the middle of the board. Each player gets sixteen pieces. In the diagrams below, the pieces bear symbols that will be easier for Western players to understand than the traditional Chinese calligraphy.

CURIOUS FACT

Throughout the world there are some 500 million Chinese-chess players. In China, the great champions tend to be professional players. Today, China boasts twenty grand masters and five grand mistresses.

The following is a list of each player's pieces, alongside their Chinese names and translations.

The red army consists of:

- 1 × Shuai (governor)—red emperor
- 2 × Shi—red mandarin
- 2 × Sang—red elephant
- 2 × Ma—red horse
- 2 × Tsjü—red chariot
- 2 × Pao—red cannon
- 5 × Tsu—red soldier

The blue army consists of:

- 1 × Tsiang (general)—blue emperor
- 2 × Shi—blue mandarin
- 2 × Sang—blue elephant
- 2 × Ma—blue horse
- 2 × Tsjü—blue chariot
- 2 × Pao—blue cannon
- 5 × Ping—blue soldier

DIAGRAM A:
The opening layout of the two armies' pieces.

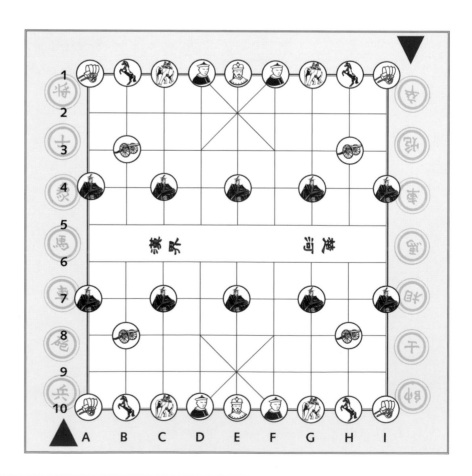

Red always begins, so players should decide beforehand which color each player will use (Diagram A).

How the Pieces Move

After the opening move, players take turns moving their pieces. Two general rules apply here:

1. There must never be more than one piece on a single square.
2. Players may not repeat moves in three consecutive turns that leave a piece on the same square as it was before.

Each piece is governed by different rules with regard to its freedom of movement.

Emperor: This piece can move one square forward, backward, or sideways, with the added restriction that it must always remain within its fortress. Its freedom of movement is therefore limited to nine squares. A crucial rule in Chinese chess is that the

two emperors must never "see" one another. This means they can never sit across from one another in a straight line, unless there is a piece between them. When a piece stands between the two emperors, it cannot be moved—it remains "chained" to its square until one of the emperors moves inside his fortress. This is a logical condition, because a player who removes such a piece puts his own emperor in check.

The Mandarin: The mandarin, too, is condemned to a life inside the fortress. It can only move diagonally to an adjacent square, and therefore has but five squares within its reach (Diagram B).

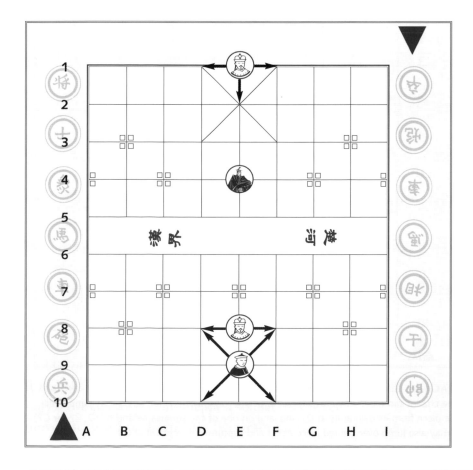

DIAGRAM B:
If both emperors are positioned directly across from one another in a straight line, they must not "see" each other; in this example, the piece at E4 prevents them from doing so. Inside his fortress the mandarin can move to any one of five squares.

Bifurcated Attacks

5 Bifurcated attacks are double attacks in which a single piece threatens two of the opponent's pieces at once. Diagram 5 shows two examples. The blue mandarin at E9 attacks the red horses at D8 and F10 while the red emperor at E2 threatens the two cannons at D2 and F2 (Diagram 5).

A game of chess in the era before the Maoist revolution.

DIAGRAM 5:
Two bifurcated attacks. The blue mandarin at E9 threatens two red horses, while the red emperor at E2 threatens two cannons.

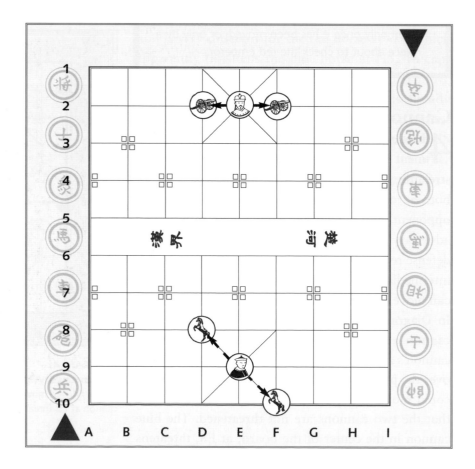

Chinese Chess: Part 2

For centuries, chess has been a source of fascination for thousands of people the world over. This interest is reflected in the immense literature on the subject, which could easily fill several libraries. In his *Schachnovelle*, Stefan Zweig writes: "Is it just a game? Or is it a science, or an art that oscillates between these two categories... It is very ancient, but at the same time, always new; its organization is mechanical, but it only works under the operation of fantasy; restricted by the geography of the board, but unlimited in the possible combinations of play; an architecture without mass but undoubtedly long-lasting in its existence...?" This almost lyrical description applies to Western chess as well as Chinese or Japanese chess, and implies that this is not a game that can be "learned in an instant, played, and then forgotten again." The fascinating learning process begins once a player studies the rules in depth. At this stage, the player tries all kinds of situations and variations on the game, and as a person learns, catches a glimpse of the hidden world of chess. Only after some time should he cautiously play his first match. Experience tells us that if he will carry on in this fashion for a long time, once one is immersed in Chinese chess, there is no end to either learning or playing.

A game of Chinese chess being played on a common paper board. Beijing, China *(Photo: Pim Smit, Amsterdam)*.

An Assault board from 1910. It depicts the war between the Boers and the British troops at Transvaal, South Africa (1899–1902). The upper part of the board depicts the negotiation of the truce between General Wood and General Joubert, while the lower extreme shows the Boers firing on British troops.

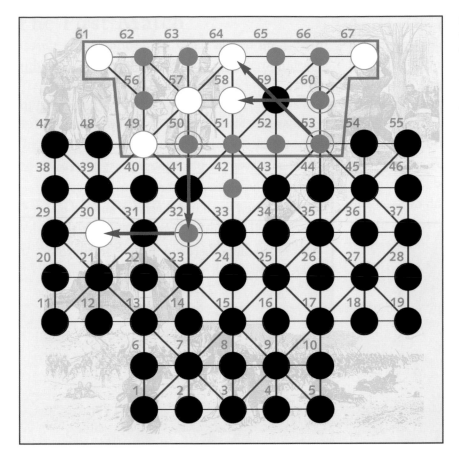

DIAGRAM C:
Capturing pieces. The French officer's move from space 50 is preferred, because it means he can capture two German pieces in a single move, whereas the officers at 60 and 53 can eliminate only one German apiece.

French Assault board, late nineteenth century.

A German in the Fortress

3 The Germans insist on pursuing the French. Because most of them are inside the fortress, the Germans decide to lay siege to it. The soldier at 53 is already inside, but he risks death, so his partner at space 35 moves to 43. Thanks to this move, the French can now choose between capturing the German at 53 or the one at 43. Whichever victim the French choose, the Germans are now assured entry into the fortress with one of their pieces. The French capture the German at 53. This is a good decision, for this soldier was already inside the fortress, and this is where the Germans must be repelled. Besides, the French official is able to return to his fortress. If the French had captured the German at space 43 with the officer at 34, the German at 53 could have entered into the depths of the fortress, while the officer would have wound up off the board. Naturally, the Germans would not have complained if the French had captured the piece at 43. But it was not to be, so this piece enters the fortress at space 52 (Diagram 3).

Manipulations

4 Nobody likes to lose pieces, but in a game of Assault it is inevitable that the German army suffer a few casualties. Besides, the Germans lose the game only if the French manage to capture thirty-four of their fifty pieces, so the loss is not so grave. If they cannot help but lose a piece, the Germans will do well to allow themselves to be captured in the manner most convenient to them. Often a situation arises where the French can capture one of the German pieces in several different spaces. In that case, the Germans can sometimes influence the French's decision. Often a German can also manipulate the course of the game by deliberately putting himself in a position in which he will have to be captured by the French officer of his choice. This is the case of the German soldier at 52. He clearly cannot avoid being captured. He must always advance toward the fortress, and there are no other Germans nearby to protect him against the officer at space 43. So the player chooses to be captured by the officer at 60. This way, he can at least free up the right side of the board for a possible siege. On the left, however, he remains blocked (Diagram 4).

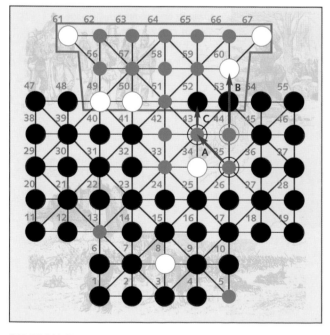

DIAGRAM 3:
A German in the fortress. In move A, the Germans put a piece on space 43. This way they ensure that either the German on space 43 or the one on 53 will delve further into the fortress.

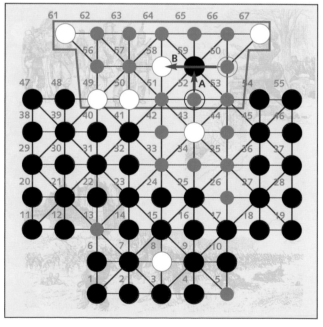

DIAGRAM 4:
Manipulations. Moves A and B show how the Germans force the French to capture them with the officer at 60 and not the one at 43.

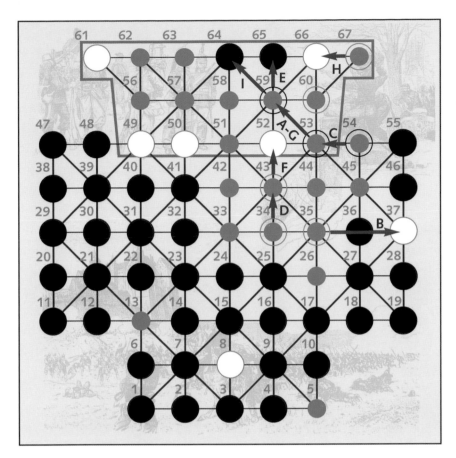

DIAGRAM 5:

Two Germans manage to entrench themselves at the end of the fortress. They arrive at this position after the following moves:

Germans: 53–59;

French: 35–37 (by obligation);

Germans: 54–53;

French: 34–43;

Germans: 59–65;

French: 43–52;

Germans: 53–59;

French: 67–66;

Germans: 59–64.

A German Advance

5 The Germans are now in a rush to occupy the fortress and surround the French. They have realized that it is preferable to enter several at a time rather than one by one. After all, a German had already entered the fortress and stayed there, only to be eliminated. The Germans have now decided to reach their goal through other means—entering the fortress in twos. The situation in the "death space" seems to permit this, because there is plenty of room on the right-hand side. The French official at 35 must capture on the next turn and move to space 37. Because of this, the two Germans have the time and space they need to enter the fortress together. The soldier at 53 initiates the attack, and with 54 entrenches himself at the end of the fortress, where they are invulnerable. The officer at 67 moves to 66 in an attempt to keep the Germans from penetrating the fortress any further (Diagram 5).

STRATEGY

Once the path to the fortress is cleared, it is a good idea to build an attack from the rear. This way, a large number of Germans will be able to enter the fortress.

Capturing Several Pieces at Once

6 Everyone makes a mistake at one time or another. So do the Germans in this match. They are so busy trying to conquer the fortress that they fail to realize that moving from 35 to 44 was not wise. They pay dearly for this mistake, which causes them to lose four pieces. The French officer at 53 captures these pieces in a single move, and moves to space 13. As usual, a move that allows a player to capture several pieces at once takes precedence over all others, so the officer at 17 cannot continue capturing toward space 5; instead, he must make a detour toward spaces 33 and 13. Naturally, he would have preferred to move to space 5 in order to free the officer at space 8 from the Germans (Diagram 6).

Escaping a Siege

7 The battle continues with the same intensity. The French are fighting with only six pieces, because several moves ago, the Germans surrounded the seventh at space 8. They have not neglected any possibilities of escape, and now is the time to do so: the officer at 13 prepares the escape, moving to 23. In the next move he can capture the soldier at 24. Once this soldier has been eliminated, the officer at 8 can flee to 24, capturing the German at 15. If this strategy succeeds, the seven officers may enter into action again.

The German could have moved from 16 to 25 without immediately breaking the fence around the officer. That way, he would have avoided, by jumping from 23 to 25, being captured by the French; but after two moves the officer at 42 will capture (jumping to 33 and then to 17), which would still allow for the officer at 8 to be freed. The Germans realize they have lost their only prisoner and decide to take a different tack. Now they seek victory by conquering all the spaces within the fortress. Because the French have occupied the lower part of the board, they have enough room to do it. The French are reinvigorated by the successful flight of their officer, and begin to play far more aggressively than before (Diagram 7).

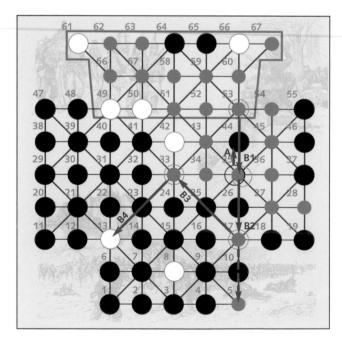

DIAGRAM 6:
A German error allows the French to capture four soldiers in one move. Moves A and B1 to B4 show how.

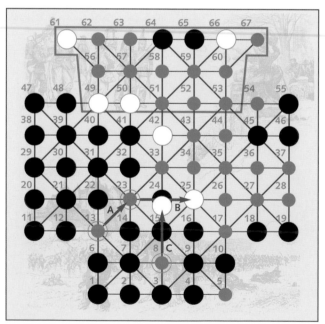

DIAGRAM 7:
The cornered officer escapes (moves A through C). The Germans can delay the liberation of the officer for a few turns, but they cannot prevent it.

The Final Battle

8 The Germans attempt to take the fortress, while the French try to take out as many Germans as possible. An impassioned battle ensues, during which the number of Germans will dwindle to seventeen. Although seven of them are already inside the fortress, ten remain outside. If they lose one more piece to the French, the game is over. Unfortunately for them, the Germans at 49 and 56 are in an impossible position (Diagram 8). The soldier at 49 is threatened by the officer at 47 as well as the one at 51. Within two turns, one of the two will be able to capture him, which will end the game. The German at 49 cannot save himself by moving to 57 because the immediate result would be the death of the soldier at 56 at the hands of the officer at 62, ending the game.

None of the other Germans is close enough to fill the gap at 48 or 50. The Germans must face defeat, and the French emerge victorious when the officer at 47 captures the German at 49 (Diagram 8).

STRATEGY

You should combine attack and defense. Sometimes both lines (of defense) are so preoccupied with developing their strategies that they lose sight of the enemy's possibilities for victory. A good player can prepare his attack without losing sight of defending himself.

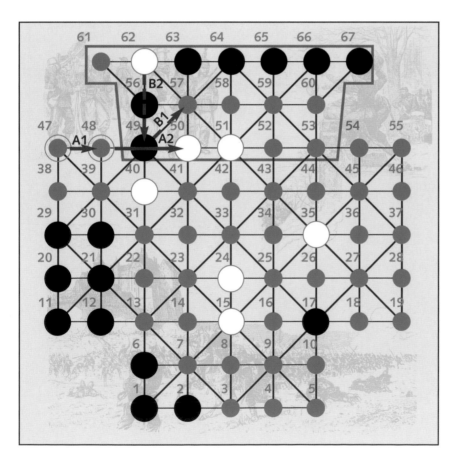

DIAGRAM 8:
The final battle. The German soldier at 49 is in a difficult situation. If he does nothing, he will be eliminated in the next two turns. But he cannot save himself without eliminating the soldier at 56 (B1 and B2). The French officer at 47 will give the *coup de grace* to the German army (A1 and A2).

Practice Makes Perfect

All good things must come to an end; so, too, must a game of Assault. Both sides gave it their all, but only one could win. The Germans' change of strategy arrived too late and cost them too many casualties. The French's game of attack in the second half of the match was very smart: they eliminated 34 Germans and were also able to rescue their trapped officers.

The German player decides beforehand if he wants to win by surrounding the French or by flushing them out of their fortress. Often it seems as though it is possible to try both strategies, but in practice it turns out that trapping the enemy requires a lot of pieces. The trapping strategy often must be carried out at the expense of an attack.

Only the French player may capture, so it is important for him to always play on the offensive. If he does not, play can quickly become gridlocked, which can make the match rather tedious.

STRATEGY

A good combat formation for the French is a closed diagonal line across the center of the board. It could move from the lower left corner to the upper right corner, or in the opposite direction. The two remaining Frenchman in this illustration could defend the "open" side of the fortress. For example, if spaces 49, 41, 33, 25, and 17 are occupied by French officers, and the two officers who remain inside take spaces 52 and 53, it will be almost impossible to break through their ranks without incurring an enormous loss. An added advantage to this strategy is that there are always enough officers near the fortress as well as behind the board to make an attack, which guarantees an entertaining and varied match.

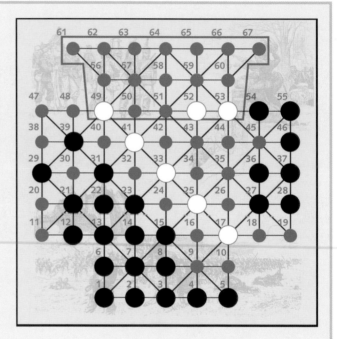

Horse Races
History of the Game

◆ ◆ ◆

Professional races were being run as early as the Classical era. On the occasion of the Olympic games in 680 B.C.E., chariot races were organized. A short while later, in 648, the first horse races took place. It should come as no surprise, then, that many people of today immerse themselves in the fascinating world of racing. Over the years there have been several different horse-racing games on the market. The race is played on round or oval boards on which there are both normal squares and squares with positive or negative attributes. Positive squares indicate higher points, either by jumping hurdles or moving more rapidly; negative squares yield setbacks, delays, and fines. The largest racing boards are divided into 150 squares. Among these are squares that include barriers, fences, and ditches. As means of transportation have increased, so too have racing game designers availed themselves of a greater number of themes for their boards.

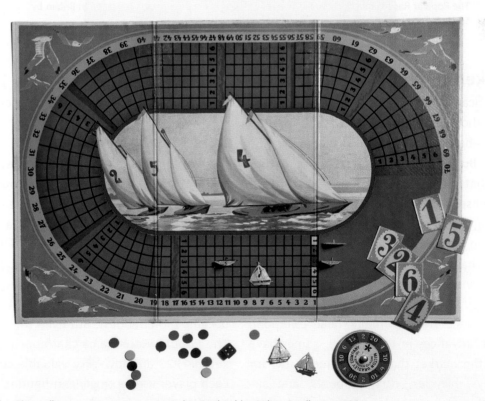

This sailboat racing game was issued in England by Milton Bradley in 1932.

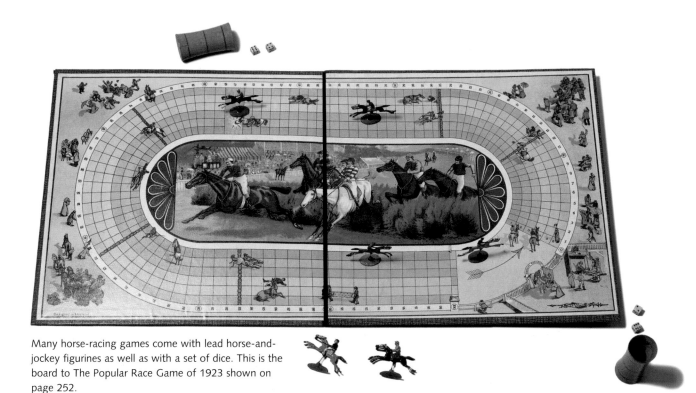

Many horse-racing games come with lead horse-and-jockey figurines as well as with a set of dice. This is the board to The Popular Race Game of 1923 shown on page 252.

An example of play:

It is now Blue's turn. He is on number 48 and rolls a ten, and so moves to number 58. That space is already taken by the yellow jockey, which must now switch with Blue and return to number 48 (Diagram B).

Special Squares

- **Square 6:** A jockey whose horse refuses to jump over a hurdle (and therefore lands on number 6) must move back to its previous position. That player must also pay one chip into the pot.

- **Square 11:** Here, too, the jockey must overcome an obstacle. If he stays on this square, he must make an additional bet, but he loses two turns.

- **Square 16:** There is a bothersome obstacle in this space—the gate. If the horse refuses to jump over it, his owner must pay three more chips into the pot.

- **Square 21:** If a jockey lands on this square by rolling a double, the player moves his jockey the corresponding number of spaces and then rolls again. If he reaches square 21 with a double-six, the player must first roll one of the dice again and then advance the number of spaces rolled. He then rolls both dice again and moves his jockey the number of spaces rolled. If a player makes two consecutive moves this way, he moves to another special square, and between the two moves must fulfill the conditions of that square before making a second move.

TIP

When playing with young children, it is common to play this game without betting and without obstacles or hurdles. The rules can also be relaxed so that a player need not reach the finish line with a perfect roll; a player who rolls a higher number than needed may cross the finish line just the same.

- **Square 27:** This square brings nothing but problems. The horse refuses to go on, and endangers the other jockeys. The jockey is disqualified. He must pay a fine of four chips and start the race all over again from square 1.
- **Square 37:** A jockey who lands here is moving with a good rhythm. He gets an extra push and moves forward to square 53.
- **Square 47:** A bad jump over the tall hurdle at 47 provokes a delay. The horse lands on the hurdle,

which now has to be repaired. The jockey must pay a fine of four chips and lose three turns before attempting to jump again.
- **Square 53:** A good jump ensures a small advantage. A jockey who lands on this space can move forward to 67.
- **Square 57:** Horse and jockey are injured. To receive treatment, they must go back to the start of the course. In compensation, the player gets two extra turns.

A satirical cartoon by Zbigniew Lengren (Poland, 1930). The caption reads: "It's hard to believe it, but his father won the Derby in London."

DIAGRAM C:

Some examples of special squares. Red rolls four points, moves to square 76, and must move back eight spaces—twice the number of rolled. Yellow lands on square 57 and has to start all over again at square 1. To make up for the delay, he gets two additional turns and lands on square 14. Blue rolls a three and moves to square 61, from which he can move right up to 74.

A scene from the French film Thérèse Raquin (1953) shows a salon where people are playing a game of horse races. The board is printed on a felt tablecloth, and the wooden hurdles sit on top of it. The pieces are figurines of a horse and jockey. Bets are placed in the center of the board.

- **Square 61:** With the finish line in sight, the horse makes an extra push and moves right up to number 74.
- **Square 70:** The jockey falls in a puddle and gets his clothes all wet. For the rest of the race, he is slowed down by the weight of the water on his clothes. From now on he can roll only one die per turn.
- **Square 76:** The horse takes a false step. The jockey must move back two times the number of spaces he has rolled.
- **Square 81:** The first jockey to land on this square can move up to 85 (Diagram C).

The Winner

The first player to reach the finish line wins. The other players continue playing until everyone, including the last jockey, finishes the race. The winner keeps the contents of the betting pot. He pays half the starting bet (not counting the fines paid out during the race by players who have tripped or fallen over various obstacles) to the player in second place, and keeps the rest. A player can win at horse races only if he arrives at the finish line by rolling the exact number of spaces required. If he rolls, say, two points too many, he must move back two spaces.

> **VARIATION**
>
> Players can decide that each jockey must complete three laps around the track before reaching the finish line. After all, real horse races work this way. But it is important not to lose track of how many laps each jockey has completed. In the first two rounds, the pieces should move from the square directly before the finish line to the very first square.

The First Game

In the game of horse races, the boxes with hurdles, the boxes before the finish line, and the "luck" factor all play important roles. There is seldom an advantage to landing on a space where there is an obstacle, for most often, these boxes cause a delay for the player. To get to the final space—the finish line—the players must roll exactly the right number of points. This means that winning or losing depends largely on the dice. This principle is shown here by demonstrating a few game situations using the same three players as before: Red, Yellow, and Blue. We will also start from the assumption that each player started with fifteen chips, six of which (two black and two white) he or she tossed into the betting pot.

Double-Sixes at Square 21

Yellow is on square 9, and it is his turn. He rolls a double-six and so moves to square 21. Since he rolled a double-six, he can roll again, but with only one of the two dice. He rolls another six, which places him at square 27. The rules say that if a player lands on this space, he is disqualified and must start the race all over again. He must also pay a fine of four chips.

Since he also landed on square 21 by rolling a double, he can roll the dice once more. He rolls seven points, which means finishing his turn at box 7 (Diagram 1).

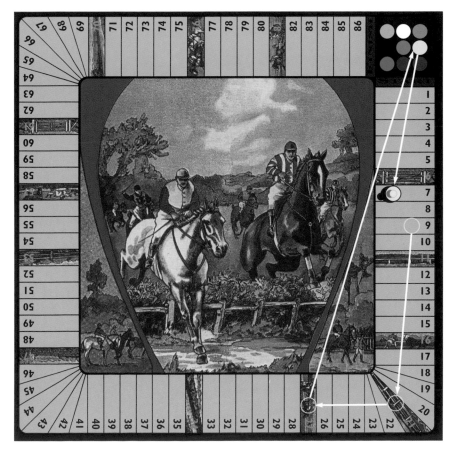

DIAGRAM 1:
It is Yellow's turn, and he rolls a double-six, which places him at square 21. The general rules of horse races say that he can roll one of the die again and move that number of spaces. He can still roll the dice once more because he landed on square 21. Because his next roll lands him on square 27, he must go back to the start, before ending up on square 7.

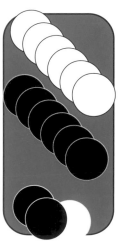

Playing Jungle:
Preliminaries

One player gets eight blue pieces; the other, eight red. Blue always goes first, so the players must decide beforehand which player will take which color. Each piece symbolizes a different animal, and each animal has a different numerical value, as follows:

Elephants are worth 8

Lions, 7

Tigers, 6

Panthers, 5

Dogs, 4

Wolves, 3

Cats, 2

Rats, 1

Pieces are generally made of wood and are richly ornamented. The board, on the other hand, is usually quite simple and made of paper. The houses are surrounded by three defense squares, and at the center of the board are twelve "water squares." At the start of the game the players put their pieces on the board (Diagram A).

DIAGRAM A:
A Jungle board with the pieces set up to start the game. The houses are at squares D9 and D1. The defensive squares are C9, D8, E9, and C1, D2, and E1. The numbers 4, 5, and 6 on columns B, C, E, and F are water squares.

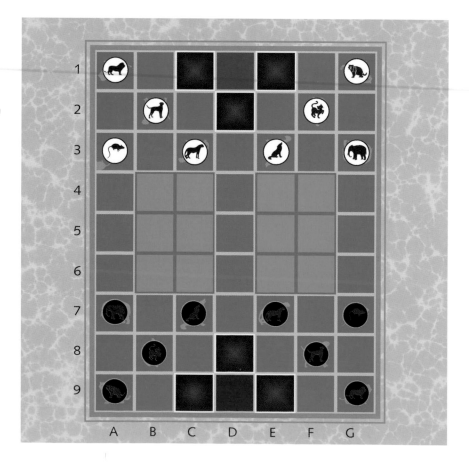

How the Pieces Move

At each turn, players move one of their pieces one square to the left, to the right, forward, or backward. As will be seen, pieces may not be moved diagonally. There can be only one piece on any given square, and pieces may not be placed in the water squares (Diagram B).

Capturing Pieces

In Jungle, players need not capture one another's pieces, although they may do so. A player captures one of his opponent's pieces by putting his own piece on the enemy piece's square. The enemy piece "dies" and must be removed from the board. When capturing, the pieces may move backward, forward, or sideways, but not diagonally. *The most important rule to remember is that a piece can be captured only by a piece of equal or greater value.* So, for instance, a cat can never capture a dog, because the cat is worth two points and the dog worth three. The only

exception to this rule is that a rat can capture an elephant even though it is worth far fewer points. According to Eastern wisdom, this exception relates to the fact that the rat can attack the elephant's brain by burrowing through its ear (Diagram C).

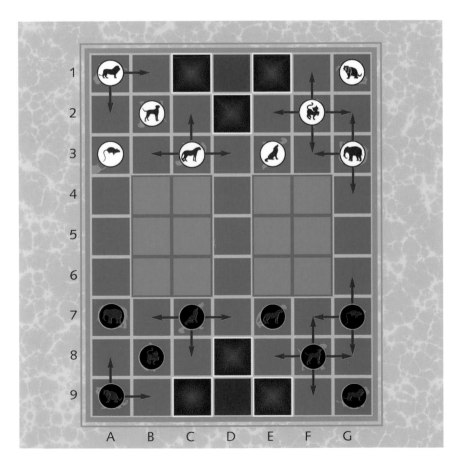

DIAGRAM B:
The motion of the pieces from their starting positions. The pieces on rows 1 and 9, the lion and the tiger, can move to one of two squares. The pieces in rows 2 and 8, the cat and the dog, can move to one of four squares, while the rest of the pieces, in rows 3 and 7, may choose from among three squares.

Home is also a special place. Players are not allowed to put any of their pieces in their home space.

The Winner

The winner is the player who manages to put one of his pieces in his opponent's home space.

A Korean variation on the game of Jungle. The game uses many more pieces, and the board consists of 11 X 12 squares with no special markings.

The First Match

A player who ventures into the game of Jungle is sure to be surprised by the many possibilities it has to offer. Each game is different and requires a great deal of concentration to reach the final goal, which is to put one of your pieces in your opponent's home square. The following pages demonstrate some interesting play situations.

The Opening

1 Blue makes the first move. He decides to move immediately into attack mode and deploy the elephant as quickly as possible toward the goal. Red, on the other hand, bases his strategy on putting his rat in the water and the lion and tiger on the front line so he can capture his opponent's pieces. After building a good defense, he will concentrate on reaching Blue's home. After three moves, Blue's elephant is in G6, beside Red's rat, which is in the water square at F6. Both pieces are safe because the elephant cannot go into the water and the rat cannot capture the elephant from there. Red's elephant moves to B7 to let the tiger through (Diagram 1).

STRATEGY

There is no need to fear losing one or more pieces. Sometimes the sacrifice of an animal piece can yield important gains.

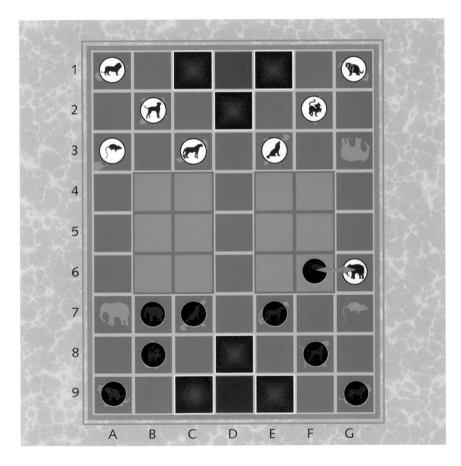

DIAGRAM 1:
After the first three moves. Blue has launched an immediate attack while Red prepares his defense. Blue's elephant at G6 and Red's rat at F6 cannot destroy one another.

Blocking

4 The game continues. Blue's rat is now in a water zone, and Blue is still unable to move his tiger forward. He decides to launch a new attack, moving his elephant from D7 to D6. This is a dangerous move for Red, who has no way of saving his tiger. What at first seemed a good strategic move for Red has backfired: Red has blocked his own tiger. If he moves it one square forward, it will be captured by the blue tiger at G5. Given that Red's elephant is in A6, the tiger cannot jump over there, either; nor can it capture Blue's elephant, because the elephant's point value is higher. In any event, Red loses his tiger and so decides to save his wolf in B7. Blue gains an extra advantage because his tiger in G5 regains its freedom of movement after capturing the red tiger (Diagram 4).

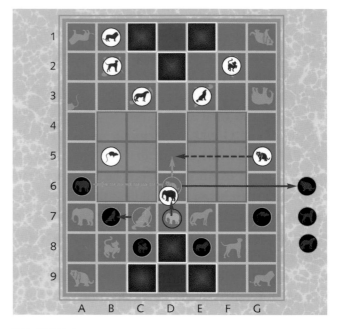

DIAGRAM 4:
Blue's elephant threatens two of Red's pieces. Blue moves his elephant from D7 to D6, where Red loses his tiger. Red has no way of saving his tiger, so he loses this important piece.

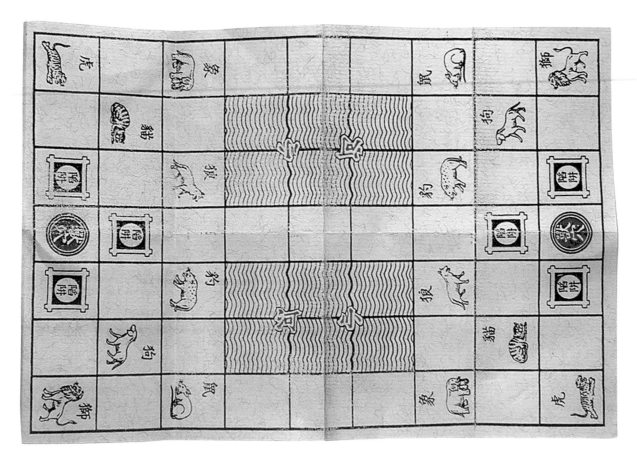

A paper game board of the kind still widely available for purchase.

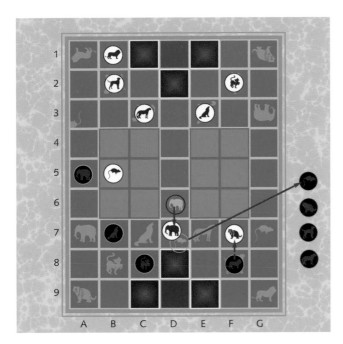

DIAGRAM 5:
A double threat. Red threatens Blue's elephant in D6 and the blue tiger in F7. Blue will have to lose one of these pieces. Blue elects to save the elephant and captures the red rat in D7.

Double Threat

5 It's Blue's turn. He soon faces a double threat: his elephant in D6 is attacked by Red's rat, and his tiger in F7 is attacked by the red lion. The elephant is Blue's most valuable piece, so he focuses on defending it. This means losing his tiger. Blue can save his elephant in D5 but would do better to capture the red rat in D7. The rat and the elephant can capture one another. Although Blue has lost an important piece, he has decimated Red's army while suffering only one loss.

The Final Phase

6 The red lion has leapt over the water to help his elephant comrade reach the goal. In his next turn he moves his piece from F1 to the E1 defensive square. In doing this, he reduces the elephant's point value to zero, but at this stage it no longer matters. Blue cannot place any of his pieces in his own house, nor can he keep Red from occupying this house with one of his pieces. Red wins the game (Diagram 6).

Evaluation

It was clear from the outset that Blue would lose the game. He chose to move directly into attack mode with his most important piece and quickly captured a good number of Red's pieces. But it would have made more sense to build up the attack slowly and surely. Blue should have attacked with a team made up of more pieces.

Because of its high point value, the elephant is clearly a very strong piece, but it cannot do very much by itself. Although Red lost more pieces than Blue, Red ultimately wins the game.

TIP

You should avoid having two of your pieces in diagonally adjacent squares unless they are both well protected. Your opponent will take advantage of this situation immediately, and will move a high-valued piece between the two as soon as possible. If he does, you will have no choice but to lose one of the two pieces.

DIAGRAM 6:
The final stage. The red elephant moves from F1 to the E1 defensive square, where it loses all its value. But this is not a problem, because Blue cannot keep Red from reaching his goal, square D1, in his next move.

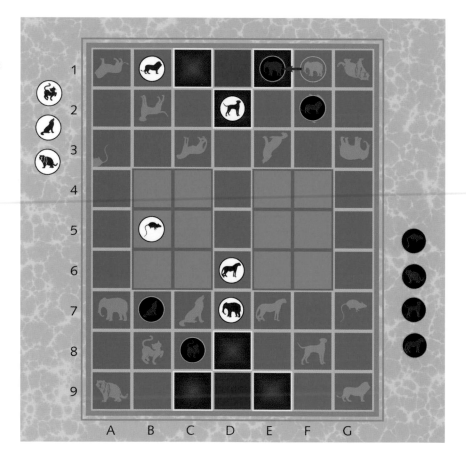

Agon
The Nature of the Game

◆ ◆ ◆

Agon is a hundred-year-old board game for two players. The board is hexagonal and divided into ninety-one hexagonal cells. Each player uses seven pieces. Six of them, called *guards*, protect the seventh, called the *queen*. Both players have the same goal: to put the queen in the center square and surround her with her guards. The first player to do so wins the game. This game is also known as *Queen's Guard*. Little is known about its origins, except that it was first played in England. It is hard to get bored with this game because there are so many permutations, and it is always a challenge to beat the other player (*agon* is the ancient Greek word for contest or challenge). The beginner will be inclined to move the queen to the center of the board as quickly as possible but will soon learn that moving fast doesn't necessarily shorten the distance. To succeed at this interesting game you must proceed with a well-considered strategy, slowly but surely, to reach the final goal.

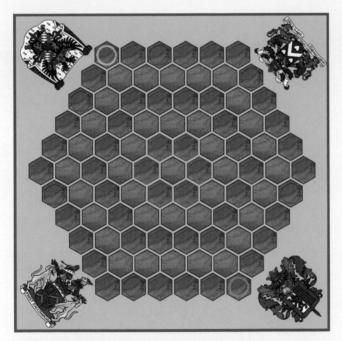

Agon is played on a hexagonal board with six white pieces, six black pieces, a queen of each color, and a die.

Players	Requirements
2	special game board
Average duration	6 each, white and black game pieces
30 minutes	1 each, white and black queens
Category	1 die
strategy	

Playing Agon:
Preliminaries

The goal of both queens is to reach the cell at the center of the board. Surrounding this cell are five concentric rings, which alternate in color and shading. Each player takes his game pieces, which he places in the outer ring of the board. The queens are placed one in front of the other at either end of a diagonal line on the outer hexagon. Players roll the die to decide who will open the game (Diagram A).

How the Pieces Move

The players take turns moving their pieces forward or to one side, into an adjacent cell. There is no difference between moving an ordinary piece or moving a queen. In the rings, a forward motion means moving to a cell closer to the center. Pieces cannot move back, away from the center. A lateral movement means the piece moves to a cell to the right or to the left within the same wing. The movement of the pieces is subject to these restrictions:

DIAGRAM A:
Agon board with the pieces in the opening position.

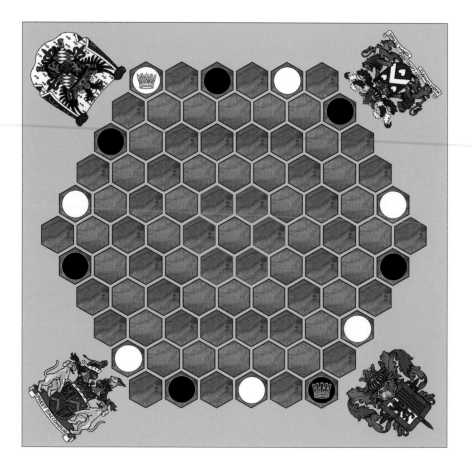

1. A player may never place a guard in the center cell. This cell is reserved for the queens.

2. There can never be more than one piece in a single cell.

3. A player may never put one of his pieces between two of his opponent's—in other words, a player may never block his own piece.

Players must think carefully before moving a piece. If a player touches a piece but then decides he would rather not move it, he loses his turn (Diagram B).

Capturing Pieces

To capture an opponent's piece, a player must block it between two of his own pieces in the same ring. This method of capturing can be used by guards as well as queens, but the consequences are very different depending on which kind of piece it is capturing.

A player cannot touch a piece he has blocked—that is his adversary's business. When a player loses a guard, in his next turn he must put that piece in a cell of his choosing on the outer ring. If a player loses his queen, he must do the same but is not free to choose the cell—his opponent chooses it. Therefore, when a piece has been captured, it must move away from the center.

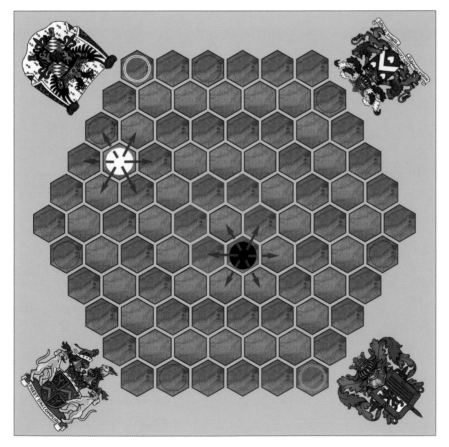

DIAGRAM B:
How the pieces move. Both Black and White can move laterally within the same ring. The white piece can also move toward the center, to a cell in the next ring, but it cannot move backward, away from the center. The black piece cannot move forward or backward because it is in the ring closest to the center, which it cannot occupy.

A queen in the center cell is not within any of the rings, so by definition she cannot be blocked in the same ring. This does not mean that by being in the center cell she is invulnerable and cannot be eliminated. In fact, a queen can be captured from the ring that borders the center square.

If several guards are blocked all at once by opposing pieces, their owner must move them one by one into the outer ring. Each time it is his turn, he must put a piece in the outer ring until none of them are blocked. (It doesn't matter in what order he moves the pieces.) When both a queen and a guard are blocked, the queen moves first (Diagram C).

Furthermore...

If the six cells in the ring surrounding the center cell are occupied by a player's guards but the center cell remains empty, the owner of those guards loses the game. Because guards cannot move backward, this move effectively blocks all play, and neither player is able to reach the center (Diagram D).

The Winner

The player who moves his queen into the center cell and surrounds it with six guards in the innermost ring wins the game.

DIAGRAM C:
Capturing pieces. Black (A) blocks the white queen. White had planned to capture a black guard by moving his piece into the next ring, but he cannot because in his next turn he must first move the queen to another square (B). Thus, he has given Black the chance to escape his threat.

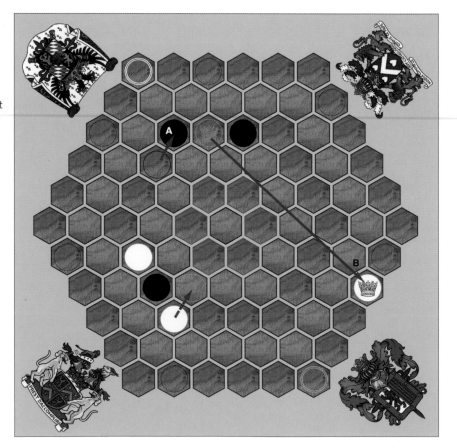

Other Openings

There are two variations on Agon whose opening position differs from the one just described. In both, the game begins with an empty board and the pieces in the players' control; each player uses six guards and one queen of the same color.

In the first variation, players take turns placing one piece in any cell on the board. At this stage it is very important to put the pieces in adjacent cells whenever possible.

The second variation appears to be a compromise between the first variation and the classic rules of the game. Players start by placing their queens on the board in the usual cell, that is, at either end of a diagonal line across the board, as in classic Agon. They then place the other pieces one by one in empty cells of their choosing.

When all the guards and both queens are positioned on the game board, the game continues according to the classic rules.

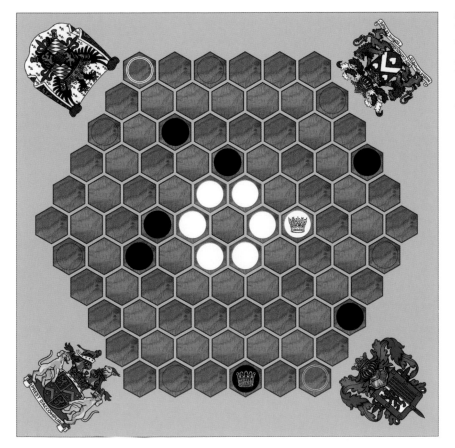

DIAGRAM D:
The game is blocked because White has put all six of his guards in the ring surrounding the center cell, while the cell remains empty. White loses the game.

The First Match

To start the first match with a solid foundation, you should not only be familiar with the rules but also have studied some interesting play situations. After all, it is always an advantage to have a sense of the game's complexity and to have thought through some of the situations and strategies that may arise. The situations described below will help prepare the beginning player.

The Opening

1 The game has begun, and it's clear that White is headed straight for the goal. After the first five moves he still hasn't moved any pieces except for his queen. He is now in the center cell. Black has moved five of his guards forward in a ring, from which can be inferred that he intends to maintain a balanced relationship among his pieces. Black builds his game carefully, while White seems entirely focused on the ultimate goal. A player who moves so quickly toward the finish is likely to end up in last place. The white queen has no guards protecting her, so her position is extremely vulnerable. You do not need much imagination to see that she will soon be blocked by two black guards and will have to begin again (Diagram 1).

DIAGRAM 1:
After the first five moves, the white queen is in a vulnerable position because she isn't protected by any of her guards. Black is busy taking a more balanced approach. He advances slowly with several guards at once.

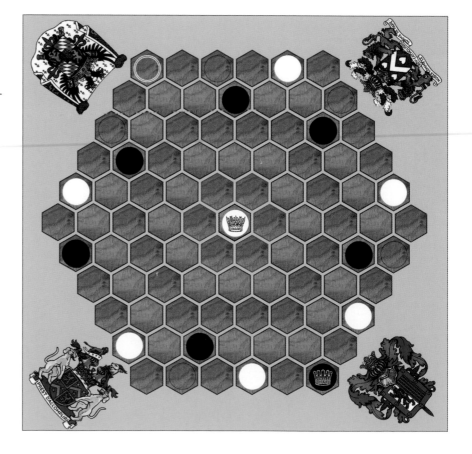

Loss by Speed

2 Black continues to move his pieces toward the center cell. White, too, begins to do this, but since he spent his first several turns moving only his queen, he has fallen behind. The black pieces are closer to the center than are the white pieces. It is now Black's turn. He takes advantage of the opportunity to block white's queen. Now the counterproductive effects of White's hasty approach in the first stage of the game become apparent. In his next turn, White will have to move the queen from the center and place it in whatever cell Black wishes. The queen must go back to the beginning. In technical terms, this is called a "loss by speed." Naturally, Black will try to make matters as complicated as possible for his opponent. He decides to return the white queen all the way to the outer ring, as far away as possible from the center cell. From the outer ring, it takes five moves to get to the center. Further, Black wants to put White's queen as far away from her guards as possible. This situation makes it clear how important it is to keep one's pieces as united as possible. It may seem like a good idea to put the queen in the center cell quickly, but it helps to keep in mind how much more difficult it is to *keep* her there (Diagram 2).

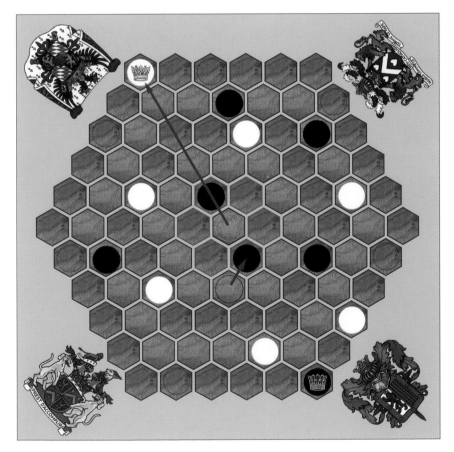

DIAGRAM 2:
Loss by speed. Black blocks the white queen and forces it to move back to the place where it started. White has wasted a lot of time putting his queen in the center square without protection.

Capturing at the Right Time

3 Players are not obliged to capture whenever they have the chance. This rule makes sense, because it isn't always convenient to capture another piece. For example, even if a player can capture a guard in the outer ring, this generally makes no sense. The same is true of capturing a guard in the second ring from the outside, where it is seldom very useful to eliminate a piece. On the other hand, capturing a queen in the outer ring can be very interesting, because the player who slays the queen can decide in what cell to place her next. The player may have good reason to put her on a completely different part of the board. All of which is to say that a player should capture another's piece when it serves a real purpose, and not simply because he has the chance to do so. It's important to try to make a series of blocks so that the other player has to keep moving his pieces back to the outer ring while you keep advancing toward the goal. Black understands this well. He sees the chance to block one of White's pieces. White must put that piece in the outer ring in his next move. Then, Black can capture another one of his pieces, and so the next time White makes a move, he must also move that piece into a different cell. This is an ideal situation for Black. While the white pieces move ever so slowly toward the center, Black has almost no obstacles as he approaches the final goal (Diagram 3).

DIAGRAM 3:

Well-planned blocks. By moving his guard forward (A), Black captures a white piece, which now has to move to the outer ring (B). In his next move, Black will move the same guard one cell to the left (C), which allows her to capture another white piece (D). Thus, Black has allowed himself some room to move and White suffers another loss by speed.

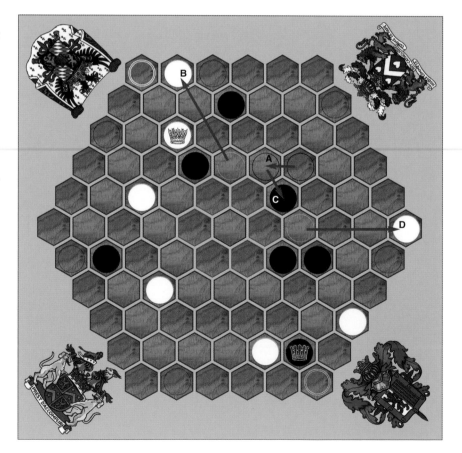

Blocking

4 One of the most entertaining aspects of Agon is that in the end, players have to put their pieces in the same cells. As they try to reach the final goal, they try to keep one another from doing the same. Constructing blocks is one way of limiting an opponent's freedom of movement. Diagram 4 shows how Black remains well ahead of White. Black's pieces are closer to the center, and they are closer together than White's. The white queen has to move forward in order to near the goal, but in the current situation this isn't possible, because she would then be blocked by two of Black's guards. If the queen moves inside the same ring toward the only other opening, the situation will repeat itself: she will also be blocked if she moves forward. As long as Black keeps his guards in the ring around the center cell, it will be impossible for the queen to reach the final goal.

Black also has a problem. In order to occupy all the cells surrounding the center, he must move his guard (A) from the left-hand side of the board, but if he does so he runs the risk of blocking himself. Black must first move this piece around in the same ring and wait for a convenient opening. The closest opening is near White's guard (B).

If White realizes in time what is about to happen, he will move this guard forward into the next ring to block the black piece. From this situation it is clear that the two players must maneuver very carefully if they want to place all their pieces in their corresponding cells (Diagram 4).

STRATEGY

Always keep in mind that pieces cannot move backward. When a player is in a situation with no way out, he can always try to make his opponent lose by allowing him to occupy the ring around the center castle without placing his queen in the corresponding space. To do this, it's important that, no matter what, he not allow the opponent's pieces any more freedom of movement; he does so by capturing some of them.

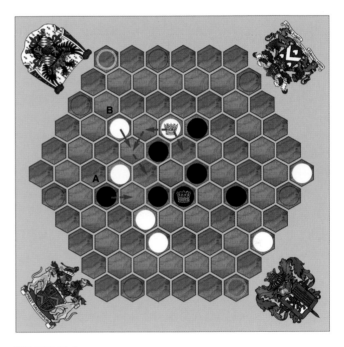

DIAGRAM 4:
How an opponent's pieces are blocked. White's queen has no way of reaching the center cell because she cannot block himself in. For the same reason, the black guard (A) cannot move forward and will have to find an opening along the sides. Moving his guard forward (B), White closes the surest opening for Black.

White's Fate Is Decided

5 Black is very close to victory. All he needs to do now is move one of his guards to declare himself the winner. It's White's turn, but he can no longer do anything to stop Black. After all, he still cannot move his queen forward. After a pointless move by White, Black closes ranks. He has won (Diagram 5).

Evaluation

At this point, one should have a good idea of the many possibilities Agon has to offer. The sample situations shown here teach that there is no point in moving one's pieces unless it is according to a good underlying strategy. Black has held the lead during the entire game, because he made sure that all his moved pieces cooperated with one another as they advanced together, toward the center. In the final stage, he made some interesting moves, positioning some of his guards strategically around the center cell, which made it impossible for White to reach that ring. One should pay special attention to blocking the center cell, because it can make the difference between winning and losing. Also, losing a piece that has nearly reached the center means losing valuable time. Even in the final arrangement, the white pieces are still scattered throughout the board because they cannot assist one another. It was therefore no surprise that White lost this game.

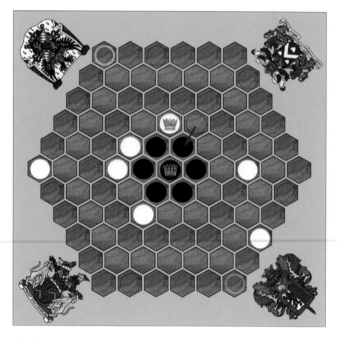

DIAGRAM 5:
The final position. White can no longer keep Black from moving his final piece to its corresponding cell. Black places his final guard in the ring around his queen, and wins.

Duodecim Scripta
History of the Game

◆ ◆ ◆

In the year 63 C.E., the citizens of Pompeii fell victim to an unexpected catastrophe: the eruption of Mount Vesuvius, which partly buried the city in lava. The catastrophe was complete when, in the year 79 C.E., a second eruption buried the entire Roman city under a thick layer of lava and ash. Everyday life came to a standstill and would not see the light of day for another 1,700 years. In the eighteenth century, what was once a horrible drama for the residents of this city became an extraordinary opportunity for countless historians and anthropologists. Their excavations yielded thousands of important findings, including two murals found in an inn. One of these depicts two men playing a board game. The man at left is holding a cup in his hand and says, "I'm out!" The other points at the dice and replies, "That's two dice, not three!" He is accusing the first man of cheating. The story continues in the second mural. An innkeeper, doubling as porter, pushes the two men outside, shouting, "If you want to fight, you can take it outside!" The fight was sparked by a game of Duodecim Scripta that got out of hand. During that time, this board game was very popular among all strata of society. Roman literature provides countless facts about this game, which is an ancestor of modern-day backgammon.

This mural was found in a Pompeiian inn almost 1,700 years after the eruption of Vesuvius buried the city under a thick layer of lava. The two men are playing a game of Duodecim Scripta, the game of twelve lines (*Photo: Pedicini, Naples*).

Rules:
Preliminaries

The board has three horizontal lines. There are twelve spaces on each line, marked by letters. Each section is split down the middle by a line, forming two groups of six spaces each. Thus, the board is divided into six groups of six spaces each. Originally the game used texts that were divided into six, six-letter words. But to make this explanation simpler, instead of using words, the six spaces are marked with the letters A through E. Also, in the diagrams shown here, each letter has been assigned a number. Sometimes a space will hold more than one of a player's

pieces. On these occasions, the number of chips is indicated by the numeral on the inside of the chip.

The players sit facing one another, and divide up the thirty chips equally. They then decide who will be the first to roll the dice and thus begin the game (Diagram A).

Rolling the Dice

The game consists of three phases: first the pieces are placed on the board, then the players move the pieces through the board, and finally, the pieces are removed from the board. In the first and second phases the players roll three dice; in the last phase, only one. In the first two phases, players take turns rolling all three dice at once. They can use the points they roll with each of the dice separately or can combine them. Thus, as a general rule, each time they roll the dice they can choose from a wide array of moves. For instance, if a player rolls the combination 1–3–6, according to the rules of the game he can:

DIAGRAM A:
A Duodecim Scripta board with six sets of six spaces each. Each player has a box of his own, which is called his home.

290 THE BOOK OF GAMES

- Move one piece ten spaces
- Move one piece one space, one piece three spaces, and one piece six spaces
- Move one piece four spaces and one piece six spaces
- Move one piece one space and one piece nine spaces
- Move one piece three spaces and one piece seven spaces

If a player rolls a double or a triple, it makes no difference with regard to how he may move.

Each time a player rolls the dice, he must move his pieces the total number of points he has rolled, even if sometimes it would be more convenient to discard one of the dice. If all such points cannot be used, the player may move none of his pieces, and must forgo his turn.

Putting the Pieces on the Board

Each player's home comprises the group of six spaces on his right-hand side marked "A." In the first stage of play, both players must place all their pieces in spaces within these sets. Players take turns rolling the dice and decide whether to use the points separately or add them all up to use at once. This means that for every turn, each player can put down a maximum of three pieces. Each space can hold any number of pieces. When several pieces are placed in the same space, they are stacked one on top of another.

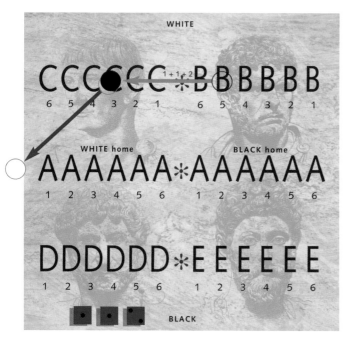

DIAGRAM C:
Capturing pieces. Black rolls 1–1–2. He decides to add the points and move his piece at B5 four spaces. He captures the white piece at C3, which must now go back and start all over again.

Blocked Pieces

A piece is blocked when it cannot be moved no matter how many points its owner rolls. Blocked pieces are called *inicti*, which means "those who cannot move." As long as the blocked player is able to move other pieces, this isn't a problem. If he cannot, however, he must pass and lose a turn.

The Final Phase

As in the first two phases, players may not enter this phase until all their pieces have finished the previous round. The player who begins the final phase should have already placed all fifteen of his pieces in set E. Now he withdraws his pieces from the board, one by one. As in the first, in this phase the pieces do not have to move through each space in set E and exit the board through the last of these. The rules say that a piece can be removed from the board when the number a player rolls matches the number of the

space on which the piece sits. For example, if a piece is on E2 and the player rolls a two, he may remove that piece from the board. If, however, his piece is captured while in the E set, its owner must return it to the first space of set A and start all over. He goes back to rolling three dice. Once the piece reaches set E again, the player can continue removing his pieces from the board. To do so he must roll the exact number of points that match the number of his space. For instance, if a player has only his final piece left in E4, he must roll exactly four in order to finish the game. If he rolls a one, he may opt to move the piece to E5, but he must then roll a five to remove the piece from the board. Sometimes this can go on for a long time, which gives the other player time to catch up (Diagram D).

Scene from a Roman tavern.

WHITE

CCCCCC ✳ BBBBB

6 5 4 3 2 1 6 5 4 3 2 1

WHITE home   BLACK home

AAAAAA ✳ AAAAAA

1 2 3 4 5 6 1 2 3 4 5 6

DDDDDD ✳ ③ E ② ● E E

1 2 3 4 5 6 1 2 3 4 5 6

BLACK ⑭ ⑩

DIAGRAM D:
The final phase. Black has already removed fourteen of his pieces from the board and must now roll a four (no more, no less) to end the game. White still has five pieces in set E.

The Winner

The first player to remove all his pieces from the board wins. The player can now call it quits but does not necessarily have to. When the same people play Duodecim Scripta regularly, they can agree on each player getting one point for every game he wins, and the ultimate winner being the player who earns ten points.

STRATEGY

A player can avoid being captured outside his house if he never puts one of his pieces on any space by itself. In other words, no piece should become a vagabond.

A sacrifice to one of the gods.

The First Match

The theory of Duodecim Scripta is actually more complicated than it appears. One of the reasons is the large number of pieces moving across the board, as well as the fact that each time a player rolls the dice he must study his options carefully. As a result, dilemmas sometimes arise in the course of play, so the game requires a great deal of concentration. The following pages describe some situations that can arise during a player's first game.

Phase One

1 Players have distributed the pieces among themselves and decided that Black will make the first move. Black rolls 2–4–6. He can put three chips in his home base—one in A2, the other at A4, and another at A6 or as close as possible—so they can move to set B soon. He decides to add up his points. He adds the four and the two, so he can place one piece on A6. The third die gives him six points, so he puts another piece in A6 as well.

Now it is White's turn. He rolls the combination 4–5–6, which goes to show that there aren't always several different options available when it comes time to put the pieces down. In this case, White cannot combine the points on his dice because each base has only six spaces. Any combination of two or three dice would yield a number higher than six. White has no choice but to put down three pieces: one at A4, one at A5, and one at A6 (Diagram 1).

Phase Two

2 Diagram 2 shows both Black and White after entering phase two: all their pieces are now "home" and about to move across the board. It seems that Black has the lead because he has already placed seven pieces in set D. Three of them are alone

in spaces 2, 5, and 6, and are therefore vulnerable to an attack by White. It would have been wiser to move the pieces more slowly, but together, toward the final set.

Now it is White's turn, and he rolls 2–4–5. Not to waste this opportunity, he moves the two pieces from C6 two and five spaces, respectively. He captures two of his opponent's pieces: those on D2 and D5. He must still move his other piece four spaces and chooses C4, which he moves to D2. This is a smart move, because now White has two pieces in D2, so they cannot be captured. The same is not true of the piece at D5, which is by itself on the space and should be protected as soon as possible. But now one should also keep in mind that Black is obliged to introduce one of his "dead" pieces on the board (in set A) before capturing any white pieces.

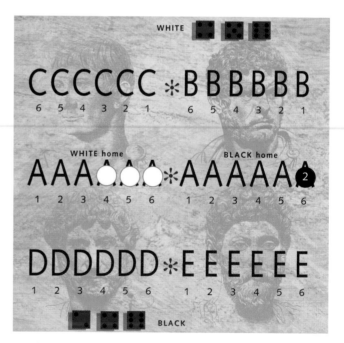

DIAGRAM 1:
Phase one. Black rolls 2–4–6 and puts two pieces in space A6. White rolls 4–5–6 and has no choice but to add a piece to A4, A5, and A6.

Blocked Pieces

3 Players keep going, and meanwhile Black's vanquished pieces are returned to the game. As shown in Diagram 3, Black has returned with a vengeance. All his pieces are now in set E and about to enter the third phase. White's fifteen pieces are still in group D, where they cannot leave in the current circumstances. Black has spread his pieces throughout E, blocking White's entrance. Thus, the four white pieces in set D6 are totally blocked because they cannot move regardless of what White rolls. The other white pieces could still move forward, but they too would soon be blocked. Black continues to play with a single die and starts removing his pieces from the board. White has no choice but to wait for a space in set E to open up, or capture one of Black's pieces.

A Grave Error

4 In Diagram 4 it is patently clear that Black has removed eight of his pieces from the board while White has removed only five. Then Black makes a grave error: he rolls a five and decides to remove his piece from E5. Thanks to this move, the other piece is left alone in its space, where it is especially vulnerable. It would have been wiser for Black to move his piece from E1 to E6. If he had, none of his pieces would risk elimination (Diagram 4).

DIAGRAM 2:
Phase two. Black has already placed seven of his pieces in set D, but three of them (2, 5, and 6) are vulnerable to attack. White captures two of them (2, 5) in a single move and ends up placing two of his own pieces in set D in a position (5) where they are completely invulnerable to attack.

DIAGRAM 3:
Blocked pieces. The white pieces in space D6 are blocked. The other white pieces in set D cannot move beyond D6.

A game of go, 1876.

Virtues

Confucius could not have imagined that his followers' attitude toward go would change so dramatically centuries later. In the era of Emperor Sung Tai Tsing (976–998), go was said to embody three of the five Confucian virtues: *Chih* (wisdom), *Jen* (kindness), and *Li* (propriety and decency). These three characteristics can still be seen displayed in the calligraphy at Asian go clubs.

Japan

Around 740, go was introduced to Japan, where at first it was played only by noblemen and clerics. According to legend, in the early eighth century, the Japanese spy Kibi no Kami spent time in China, where he attempted to decipher that country's deepest cultural secrets. When the emperor Hsuang-Sjung of China discovered his intrigue, he decided to test Kibi no Kami and suggested a game of go with one of his ministers. When it started to look as though victory would go to the Japanese visitor, the minister's wife tried to avoid humiliation by surreptitiously moving some of his pieces. She had hoped the game would at least end in a draw, but the cheat was discovered immediately. The lady was about to be punished, but Kibi no Kami saved her life. The minister's wife was so grateful that she helped him escape from China safely—taking the game of go in his luggage back to Japan. The museum at Nara, Japan, still holds two of the go boards that Kibi no Kami brought back from his trip.

Europe and North America

Although by the seventeenth century, go had already been described by Westerners returning from their great, exotic trips through the Far East, the game was not played in Europe until the late nineteenth century. After spreading slowly, go is now played in virtually every European country as well as in North America. The European Go Federation and the American Go Association promote the game and support the development of go players, including information, classes, workshops, local chapters, and national and international tournaments. The number of players and their skill levels are still on the rise.

Playing Go

The fascinating game of go has many passionate fans the world over. Numerous books have been written about this game, and there are many local and national go clubs and federations, which is why people often speak of a certain "go culture." The game of go can be nicely defined by the expression, "learn as you go," because even if you haven't mastered all the rules, it is a good idea to start playing right away. The experience you acquire by doing so makes it easier to understand what steps to follow. You quickly get an idea of the game's countless possibilities and its always surprising changes.

The official go board is a grid made up of nineteen horizontal lines and nineteen vertical. Beginners are advised to take their first steps on a smaller board so they can follow the unfolding of the game more easily even as the rules remain the same. For this reason, this book demonstrates on a board with nine-by-nine lines. Both players gain points by taking over areas of the board and by capturing each other's pieces. The winner is the player who earns the most points by the end of the game.

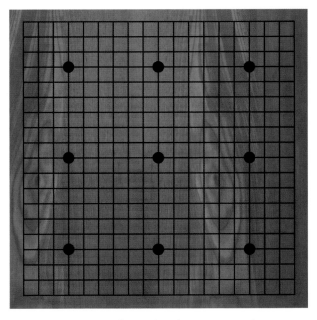

The fascinating game of go is played on a nineteen-by-nineteen grid. The game requires 181 black pieces and 180 white pieces.

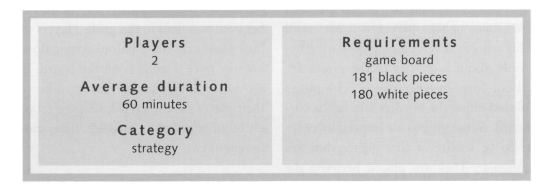

Players
2

Average duration
60 minutes

Category
strategy

Requirements
game board
181 black pieces
180 white pieces

Territorial Go

It is time to play a few games of go to practice the rules explained above. In territorial go, the goal is to conquer territories and capture pieces. The game is played using the basic rules of go, as in capture go, except that there are two additional rules. The first is the ko rule. The second is that players have a right to pass when they have no move to make. If a player passes, and his opponent responds by doing the same, the game is over. The winner is the player who has earned the most territorial points and captured the most pieces. Territorial points depend on the number of empty squares left at the end of the game, so the players count all the empty squares that are surrounded by a single player's pieces.

Groups: Living and Dead

The introduction of living and dead groups means delving deeper into the rules of go. A group is "living" if it consists of pieces the opponent cannot capture under any circumstances. Diagram E (A) shows an example of a living group. There is no way for White to capture Black's group: he cannot put a piece on X or Y, because doing so would be suicide. This would change if he could place a piece on both squares at the same time, but that is not allowed. The group's two liberties, that is, the two squares separated by a single piece and otherwise completely surrounded, are called "eyes."

Thanks to them, the group can no longer be captured—it is a living group. A group is also deemed living if at any given time it is able to create two eyes. Eyes also can be larger than two pieces. If an eye covers three squares, the player can simply split it in two by putting another piece in between. In fact, his opponent could also interpose a piece, thereby capturing the group. This is why a large group is truly alive, regardless of whose turn it is, only if its eye consists of at least four squares in a row.

EXTRATERRESTRIAL GO?

The former chess world champion Emmanuel Lasker once said, "Chess is earthbound, whereas go is universal. If there is intelligent life somewhere in space, it undoubtedly knows the game of go."

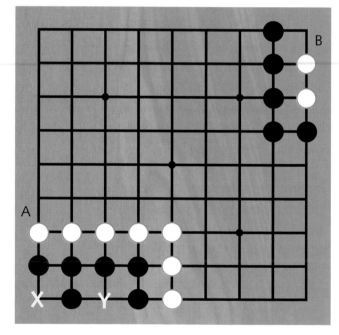

DIAGRAM E:
A living group and a dead group. White cannot place any pieces in X or Y—so the black group (A) lives thanks to its two "eyes." The white group (B) will be eliminated immediately—it is a dead group.

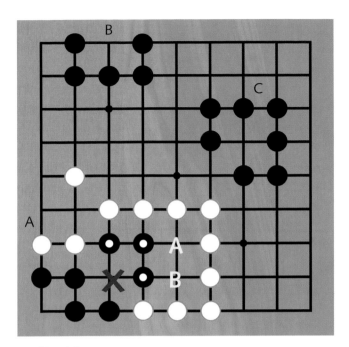

DIAGRAM F:
True eyes and false eyes. The eye in square X is false, for White can put one of his pieces in it if he pleases. B and C, on the other hand, depict true eyes.

The opposite of a living group is a dead group. A group is considered "dead" if the opponent can capture it whenever he pleases, and there is nothing to be done about it. The white group in Diagram E (B) is dead: the white pieces are in *atari*, and White cannot save them from elimination (Diagram E).

True Eyes and False Eyes

The group shown in Diagram F (A) appears to be living, but it really is not. If pieces are placed on A and B, the three marked black pieces are in atari. In his next turn, White puts a piece on square X and eliminates the black chain. Something happens to the "eye" in square X: it turns out to be false! To form a true eye in a corner or around one of the sidelines, a player must occupy every single square surrounding the space. To form a true eye in the center of the board, he must place his own pieces on each of the four diagonal corners of the eye. B and C in Diagram F show examples of true eyes (Diagram F).

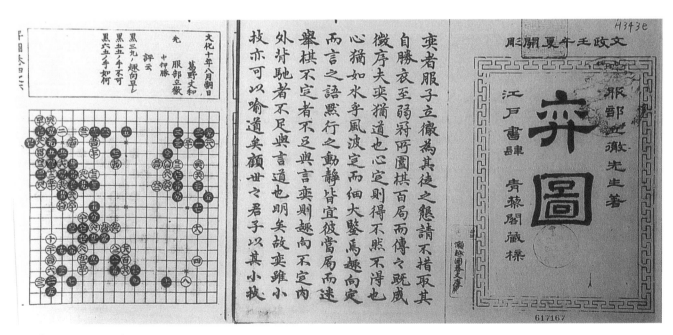

Page from a go manual circa 1935.

Kobayashi Koichi, at right, wins the first title match at Meijin in 1985 *(Photo: Archive, European Go Center, Netherlands)*.

Counting Points

If, after passing, the two players have several options with regard to the life or death of their groups, the game must continue. A player who claims a group is dead must prove it by actually capturing it. If he does, it means he was correct. If not, he confirms that the group is in fact alive. After a few games, these situations will cease to arise. Once a difference of opinion is resolved with regard to the life or death of a group, players can start counting their points.

DIAGRAM H:
A double atari. If White puts a piece on square X, in his next turn he can take Black's last liberty at A and B.

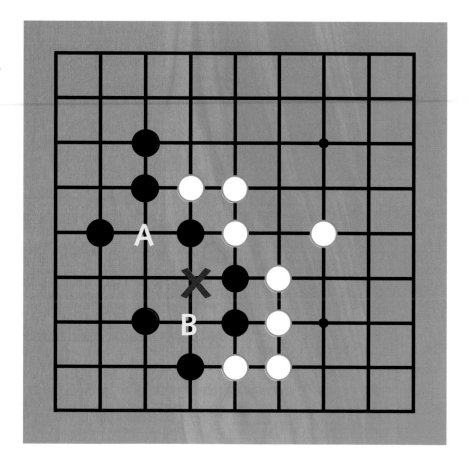

Diagram J shows a possible final scenario in a game of go. Players have both taken a pass because neither can move any of his pieces, capture one another, or conquer a new territory. White has captured two of Black's pieces, while Black has taken only one of his. In the diagram, the marked pieces are dead—they can be captured by the opponent at any time. Players remove these pieces from the board so that the board looks as it does in Diagram K. Once the board is cleared of dead pieces, it becomes evident that Black has earned twenty points with his territories. Added to the nine dead pieces he removed from the board, and minus only one lost piece, Black's total is thirty points. White has earned fifteen points with his territories.

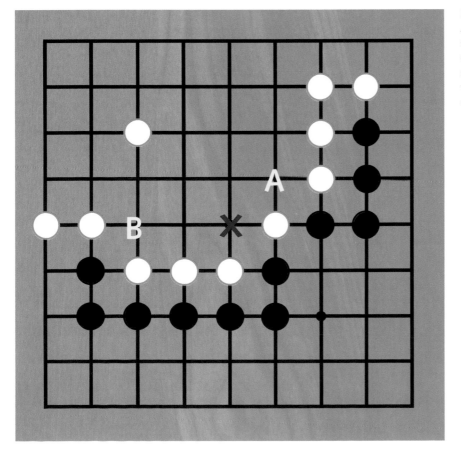

DIAGRAM I

A serial atari. Black gives atari at square X. White joins his threatened piece with the piece at square A, and then Black blocks three white pieces by putting one of his in square B.

Also, the arrangement of the pieces must guarantee that they can easily and successfully repel an enemy attack (Diagrams F and G).

Grouping Too Much

The following piece of strategic advice is very important: always limit the number of groups. There are two reasons for this: safety and efficacy. It is clear why fewer groups mean greater safety—since neither player wants to see his groups captured, he must develop living groups. If he has several groups, he will have to create eyes for two groups at a time, which simply isn't possible. After all, he can place only one piece on the board per turn.

Diagram H shows why it is more effective to have fewer groups. This is the final phase of a game of go. White immediately attacked and tried to overpower the black piece by removing as many of its liberties as possible. But after a few moves, the arrangement of Black's pieces has become far stronger. They form a chain with a total of six liberties, while White has three loose chains with no more than two or three liberties apiece. In terms of territory, it is usually more efficient to occupy one large space instead of two or three smaller ones. As Diagram D shows, the same number of pieces can cover a much larger territory in a corner than in the center of the board (Diagram H).

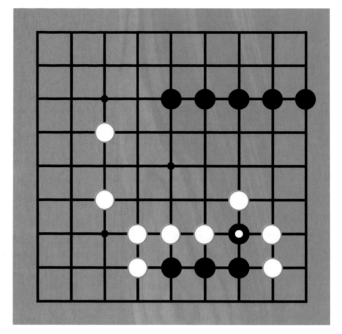

DIAGRAM G:
Black tries to separate the white pieces by putting the dotted piece between them. The result is a chain that cannot be converted into a living group, and that has fewer liberties than the white pieces around it.

STRATEGY

As a general rule, you should never have more groups than your opponent.

Ladies absorbed in a game of go. This image from 1856 is rather special because, at the time, go was played almost solely by men.

One More Group

The exception proves the rule, so sometimes rules are made to be broken. It's a good idea to create as few groups as possible, fewer than your opponent, but sometimes it becomes strategically necessary to form a group in a given place on the board even if it means having more groups than your adversary. In Diagram I, Black has started developing a territory on the right-hand side of the board. White is busy taking over the territory on the left. If White persists, and puts a piece on square X, Black will probably put one of his pieces on square Y. If he does, he will have conquered a territory twice as large as White's, which will make it impossible for White to develop a living group on the right-hand side of the board. Black will inevitably win the game with an enormous lead. That's why White should not put his piece on square X. It would have been better to attack Black's potential territory by occupying square Y. Although that would mean White having one group more than Black, here it is apparent that the rules needn't always be followed to the letter (Diagram I).

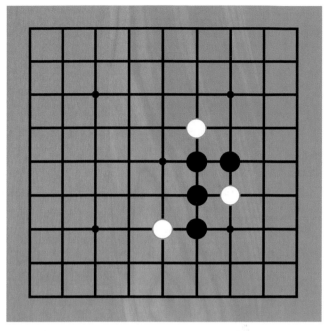

DIAGRAM H:
A limited number of groups. A large group with six liberties is more effective than three vulnerable chains with two or three liberties apiece.

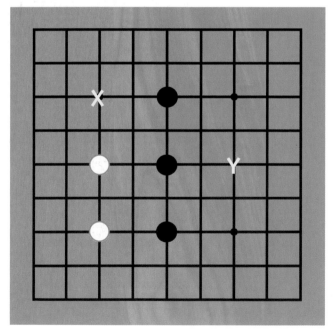

DIAGRAM I:
One more group. White has more chances of winning if he attacks the potential Black territory at square Y, even if it means having one group more than his opponent.

Divide and You Shall Conquer

While it is a good idea to limit the number of your groups, by the same token, you want your opponent to have many smaller, vulnerable groups. You can help this process along by separating your opponent's pieces. In go, the old adage "Divide and you shall conquer" is as true as ever. In Diagram J (A), Black has just placed the dotted piece on the imaginary line between the two white pieces. This way he splits them into two independent chains while keeping his piece from being blocked in a corner. If White reacts by putting a piece on square X (B), Black will immediately put one in square Y, effectively killing the white piece at Y. White still has an option: he, too, can add a piece to Y, but then another one of his pieces will be in trouble. Black can then add a piece to X, thereby threatening the white piece to its right. It's clear, then, that White's arrangement in Diagram J (A) was faulty from the start. He would have done better to add a second piece to the center square as shown in Diagram J (C). If he had done so, players' roles would have been reversed, and White would have successfully divided Black's pieces. Then at the very least he could have blocked one of Black's pieces. If Black had added a piece to square X, White would have added one to Y, blocking the black piece underneath. Conversely, if Black responded by putting a piece on Y, White would have blocked the black piece at X (Diagram J [C]).

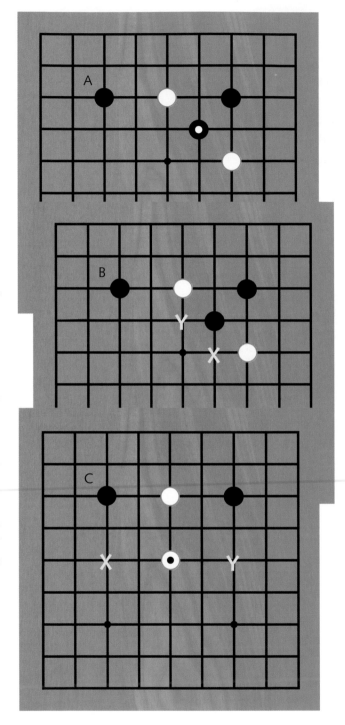

DIAGRAM J:
Dividing the opponent's chains. Black divides the white pieces into two separate chains, which at the very least will cause problems for both of them (A and B). On the other hand, if White adds a piece to the center square, he can instead divide Black's pieces (C).

Atsumi

The great black wall that stands out like a rock among the waves in Diagram K is what is called *atsumi*. This means it has very few weak points and is virtually invulnerable to attack. Atsumi groups radiate great power, felt throughout the right-hand side of the board in Diagram K. If White decides to put a piece within Black's sphere of influence, Black will push toward it, weakening White's position. It is generally true that it is never a good idea to play close to an atsumi. Its strength is hard to express in point values, but its influence can be felt to be that of a vast territory. To play with or against an atsumi is a subtle and complicated task that requires a great deal of experience with the game (Diagram K).

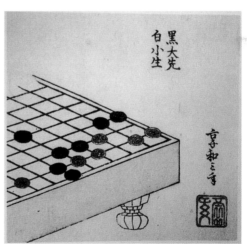

An instructional illustration of a go situation from an 1867 book.

At left, a go scenario in eighteenth-century China. According to legend, the Japanese learned to play go from the Chinese. Here, Japanese are playing against Chinese.

International go tournament, Tokyo, 1995.

STRATEGY

Experienced go players always try to make moves that accomplish several goals at once. You can adopt this habit by conquering territory and attacking your opponent in the same move, for instance.

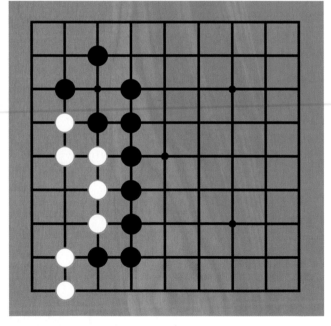

DIAGRAM K:
Atsumi. The black wall rises like a great rock over the tide—it is *atsumi*.

Go: Part 3

The European Go Federation is the association that connects the different go circles throughout Europe as the American Go Association does for North America. Every year, the European go championship and various related tournaments are held in a different city in Europe, drawing more than 500 go players. For most players, this is their vacation. The most important tournament besides the European championship is the Fujitsu Finals, held each December, where players compete for a place in the world championship in Japan. The Fujitsu Finals are organized at the European Go Center in Amstelveen, Netherlands. The center was donated by Iwamoto Kaoru, a first-rate Japanese pro who, at the end of his long career as a go player, sold his house in Tokyo and with the proceeds built three go centers in different parts of the world. The European Go Center offers support to all go circles in Europe and provides promotional material and literature in sixteen European languages, used in twenty-four countries.

Kato Masao and Hikosaka Naoto, absorbed in a fascinating competition (*Photo: Nihon Ki-in, European Go Center*).

The First Match

At this point, the reader who has been learning to play go by following the rules will have gained some experience by playing several practice matches. It is also interesting and instructive to study the moves made by professionals in tournament matches. It is a well-known fact that the number of possible go matches is virtually infinite. The following pages describe a professional go match, in order to provide as broad a perspective on the game as possible. This match was played on a nine-by-nine board and was transcribed under the direction of Dutch player Frank Janssen, who holds a sixth-degree dan. Although professional go is usually played on 19 × 19 boards, nine-by-nine boards are not uncommon; however, the latter they do give the opening player a certain advantage. To fix this problem, players use the *komi* system, in which White receives a certain number of points at the end of the match; these points, usually numbering five, are called *komi*. A game is always more fun if it doesn't end in a draw, so often the players agree to award 4.5 or 5.5 komi points to avoid a tie.

It is recommended that you play the following match yourself, following the description to the letter. Then try to remember, after each move, the reasoning that went into it.

Preliminaries

This match is a clear example of what a professional go match looks like: constantly changing planes, and a broad spectrum of intelligent moves to get the most out of the pieces' positions. In the diagrams, moves are indicated as follows: 1 is Black's first move, 2 is White's first move, 3 is Black's second,

and so forth. Every single move is shown on the board to give the reader the opportunity to follow the entire match on a board of his or her own.

The First Moves

1 It is clear from Diagram 1 that Black has started to conquer a large territory on the right-hand side of the board. Meanwhile, after two moves, White claims a modest area on the upper left-hand side. If the territory really ends up being divided this way, White will be in bad shape. The difference between these two territories is worth about twenty points. To counter this, White will have to place one of his pieces inside Black's sphere of influence (Diagram 1).

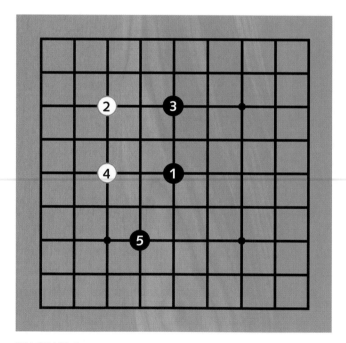

DIAGRAM 1:

The first moves. Black immediately claims a large territory on the right-hand side of the board, while White has the option of controlling a modest number of squares on the upper left-hand corner of the board.

Black's Sphere of Influence

2 In the strategies already discussed, it was noted that sometimes a player cannot help but have one group more than his opponent. The present situation is a good example. It's White turn, and he places a piece on square 6, even though it means forming one more group (Diagram 2). This way he has penetrated what could be Black's territory. If he puts a piece on square A, Black will add one to square 6, backing White into a corner. The same thing happens if White puts a piece on square B—Black

would react by adding his piece to square 6 and blocking White. On the other hand, if White adds a piece to 6, the corner is his for sure because he can always move to A or B. This way, his position is much less precarious than if he had played A or B.

A Threefold Objective

3 Once White has put a piece on 6, Black decides to look toward the right. If he places a piece on 7, he will have made a highly strategic move that serves a threefold goal: it blocks White's downward expansion, it attacks the white group, and it begins developing the territory in the lower left-hand side of the board (Diagram 3).

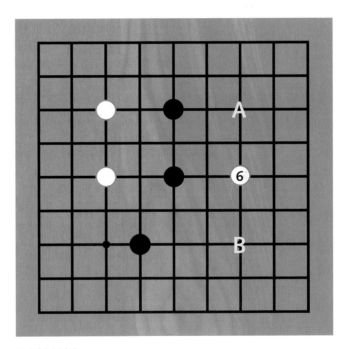

DIAGRAM 2:
Black's sphere of influence. White penetrates this potentially Black territory by moving to 6, which opens up several options for him.

Kaoru Iwamoto, Japan's highest ranking professional player. Iwamoto dedicated his entire life to go. His world tours have earned him a worldwide reputation as a go master. At seventeen, he wrote the best introductory book on go, which is still considered an important work. He has founded many go centers, and his goal is to open one on every continent.

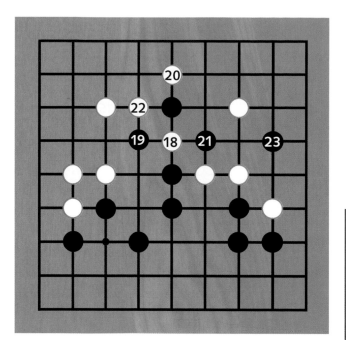

DIAGRAM 6:
A territory for White. White finally manages to join his pieces in the upper left-hand side of the board, but now Black has a chance to penetrate his territory on the right.

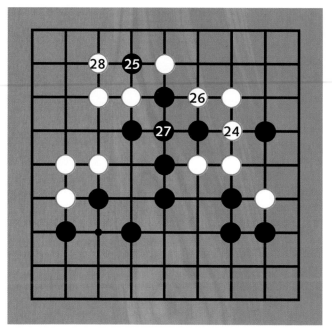

DIAGRAM 7:
A sacrifice. White joins together a few of his pieces, and Black sacrifices the piece at square 25.

A Sacrifice

7 White joins together some of his pieces after putting one in square 24. In his next turn, Black sacrifices his piece at 25. The purpose of this move will become clear at a later stage of the game. The black piece at 27 is situated to keep White from putting a piece on that square and capturing two of Black's pieces (Diagram 7).

TIP

It is a good idea to play with a more experienced player at some point. Make sure to ask his opinion at the end of the match. Most go players enjoy explaining the game.

A POPULAR SAYING

There's a saying that goes, "Don't build territories over weaknesses," which is to say, it is unadvisable in go to play close to an opponent's wall.

The Final Frontier

8 By playing square 29, Black conquers the dotted white piece on the square below it. In his next move, on 31, he penetrates the white zone on the left-hand side of the board. Professionals go a bit further when establishing their final frontiers (Diagram 8).

A Noteworthy Turn of Events

9 The board is filling up; meanwhile, both players expand their territories with each move. Then something noteworthy happens: White captures one of Black's pieces from square 40, and Black surrounds the center square by putting a piece on 41. It is worth asking whether White could have prevented this by putting a piece of his own on that space (Diagram 9).

An 1860 Japanese etching showing a family playing go.

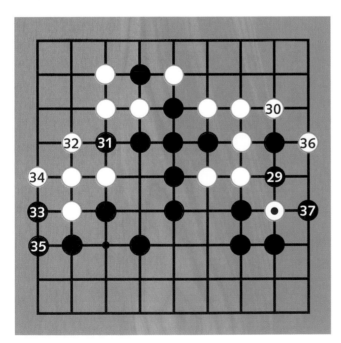

DIAGRAM 8:
Both players establish their final frontiers.

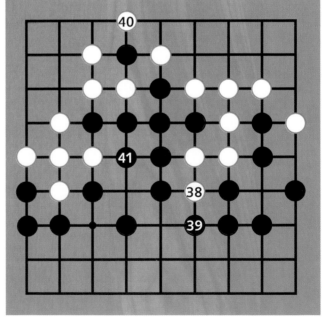

DIAGRAM 9:
A noteworthy move. Why didn't White keep Black from surrounding the center square by putting his own piece on 41?

What If...?

10

Diagram 10 (move 1) shows what might have happened if in Diagram 9 White had moved one of his pieces to square 41. Black would then have given him atari with the piece at square 4 and tried to enter the white zone on the top half of the board. White's reaction would surely have been to try to join his pieces, so it would have made sense to move to 5. But then Black would have given atari from square 6, capturing ten of White's pieces by putting a piece on 8 and another on 10. Now it is clear why move 25 in Diagram 7 made sense—it made it possible for Black, if necessary, to atari at 6 (Diagram 10).

The Final Moves

11

If White does not join his pieces after putting one of them on square 42, Black will take five White pieces and move into 42 himself. White can now calmly protect himself from atari at 43 with his piece on 44. After all, a black piece on square A does not pose the threat of an atari, because now White can simply answer from square B. After setting down piece 44, neither player has the chance to take over more territory or to capture the other's pieces. They call an end to the match (Diagram 11).

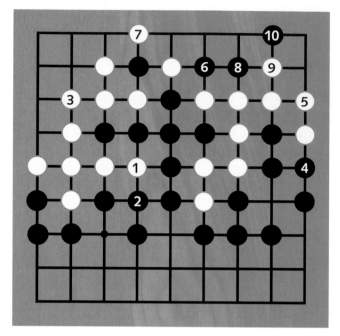

DIAGRAM 10:
What if White had played 41 (move 1 in this diagram)? This would have meant a loss of ten pieces, because move 25 in Diagram 7 allows Black to atari at 6.

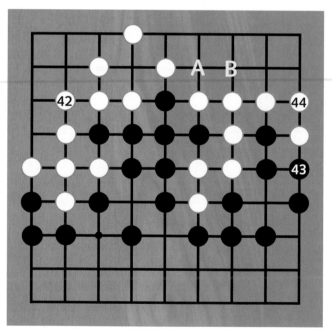

DIAGRAM 11:
The final moves. To avoid losing five pieces all at once, White must join together his pieces at 42.

Back to the Game Board

12 Both players have passed on their turns, so now it's time for the final tally. First the dead pieces are placed inside their respective territories. Black has taken two of White's pieces, and White has taken one of his. White puts an additional four pieces in Black's territory (on the lower left-hand part of Diagram 12) because he still has four komi points. He still needs half a komi point, but he cannot put half a point on the board (Diagram 12).

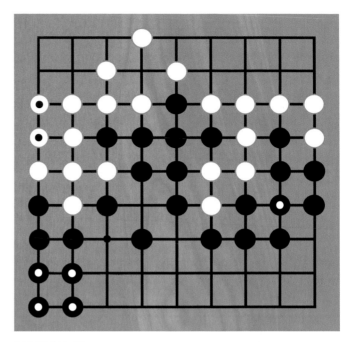

DIAGRAM 12:
Back to the game board. Both players put the dead pieces in each other's territories, and White adds four black komi pieces.

CURIOUS FACT

In Japan, five hundred or so professional go players earn a good deal of money playing their favorite game. Top and midlevel pros supplement their winnings by teaching, writing articles, and other arrangements. Korean and, to a lesser degree, Chinese pros also earn significant prize money, and in international competition some Korean players are now stronger than the top Japanese players. Frank Janssen, a member of the European Go Center, provided the list below from the Nihon Ki-in, the Japanese foundation of go professionals, for top Japanese player prize earnings in 2004 (in italics is the rank or title held that year, when 100 yen was slightly more that one U.S. dollar):

1. Cho U, *Meijin Honinbo*: ¥ 104,956,528
2. Hane Naoki, *Kisei*: ¥ 67,830,604
3. Yamashita Keigo, *Tengen*: ¥ 57,101,390
4. Yoda Norimoto, *Gosei*: ¥ 53,288,550
5. Kobayashi Koichi, *9-dan*: ¥ 38,270,000
6. O Rissei, *Judan*: ¥ 34,049,100
7. Cho Chikun, 25th *Honinbo*: ¥ 27,660,004
8. Mimura Tomoyasu, *9-dan*: ¥ 26,537,040
9. O Meien, *9-dan*: ¥ 24,770,488
10. Takao Shinji, *8-dan*: ¥ 17,149,060

Ladies absorbed in a game of go during the Qin dynasty, 200 B.C.E.

Rules:
Preliminaries

The Wari game board has six pits on each side. It sits horizontally between the players. Each player uses the row of pits on his side. Each player gets twenty-four chips. It does not matter what color they are, because the players do not need to distinguish whose pieces belong to whom—what matters is whose side the pieces are on. (However, for greater clarity, the diagrams distinguish between the players' respective pieces and have the number of pieces in each hole marked on one of them to make matters easier.) At the start of the game, players sow four pieces in each pit. They draw to decide who will begin (Diagram A).

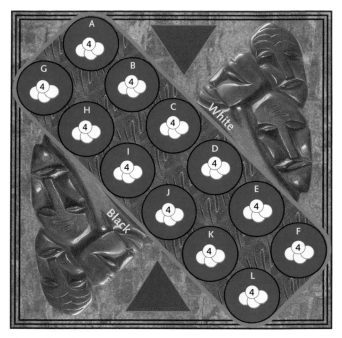

DIAGRAM A:
Wari board at opening.

Craftsmen in Ghana making Wari boards *(Photo: Pim Smit, Amsterdam)*.

How the Pieces Move

The player who starts takes the pieces from one of the pits on his side of the board and places them, one by one, in each of the next consecutive four pits, moving counterclockwise. When Black begins and moves the pieces from pit J, he creates the situation shown in Diagram B1. If White then moves four pieces from pit A, the board will look as it does in Diagram B2. Players take turns moving all the chips from one of their pits. Though the pieces do not belong exclusively to him or his opponent, he must play with the pieces that are on his own side of the board (Diagrams B1 and B2).

Capturing Pieces

In Wari, there is a special method for capturing pieces. When a player puts the last piece of his turn in one of his opponent's pits where there are only one or two pieces, he removes those pieces from the hole and puts them in a pile between himself and his row of holes on the board. The pieces that have been removed from the board will not reenter the game (Diagrams C1 and C2).

CURIOUS FACT

Many wooden mancala boards are carved and decorated with symbols, and have typically been passed from father to son.

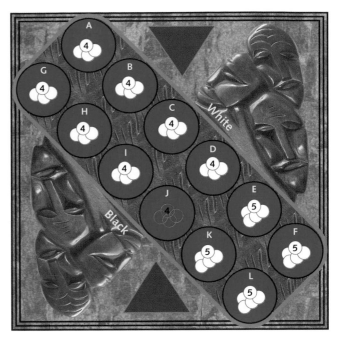

DIAGRAM B1:
How the pieces move. Black takes the pieces from pit J and one by one puts them in the next four pits over (K, L, F, and E).

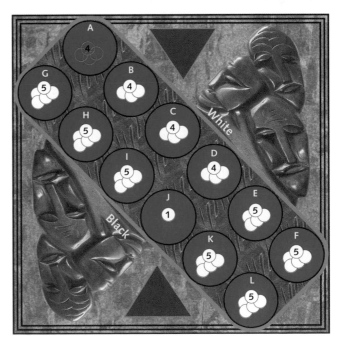

DIAGRAM B2:
White is the second to play. He takes the pieces from pit A and puts them one by one in the next four pits (G, H, I, and J).

Mancala players. Woodcut by Thomas Bewick, circa 1790.

Finishing

When very few pieces are left on the board, players may opt to call it quits. In practice, this happens when there are only two or three pieces left in play and the chances of capturing any pieces are virtually nil. Each player removes the pieces from his row, and adds them to the pieces he has captured.

The game also ends when a player is unable to make any move during his turn because there are no pieces left in his row. The player who still has pieces in his row adds these to the pieces he has captured (Diagram E).

The Winner

The winner is the player who has captured and removed the most pieces by the end of the game.

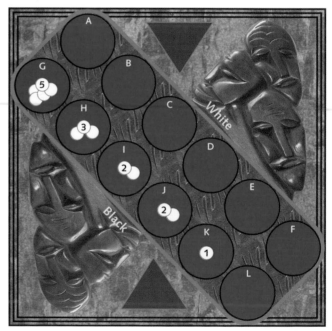

DIAGRAM E:
Finishing. Black can no longer "feed" White. When White's turn comes, he will not be able to move at all, so the game will be over.

The First Match

When you start playing Wari, you'll immediately be surprised by the many quick changes that occur in a single game, and the myriad possibilities the game offers. You will learn tactics such as threat of the capture, defense, and counterattack. Wari is a game with many strategic options that a beginner will only begin to understand little by little, by playing a few matches. In general, the game is divided into three phases: opening, midgame, and endgame, as described below. It's a good idea to try these out for yourself on the board as you study them.

Opening: Basic Principles

As with many other games, in Wari there is no single correct way of opening. There are different ways to play this game in a balanced and thoughtful manner, but all of them are based on these principles:

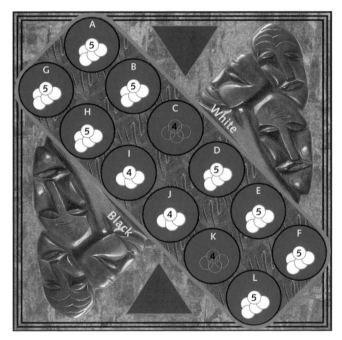

DIAGRAM 1A:
The first moves. Black has played the pieces in K and White has emptied pit C.

1. It's important to maintain alternating free and occupied pits, to keep your opponent from capturing multiple pieces.
2. You must decide early in the game where you want to build your buffer.
3. Losing a few pieces is not a problem as long as it means gaining some other advantage.
4. From your very first move you should always think about how your opponent will react.

The First Moves

1 In keeping with the first principle of opening, the obvious thing to do is to empty out K, I, and G in the course of the first few moves. In Diagram 1A, Black has started doing this by moving the pieces from pit K. White has removed his pieces from pit C. It's Black's turn again, and in line with the basic principles, he must next move the pieces in I. But if he does, White will immediately capture two pieces. The same thing would happen if he moved the pieces in G, H, or J. In each case, one of the pieces would end up in pit K, and all White would have to do is move the pieces from A to capture that piece. So Black decides to move the pieces in L instead, and White reacts by removing the six pieces (5 + 1) from F. The result is the situation in Diagram 1B. Anyway, in his next move Black will put one of his pieces each in pits K and L. Then White will play from pit A and capture four pieces.

The attack on Paris took place house by house. Homes were conquered and recaptured according to the advances and retreats of the battling armies.

Because of these surprising and unusual characteristics, this timeless game was, unfortunately, relegated to oblivion after a brief period of great popularity. Perhaps this is owing to the amount of time it takes to master the rules, which can be rather complicated. Or maybe people wanted to forget the events that inspired the game, and stop thinking about this moment in history. One hopes the game will awaken the interest of new players who can rekindle the popularity it once enjoyed.

The Board

Siege of Paris is played on a sort of enlarged chessboard with alternating light and dark squares and a citadel in the center of the board. Boards can vary widely in appearance, from simple cardboard models to exquisite collector's items made with fine woods and excellent finishes.

French antique dealers sometimes carry truly precious Siege of Paris boards and game pieces. Finding an antique set can be a fun challenge for collectors and game connoisseurs alike.

The Pieces

The pieces, like the board, vary from the very simple to the elaborate. Nonetheless, the special thing about the pieces isn't just their decoration, but their function on the board. The mobility of the pieces is restricted, as in most games of strategy, not only by the pieces' appearance but by the camp (invading or defending) to which they belong and their corresponding objective in the game.

The Game's Identity

Despite its apparent similarity to several other games, Siege of Paris, like the historical events on which it is based, is a game with a strong identity of its own. Its rules include innovations that cannot be found in any other board game. It also offers the peculiar option of being played with either two or three players. Few games of strategy allow this. Also, the creator of Siege of Paris added another dimension to the game by limiting the freedom of movement of some pieces on both sides, black and white.

Playing Siege of Paris

Siege of Paris is an intriguing board game which was usually played by two people, though it is ideal for three players. Two of the players direct their respective armies, which attack the citadel from different sides. The third defends the citadel and tries at the same time to capture the opponents' pieces. The invaders can win the game in two different ways, so they must decide either together or separately which campaign they will pursue. The same is not true for the defender—first, because he works alone; second, because he has only one way of defeating his adversaries. It doesn't matter which role the players assume—to win, they will simply have to call on their strategic ability. The board is divided into twelve by sixteen squares in alternating light and dark colors. The citadel covers an area in the center of the board of six by six quares and contains eight round spaces connected by several lines.

To play this unique game of strategy, you need both a special game board and special pieces, totaling eighteen black, eighteen white, and eight red pieces.

Players	Requirements
2 or 3	special board
	18 each, white and black pieces
Average duration	8 red pieces
45 minutes	
Category	
strategy	

The First Match

Anyone playing Siege of Paris for the first time will quickly be captivated by the immense variety of possible gaming situations it has to offer. The player will discover that there is no point in moving pieces for its own sake but will instead need to plan a strategy. The attacking pieces must cooperate to shield themselves from attacks from the opponent. The defending team, meanwhile, runs the risk of losing sight of the big picture when it tries to keep from getting trapped, while at the same time hunting down the opponent's pieces and trying to guard the citadel. The following pages present guidelines a beginning player can follow to give a sense of direction to his or her first few games.

The Opening

The defensive camp has three game pieces, which occupy the eight spaces inside the citadel. The defender opens the game, so it is both logical and inevitable that one of his pieces leave the citadel in the first move. The attacker can decide to concentrate on trapping the defensive pieces. If he opts for this strategy, it's important that he control the access roads to the citadel as soon as possible so that the fewest number of defensive pieces are able to exit. Of course, he must also take care not to let his pieces be captured. If the attacker elects to enter the citadel with three of his pieces, they must always move in that direction. In that case, speed is not as important as ensuring the balanced movement of troops toward the citadel and making sure the pieces cover one another to avoid capture.

General Von Moltke, German commander in the Franco-Prussian War.

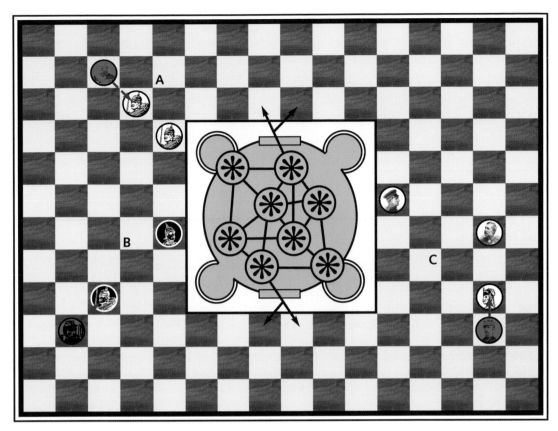

DIAGRAM 1:
The importance of covering. The defender is unable to capture a piece in any situation shown here. All the attacker's pieces are covered by other pieces.

The Importance of Covering

1 The Germans, as a group, control a total of thirty-six pieces. That may seem like a lot, but the defending camp can win only by capturing the opponent's pieces and will do whatever it can to accomplish this. For the attackers, then, the most important thing is to cover their pieces. In Diagram 1 (A), the defending general cannot capture the attacking soldier because it is already covered by another attacking soldier. In Diagram 1 (B), a defending soldier tries to capture a German soldier but cannot do it here, either, because the German is covered by a lieutenant, which can move two squares diagonally. Nor can the defender capture a piece in Diagram 1 (C), though it may appear at first glance as though he can. In the beginning, the

colonel can move sideways but not into a square already occupied by the attacking captain. The general in the square next to the citadel cannot protect it because it cannot move backward. It is the colonel providing cover here, for it can move two squares to the side. These scenarios show that the attacker must ask himself before making any move whether one of his pieces is without cover (Diagram 1).

Stalemate

2 When an attacking soldier enters the citadel, the game halts and ends in a draw. This means that only the German armies can force a stalemate. They will try to do so when they are threatened with defeat and believe they can no longer win the game using a new strategy. Diagram 2 shows the attacking armies reduced to two soldiers and six other pieces, so the two attacking camps have a total of eight available pieces. The defender need only capture two more soldiers to win the game. The defensive pieces are dispersed throughout the board and only one of them is inside the citadel, so the attacker will not be able to trap them all inside. Because the German army has no chance of putting three of its pieces inside the citadel, it decides to force a draw. To this end, it takes advantage of the rule that the defensive camp has a duty to capture. The attacker has positioned a soldier near the lower entrance to the citadel where the defender will be forced to capture it in his next turn. The defender realizes the danger of a tie. He would prefer to move one of his soldiers into the citadel to block the attacker's entry, but has to capture the piece below, so in his next turn the attacker can move his soldier into the citadel and force a tie (Diagram 2).

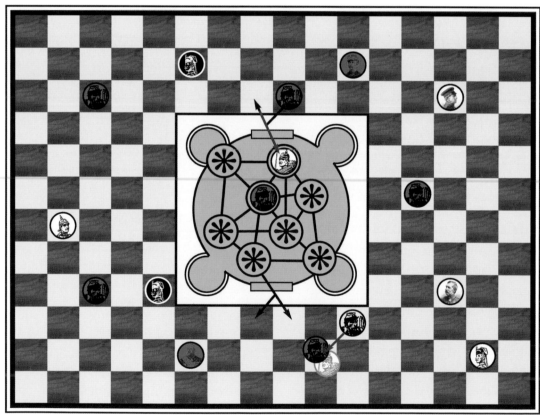

DIAGRAM 2:
A draw. The defensive army is obliged to capture the German soldier to the right of the citadel, which means the German soldier has the chance to enter the citadel through the left-hand side, forcing a draw.

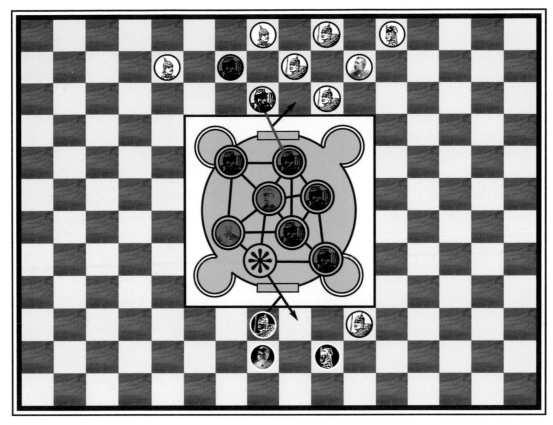

DIAGRAM 3:
The attackers win. The defense is unable to capture any pieces, and the attackers have managed to trap all his pieces inside the citadel.

Attackers Win

3 Diagram 3 shows that the attackers' remaining pieces have clustered around the doors of the citadel. They clearly intend to win the match by trapping the defender's pieces inside. The defender's pieces cannot leave the citadel through the lower entrance because it is totally blocked. There are two defense pieces near the upper entrance to the citadel. It is the French army's turn, but this side cannot capture any of its adversary's pieces because they are covering one another. In this situation, the defender will not be able to avoid eventually moving one of his soldiers into the citadel. He will now have to put his last soldier in front of the citadel door—the only available square. Finally, the attackers will force him to move this piece inside, and will win the match by trapping him inside (Diagram 3).

Defenders Win

4 In Diagram 4, the defender has managed to capture all twenty-four enemy soldiers as well as five other pieces, reducing the German armies to only seven men. The attackers are no longer in a position to force a draw, because they do not have enough soldiers to enter the citadel. The attackers have allowed themselves to be eliminated! Now all the defense has to do is capture one more piece and he will win the game, as he is isolating the enemy captain using all his soldiers. He can capture the captain by moving just one of his pieces. The captain can move only one square forward or to one side, and will inevitably be captured by the defender when the latter makes his next move, winning the game (Diagram 4).

ATTACKER'S STRATEGY

The attacking lieutenants and soldiers can move backward, but the other attacking pieces cannot. This means the players must be careful not to advance too many of their pieces, lest they become useless.

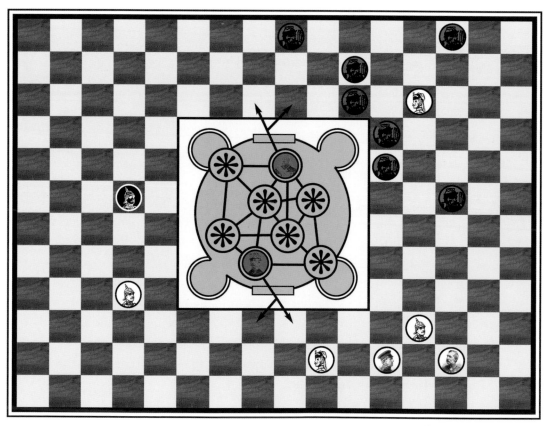

DIAGRAM 4:
Defenders win. In the situation pictured here, the attacking captain cannot avoid being captured by the defender's next move.

Polish Checkers
History of the Game

◆ ◆ ◆

Our knowledge of the history of checkers rests largely on linguistic facts. Based on these facts, the British historian of board games Harold Murray (1868–1955) carried out the most comprehensive historical study of checkers. In carrying out this task he was aided by renowned linguists. The results were published in his book, *A History of Board Games Other than Chess*, in 1952. And a 1916 manuscript found among his belongings, entitled *Preliminary Investigations into the History of Draughts*, is a significant contribution to our understanding of where, when, and how the game of checkers (known as draughts in many countries) was born and how it would later develop (see also English checkers, page 153). Historians agree that it is descended from another board game, but they do not agree on which. Two games are considered precursors to checkers: some believe it is descended from chess, while others think Alquerque (see page 199) is the only board game that could possibly be related to checkers' origin. Alquerque is one of the medieval games described in the codex of King Alfonso the Wise, which he completed in Seville in 1283. It is assumed that with the arrival in Europe of checkers, in which the pieces are obliged to capture, the game of Alquerque disappeared.

A humorous etching from *Caricatures Parisiennes*, 1810. The cartoon suggests that political decisions were made at the checkerboard.

Alquerque or Chess?

The oldest known literature on the game of checkers was published in Spain. Based on this fact, Professor Van der Linde (1874), the chess historian, believed that checkers developed from constructions derived from the endgame in traditional pan-Arabic chess, in which pawns were crowned. Professor Daniel Willard Fiske shares this opinion, which he defended authoritatively in 1905 in the following terms: "Checkers is a very simplified version of chess, and it is therefore logical that its direct and only origin lies in this game." In his 1917 book, *The Chess Amateur*, the specialist W.S. Branch relates the game to Alquerque and chess thus: "The game of checkers was born from experiments carried out on a chessboard using the rules of the game of Alquerque."

The Name

The Roman game *ludus latrunculorum* takes its classical Latin name from the pieces that were needed to play the game. Likewise, in Medieval Latin the name of a board game was formed by taking the collective name of the pieces used to play it. Thus, chess took the name of one of its pieces, ignoring the individual names of particular pieces. In French, checkers is called *jeu de dames*, and it is formed according to the same rules as Latin games—after the pieces, which are called *dames* ("ladies" or "damsels"). Similarly, in Spain the game is known as *juego de damas*, where each piece is called a *dama*. The name refers not only to the queen (*dame or dama*) in chess, but also to "ladies of high society."

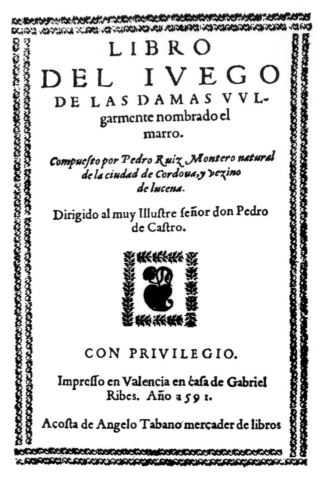

Frontispiece of an antique checkers manual (1591).

Popularity

The popularity of checkers can be divined, among other things, from the many paintings of inns in which travelers are pictured passing the time and resting by playing a game of checkers. From the moment of its appearance in Europe, checkers has been played by young and old in all strata of society. While women would usually gather in homey settings to enjoy a game of checkers, men usually played it outside the home.

Playing Polish Checkers

English checkers, or draughts, is one of the most popular versions in the world, but Polish or continental checkers is a close second in popularity and dissemination, among both children and adults, amateurs and professionals. Polish checkers is so widespread that as a general rule, it is referred to simply as "checkers" or "*dames*," and is widely known as *international checkers*, for the game is played on all five continents, where many countries belong to the World Checkers Federation, founded in 1947. The basic rules of the English version apply to the Polish version as well, but some of the differences (such as the power of the largest king) make Polish checkers more complicated. Polish checkers involves many complex strategies, which ambitious players study closely. It is played on a ten-by-ten board, using two sets of twenty pieces of two different colors. Players aim to capture or immobilize all their opponent's pieces as soon as possible.

A game of checkers on the streets of New York *(Photo: Pim Smit, Amsterdam)*.

Polish checkers is played on a board of ten by ten squares. The game also requires twenty white pieces and twenty black.

Players	Requirements
2	special game board,
	ten by ten squares
Average duration	20 each, white and black pieces
30 minutes	
Category	
strategy	

A tough move. This is a cartoon from shortly after the French Revolution. The game of checkers was very popular in France at the time and was often used in political satires such as this one.

Rules:
Preliminaries

The players in a game of checkers sit across from each other with the board between them so that, as in chess, the white square is at their right. Both players put their pieces on the black squares in the first four rows of each side. They draw to decide who will play with which color, because White always makes the first move. After each game, players switch colors (Diagram A).

How the Pieces Move

The pieces move diagonally from one square to another toward the opposite side of the board, so they can move only along the dark squares. At the start of the game, both players can choose among nine possible moves. When a piece reaches the opposite end of the board, it is crowned and becomes a king.

Capturing Pieces

In Polish checkers, the pieces are obliged to capture. A player can capture by jumping diagonally over his opponent's piece and into the open square behind it.

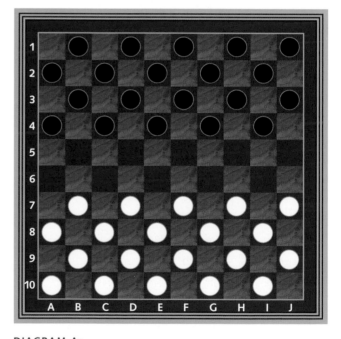

DIAGRAM A:
The opening position of the pieces in Polish checkers.

If a player can capture several pieces in a single turn, he must do so. The pieces can capture one another by moving either backward or forward. If a player can capture in several different places, he must choose the option that allows him to capture the

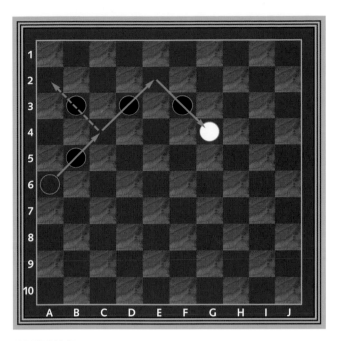

DIAGRAM B:
Capturing pieces. White may prefer to capture two pieces and land in A2. That would allow him to crown the piece more quickly, but the multiple jump has preference, so White must capture the three pieces.

most pieces. If the number is the same in all cases, he must choose the strongest move, meaning the one that will allow him to capture the most kings. When capturing, a piece may not jump over the same piece more than once. Sometimes a player forgets to capture a piece. In many homes, this means applying the huff rule, which means the other player can remove the piece that the other player neglected to capture. The official rules do not acknowledge the huff rule. If a player forgets to capture or doesn't finish a multiple jump, his opponent can do one of two things:

- He may insist that the player return the piece he has just moved and complete the omitted move;
- He can accept the omission. In this case, if possible, in the next turn the opponent will still be obliged to capture (Diagram B).

The Coronation

A piece becomes a king only if it lands on the last row of the board at the end of a move. If it does, but the player abandons the piece again at the end of his turn because it has to continue jumping, the piece cannot be crowned in that move. A king can move forward and backward any number of spaces, always in a diagonal line. After capturing it can land on any empty square behind the piece it has just captured, in the same direction. It can begin its jump several squares before the piece it intends to capture, but it cannot jump over two adjacent pieces in the same turn. A queen is a powerful weapon: it can capture by moving either backward or forward all along a diagonal line, without having to start or end on a square next to the piece it intends to capture. Her opponent must protect himself from her at all times (Diagram C).

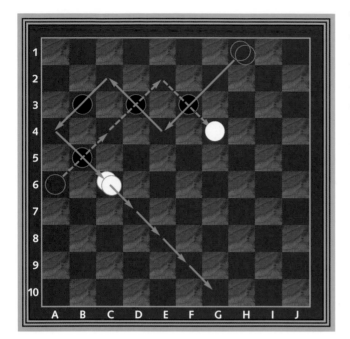

A king attacks. White can capture more pieces with his king than with the other piece (four rather than three). The king can land on any of the squares in the diagonal line between C6 and G10.

The Winner

The winner is the player who captures all his opponent's pieces, or who has put his opponent in a position where he can no longer move at all. The game often ends in a draw. Players can decide to call an end to the game at any time if they agree on the final result.

An Asian variation on chess and checkers, played on a twelve-by-twelve board. Singapore, 1984 (Photo: Pim Smit, Amsterdam).

The First Match

It does not take long to learn the rules of the game, which means a person can play the first game of checkers immediately. But as mentioned, Polish checkers is a difficult and complicated game. Like so many other games, checkers requires a solid theoretical base if one is to play it well. A game of checkers covers three stages: the opening, the midgame, and the endgame. Each stage has its own set of moves, threats, and strategies. The following pages depict a few situations from each of these stages so the beginning player can begin to appreciate these nuances.

An Opening

1 The pieces are on the board in the opening position. The following moves are made:

1. White D7–E6. Black E4–F5.
2. White C8–D7.

After this move by White, the situation on the board is as shown in Diagram 1.

1. White's second move is a mistake, because now Black will make a single move in which he captures two White pieces.

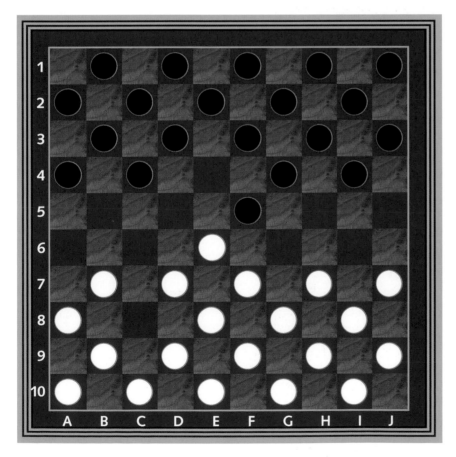

DIAGRAM 1:
It is Black's turn. After making a series of moves and sacrificing two pieces, he can capture three of White's pieces in a single move. This is known as the *Haarlem move.*

A game of checkers. Lithograph by Julien Boilly, circa 1850.

Black makes his move: F5–G6.

White can capture in one of two ways: H7 to F5, or F7 to H5. The result will be the same either way. In his third move, White chooses the first option and moves H7–F5.

3. White H7–F5. Black C4–D5.
4. White E6–C4. Black G4–A6.

Black first sacrificed two of his pieces, one after another, but was then able to capture three of his opponent's pieces in a single move, meaning he has taken one more piece than White has. Also, in C4 another White piece is threatened. There is no way to protect it, so Black will end up taking two more pieces. If he keeps playing like this, White will win the game. To confirm that the moves H7–F5 and F5–H7 really do lead to the same result, you can move the pieces back to the position shown in Diagram 1:

1. Black moves from F5 to G6 as before.
2. White now makes his third move and this time chooses the second option, moving F7–H5.
3. Black I4–G6. He does not move G4–I6 because it would still allow White to escape.
4. White H7–F5. Black C4–D5.
5. White E6–C4. Black G4–A6.

The result is the same. Black has captured four pieces and White has captured three. Again, this time a White piece is left on the board and it will surely be captured in the next turn. This combination is known as the Haarlem play or "green play." It is an important move and should be committed to memory (Diagram 1).

Another Opening

2 The pieces are back to their opening position on the board. This time the first moves are as follows:

1. White F7–E6. Black E4–D5.
2. White G8–F7.

In this way, the scenario in Diagram 2 develops, which is actually just an inversion of Diagram 1. White's last move is a mistake, because it gives Black the opportunity to develop the Haarlem play. Black makes the play with the following move: D5–C6.

White now has two ways of capturing, and the result is the same either way. But first he opts for:

3. White B7–D5. Black G4–F5.
4. White E6–G4. Black C4–I6.
5. White J7–H5. Black I4–G6.

The white piece on G4 is threatened, and there is nothing White can do to save it. Black captures two more pieces, just as before.

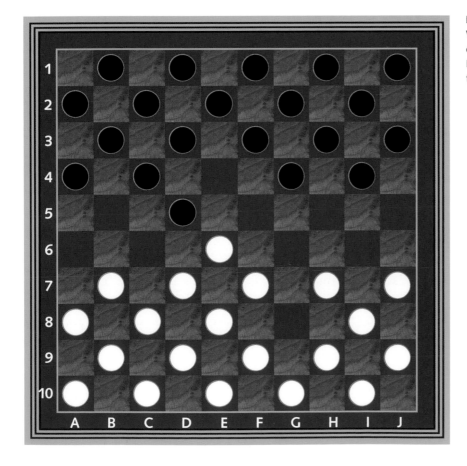

DIAGRAM 2:
With this opening, too, Black can develop the Haarlem play. He captures two more pieces than White.

Notice what would have happened if, after Black's second move, White had decided to make the following moves:

3. White D7–B5. Black A4–C6. Black does not choose the move C4–A6 because he has nothing to gain from it and the game would remain the same.
4. White B7–D5. Black G4–F5.
5. White E6–G4. Black C4–I6.
6. White J7–H5. Black I4–G6.

(Diagram 2).

A Play of Positions

Playing well in checkers means attaining a deeper understanding of the game, beyond knowing how to gain a material advantage by capturing a piece, or sacrificing one, two, or more pieces after capturing three, four, or more of your opponent's. A player should not reduce his game to this limited dynamic,

because it means neglecting his position. "Position" means the strategic arrangement of one's pieces. The aim is to group and arrange your pieces such that they are more dominant with each move, to progressively corner your opponent, and finally, to win. This strategic game is called the "play of positions," and capturing pieces by jumping over them is a key element in it. This—and not the limited play of capturing—is the ideal tactic, for it takes advantage of all the game's possibilities. Capturing an opponent's piece should be a means, not an end. A player should be careful that the former does not cost him the latter, and should maintain a balance between capturing and positional play.

Chinese courtesans before a checkerboard. Painting by Giuseppe Castiglione (1698–1768).

A Midgame Combination

3 Diagram 3 shows the well-known strategy attributed to the nineteenth-century French champion Raphael. White wins this game elegantly by making the following moves:

1. White H7–G6. Black F5–H7.
2. White E6–F5. Black G4–G8.
3. White C8–B7. Black A6–E6.
4. White G10–H9. Black B5–F9.
5. White H9–B3. Black A4–C2.
6. White captures five pieces (from E10 to C4) and wins. It does not matter what piece Black uses—he will be captured no matter what, and will lose his last piece in the next turn (Diagram 3).

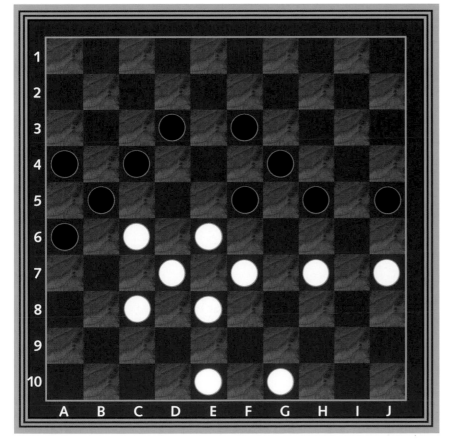

DIAGRAM 3:
A midgame combination attributed to the champion Raphael. White wins.

Another Midgame Combination

4 The arrangement in Diagram 4 contains one of the most fantastic known combinations in checkers. It would allow Black to move F5–G6, and White to reply with J5–I4. This original opening, in which White sacrifices three pieces (Black captures with H3 and moves all the way to F9), and the rest of the combination, took the world of checkers by surprise. It consists of the following moves:

1. White A8–B7. Black G6–E8.
2. White E6–D5. Black C4–E6.
3. White D7–F1. Black B5–B9.

STRATEGY

From the very first moves, a favorable disposition of the pieces is a key factor in the game's development. It is therefore always a good idea to use all the pieces.

---

4. White F1–J5. Black A6–C8.
5. White J5–A8, capturing seven pieces as he moves through F9, C8, F3, I2, H5, E8, and B9, thereby gaining an advantage. This play was made by Russian champion Z. Tsirik in several matches during the 1950s (Diagram 4).

Endgame

5 Someone once astutely observed about checkers, "As the number of pieces decreases, the possibilities increase." Put differently, what at first appears to be the easiest is in fact the hardest. Diagram 5 shows a simple arrangement consisting of few pieces. At first glance it appears as though this situation will lead quickly and easily to victory. Nothing could be farther from the truth, as the following hypothetical situation shows:

Two people sit down at a checkerboard with their pieces in the position shown in Diagram 5. When White is asked to win the game, he does.

DIAGRAM 4:
This famous midgame combination takes the White player to victory.

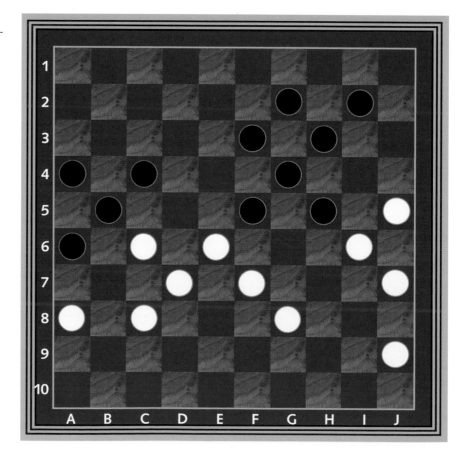

Then the same thing is asked of Black, and he also wins, although White made the first move. Then Black makes the first move and the game ends in a draw. White wins the next few times.

White won, tied, or lost, and yet could have won in every situation, regardless of who made the first move, if he had played the game well. This can be proven using the following five variations on this endgame:

Variation 1: White starts and wins.

1. White F7–G6. Black D1–C2.
2. White G6–H5. Black C2–D3.
3. White H5–G4. Black D3–C4.
4. White G4–F3. Black C4–D5.
5. White F3–E2. Black D5–E6.
6. White E2–F1. Black E6–F7.
7. White F1–J5. Black F7–E8.
8. White J5–E10. White wins this time. He earned a king at F1, but Black could also have done so at D1, H1, or J1. There, too, he would have won this time.

Variation 2: White starts, Black wins.

1. White F7–E6. In the first variation, White made this move correctly, but this time makes a mistake, because here Black will follow with D1–E2.
2. White E6–F5. Black E2–F3. Black wins because, no matter what piece White moves, he will capture White's piece in his next move.

Variation 3: Black starts; no one wins.

1. Black D1–C2. White F7–E6.
2. Black C2–B3. White E6–F5.
3. Black B3–C4. White F5–G4.
4. Black C4–D5. White G4–H3.
5. Black D5–E6. White H3–62.
6. Black E6–F7. White G2–F1.
7. Black F7–E8. White F1–J5.
8. Black E8–D9. Now nothing can stop Black from gaining a king, as in the first variation; therefore, both players have a king and the game ends in a draw. Variation 4: Black starts, White wins.

The first moves are the same as in the third variation, but this time White, instead of moving E6–F5 in his second turn, moves E6–D5. Thanks to this, Black is forced to move B3–A4. Next, White moves D5–C4 and wins the match.

Variation 5: Black starts, White wins.

1. Black D1–E2. White F7–E6. White wins again: E2–F3 is followed by E6–F5, and E2–D3 is followed by E6–D5 (Diagram 5).

Another Endgame

6 Diagram 6 shows another endgame position. In this situation, White is closer to the kings' line. He can also reach four squares in Black's kings' row: D1, F1, H1, and J1. But the situation can vary depending on where White is able to crown his piece. If he does so on F1, H1, or J1, he will lose the game. He can win only if he crowns his piece at D1. Suppose that White crowns a piece at H1:

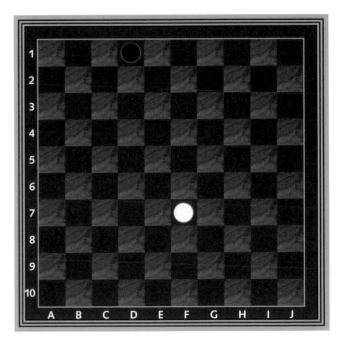

DIAGRAM 5:
An endgame. Regardless of who begins the game, White will win.

Rules:
Preliminaries

Each player gets five pawns of a single color, each of which should be of a different color than the other players'. At the foot of the mountain are five base camps, one for each player. At the start of the game, players put their pawns in their respective bases. The thirteen obstacle pieces are arranged on the board in their starting positions. To determine who will start, players take turns rolling the die. The highest roller begins and the lowest roller moves last (Diagram A).

Moving the Pawns

The pawns leave the base camp, pass through the nearest space, and then move sideways, forward, or backward. They move as many spaces as they rolled on their turn, always along the lines that connect the spaces. This means they never move diagonally. The pawns may enter the game whenever the player wishes, so all five of a player's pawns may be on the path at the same time. A pawn can change direction any time, moving sideways and then forward or backward, though never forward and then back in the same turn. There must never be more than one pawn in a single space, but the pawns can pass over each other.

DIAGRAM A:
A Chimera of Gold playing board in the opening position. There are five pawns in each base camp. The obstacles, which move during the game, are marked with the dark blue pieces with the red circles.

There are 138 spaces between the base camp and the summit, and at any given juncture, there will be many pawns on the board, all moving toward the same goal and more or less in the same direction. It is unavoidable that they will run into one another regularly. When this happens, one of the pawns simply passes over the other, regardless of whether the pawn is one of the player's own or his opponent's. If the player rolls enough points on the die, he can pass over several pawns in one turn. The space or spaces over which he passes are simply counted as though they were empty. But the pawns may never pass over an obstacle (Diagram B).

Capturing Other Pawns

If a pawn lands on a space in which there is already another pawn, he captures that pawn, forcing it to return to its base camp. The defeated pawn has to start all over again. Also, when a pawn lands on a space that is already taken by an opponent's pawn *and* in which there is an obstacle, he captures the pawn that was already there and is sent back to his own base camp. But players are under no obligation to capture their opponents' pawns when given the chance (Diagram C).

DIAGRAM B:
The pawns move from side to side, forward, or backward. They may never pass over an obstacle.

Obstacles

A pawn may not pass over an obstacle, but the placement of the obstacles in the opening position tells us that the pawns are going to run into one of them as soon as they leave their camps. To overcome obstacles, a player must stop on the space where the obstacle sits and wait there until his next turn. If his pawn isn't eliminated, he can then continue on his way and leave the obstacle behind. Plus, that player now has an important resource, namely that he can move the obstacle to any empty space he chooses. He does not have to do so, and can leave it where it is if he is convinced that the obstacle is already in a good strategic position. But there are two cases in which moving an obstacle can be advantageous:

- if the obstacle can be used to block one or more of an opponent's pawns;
- if the player can use it to protect his own pawns.

Players may not place an obstacle in the first row of spaces (the row closest to the camps).

TIP

There can never be an obstacle in the first row of spaces. If a player wants to avoid losing because all his pawns are blocked, he might consider leaving one pawn at his base camp until all the others have reached the summit. If he does, however, he must be sure that this pawn will also be able to reach the summit.

DIAGRAM C:
Capturing pawns. Red rolls a three and captures the blue pawn that's occupying a space with an obstacle in it. Green rolls a five and forces Yellow to return to its base camp.

Finishing

The goal is just beyond the space marked with a flag. To get there, the player must roll the exact number of points. When a player has a pawn in the space with the flag and rolls more than a one, he must move a different pawn. If that isn't possible, he must move the pawn at the penultimate space, but has to move it sideways. If that isn't possible, either, the player must abandon the game, because according to the rules, if a player cannot make use of his move, he loses. Once the pawns have reached their goal, they no longer move and cannot be attacked (Diagram D).

The Winner

The winner is the first player to get all his pawns to the summit. The others can keep playing and compete for second and third place and so forth. Or they can call it quits and count for each how many pawns reached the summit. If two or more of the other players have the same number of pawns at the top, they can keep playing to break the tie.

VARIATION

This variation on the Chimera of Gold has the same rules, except with regard to how the obstacles are used. When a player overcomes an obstacle, he need not leave it in its present site or immediately move it to another space. He can remove the obstacle from the board and return it whenever he pleases. The only condition is that he must do so at the beginning of his turn. This adds tension, for now at any time, an obstacle can appear anywhere on the board.

DIAGRAM D:
Arriving at the summit. Red has taken three pawns to the goal and must now roll a one to move his fourth pawn into the flagged space. He rolls a six. His fifth pawn is completely blocked by two obstacles, and moving to the right is impossible with his fourth pan. Thus, he has no choice but to move his fourth pawn to the left.

Evaluation

Chimera of Gold demands that players constantly think of their different options and possible movements in order to evaluate their best move at any given time. If a play isn't well considered, it can cause a considerable delay.

The diagrams on the preceding pages simplify the reality of this game, for they do not represent all the pawns at work on the board. Altogether, there may be as many as twenty-five pawns on the board at one time. This means the real game is an even greater challenge for players, insofar as it demands they take in the whole situation and foresee the consequences of each move.

STRATEGY

Because of the rush to be first to reach the top of the mountain, there are often one or several obstacles left in one of the rows closest to the base camps. If a player temporarily leaves a pawn in his base camp, he can capture an obstacle fairly easily whenever he needs one.

DIAGRAM 4:

Approaching the end. Green is close to victory because he need move only his last pawn into the summit. But Purple can build an obstacle and decides to place it to the left of the fifth green pawn, which is now trapped between two obstacles. Green fails to roll a one, thus losing the game.

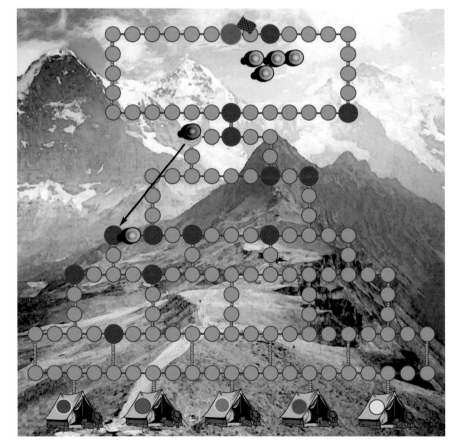

Mikado
History of the Game

◆　◆　◆

For centuries, the Chinese have been known for their surprising magic tricks and their complicated games of skill and patience. The Chinese are especially good at designing games that require few accessories. The game of Mikado, which is known around the world, exemplifies these traits, so it comes as no surprise that, although it bears a Japanese name, it is generally believed to have been invented in China. There it was played with sticks and wands shaped like spears, saws, a serpent coiled around a stick, a cloverleaf, a miter, a bird on a tree, a trident, a fork, a horse's head, a bucket yoke, and so forth. The value of each of these wands was proportional to the difficulty a player would have manipulating it on account of its shape. The saw was the most difficult to take away, so it was worth more than all the others (fifty points). On the other hand, the simpler wands had a lesser value. The wand with the woman on it was worth two points, for instance. There were two wands of each kind, which were usually carved crudely out of cane or bone. More affluent people played on magnificent, carefully carved Mikado boards made of ivory. The game also included a wand with a hook, used to remove other wands from the pile and handed from one player to another as they took turns (see the photograph on page 410).

Woman and child playing Mikado in an illustration from the late nineteenth century.

Rules:
Preliminaries

Mikado is played using forty-one sticks sharpened to a point at both ends. The game is named after the most important of these sticks: the white stick or Mikado. There are others of different colors: blue, green, red, yellow. Each color has a specific value. The 41 sticks in a game of Mikado are distributed as follows:

- one white stick or Mikado, worth 20 points;
- five blue sticks worth ten points each (50 points total);
- five green sticks worth five points each (25 points total);
- fifteen red sticks worth three points each (45 points total);

- fifteen yellow sticks worth two points each (30 points total).
- Altogether the sticks add up to 170 points (Diagram A).

The Pile

The sticks are mixed up and then held tightly together like a bouquet of flowers. One of the players holds them in his hand and sets the bunch down vertically on the table. He then opens his hand and the sticks spread in all directions, forming a pile. If the sticks don't form a pile in all directions, or if one or more of the sticks lands on the ground or stays in the player's hand, the same player drops them again until there is a pile that all can play from.

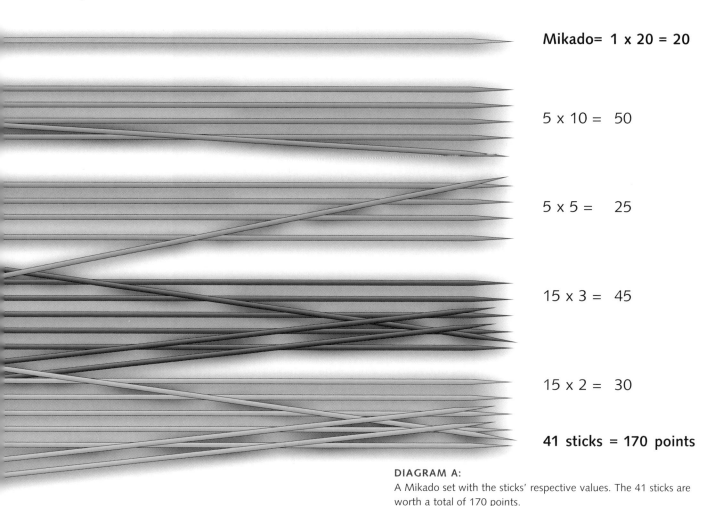

Mikado= 1 x 20 = 20

5 x 10 = 50

5 x 5 =   25

15 x 3 = 45

15 x 2 = 30

41 sticks = 170 points

DIAGRAM A:
A Mikado set with the sticks' respective values. The 41 sticks are worth a total of 170 points.

It's important to make the pile in the center of the table so the sticks do not fall off the edge and every player can get close enough to the pile. Before beginning, players draw to see who will drop the sticks. For prudence sake, that player cannot start the game, because he might try to drop the sticks in the way most advantageous to him. Usually the players agree that his neighbor to the left will open the game (Diagram B).

Drawing the Sticks

Being the first to draw is always an advantage, because at first there will be a few sticks that aren't touching any of the others and can therefore be removed easily. Of course, the first player will take them immediately, or else they become a gift to the next player. Then the player decides how to proceed. He can take the stick that seems easiest to get, or might consider the value of the different sticks and choose the one that's worth the most, which may not be as easy to remove as a lower-valued stick. It does not matter which option he chooses—the important thing is that he carefully consider the position of the stick he wants to remove, and its point of contact with other sticks. If a player touches or removes a stick, he cannot go back and change his mind. This means he cannot drop the stick to pick up another. Once the player chooses one, he must remove it from the pile. If he manages to do this without touching the other sticks, he may continue. The same player decides again which stick he wishes to pick up next, and tries to remove it.

DIAGRAM B:
How to make a pile. The bunch is dropped in the middle of the table. If you open your hand quickly, the sticks will scatter in all directions.

A Mikado box from the 1950s. The hook-shaped tool is clearly visible here. The sticks are all shaped like tools or utensils.

A Variation

In this variation on Mikado, several players may use a tool to help them remove the sticks: besides the person who takes the white stick, any player who picks up a blue stick can use it to help remove the rest of the sticks. The blue sticks, then, serve the same function as the Mikado. The original name for the blue sticks is "samurai." So in this variation, it is a strategy to try to take a blue stick even if it is in a difficult position, and the players should weigh the benefits of this move and always consider making it. In the beginning, there are only five of these sticks, and it is worth asking whether there will be any left in the next turn. The other rules stay the same, so in this variation the players must still remove the sticks one by one.

The First Match

To get the most enjoyment out of Mikado, it is important to proceed with calm and concentration. A player who can do so has a decisive advantage. Skill is also important and can be gained only by much practice, which means it is time to play the first match. Two techniques and an example of tallying are provided here so the new player can start his first game well prepared.

Finger Technique

1 Fingertips are the primary tool for picking up sticks. The more fingers you use to hold a stick, the more unstable it will be, and the greater the risk of touching other sticks. To reduce the risk of touching or shifting other wands, it is a good idea to use as few fingers as possible. The sticks are pointed at both ends. If you squeeze one of these points against the tabletop with your fingertips, the other end will rise, like a seesaw. If you then grab the stick by the freed end with the thumb and index finger of your other hand, you can lift it from the pile, but carefully.

This is the surest way to pick up sticks but requires a bit of practice. At first, the stick will rise and tilt to one side. The stick will move directly upward only if you apply pressure to the right spot (Diagram 1).

Mikado Technique

2 The technique of picking up sticks described above will not always work. Say, for instance, a stick is resting on a row of other sticks without touching the table at either end. In a situation like this, it is impossible to apply pressure to one of the tips without moving the other sticks. Thus, the Mikado comes in very handy. First the player must find a space wide enough to insert the Mikado safely. He must place the Mikado under the stick he wants to remove. If he picks it up in a swift, oblique motion, the stick will literally fly up and land to the side or in front of the pile on the table. Then the player can pick it up between thumb and forefinger and add it to his reserve. This technique takes a bit of practice. At first the stick will fly up but will land on top of the pile (Diagram 2).

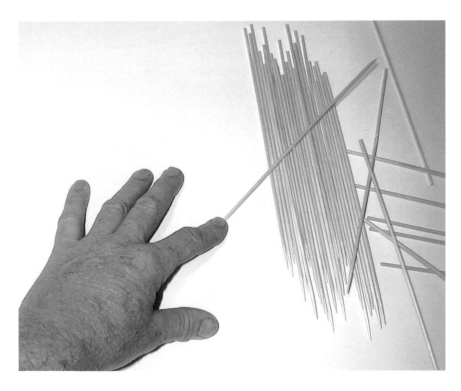

DIAGRAM 1:
Finger technique. If you press one of the tips of the stick against the table with your fingertip, the other end will rise. You can then remove it from the pile by holding it carefully with your other hand.

Player A

$$7 \times 2 = 14$$
$$6 \times 3 = 18$$
$$2 \times 5 = \underline{10}$$
$$42$$

Player B

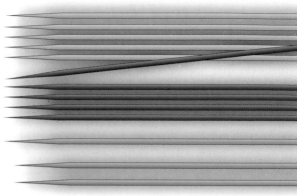

$$5 \times 2 = 10$$
$$5 \times 3 = 15$$
$$1 \times 5 = 5$$
$$2 \times 10 = \underline{20}$$
$$50$$

Player D

$$1 \times 5 = 5$$
$$1 \times 20 = 20$$
$$1 \times 10 = \underline{10}$$
$$35$$

Player C

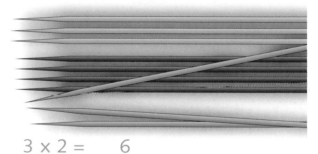

$$3 \times 2 = 6$$
$$4 \times 3 = 12$$
$$1 \times 5 = 5$$
$$2 \times 10 = \underline{20}$$
$$43$$

DIAGRAM 3:
An example of how to tally points. Player B does not have the most sticks but does have the most points, thus winning the round.

Renju
Nature of the Game

◆ ◆ ◆

Renju means "row of precious stones," a lovely name for a fascinating game of positions in which the players try to arrange their pieces in a line. Renju may be considered a game of intelligence, for the players engage in mental combat where a single slip can mean the difference between victory and defeat. Renju was given its name in 1899, as an outgrowth of go-moku, a game whose name recalls that of go. But although its rules resemble those of go, and it is played all over Japan, there is no direct relationship between the two games. The only significant resemblance among them is in the materials required for play, for both go-moku and renju require a go board and a set of go pieces. A game of go-moku between two experienced players will always be decided in favor of the player who makes the first move. For both players to have the same odds of winning, renju unfolds in a more sophisticated manner. It is an appealing game in which both players pursue the same goal, but submit to different rules. Which set of rules each player will follow depends on who opens the game.

There are many similarities between go, go-moku, and renju, especially in the opening stages of play, so it is impossible to tell which of the three games is being played in this illustration.

Players	Requirements
2	go game board
	25 each, white and black go pieces
Average duration	
20 minutes	
Category	
ancient, strategy	

Rules:
Preliminaries

The board is a grid of nineteen vertical and horizontal lines. The game is played on the intersections of the lines, which will be referred to from now on as "spaces." The two players sit across from one another with the board between them. The board is empty at the start of the game. After agreeing what player will use which color, each player knows which set of rules he must follow during the game. It's impossible to anticipate how many pieces each player will need, but twenty-five is a reasonable estimate. Go has a total of 181 black pieces and 180 white, which is plenty. In renju, the player using the black pieces (stones as they are called) always opens the game.

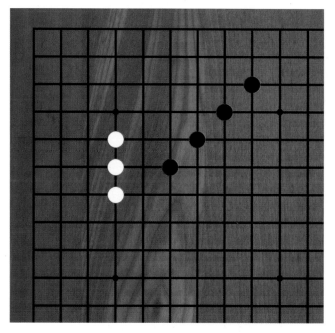

DIAGRAM A:
An open three and open four. Regardless of what move White makes next, Black will win the win the game.

Placing the Pieces

Black starts by placing one of his pieces in any open space on the board. Then it is White's turn to put one down. Players thus take turns putting pieces on the board one at a time. There cannot be more than one piece allotted to each space. Players should think carefully before making a move, because once a piece is on the board it cannot be removed, moved, or eliminated. Both players try to put their pieces on the board so as to form a continuous vertical, horizontal, or diagonal line of five pieces. At the same time, each player tries to keep his opponent from forming such lines.

Open Threes

An open three is a line of three pieces of the same color with an open space at each end. If the owner of an open three adds a piece to either end in his next turn, he'll have four pieces in a row. If this row also has an open space on both sides, it's called an "open four." It is clear that the first player to get an open four will win the game. After all—his opponent can put only one piece on the ends of his own row at a time, and cannot keep him from adding a fifth piece to one side or another of his row in the following turn. This means you must try to avoid open threes if your opponent will be able to extend it to an open four on his next move (Diagram A).

Two Open Threes

As a player becomes more familiar with renju, he will no longer try to attain an open three, but an open two. Experienced players try from the very start to arrange their pieces on the board in such a way that they can quickly form two threes at a time. Often the first four pieces are placed in such a way that they form two open threes as soon as the fifth piece is set down between them. The resulting arrangement is ideal, for one of these two open threes can always be transformed into a four regardless of the opponent's next move. If the player manages to form an open four, he will win. You can see this in Diagram B. If a piece is added to space A, the

white pieces form two open threes at once. As a result of Black's next move, the white pieces will turn the vertical or diagonal rows of three into a four. Black will inevitably lose the game, because both rows are open (Diagram B).

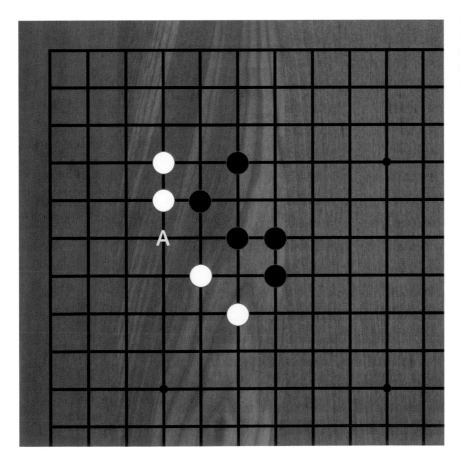

DIAGRAM B:
Two open threes. If a piece is added to space A, the white pieces form two open threes at the same time.

Forbidden for Black

The creation of open threes and fours is an interesting tool of which both players should be mindful. Obviously, it's more interesting to form two open threes or fours at once, but Black is forbidden from doing so because he always opens the game and therefore already has an advantage. As said before, renju offers both players the same chances of winning, so there are certain restrictions in place for Black.

The black pieces can form an open three or four, but never both at once. The restriction is even stronger with respect to double-fours, which can never be formed at the same time, even if they are only "semi-open" (open on only one side or in the middle). The third restriction imposed on Black is that a black row must not consist of more than six pieces (Diagram C).

DIAGRAM C:
Forbidden for Black. Black creates two open threes and one seven-piece row if he adds a piece to space A. Both constructions are prohibited.

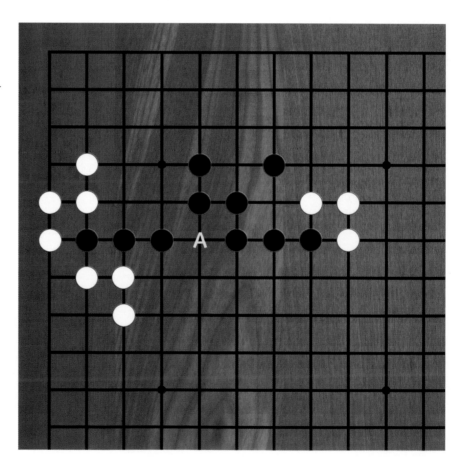

Scene from a Japanese tea-house. In the foreground two men play a combative game of shogi. The people in the center are most likely playing go-moku or renju. The women, meanwhile, prepare the tea and play musical instruments.

Black and White

From the foregoing, it is clear that White can form open threes and a four at once, while Black's mobility is restricted by a series of prohibitions that level the playing field. But Black enjoys a great advantage because he gets to make the first move in the game. To summarize, the rules of the game include the following differences between the two players:

- Black starts the game, so White always plays second
- White can form two or more open threes at a time, but Black cannot. In a single move, Black can form a maximum of one open three or two semi-open threes

- White can form two or more open fours, while Black can form a maximum of one per turn. Black is also forbidden from forming two or more semi-open fours at the same time

- White can make his lines as long as he pleases, provided their length allows for a Black row that is composed of six pieces at most

Finishing

It's possible that Black might overlook one or more of the rules to which he must adhere. He might be so absorbed in the game that he accidentally forgets one of them. If White notices, he immediately informs his opponent. Black then removes the offending piece so he can then make a legal move. If White does not notice the violation until he himself has taken his turn, several things can happen. At the outset, players themselves agree on the sanctions that will apply, which may depend on the violation:

- If the illegal move results in a win for Black, the game can be declared null
- In all other cases, the game goes on
- By mutual accord, players may arrive at a different arrangement, but it's advisable to agree on such an alternative rule ahead of time

The Winner

The winner is the first player to form an unbroken line with five of his own pieces, whether it be horizontal, vertical, or diagonal. Note that the five-piece rule is an absolute condition for winning the game. A row of more than five has no value. Often the players agree beforehand that each game is worth one point and that the first player to reach ten points is the final winner (Diagram D).

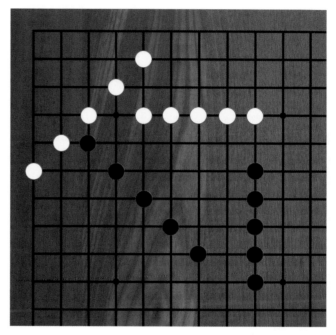

DIAGRAM D:
The various ways the players can form an unbroken line with five of their own pieces; horizontal, vertical, or diagonal.

The First Match

In renju, risks and opportunities can arise quickly, so players should be constantly alert. Because the rules of the game differ for the two players, they will each fight for victory in different ways. The goal is to create a strategy of your own while trying to thwart your opponent's plans. All this is not easy, but it's a fascinating challenge. If a beginner pays attention to the explanations on the following pages, he will be better prepared to play his first match.

Openings

1 Black starts the game by putting one of his pieces on any of the spaces on the board. It's best to add the piece to the center of the board and to try to arrange the pieces so they can be joined in different directions. If he puts a number of pieces compactly in the middle of the board, he can try to form a row of five in different places. This is especially important for Black, whose restrictions put him at a disadvantage. Later on, it will be harder to join several pieces.

At first glance, Korean chess also bears a resemblance to renju.

THE MATCH MOVE BY MOVE

The preceding text and diagrams are based on an actual renju game. The following are all the moves made in that game.

1. **B: D4, W: D3**; 2. **B: E2, W: C2**;
3. **B: B1, W: E4**; 4. **B: F5, W: E5**;
5. **B: F6, W: E6**; 6. **B: E7, W: D6**;
7. **B: C6, W: C7**; 8. **B: B8, W: B6**;
9. **B: C4, W: G3**; 10. **B: F4, W: F3**;
11. **B: E3, W: G2**; 12. **B: H1, W: G4**;
13. **B: G1, W: G6**; 14. **B: F7, B: G5**.

Now it's White's turn. For him, the most important thing is to limit Black's mobility. If he puts his first piece far away from Black, he will run into trouble. He may intend to occupy a space of his own, but at the same time is conceding another space to his opponent. White always moves second, so he should never pass up a chance to get in Black's way. If each player forms a row of five pieces in a different part of the board, Black will always be the first to finish. Therefore, in his first move White should always put his piece in a space adjacent to the first black piece, either on one of the lines of Black's space or diagonally from it. If he puts his first piece in a straight line relative to Black, it is called a *kagetsu* opening. If the first white piece is situated diagonally from Black, the opening is called a *hogetsu*. Black can respond to either of these openings in several ways.

Capturing and Jinxing

A player captures his opponent's piece when he reaches that piece's space with one of his own. The eliminated piece is removed from the board immediately. Although capturing pieces is not mandatory in Jinx, a player can be forced to eliminate a threat. Players often make a move that will allow them to capture their opponent's piece in the next move. When a player makes this kind of move, he can call "jinx"; he doesn't have to, but if he does, he must do so immediately after making his move. He thus forces his opponent to move the threatened piece. Sometimes more than one piece is threatened after a player calls jinx. If so, his opponent may decide for himself which of the threatened pieces he wants to move, and the "jinxer" cannot call jinx again until his turn

is over. To capture a piece, the player must move one or two spaces, depending on the color of the lines. A player who is obliged to move a jinxed piece can move it to any space as long as he follows the rules for moving pieces. The threatened piece is free to capture the opponent's whenever possible, including the piece that is threatening it (Diagram C).

DIAGRAM C:
Capturing pieces. When a piece moves into a space where an opponent's piece already sits, the latter is eliminated and removed from the board.

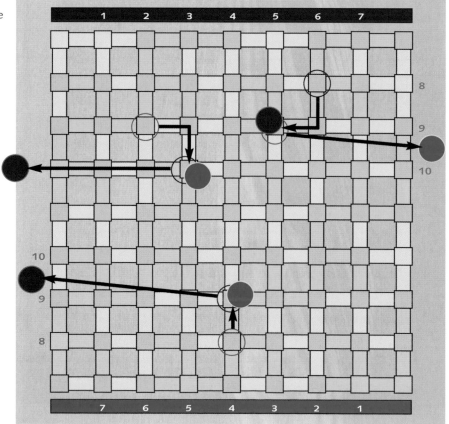

Finishing

The players do not have to jinx one another, but an important reason for doing so is that it limits the opponent's mobility by forcing him to move the threatened piece. This means the jinxer has one turn in which he can calmly develop his plans. When one player has only one piece left and the other has two, they can no longer call jinx.

The Winner

The winner is the player who captures all his opponent's pieces. A game of Jinx can end in a draw. This happens, for instance, when both players still have one piece but feel they can no longer capture one another. Players then agree to end the game.

Jinx for Four

When four people play a game of Jinx, they form two teams so there are two players on each side of the board. Usually when we think of a team we think of cooperation between the two players, but this rarely happens in Jinx. In fact, the members of a team may not agree beforehand how they will

move. When there are more than two people playing, the stars on the game pieces play a very important role. A piece with the star faceup is known as a "star piece." A piece with the star facedown is called a "neutral piece."

In Jinx for four, there are six red pieces and six green. Each player receives three of a single color. In teams, one player puts his starred pieces in spaces 8, 9, and 10. His teammate puts his in spaces 1, 2, and 3. Players draw to see which team will start the game. Then, play proceeds in the following order:

- first team, player with neutral pieces
- second team, player with neutral pieces
- first team, player with starred pieces
- second team, player with starred pieces

A player can jinx only the player whose turn immediately follows his; conversely, a player can be jinxed only by the player whose turn immediately

---

STRATEGY

It is possible that a player's piece threatens his opponent's piece that he does not want to capture. In such a case, it is a good strategy always to call jinx, so that the opponent must eliminate the threat and create an open space.

DIAGRAM D:
The opening position in Jinx for four.

The Winner

The winner is the last remaining player to hold tokens besides the banker (who isn't really a player), once all the others have been eliminated. The other players are classified according to the moment when they had to withdraw from the game; the loser is the first player to withdraw. Players can also agree to compete over ten games. Then everyone will have played nine games, because each player must play the banker for one game. After each game, players write down the name of the winner and the number of tokens they had at the end of the game. After ten games, the totals are added up, and the player with the greatest number of tokens is the final winner.

DIAGRAM D:
A loser. One of the players has only two tokens left. He bets both of them on the sun. The sun does not appear on any of the dice, so the player must leave the game.

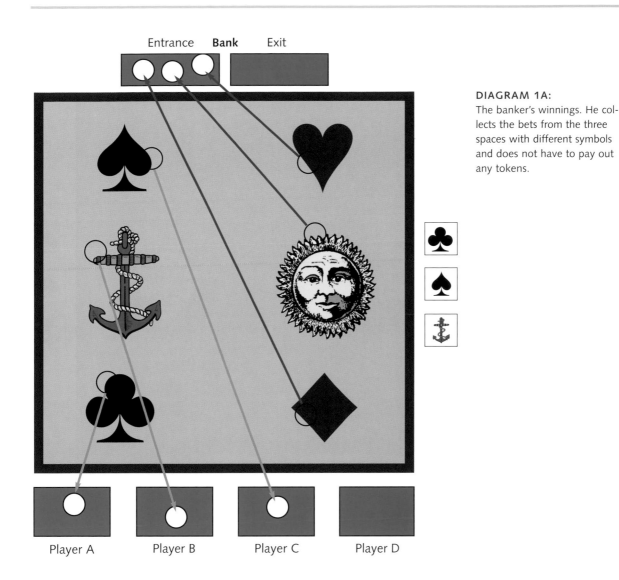

Entrance **Bank** Exit

DIAGRAM 1A:
The banker's winnings. He collects the bets from the three spaces with different symbols and does not have to pay out any tokens.

Player A   Player B   Player C   Player D

The First Match

In Sun and Anchor, chance or luck decides in large measure who wins or loses. What combinations does the banker roll, and to what degree do they match the symbols on which the players bet their tokens? The rules aren't complicated, there isn't a single optimal betting strategy, and no special skills are required on the part of the players. For these reasons, Sun and Anchor is an easy-to-learn social game that children and adults alike can enjoy. The following pages provide a few interesting additional facts and ideas that can be useful when playing the game for the first time.

An Example of Play

In Diagram 2, Player D still has two tokens when his turn comes to play the banker. The other players wager, and then D rolls the dice. He rolls two hearts and an anchor. Player B wagered two tokens on the heart. Therefore, the banker must pay him four tokens from his own reserve, and B receives six tokens altogether, including the ones he wagered himself. D no longer has four tokens in his reserve, but as luck would have it, wins the tokens he needs in this round anyway—by collecting the wagers on the spade, the club, the diamond, and the sun. Thanks to this, the bank can pay out exactly the amount

owed to B without touching his own reserve. He breaks even in his round as banker. The tokens on the anchor are returned to A, because this symbol appeared on one of the dice (Diagram 2).

> **TIP**
>
> It is a good idea to play with a limited number of tokens for each player. When many tokens are used, it simply means the players will wager more. In the end, the game remains the same and is just as exciting when played with fewer tokens.

DIAGRAM 2:
A money exchange. D is the banker. He collects four tokens, which he immediately has to pay out to B. D begins and ends this round with two tokens.

Entrance **Bank (Player D)** Exit

Player A   Player B   Player C   Player D

Hex
Nature of the Game

◆ ◆ ◆

The object of the board game Hex is clear and uncomplicated: Join the two opposite sides of the board with a single, unbroken line of game pieces. If you accept
the challenge, you will soon conclude that the goal is quicker and easier to for-
mulate than it is to attain. Your opponent's pieces constantly block your way, so
you have to keep changing direction and renew your search for the shortest
route. At the same time, you must always keep an eye on your opponent's intentions and try to keep him from reaching his goal. Children approach this game
differently than adults but what makes this game fun is that the difference in
approach is completely unimportant; Hex is always a challenge if the two players
have a similar skill level. Hex originated in Denmark, where it was known as
Polygon, invented in 1942 by Piet Hein, and was also created independently by
John Nash at Princeton University.

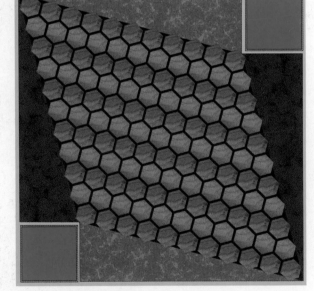

Parker Brothers marketed a commercial version that is no longer
produced as Hex, and the name
stuck. It is played on a board that
looks like a honeycomb.

DIAGRAM A:
A Hex game board. Two of its borders are blue,
the others are red. Each player has sixty-one
game pieces and must agree on who starts (usually by a coin toss or roll of dice).

Players	Requirements
2	special game board
Average duration	61 each, white and black go pieces
20 minutes	
Category	
strategy; connection	

Rules:
Preliminaries

The board consists of a rhombus made up of eleven-by-eleven rows of hexagonal cells. Two of the facing borders are blue, the other two are red. The blue margins are used by the player with blue chips, and the red margins are for the player using white. Players choose their colors and sit at the table. Go pieces can be used to play the game. Players distribute the pieces and set the board down between them, black on the blue side, white on the red. This means that the players do not exactly face one another. The board is empty at the start of the game. The most pieces a player can have at any time is 61, so there are a total of 122 pieces between the two colors. This also means that there is one more piece than is needed to fill the board (which has only 121 cells). In practice, each player will need far fewer than 121 pieces. Hex has no established rules that determine which player begins the game, so the players must agree beforehand who will make the first move. It is usually decided by a coin toss or a roll of the dice (Diagram A).

TIP

It's a fun challenge to set a personal record and then beat it. To this end, you count the number of pieces in the winning row and try to win the next match with a row made up of fewer pieces.

DIAGRAM B:
Arranging the pieces. The pieces are placed on empty cells, which the players may choose freely. Most cells are surrounded by six other cells. The cells along the sides are flanked only by four.

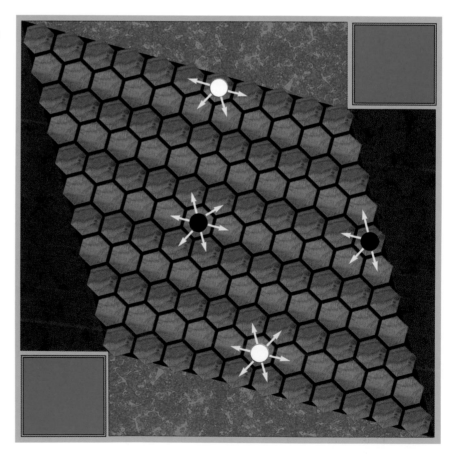

Positioning the Pieces

The first player puts one of his pieces on the board. He can place it anywhere he likes, as long as the cell is empty. One should consider each move carefully before making it, because once a piece is on the board and the player's hand is no longer touching it, the piece cannot be removed. There is no capturing in Hex, so the pieces cannot be eliminated that way. After the first player puts a piece on the board, it is his opponent's turn, and he also puts one of his pieces in any empty cell he likes. Players continue in this fashion, taking turns putting pieces on the board one at a time. Since the cells are hexagonal, they are each surrounded by six other cells, except for the cells on the outer rows of the board, which have only four cells around them (Diagram B).

STRATEGY

Whenever possible, it's a good idea to play on cells that are surrounded by empty cells. Players should avoid putting a piece in one of the corners, because these have only two or three cells around them and a piece can easily end up blocked in.

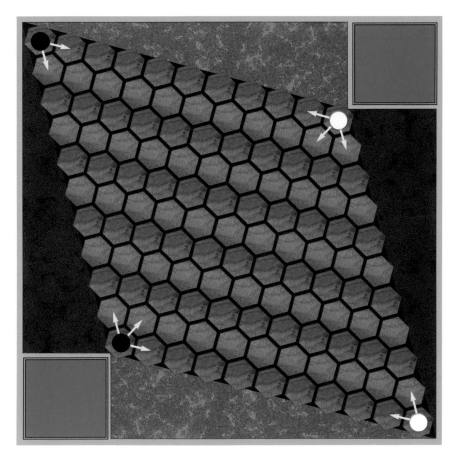

DIAGRAM C:
The corner cells. Two of the four corners have only two contiguous cells, while the other two are flanked by three other cells. The black piece in the lower left-hand corner belongs to the blue side; the white piece on the right-hand side is Red's.

Women absorbed in a game. English drawing, 1810.

The Corner Cells

The four corner cells have a special position, because they each neighbor both a blue side and a red side, and because they are flanked by only two or three cells. It is relatively easy, then, to block a piece in a corner cell with only two adjacent cells. The corner cells are not reserved for either player; like the other cells, they can be used by anyone. When a player puts one of his pieces in the corner, he considers the piece to make up border of his own side, so an uninterrupted line from one end to another may include a corner cell at the beginning or the end (Diagram C).

A Good Row

When putting the pieces down on the board, players should try to form a line that joins two same-colored sides on the board. Players have total freedom with regard to how they accomplish this goal. They needn't always put a piece on a cell adjacent to the one before it, and can scatter the pieces here and there throughout the board. In the end, the line must consist only of the player's own pieces. If his opponent is able to interrupt the line with one of his pieces, the row is rendered worthless. If this happens, the owner of the line should start building a new one or try to continue an existing line, going around his opponent. The line, therefore, need not be straight. It doesn't matter if it curves, and it makes no difference how many pieces it takes to complete it. But the line must always meet two conditions:

- It must be unbroken
- It must be made up entirely of one player's pieces (Diagram D)

The Winner

The winner is the player who manages to join his two sides of the board with a single unbroken line of his own pieces. Since the pieces divide the board in two, it is absolutely impossible for both players to join their respective sides of the board—in other words, in Hex there can be only one winner.

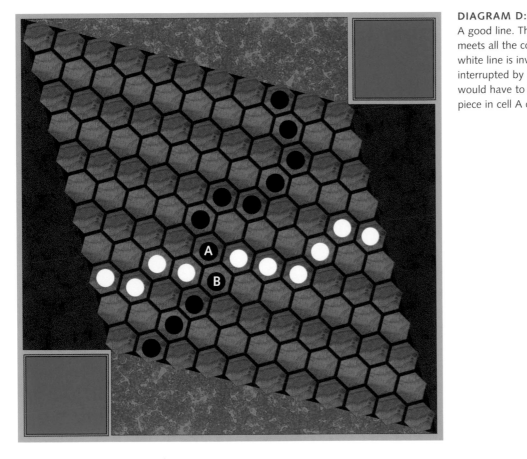

DIAGRAM D:
A good line. The black line meets all the conditions. The white line is invalid because it is interrupted by a black piece. It would have to have a white piece in cell A or B.

The First Match

The saying "practice makes perfect" applies to the game of Hex. With every game, players increase their knowledge of certain mechanisms and possible strategies. They also pick up more ideas about how to position their pieces so that their objective is less transparent to the opponent. The following pages describe some interesting game situations.

The First Moves

1 White opened the game, adding one of his pieces. Each player has now added four pieces. One can begin to see a difference in the two players' playing style. Until now, White has added pieces only to contiguous squares, whereas the black pieces are scattered throughout the board. The white pieces are all in the middle of the board. Black has put one piece on each blue end of the board. He has done this on purpose, because the players have fewer chances of eluding an opponent on the ends of the board than in the middle. White would like to reach his goal with the straightest line possible, while Black's arrangement reflects a more flexible attitude. It's easy to figure out which cells White intends to fill. Black assumes that in White's next move, he will try to add a piece to D5 to lengthen the line he already started. He decides to halt this process, and puts one of his own pieces in D5 in his fourth turn (D1).

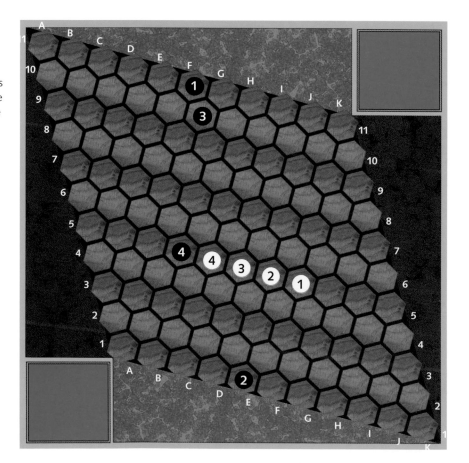

DIAGRAM 1:
The first moves. After four turns, Black has marked the starting and end points of his line, and has arranged his pieces more flexibly than White. White has formed a straight line in the middle of the board.

The Next Several Plays

2 It is White's turn, so he puts down his fifth piece (Diagram 2 shows where). Since D5 is taken by a black piece, he has to make a detour and chooses D4. Black believes his next move will be to add a piece on C4. This makes sense, because in this cell, White would be only two cells away from the red border. To stop this, in his next move Black puts one of his pieces in that cell. White must take another detour thanks to Black's move. Black can now continue to block his opponent to keep him from reaching the red border. Black is convinced that he has started on a relatively straight path to the blue border, and at the same time is forcing White to follow a fairly roundabout course. He's right, because with

each move, White has to keep shifting farther away, toward the blue side. But once he reaches the corner cell, Black realizes he has a problem: after White's seventh move, he cannot keep him from reaching the red border. White has only one piece to go. And he can choose between the corner A1 or A2. Of

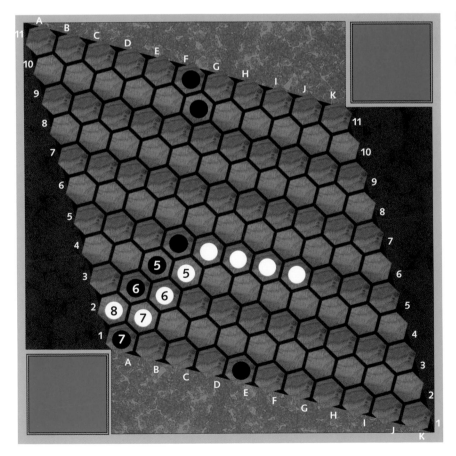

DIAGRAM 2:
The next several moves. Black cannot stop White from reaching one of the two red borders. He minimizes the damage by putting his seventh piece on A1.

course, Black will put a piece in one of those two cells, but White can use the other cell anyhow. It's worth asking which of these two cells is the best choice for Black to add his seventh piece. If he chooses the corner, he will reach the blue border, but White will also reach the red by taking A2 in his next move. Then White will have an unbroken line that touches one of the two red sides. Meanwhile, Black's line is discontinuous. If Black puts his piece on A2, the eighth white piece will undoubtedly end up in the corner cell, cutting off Black's path to the blue border. He will have no way of reaching blue, even with a discontinuous line. In that case, he will have to run a very long course and try again on the other side. It is clear that Black's situation is far from ideal, but the best move he can make is to take the corner cell. Predictably, White immediately adds a piece to A2. Now Black has no other choice but to form a line around the four white pieces in the middle of the board from E5 to H5 (Diagram 2).

The Final Moves

3 It is Black's turn to put his final piece on the board. He realizes that White is only three cells away from victory. If he manages to extend his line across the center of the board by putting his three pieces in I5, J5, and K5, he will link the two red sides with an unbroken line of white pieces. Black tries to stop him by adding a piece to I5. White responds by putting one in I6, so he moves forward

in spite of Black's efforts, for I6 is only two cells away from the red border. Black severs one of these routes, adding a piece to J6. History repeats itself, for when White was trying to reach the other red border, Black did nothing but try to stop him, and did little to form a winning line for himself. Black responds to each of White's moves with a defensive move of his own. Although Black realizes he runs the risk of losing, he's not sure how to tip the balance in his favor. White is just one cell away from victory. For his final, decisive move, he can choose either K7 or K8. This means Black can no longer stop him from winning. He puts a piece on K7, after which White brings the game to a close by putting his final piece on K8 (Diagram 3).

A SAMPLE MATCH

It's a good exercise to play the Hex match described in these pages from start to finish, following the numbers in the diagrams.

1. **W: H5, B: F11**; 2. **W: G5, B: E1**;

3. **W: F5, B: F10**; 4. **W: E5, B: D5**;

5. **W: D4, B: C4**; 6. **W: C3, B: B3**;

7. **W: B2, B: A1**; 8. **W: A2, B: I5**;

9. **W: I6, B: J6**; 10. **W: J7, B: K7**;

11. **W: K8**.

Evaluation

4 The match just described was started and won by White. Though it may seem as though the player who makes the first move has an advantage, it isn't always so. White kept his pieces together from the start. He gave the impression that, because the arrangement of his pieces was inflexible, Black would have an advantage. In the end it appears that Black wasted precious time scattering his pieces throughout the board. Each time it was his turn, he added a piece right next to the cell his opponent had just occupied. His entire game was defensive. It probably would have made more sense not to put his seventh piece on A1. After all, it was inevitable that White should reach the red border on the left-hand side of the board. He could have put his move to better use had he blocked the white line on the right-hand side by putting a piece on I5. Then, in his

next turn he could have added one to I6, which would have cut off White's path to the red border for good, and would have trapped him on a blue side. The situation would be completely different if Black put his eighth piece on H4 instead of I6. The white line would then be blocked on both sides, though Black could not stop White from completing his line from above, using cells I6, J7, and K6 or K7. It's a good exercise to repeat these moves on an actual board (Diagram 4).

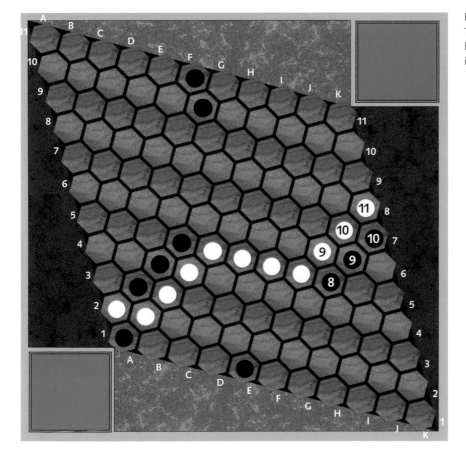

DIAGRAM 3:
The endgame. Black is unable to block his opponent. White wins in eleven moves.

Rules:
Preliminaries

On each side of the square game board are two rows with nine boxes each. The boxes are numbered 1 through 9. The upper line is green; the lower one, white. Around the center of the board, on the green row, are four scorekeeping spots for each player. The space in the center of the board is blank—this is where the dice are rolled. Each player sits in front of a double row on one of the four sides of the boards. They each receive four game pieces of the same color, for scorekeeping purposes. They leave them in the corner to the right of their rows. At the start, each player makes his own game and everyone

takes a turn, so deciding who goes first is not particularly important. Still, before the game begins, players usually roll one of the dice, and the high roller generally makes the first move (the player with the lowest roll usually goes last). If two players roll the same number, they roll again until the final playing order is decided.

The first player takes nine playing pieces and places them in the boxes of his white row. He will try to move as many of these pieces as possible into the corresponding green boxes. One of the players assumes the role of secretary, and at the end of each player's turn, he writes down the total points has earned (Diagram A).

DIAGRAM A:
A Shut the Box game board with all the required accessories. It is Player A's turn, and he has already put his black playing pieces in the white boxes.

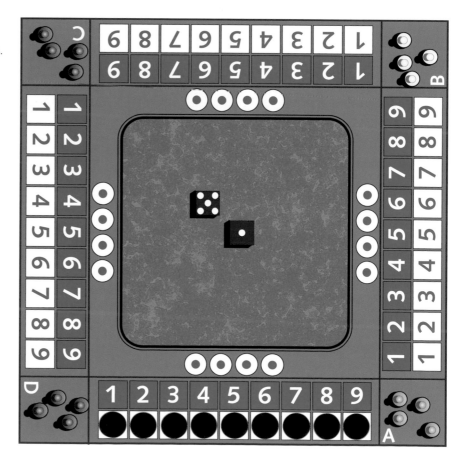

The First Roll

In this game of Shut the Box, the player can roll the dice by hand or using a dice cup. The first player rolls both dice and then adds up his points. The total rolled determines the possible combinations of numbers, and he examines which box or boxes he can cover with them, weighing the pros and cons of each possibility and settling on one. He moves one or two pieces from the white boxes into the corresponding green boxes. The sum of the numbers in the boxes should match the total points rolled. If, for instance, he rolls a two and a six, he can move a piece from white box number 8 to green box number 8. But he can also opt to move his pieces within the white row:

- 7 and 1
- 6 and 2
- 5 and 3

This example shows that the player has four possibilities. If he occupies the green boxes numbered 1, 3, and 4, these too will add up to eight points. But a player may not fill more than two boxes per roll. This also means that he cannot move any pieces to green box 4. To add up to eight, he would have to put two pieces in the same box, which is against the rules—each box can be occupied by only one piece at a time; nor may he add only the one piece, for players are required to use all the points they roll in that move (Diagram B).

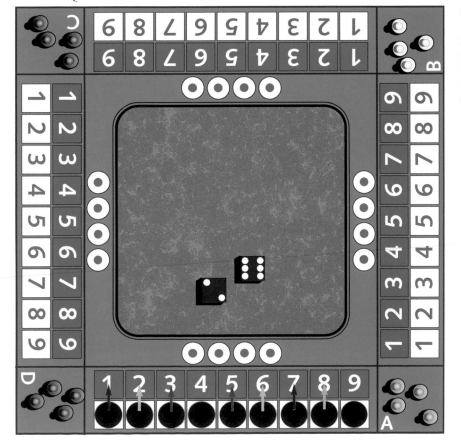

DIAGRAM B:
Possible combinations when a player rolls a two and a six. This player can move only one piece into box 8, or two pieces into boxes 7 and 1, 6 and 2, or 5 and 3.

Endgame

3 The first player rolls a five and a one on the fifth try. This is lucky, because he can use those six points. He has only one option, since a piece is already in box 6 and combinations of other boxes are already taken: he must move into 5 and 1.

The game becomes more exciting as the number of boxes grows smaller. On his sixth roll he gets a four and a two, which also add up to six. In an earlier roll, he had only one option for using this number, but now has none. He has been unable to fill boxes 8 and 9, so the secretary jots down his total as 17 points (Diagram 3).

Conclusion

4 The first player has not had a good turn, ending up with a rather high score. The reason is that he was unable to fill the highest numbered boxes. He can chalk this one up to bad luck: he rolled no higher than a six in his first six rolls, and so was also unable to choose between one or two dice.

Such situations present an obvious lesson: you should always try to fill a single box first, and start moving two pieces at a time only when you absolutely have to. The importance of this principle is underscored if you repeat the moves made by the player in this example but ignore this piece of advice. The first roll yielded a six and a one. Suppose he had moved two pieces into boxes 6 and 1. With his second roll, three and three, he could also have filled two boxes (4 and 2). In his third roll, two and one, the only choice was to fill box 3. And with this, the game would be over for him because his final roll yielded six points (a four and a two). He would have been unable to use these numbers in any way, so his final points would have added up to 29—a much higher number than scored here (Diagram 4).

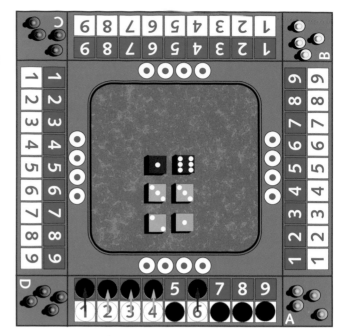

DIAGRAM 4:
In conclusion, you should fill two spaces at a time only if it is absolutely impossible to fill just one. Had the player filled two boxes from the first round onward, he would have ended up with 29 points.

TIP

For variety's sake, players sometimes agree that the winner will be the player with the fewest open green boxes. This scorekeeping system often yields a tie between two or more players, so a winner can be determined with the tied players having an extra turn, like an elimination round.

Chinese Checkers
History of the Game

◆ ◆ ◆

The name of this game implies that it is a very old, Chinese version of checkers. Not so. Everything seems to indicate that this game, like Halma, originated in nineteenth-century England or America. An English game "Hoppity" is thought to be the inspiration for Halma. A Halma board was published by E.I. Horsman, New York, copyrighted 1885, and the game manufacturer Ravensburg published Stern-Halma in 1892 that bore many similarities to it with the board shaped like a star. The star-shaped board and its many colors attracted much attention. The widespread popularity of Halma in Britain can be gleaned from a quotation from the famous Irish playwright George Bernard Shaw, who in 1898 wrote: "The Englishman stays at home, with his family, in his chambers; there they sit in silence with a book, a sheet of paper, or a game of Halma."

An English family enjoying their board games. Eighteenth-century copper etching.

jump must be in a straight line. A piece does not have to jump over another simply because it can, and the player has the freedom to stop after one or more jumps, even if he is able to keep jumping.

At each turn, players choose one of the two possible moves. A jump isn't necessarily preferable to a simple move. Players can always decide whether to move a piece or use it to jump over another. But they may not do both in the same turn. This means it's against the rules to first move a piece and then use it to jump over another (Diagrams C and D).

DIAGRAM C:
Possible moves. In each turn, players can move a piece in any direction into an adjacent space. In theory, they can choose to move into any of two, four, five, or six spaces.

The Winner

The winner is the first player to move all one's pieces into the opposite garden. If he plays with ten pieces, he must place all of them in the spaces farthest from the center, what would have been their starting positions in that corner of the board. When more than two people are playing, the others can keep playing to decide who will end up in second, third, fourth, fifth, and sixth place. When four people are playing, they usually form two teams. The members of a team may occupy either adjacent or opposite corners of the board. If they choose the latter, they have more opportunities to help each other move their pieces.

But even when playing in teams, each player moves only his own pieces. A match between two teams certainly cannot be won by an individual player. The match is decided when both members of a team have put all their pieces in their opposite gardens.

CURIOUS FACT

When players of the same skill level face off in Chinese Checkers, it often becomes a very close race, so making the first move becomes important.

DIAGRAM D:

Moving the pieces: jumping. You can jump over your own pieces or over your opponent's, as long as the space you are jumping into is empty and forms a straight line with the other two spaces. Players can jump several times in a single turn.

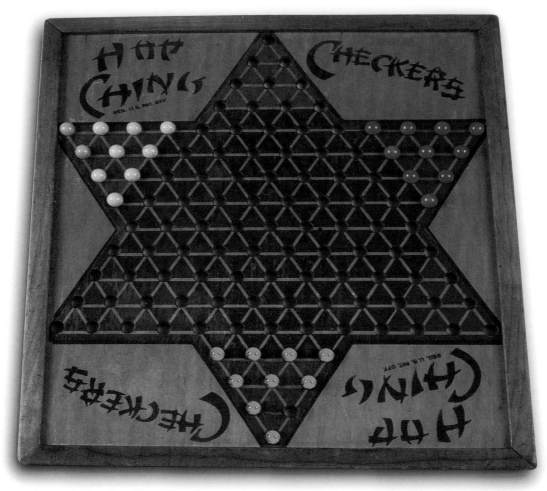

A Chinese Checkers board from the early 1900s, United States.

The First Match

Your first game of Chinese Checkers ceases to be daunting once you know the rules. Playing often is the only way to get a sense of the game's complexity and permutations. Chinese Checkers is never boring, if only because you can play it on many different levels. It also offers many different possibilities because it can be played by several people. For example, when playing one-on-one, all the pieces must be moved to the opposite player's garden. It's very likely that one of the players will leave one of his pieces in the garden for a long while. The rules of the game allow this tactic. As a result, the other player cannot fully occupy that garden. When three people are playing, the problem does not arise, because the target garden is empty from the start. Regardless of the number of players, the object of Chinese Checkers is always the same. Every player can have his own philosophy and strategy, but there are two essential ones, explained below in several game situations.

A Ladder

1 Players try to take the shortest path to the goal. Often this means using a "ladder," or series of pieces arranged so that one or more pieces can move quickly through the board by jumping over them.

Diagram 1A shows a ladder. Red can advance six spaces in a single turn with his top piece by making three jumps. The piece in the lowest space can also advance six spaces in one turn by jumping over the same three pieces. Without the ladder, making the same move with thcsc two pieces would have taken twelve turns.

Players can use an opponent's ladder, as well. This becomes interesting when two players have to move their pieces into their opponents' gardens. Diagram 1B illustrates this situation. When one of the players forms a ladder, the other is delighted to use it. A ladder is an ideal resource, but has its drawbacks. One or more pieces must be placed in its lower extreme, and a space must be reserved at the end of the ladder for the pieces to land. This takes valuable time, and time is of an essence in Chinese Checkers. Every player reaches the final goal sooner or later, but only one can be first. Finally, the possible advantage of a ladder can be annulled because the opposite player can likewise use it or block it (Diagram 1).

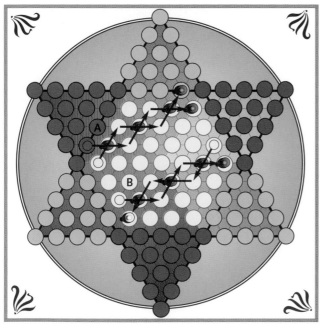

DIAGRAM 1:

1A: The ladder, made up of three pieces, allows others to move several spaces at once.

1B: The other player can also avail himself of the ladder.

A Closed Formation

2 The other strategy often used to move pieces quickly across the board consists of maintaining a closed formation. Closed formations can be moved quickly and effectively. An added advantage is that the other players cannot interfere with your game as much. As a united group, pieces of a single color help one another as they move toward the final goal, jumping over one another whenever possible. In order to advance as a block, players make an effort to jump with the piece furthest to the back. This possibility is shown in Diagram 2, in which the spaces are marked by letters and numbers. The letters refer to the intersection where a piece lies, and the numbers mark the corresponding row. The four pieces in the yellow corner are in spaces fg2, gh2, fh3, and gi3. The yellow player can then move them, one by one, to the goal, with no trouble. After a few turns, he will undoubtedly encounter enemy pieces, which he can jump over, but this would take up a lot of time. It is much more effective to jump over one's own pieces whenever possible. Thus, Yellow makes one jump per turn: gh2–eh4, gi3–eg3, and fg2–dg4. Naturally, he will also try multiple jumps. This way, he keeps his pieces together and advances quickly toward the finish (Diagram 2).

STRATEGY

You should never move your piece too quickly. It is better to first figure out if there's anywhere you can jump, and to jump rather than making a simple move; multiple jumps are more advantageous than single jumps, as long as they move the piece in the right direction.

Evaluation

Time and speed are important factors in Chinese Checkers. Pieces move more quickly across the board by jumping than by making a stepwise move, so it's always wise to jump, jump, jump. A well-considered strategy for facilitating these moves will use both ladders and closed formations. A good strategy also means compromising between deploying your pieces quickly and blocking your opponent's moves.

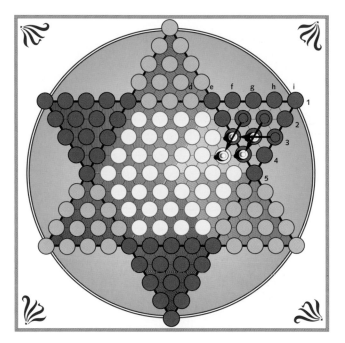

DIAGRAM 2:
A closed formation. The groups of pieces can move quickly and effectively across the board by jumping.

Saxon Hnefatafl
History of the Game

◆ ◆ ◆

A Saxon Hnefatafl game board was found in a Roman tomb from the Iron Age in Wimose, Funen, Denmark's largest island. There are eighteen boxes on one side. If the board was symmetrical, it must have consisted of at least eighteen by eighteen boxes measuring about 1 by 1 inch (2.5 by 2.5 cm). The Iron Age ended in approximately 400 C.E. in northern Europe, which tells us that Saxon Hnefatafl was played in Scandinavia well before this time. The game was very popular among the Normans or Vikings. The Vikings were feared, as evidenced by the prayers that monks repeated constantly in the monasteries: "O Lord, save us from the fury of the Normans." Villagers on the coast of the North Sea were also known to make such prayers. They lived in fear of the Vikings—those audacious warriors who traversed the seas in search of gold, treasure, and new lands. Around 800 C.E., the Vikings fortified various merchant cities, from whence they embarked on voyages to faraway lands. On these voyages they played Saxon Hnefatafl. In 870, the Vikings arrived in Iceland; in 985, they landed in Greenland; and finally, in 1001 they set foot on Terranova, the North American continent. They left behind settlements in each of these lands.

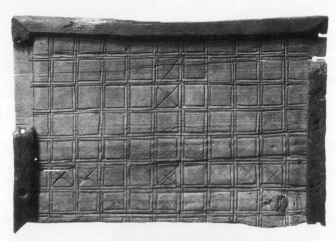

Fragment of a Saxon Hnefatafl board, circa 1100. The board was carved in wood and ivory, and the opposite side could be used to play tric-trac (an old form of backgammon played with pegs).

The challenge and variety of Planks is even greater if you play with more people. Next will be discussed in more detail the differences that arise in a game among three or four players (Diagram E).

Distribution Among Three Players

When three people play a game of Planks, they use three sets of pieces: sets A, B, and C. One player takes a piece from each of these sets. He places them upside down on the table and mixes them up. Then each player picks three. The player holding a piece with the letter A opens the game. The player with the letter B sits to the left of the first player, so it will be his turn next. Player C sits to the right of Player A. When playing several games, each player will use the same pieces in each round. It suffices for the players to agree that Player B will open the next

STRATEGY

It is wise to bring the pieces into play in a certain order. For example, try not to use the two red pieces in your first two turns. More than likely, you will soon need a red piece to counter the threat from your opponent.

round and C will open the third. The strips are placed facedown on the table and mixed up. They are then divided equally among the players, so that each of them gets four. Each player places his strips, with the colors faceup, in front of him on the table. The game can begin after the players agree on how many rounds they will play.

DIAGRAM E:
More players and more blocking. Player A can form a winning line if he puts a white piece on strips 2 or 3. Players B and C can stop him by each putting a piece on those squares.

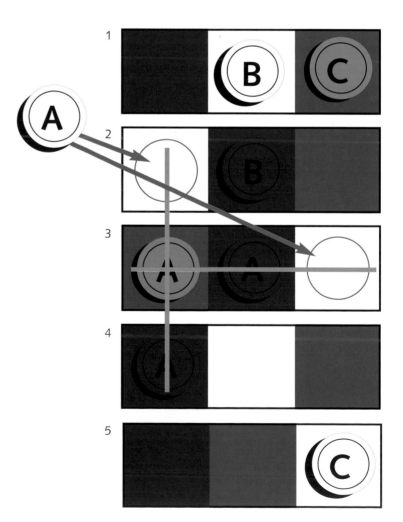

Penalty Points in a Three-Player Game

Three-player Planks produces an interesting phenomenon typical of games of strategy, in which each player wages battle alone against the others. A situation can arise in which one of the players threatens to reach the final goal, and it is necessary for the others to stop him. Often his two opponents are in a position to do so, but neither of them is particularly motivated. One maneuver for blocking a player who is about to win actually frustrates the progress of the other players, because generally, a player cannot both stop an opponent from winning and continue to work at forming a three-piece line at the same time. Suppose Player A must be stopped. Player B will inevitably be tempted to follow his own path and leave this problem to Player C. Player C has no choice but to block Player A, because he cannot leave this task to the other player. After all, once his move is over, it will be Player A's turn. The U.S. games expert Sid Sackson acknowledged this phenomenon

and adapted the original rules of Planks to prevent this situation from occurring. In order to motivate Player B to stop Player A, he established that the player to the left of the winner gets two penalty points, while the third player gets only one. The winner gets no points either way. Sackson's additional rule ensures a fair distribution of penalty points among the players. When one player threatens to win, the player whose turn it is next can decide to do nothing to stop him. But if that player makes good on his threat to win, the player to his left will be penalized two points.

Here's an example:

Player A can form a winning line in his third turn by putting one of his pieces in strip 3. Player B

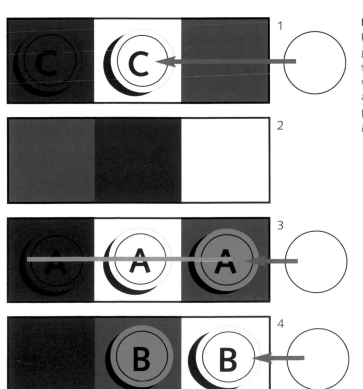

DIAGRAM F:
Penalty points in a three-player game. Players B and C do not stop Player A from forming a winning line in his third turn. As a result, Player B is assessed two penalty points, while Player C gets only one.

Finishing

As mentioned, the object of Hasami shogi is to form an uninterrupted line of five pieces. Players can construct this line either vertically, horizontally, or diagonally. But the spaces in rows 1, 2, 8, and 9 are off-limits. This means a winning line cannot include any pieces on the lines that were already filled at the start of the game. A Hasami shogi match ends in a draw when one of the two players has only four pieces left—after all, it is now impossible for that player to form a winning line. This makes it clear that a player who captures fourteen of his opponent's pieces is not rewarded with victory. Hasami shogi is first and foremost a game of position, and not a war game (Diagram D).

TIP

It is good strategy first off to prepare a winning line and then finish it in five consecutive turns. This way it will be harder for your opponent to know what you are plotting.

DIAGRAM C:
Capturing pieces. Pieces are captured by surrounding them. A piece that is voluntarily placed between two enemy pieces has not yet been captured, although it is in danger.

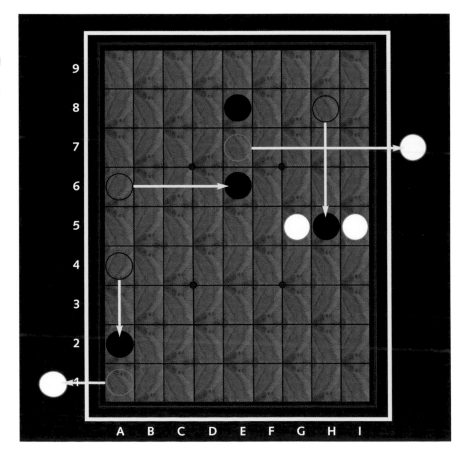

The Winner

The winner is the first player to form a winning line of five pieces. Sometimes players agree to a certain number of rounds, and only when these are over do they determine the winner. If so, the loser of a round continues playing by himself, and the players count how many moves it takes him to form a winning line of five pieces. The number of turns equals the number of penalty points the loser receives. The winner is the player with the fewest points at the end of the agreed-upon number of rounds.

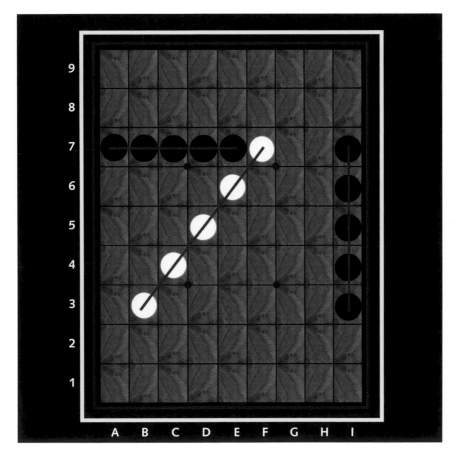

DIAGRAM D:
Some winning lines. A winning line consists of five of a player's pieces, none of which may be in rows 1, 2, 8, or 9. The line can be vertical, horizontal, or diagonal.

The First Match

Any Hasami shogi player would do well to decide on a strategy before starting a match. Hasami shogi is strategic in nature; thus, it's a good idea to be well prepared at the start. When deciding on the best way to play, it is sensible to choose one of the spaces on which you want to form a winning line. Also, in the course of the game, you have to concentrate on your opponent and his moves at every moment. A player who neglects this will almost certainly be met with sudden jeopardy. The following pages describe a few interesting play situations culled from a match between two beginners.

Initial Reflections

Black and White have distributed the pieces between themselves and placed them on the board. Each player decides, on his own, that he will capture his opponent's pieces only when it serves some (other) purpose. Players each want to concentrate on forming a winning line and on keeping the other from doing the same. White chooses spaces A3 to A7, because pieces are less vulnerable in the spaces on the sides of the board: after all, the opponent cannot surround a piece on these spaces or capture them horizontally.

Black decides to form a diagonal line in spaces C3, D4, E5, F6, and G7. He thinks a diagonal line will be less perceptible than any other, and therefore his opponent will not discover his plan immediately. As a general rule, Hasami shogi players should be ever aware of the possibilities of forming a winning

line and of the pros and cons of their various options. None of the spaces in rows 1, 2, 8, and 9 can be part of a winning line. Thus, in a vertical direction are just enough spaces to form a winning line, and no other way to evade the opponent if he chooses to take one of them. If one is taken, no choice is left but to capture or form a line someplace else. This is not so for the horizontal lines, because in principle, all nine spaces can be used, and there is ample room to evade the opponent. The same thing happens with diagonal lines as with vertical lines. The player can use exactly five spaces. A diagonal line can begin in any five of the nine spaces in row 3 or 7.

Watercolor after an 1845 etching showing a professional player accompanied by a porter, who carries the game board on the way to the next match. This could be a go player, but since the board has only nine-by-nine spaces, it could very well be a Hasami shogi board.

CURIOUS FACT

The method of capturing in Hasami shogi is called technically called *custodian capture* (literally, house arrest). Here the word *custodian* means "watchman" and *capture* signifies arrest.

First Moves

1 White begins. He tries to reach his goal, and Black does the same. The difference is that White cannot place all his pieces in the spaces where he wants them to be in the end. Instead, he must keep his plans hidden as long as possible. Black, however, can put his pieces where he wants them to be at the end of the game. After each player takes three turns, White can infer from the position of Black's pieces that his opponent wants to form a diagonal line. There is even a row of five black pieces on the board, but it does not meet the requirements for a winning line. The reason Black chose a diagonal line early in the game seems no longer valid. It is more difficult, however, to infer anything from the arrangement of White's pieces.

At this stage, it's impossible to say which player has an advantage. Players have not yet blocked one another, have not captured any pieces, and the game can still unfold in many different ways (Diagram 1).

A Change of Plan

2 Since White has guessed that Black is trying to form a diagonal line, White decides to block him by putting a piece on space D4 (Diagram 2). If Black still wants to form a diagonal line, he will have to capture the White piece that stands in his way, which will cost him at least three turns. Black decides not to do so, and changes his original plan of forming a diagonal line. Instead, he tries to form a horizontal line with five pieces in row 6. He gets to work immediately on his goal, moving his piece from D8 to D6. White fears that his piece on space C6 will be eliminated by his opponent in the next turn, so he moves it to A6, one of the spaces where he wants to form a winning line. This way, he rescues the piece, though his piece on C7 runs the same

risk of elimination (to do so, Black need only move his piece from D6 to C6). But Black reminds himself that he has set out to make solely functional moves. In this situation, it's more advantageous not to capture the piece on C7, but to jump over it instead, which allows Black to reach space C6, which White has just abandoned. As a result, there are three black pieces in row 6. If Black had captured the white piece, there would be only two.

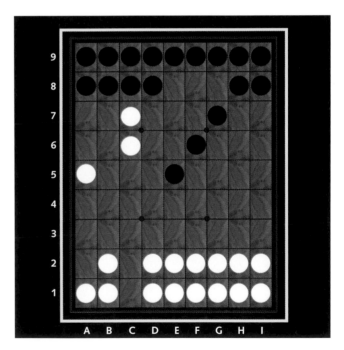

DIAGRAM 1:
The position of the pieces after three moves. It's likely that White will guess that Black wants to form a diagonal line, whereas White's goal is less obvious.

The Danger of an Open End

3 White must do something immediately to stop his opponent from forming a winning line. He recognizes the danger posed by four enemy pieces in a line with two open ends. Black could attain this position if in his next move he puts a piece on space E6. If given this opportunity, White will certainly lose. In that case, all White could do is block that line one turn at a time, so Black could add a piece to the other end and win. White decides to defend himself by capturing one of the black pieces in row 6. However, Black immediately puts another piece in that row, so there are once again three pieces in row 6.

History repeats itself, because White must once again stop his opponent from forming a four-piece line with two open ends. He blocks one of the open ends, putting a piece on space C6 (Diagram 3). Black adds a piece to the other end, and so is able to form a four-piece line with an open end. As expected, White now puts a piece at the other end in space H6, so the four black pieces are now surrounded by two white pieces. Black decides to put an end to this situation by capturing the piece White just added. As a result, he has an open end once again.

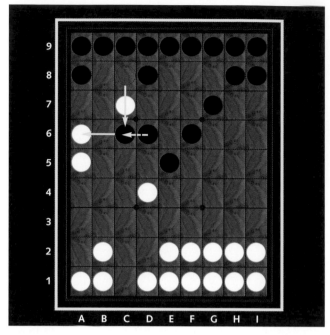

DIAGRAM 2:
A change of plans. Black opts to form a horizontal line instead of a diagonal one. Instead of capturing the white piece on space C7, he jumps over it with the piece on C8; now he has three black pieces in row 6.

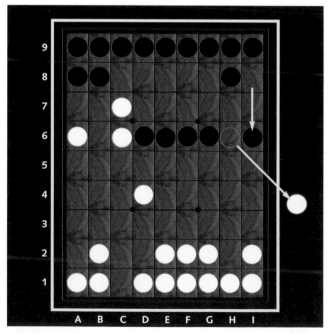

DIAGRAM 3:
The danger of open ends. Black has four contiguous pieces in row 6. He hopes to clear the way by capturing the white piece on H6.

The following is a transcript of all the moves in the first Hasami shogi match described here. The (x) indicates that a piece has been eliminated.

1. W: C2-C7, B: G8-G7
2. W: C1-C6, B: F8-F6
3. W: A2-A5, B: E8-E5
4. W: D2-D4, B: D8-D6
5. W: C6-A6, B: C8-C6
6. W: A5(x)C5, B: E5-E6
7. W: C5-C6, B: G7-G6
8. W: H2-H6, B: I8(x)I6
9. W: H1-H6, B: I6-I8
10. W: I2-I6, B: B8(x)B6
11. W: C7(x)C6; B: B9(x)B6
12. W: D4-A4, B: B6-C6

Behind the Lines

4 White stays on the defensive by trying to stop his opponent from putting a piece on space H6 and forming a winning line. He can do this only by taking that space himself, so White voluntarily moves between two enemy pieces (Diagram 4). Black knows he cannot capture this piece.

Black moves one of the neighboring pieces, from I6 to I8. His purpose is to return this piece to I6 in his next turn, which will allow him to capture the piece in question.

White appears to have read his opponent's mind, and sees only one way of avoiding capture. He moves his piece from I2 to I6. As a result, Black's possibilities on the right end of his line diminish considerably. After all, his pieces are all on the same side of the line: near or on the baseline. To capture one of the white pieces in space H6 or I6, he has to surround them on both sides.

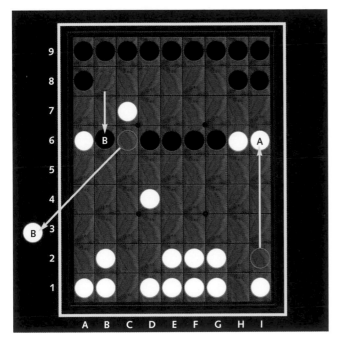

DIAGRAM 4:
Behind the lines. In his tenth move (I2–I6), White blocks the black line on its right end. Black will have a hard time breaking through this block, because all his pieces are arranged along one side of the line.

The Final Battle

5 Black sees a chance to create an opening on the left side of his line. To do this, he moves a black piece from space B8 to B6, capturing the white piece on C6 (Diagram 5). White realizes that he has to keep blocking this side of the line at any cost. He takes C6 again, this time with his piece from C7. This way, he not only blocks the end of the black line, but also captures the black piece on B6. Black still does not give up. He retakes space B6 using the piece on B9, and captures the white piece on C6 a second time. This time White's situation is less hopeful. Before, White could block this open end by adding one of his own pieces. Now he cannot, because he has no pieces left in column C. White knows he has lost the game. He has no way of stopping Black from completing his winning line in his next turn, by placing the piece from B6 in C6.

Evaluation

In the game just described, Black quickly took the lead and maintained it during the entire game. After the first three moves, White had to play on the defensive and had no chance of forming a winning line of his own. In part, this situation developed because Black chose to form a horizontal line. In this direction, it's possible to form a line with one or two open ends: a great opportunity for the maker of the line and a serious threat for his opponent. In the case of vertical and diagonal lines, it isn't possible to form lines with open ends. From this, one can safely assume that the decision to form a horizontal line is a good one.

A second conclusion is that it's very important to distribute the pieces evenly in rows 1 through 9. Black was blocked in on his right side in the tenth

move, because his pieces were bogged down on his own side of the board.

A third observation is that it's very important to ensure there is one piece in every column. Toward the end of the game, White no longer had any pieces in column C, and lost the game as a result.

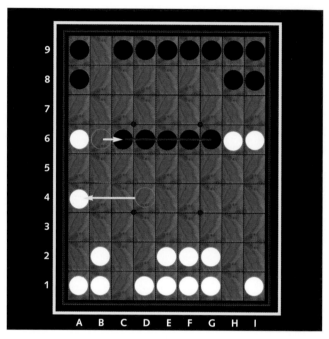

DIAGRAM 5:
The final battle. It is White's turn. Since he has no pieces left in column C, he cannot stop Black from forming a winning line in his next move.

A VARIATION FOR BEGINNERS

Sometimes Hasami shogi is played on condition that a player may move a piece only one space per turn. In this variation, it is not possible to jump over one another's pieces. This rule makes the game slower and less confusing, so it's a good variation for beginners.

Hasami Shogi: Version 2

The game of Hasami shogi just discussed is one of the two popular board games from Japan with this same name. Although the version here resembles the other in some respects—especially with respect to the game materials—they are in fact two different games. The Hasami shogi described below is a war game. The rules are quite simple, and this is probably one of the reasons the game is so popular among children in Japan. (It would be more accurate to say,

"among Japanese boys," for according to tradition, board games are mainly a pastime for males.)

This game, in which players must work with a clear strategy, is also a fun challenge for adults. Players can use part of a go board for Hasami shogi, and may also use go stones, but it is more common to use a shogi board and the usual black and white chips. The object is to eliminate all the opponent's pieces.

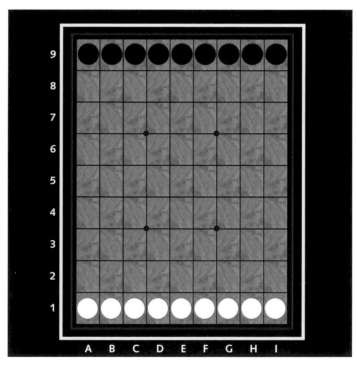

DIAGRAM A:
A Hasami shogi board with the pieces in the opening position.

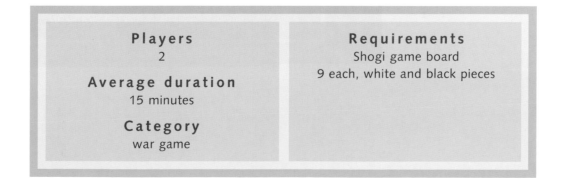

Players	Requirements
2	Shogi game board
	9 each, white and black pieces
Average duration	
15 minutes	
Category	
war game	

A Reversi tournament held on August 15, 1886, in the Belgian town of Vilvoorde. The checkers club would regularly match wits with other clubs by playing Reversi.

The Board

Othello was introduced to other European countries in the early twentieth century. In Germany, people began requesting the game in 1907. There was no specific need for a special board, because a checkerboard with eight-by-eight squares can be readily used to play Othello. Even so, the game manufacturer Ravensburg designed a special board for it in 1898. The game was published under its "original" name of Reversi. The plastic board with little holes appeared on the German market in 1968. Its launch involved a great deal of publicity, which was responsible for the rise in the game's popularity.

Reversi and Othello

The original commercial name of this game undoubtedly comes from the term *to reverse*. This choice has a logical explanation: in Othello, captured pieces are not removed from the board but are reversed or turned around.

Around 1970 in Japan, Goro Hasegawa created the same game and gave it the name Othello, which alluded to the Shakespearian play and to its English origin. Othello was launched amid a spectacular advertising campaign, which led to its quick spread throughout Japan, the United States, and some European countries.

Tournaments

In Japan, board games are usually not played socially or at home with the family. This is also true of Othello, which is considered a serious game in Japan, and is played mainly in clubs or associations. Players are usually male. Players regularly match wits in various tournaments. It is even possible to become a great champion by winning an Othello grand championship.

Playing Othello

Othello is an appealing game involving capture. It can keep two players busy (and entertained) for a good long while. The most noteworthy aspect of this game is the method of capturing pieces. First, because of how often this occurs in the game, players have the obligation to capture once per turn, so a player who cannot do so loses his turn. Second, captured pieces meet a curious end: whereas in many other games they disappear from the board, in Othello, captured pieces are simply turned around and become the opponent's, because the pieces are a different color on each side.

Othello is played on a board that is gradually filled up in the course of the game. The game is over when all the spaces are filled up, or when neither player can capture any more pieces. If at this point there are more red than yellow pieces on the board, Red wins; if there are more yellow pieces, the honor goes to the player who is using that color. (Othello is also played with black-and-white pieces.)

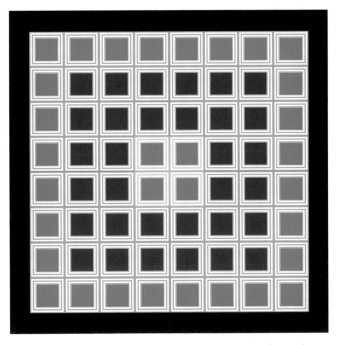

An exciting game of Othello calls for a special board and sixty-four pieces with a different color on each side.

Players	Requirements
2	special game board
	64 chips with one side dark
Average duration	and one side light
25 minutes	
Category	
positional	

The Winner

The winner is the player with the most pieces on the board at the end of the game. A game of Othello can end in one of two ways. The first is when the sixty-four pieces are all on the board; the second, when there are still pieces left to play, but neither player can capture. The number of red and yellow pieces are counted, and the player with the most pieces wins. Players can make different arrangements with regard to the tally. Suppose they have put all the pieces on the board and there are forty-three red pieces and twenty-one yellow pieces left on the board (Diagram D); Red gets forty-three points and Yellow gets twenty-one. Players can then agree that the first player to reach a certain number wins, or they can elect to award the winner the difference in points between forty-three and twenty-one: twenty-two points. Also the players can establish beforehand how many points are necessary for a player to be the definite winner. The same tally can be made when all the pieces are not yet on the board.

VARIATION

To introduce younger children to the game of Othello, you might consider using fewer than sixty-four pieces.

DIAGRAM D:
The final position. There are forty-three red and twenty-one yellow pieces on the board. Red is the winner.

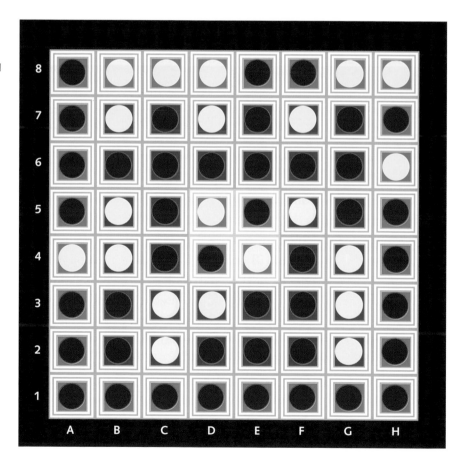

A group of Moroccan men play on an eight-by-eight board. This is a variation on Reversi (Othello), played with a limited number of pieces.

The First Match

Many games from the late nineteenth century have fallen into oblivion, or are known only on a very limited scale. Such is not the case with Othello, which is an example of a game that has always enjoyed the fervent enthusiasm of players all over the world. The theory of this ingenious game can be explained very quickly, so it's possible to start playing right away. In practice, players learn that, although the game appears to be very simple, it requires a well thought-out strategy. To guide the beginner, several interesting examples of play are provided below.

STRATEGY

It makes sense to consider, before starting to play, which strategy you want to apply, but it is never a good idea to adhere to it strictly. If circumstances call for it, you should be flexible enough to change strategies.

A Short Game

1 As mentioned, a beginner can quickly move on to the first game. But a first game can also conclude very quickly. It is even possible for a player to win within five moves. A game of this length is shown in Diagram 1. In the opening position, the yellow and red pieces are in diagonal lines. The coin toss gives the first move to Red. The number on the piece indicates the respective players' turns. The yellow piece marked with a two is the second to move in the game, by the yellow player. To be clear: under no circumstances should the players expect this piece to remain yellow for the rest of the game. To know which color a piece is at the end, the plays must all be repeated in order. If a game is repeated, players must not forget to turn over the pieces once they are captured. After Red's fifth turn (move 9), only red pieces are left on the board. It is then

> **TIP**
>
> It is possible, and should pose no problem, for two people of different skill levels to play a game of Othello. If, furthermore, players want to level the playing field, one may grant an advantage to the weaker player. This action has no impact on the course of the game. Another possibility, which does affect the game, is to allow the weaker player to occupy one or more of the corner squares at the start of the game.

Yellow's turn, but it is impossible for him to capture a piece, because he would have to have a yellow piece on the board. In this situation, Red cannot capture any pieces, either, so he wins this short game (Diagram 1).

DIAGRAM 1:
A short game. Red wins after only five turns.

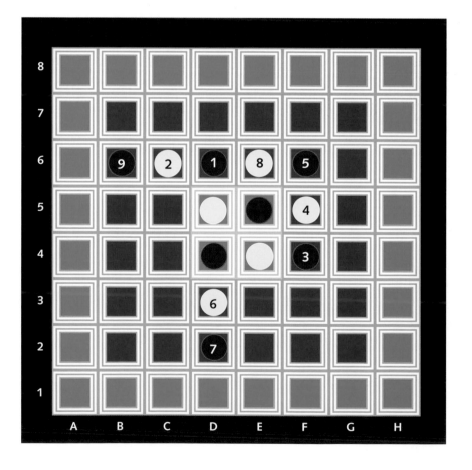

This pocket game of checkers, recommended in the Johnson & Smith Co. catalog of 1929, also includes Othello pieces and a set of rules.

Unequal Strength

When, after a game, the pieces left on the board are all the same color, as in the game described above, the keeper of those pieces usually receives sixty-four points. You might call this a victory *cum laude*. In particular, if players are unequal in strength, this type of victory occurs regularly. Othello can remain interesting even in competitions where the players are not equal, and in which the same player wins repeatedly. The loser takes up the challenge of winning at least once. For the winner, the challenge lies in winning the game in the fewest possible moves, or beating his previous score.

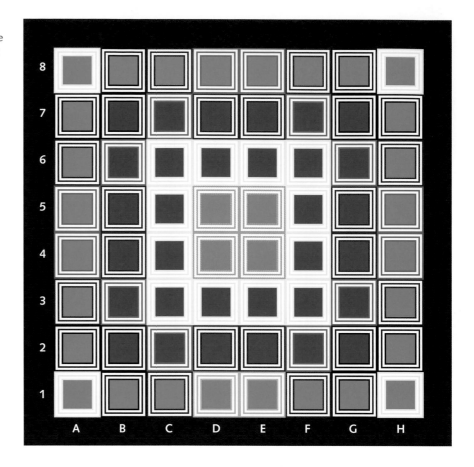

DIAGRAM 2:
The value of the squares. These general guidelines show that it is better to avoid the black squares on the board.

■ = safe

■ = mostly safe

■ = risky

■ = dangerous

The Value of the Squares

2 In recent years, experts have conducted studies of Othello. These studies have not yielded a mathematical solution the game, such as finding a single correct strategy or the outcome of perfect play. Nonetheless, they have helped to confirm some received wisdom and to establish some clear general guidelines. With regard to the value of certain squares, the studies established that the corner squares are the most valuable. A piece on one of these four squares serves as a sort of anchor in three directions. Since capturing must always be done in a straight line, a piece on a corner square is impossible to seize. The game inevitably progresses from the center of the board. A good strategy consists of trying to avoid the weaker squares rather than taking over the strong squares. The twelve squares surrounding the four center squares are considered safe. Squares become increasingly unsafe the farther they are from the center, and the most risky squares are the ones immediately to the sides of the corners. If a player puts a piece on one of these, in his next turn his opponent might take the opportunity to seize one of the coveted corner squares. Diagram 2 provides general guidelines with respect to the value of the different squares. It is worth mentioning that, for tactical reasons, these rules should be applied judiciously, not rigidly.

Simple Attack

Beginning Othello players tend to try to make only multiple attacks at the start of the game. But this enthusiasm, although understandable, tends not to be effective in practice. A player shows good strategic understanding if, during his first few moves, he makes only simple attacks, because if several of an opponent's pieces are flipped over in a single turn, the opponent can choose among several more squares in which to put his next piece. It is much more sensible to limit as much as possible the opponent's choices of where to move, and to make a multiple attack only when it is sure to be effective. The patient player will be rewarded for it.

Strategy Tips

The study of Othello provides us with some tips in regard to strategy. One of these has to do with the disadvantages of filling up squares on all sides of the board too quickly. Experience shows that these pieces are usually captured in a multiple attack. This contradicts the first principle, which holds that during the first few turns, a player should try to carry out simple attacks, saving multiple attacks for later.

A second tip is that there is no need to pay too much attention to the corners. These squares are no doubt interesting, but it is inadvisable to try taking them at any cost.

It's important to keep some pieces among a concentration of the enemy's pieces. These pieces are in a strong position, because the enemy cannot capture them. In the final stages of play, these pieces can often be used to surround an opponent's pieces.

A Championship Tournament

3 A match played during a championship tournament in Japan in 1982 is shown in Diagram 3A. In Diagram 3B, Red has won the game with forty-one pieces versus twenty-three. It is a good exercise to repeat this game. This way, a beginner can get a good idea of the various situations that can arise. He will also see that luck can be very fickle in this game. At one point, Yellow has a clear advantage, and at the next moment, the situation has reversed completely. It is fundamental to turn over a piece as soon

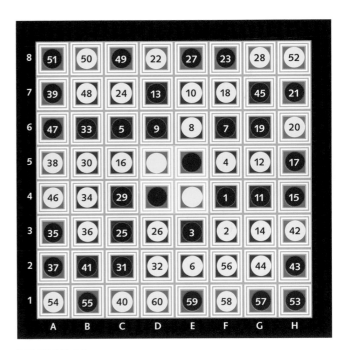

DIAGRAM 3A:
A match between master players played in Japan in 1982.

as it is captured. If a player forgets to flip over the newly captured piece, the game is now disqualified and must be started over. In any event, this is a good exercise because it forces the player to control the pieces he has captured, in all directions. It is worth mentioning that Yellow made a multiple attack in his second turn (move 4), and Red made none until his sixth turn (move 11). In each of these moves, the player captured and flipped over two pieces. As the game moved forward from each multiple attack, more pieces were captured. On the forty-eighth move of the game, Yellow captured five pieces by putting one of his in square B7. In his next turn, Red beat this number by putting one of his pieces in C8.

Red was the first to put a piece on a square on the edge of the board. He accomplished this in his eighth turn (move 15), putting a piece on square H4. In addition, he was first to put one of his pieces in a dangerous square—square H7, which borders a corner square. Red placed a piece on this square on his eleventh turn (move 21). At this point, Yellow could not directly fill the corner square at H8, because he could make no direct attack from there.

T I P

If over time you lose the original game pieces that came as a set, you can replace them with coins of the same size. Coins are ideal because they have two distinct sides (heads and tails).

Toward the end of the game, in Red's twenty-sixth turn (move 51), he put one of his pieces in the corner square A8. Luckily for Yellow, he was able to put a piece on the corner square H8. Had he not been able to do so, he would have lost every piece in row 8, because Red would undoubtedly have put a piece on that very same square (Diagrams 3A and 3B).

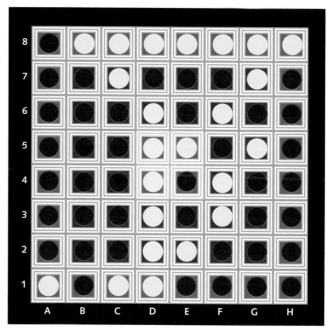

DIAGRAM 3B:
Outcome of a match between master players. Red has forty-one pieces versus Yellow's twenty-three.

Craps
History of the Game

◆ ◆ ◆

Craps, incredibly popular in the United States, originated not in North America, but in Britain. It developed from an English game called Hazard, which is the ancestor of many casino games including craps, faro, the Macao, and *trente et quarante*. In North America, Hazard began to spread, starting in 1800 among the black residents of New Orleans. The rules of the game were modified and stabilized from there, and little by little, craps developed from it. At first, the game was known only to longshoremen and sailors, who played it regularly. Men would gather in narrow alleyways to try their luck. Toward the end of the nineteenth century, craps made its debut in gambling houses. As soon as the first casinos opened their doors to this game, it became official and respected. The casinos and gambling houses where it was first played were divided into two categories. People from the upper echelons of society played craps at elegant gambling houses known as "carpet joints." The man on the street took refuge in noisy "sawdust joints."

During World War II, craps was very popular among U.S. and Canadian troops. The game was forbidden, and still is, at French casinos. So much money is wagered on craps that some consider it the most important game of chance in all of history.

A typical "carpet joint" in 1843. This American gambling house takes its name from the already famous, luxurious London gambling establishment of the eighteenth century, Crockford. Although the apparent calm of these gentlemen would seem to suggest otherwise, they are betting very large sums of money.

Agua Caliente (literally "hot water") was a resort area situated in southern Tijuana, Mexico. Both were places where game aficionados met, as well as other "high rollers," during the 1920s and 1930s.

Agua Caliente Resort

Although craps is predominantly a U.S. game, it was also played in the casinos of Mexico, particularly in the idyllic tourist destination of Agua Caliente in Tijuana, near San Diego. This complex, among others, consisted of a first-class hotel, expensive restaurants, swimming pools, golf courses, and a magnificent casino. Agua Caliente first opened its doors in 1928. The casino, and the game of craps itself, owed its popularity in large part to its proximity to Hollywood.

The Gold Room

The Gold Room was the most coveted room at the Agua Caliente casino. There, millionaires would gamble astronomical sums of money. As a nod to their favorite game, these gamblers were known as "high rollers."

Many dreamed of playing craps in the Gold Room. A person who was invited to play a game in this room, and then to dine in the exquisite restaurant next door, was undoubtedly a member of the most privileged class. It was a compliment to one's financial position, and naturally, something to brag about. Famous playboys and film producers, such as Carl Laemmie, founder of Universal Pictures, threw private parties at this establishment. When the casino's doors closed, the focus of casinos and craps became Las Vegas.

The Dice

Seeing that great sums of money routinely pass through the craps table at any casino, a great deal of attention is paid to the materials required for the game. The dice should be manufactured by a respectable company with a special license from state gaming authorities. Both the manufacturer and the casino are very demanding with respect to the manufacture of dice, typically measuring the dice with a micrometer. The dice must be perfect cubes to within 1/10,000 of an inch. If a die does not fulfill this requirement, it will not be used for craps.

Playing Craps

Craps is one of the most exciting and fast-paced games of chance. It is especially well suited to people who believe in the magic of dice. There are many variants of this game. Herein is described the most important version: bank craps. It is known as a casino game, popularized in many movies; there also exists a home version of the game that can be played by as many people as wish to take part. The home version requires a special game board; the players can use poker chips or simply make use of go pieces, dry beans, or matches as tokens for betting. When the players lose, they pay their wagers to the bank; when they win, the bank pays them. This means that the players never have wagers among themselves. No roll is good or bad in and of itself; rather, it depends on the combination of points on the dice and on the square on which the players are betting. At first glance, the large number of possible bets can make it seem as though craps is a very complicated game. In practice, this simply isn't the case, especially if you take the time to study the rules calmly and in depth before trying your hand at your first game.

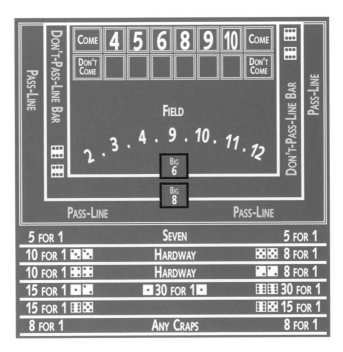

In casinos, craps is played on tables designed especially for this game. The board used in the domestic version is somewhat different. Besides the game board, players need enough chips to place their bets. When there are no more than four players, they can make do with pieces from a go set.

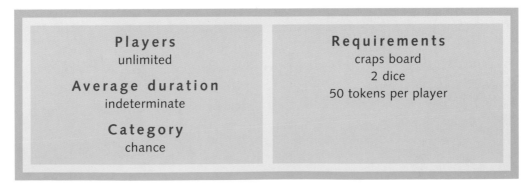

| Players |
| unlimited |
| **Average duration** |
| indeterminate |
| **Category** |
| chance |

| Requirements |
| craps board |
| 2 dice |
| 50 tokens per player |

Rules:
Preliminaries

In theory, a game of craps need never come to an end. Players can keep betting and rolling the dice as long as their reserves do not run out. Therefore, it's a good idea to agree beforehand on when the game will end. The simplest way is to agree on a certain amount of time, such as a half-hour.

It is important that the players and the bank have an ample number of pieces. If there are four players, they can use a set of go pieces; if there are more than these, they can use poker chips, dry beans, buttons, or matches. They can also use pieces of various colors for different values. As a general guideline, though, fifty pieces per player are enough. In any event, players must all have the same number of pieces, and the bank should always have a good-size reserve. Players roll the dice to decide who among them will begin. Players take turns clockwise, so that each player passes the dice to the person to his left.

Rolling the Dice

The dice are shaken in a closed hand. According to the official rules of craps, they are then tossed against the edge of the table or against a wall, so that they bounce on the board or on the sides of the table. For this reason, it's a good idea to position the table with the edge against a wall. If only one of the dice bounces off the wall, both dice must be rolled again. This also holds true when one or both dice fall off the table. Sometimes, one of the dice touches the wall and then touches an object or a player before landing on the table. In that case, the roll is valid. The result of the roll is the sum of the numbers on the two dice (a minimum of two, a maximum of twelve).

A game of craps in a Las Vegas casino. The surface of the table is somewhat deep so that the dice do not roll off. At the side of the table stands a "box man," who pays the winnings out to the players. The three dealers are in charge of placing bets on the table and collecting the wagers lost by the players.

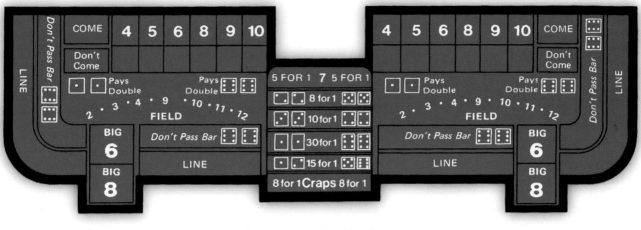

Typical example of the possible wagers on craps, as they appear on the tables of most casinos.

Three Initial Rolls

Each turn begins with a player rolling the dice, and it ends as soon as it is decided whether the roll is a gain or a loss. For this reason, the dice can be rolled several times in the same turn. Also, players often take several consecutive turns. The first roll of the dice in each turn is called the "come-out roll," because after the dice yield a gain or a loss, this is the first time they are rolled again.

There are three possible come-out rolls:

1. **A natural:** When the sum of the points on the dice is seven or eleven, it is called a "natural." This is a winning roll, sometimes also called a "pass." The same player gets another turn, which also starts with a come-out roll, because the last turn ended with a win-or-lose decision.

2. **Craps:** A total of two, three, or twelve points is known as "craps," which means "foolishness" or "junk." It's a fitting name, because craps is a losing roll, also known as a "miss." Still, a player who rolls craps is entitled to another roll.

3. **A point:** The third and final come-out roll can consist of any of these totals: four, five, six, eight, nine, or ten. If a player rolls one of these numbers, a point is established. In this situation,

TIP

It can be practical to find someone who isn't playing and is willing to act as banker and referee.

the seven plays a special part. In theory, a point does not mean any particular gain or loss. To turn it into a winning roll, the player is obliged to roll the same number again, and so a single turn consists of more than one roll. The player must roll the same point again before he rolls a seven. Suppose a player rolls a five. This is his point. His next roll is a six; this roll is neither a winner nor a loser, and he must keep rolling until he rolls a five or a seven. If the player rolls a five—his point—before rolling a seven, he has a winning roll. This can be compared with a natural and is also known as a "pass." The player who rolls this gets another turn, so he has another come-out roll. But if the player rolls a seven before he rolls another five, he has a losing roll. In craps terminology, this is known as a "seven out." The player does not get another turn and must pass the dice to the player to his left (Diagram A).

An Example of Play

For greater clarity, we will here demonstrate a game from a player's first come-out roll to the moment he passes the dice on to the next player. For greater convenience, this player will be called "A." He rolls the dice a first time, or in other words, makes his come-out roll. His points add up to two, which is a craps. The second roll by Player A is also a come-out roll. This time he rolls a seven—a winning natural. The third time, he rolls a five. Player A rolls again—an eleven. Since this is no longer a come-out roll, it does not qualify as a natural. In this situation, the number eleven has no value, and Player A must keep rolling the dice. Next he rolls a nine, a ten, and finally, a five. He didn't roll a seven, and so was able to turn his point into a winner. Now, Player A keeps rolling the dice and makes his fourth come-out roll, which yields a twelve, for another craps. His come-out roll in his fifth turn again yields a point, this time an eight. Next, Player A rolls a two and then a seven. This is a seven-out, for he has rolled a seven before rolling another eight, his point. This means that Player A's turn is over. He passes the dice to his neighbor to the left (Diagram B).

DIAGRAM A:

Naturals and craps. A player who rolls a seven or an eleven in his first roll has a winning natural. A two, three, or twelve is a losing roll, or craps. The other come-out rolls are points, which indicate neither a win nor a loss at first.

Players bet assiduously at a craps table. An image from 1950s Las Vegas.

The Next Player

After his seven-out, the player passes the dice to the next player. There are two other situations in which the dice can be passed voluntarily from one player to another. One is when a player receives the dice from the previous player and immediately passes them to the next, forfeiting his turn to roll. He can also pass them after a decisive roll of the dice. Thus, a player is never forced to make a new come-out roll.

The Craps Board

The craps board is not as complicated as it may seem at first glance. It features many spaces on which the players can bet. Each square has a name, a number, or a picture of two dice. The shape of the different spaces varies. There are square spaces of different sizes, as well as rectangular spaces, and long, curved spaces (Diagram C).

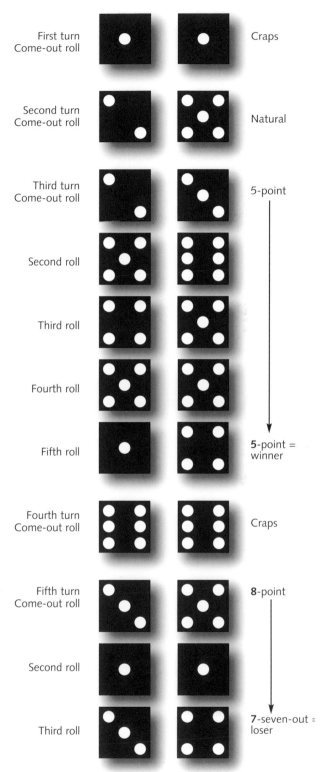

DIAGRAM B:
An example of play. Player A rolls craps, a natural, a winning point, and another craps. In his fifth turn, he gets a seven-out. He then must pass the dice to the next player.

Wagers

The players all play against the bank, so they may not make any bets among themselves. Before rolling the dice, players always have a chance to bet. The player who makes a come-out roll must indicate by a wager on the pass line or on the don't-pass line whether he intends to try for a winning roll (natural or point) or a losing roll (craps or seven-out). The other players must also bet. As mentioned, there are many spaces on which the players can bet, which will be discussed later on.

Calculating Probabilities

During a game of craps the players are constantly deciding where to bet. To do this, it helps a lot to know some basic rules of math. In the first column in Diagram D (A), several possible totals are marked. Next to it (B) is indicated how many ways there are to obtain each total. In the case of twelve, there is only one way to obtain it: by rolling double-

sixes. Altogether there are thirty-six possible combinations. The next column (C) shows the odds of getting that number in any given turn. To calculate, you compare the number of ways to obtain a given number with the number of ways of getting any other (thirty-six minus the number of ways to roll the number in question). Column D shows the chances of rolling a given number before rolling a seven. This is relevant for a player who has rolled a point and wants to turn it into a winner. The final column (E) shows the odds of rolling a high number and then a low number. The odds of rolling a twelve before a four, for instance, are 3 to 1 (Diagram D).

DIAGRAM C:
A craps board.

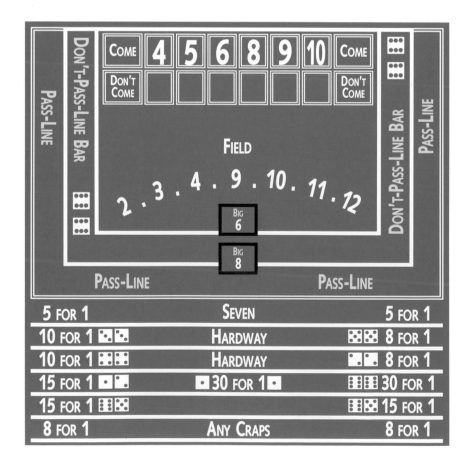

Calculation of probabilities

A Totals	B Combinations	C One roll	D Before the seven	E High before low											
12	1	35-1	6-1	**12**											
11	2	17-1	3-1	2-1	**11**										
10	3	11-1	2-1	3-1	3-2	**10**									
9	4	8-1	3-2	4-1	2-1	4-3	**9**								
8	5	31-5	6-5	5-1	5-2	5-3	5-4	**8**							
7	6	5-1	-	6-1	3-1	2-1	3-2	6-5	**7**						
6	5	31-5	6-5	5-1	5-2	5-3	5-4	1-1	5-6	**6**					
5	4	8-1	3-2	4-1	2-1	4-3	1-1	4-5	2-3	4-5	**5**				
4	3	11-1	2-1	3-1	3-2	1-1	3-4	3-5	1-2	3-5	3-4	**4**			
3	2	17-1	3-1	2-1	1-1	2-3	1-2	2-5	1-3	2-5	1-2	2-3	**3**		
2	1	35-1	6-1	1-1	1-2	1-3	1-4	1-5	1-6	1-5	1-4	1-3	1-2	**2**	

DIAGRAM D:
Calculation of probabilities. Some knowledge of this subject area is useful when making decisions on wagers.

Betting on the Pass Line

A player bets on the pass line when he thinks the next roll is going to be a winner. Anyone can bet on the pass line, not just the player rolling the dice. If the roll actually turns out to be a winner, the bank pays the value of the wager one to one. For example, if someone has bet two chips, he will get two from the bank. He can take them himself from the pot. If the roll is not a winner, anyone who bet at the pass line loses his wager to the bank. Players are not permitted to withdraw their bets if the player rolling the dice gets a point—they must wait and see whether chance decides for or against him.

Bets on the Don't-Pass Line

Putting one or more chips on the don't-pass line is the opposite of betting on the pass line. It means that the player expects the next roll to be a loser. It is a bet on a craps or a seven-out. But if the craps is a double-six, the wager is void, because this combination is barred by the bank. This is indicated on the board, where to the side of the space for the don't-pass line, there is an image of a double-six with the word "bar" next to it. When the player rolling the dice rolls a double-six in his come-out roll, there is no gain or loss, and the players withdraw their wagers from that space. If a player bets on the don't-pass line, he wins when the player rolling the dice gets a losing roll. The payout is the same as on the pass line: one to one.

CURIOUS FACT

In Britain the board does not feature the "big six" or "big eight" spaces.

Come Bets

Come bets are very similar to those wagers made on the pass line. The difference is that wagers on the pass line are made before the player makes his come-out roll, whereas with the come bet, they are made after the come-out roll. When the come-out roll is a point, the player must roll again and let luck take its course. Before the next roll, and before any roll, the roller must give the other players the chance to place their bets. Before making the second roll,

players place come bets. Players can place come bets only if the roller gets a point on his come-out roll.

Come bets are always made on a winning roll. After the second roll, players look to see if chance has decided on the first roll, which is related to bets on the pass line and the don't-pass line. At the same time, they look to see whether the roll is a winner or a loser with respect to the come bet. If the roll is craps, the come bets are lost. If the roll is a seven or eleven (a natural), players win their bets.

Ladies from good families also wagered once in a while. In the United States, there were special rules for "the weaker sex." At this carpet joint, the ladies enjoy a game of faro; this game developed from Hazard, which means it has the same root as craps.

A croupiers' school at Nice, France, in the year 1905. The apprentices learn their profession by training daily for six months.

Suppose someone has placed a come bet and the roll is a natural. Since the payout is one-to-one, the player gets one chip from the bank. He takes it from the pot and places it to the side of the come box. Now he must decide, before the next roll, whether to put down two chips in the come box. He can also take them both out or leave only one.

Betting on the Don't-Come Box

Betting on the don't-come box is the opposite of betting on the come box. When placing a don't-come bet, the better assumes that the player rolling the dice will roll a losing combination. In this square, you win if the roll is a craps or a seven-out. As with the pass line, one of the possible rolls, the double-six, is blocked. If the player gets this roll, it is neither a win nor a loss.

Example of a Bet

Before discussing the other betting squares, an example of play is provided to clarify some of the possibilities just described. Suppose it's Player A's turn. He bets one chip on the pass line. Player B follows his example, and Players C and D each bet one chip on the don't-pass line. A's first roll is a double-four. This is neither a natural nor a craps, but a point. Therefore, the bets simply remain on the board and A must keep rolling the dice. First, everyone has the opportunity to bet on the come or don't-come box. A and B put down one chip apiece at the come box, and Players C and D keep betting on a losing roll, each of them putting a chip on the don't-come box.

STRATEGY

You should never bet on the "big" squares, and always choose a place bet instead.

VARIATION

To minimize the bank's advantage, players sometimes make different agreements regarding "field" wagers. As a general rule, players agree that the bank will pay out double or even triple for the numbers two and twelve.

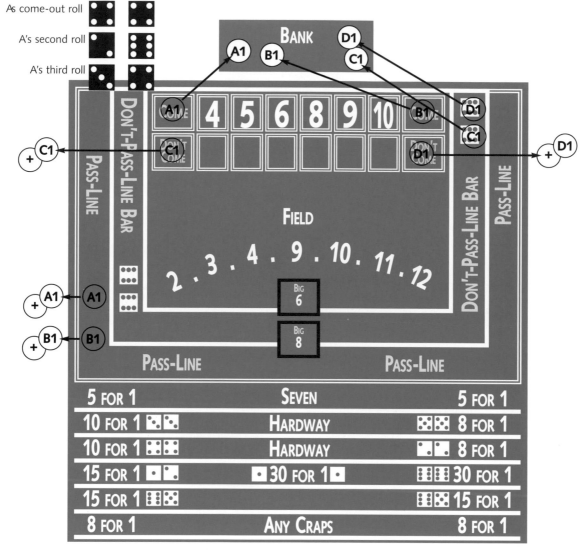

DIAGRAM E:
An example of betting. A and B bet on the pass line, while Players C and D bet on the don't-pass line. The come-out roll is an eight, after which A and B bet on the come box and C and D bet on the don't-come box. The second roll is also an eight. A and B win the bet on the pass line; C and D lose. The third roll is a seven-out. C and D win, while A and B's wagers on the come box revert to the bank.

In his second roll, Player A tries to roll another eight, the same point he got in his come-out roll. After all, he bet on the pass-line based on the assumption that he was going to win. The same roll serves as a come-out roll for the wager on the come box and the don't-come box. Player A rolls a two and a six. This is a repetition of the eight, so the point from his come-out roll has become a winning point. Players A and B take one chip each from the bank, since their bet was on the pass line. They also remove the chip they have on the pass line. Players C and D's wagers on the don't-pass line go to the bank.

For the come and don't-come bets, Player A rolled an eight point. Player A keeps rolling. In his next roll the dice show a three and a four. It's a seven-out, so Player A isn't able to turn his point into a winning point. C and D have won the bet. They each take a chip from the bank and add it to their reserves, together with the token from the don't-come box. Players A and B are obliged to turn over their token from the come box to the bank. They had bet on a winning point. Since Player A rolled a seven-out, he too has ended his turn. He must pass the dice to Player B (Diagram E).

Place Bet

A place bet means betting on a numbered square, between the come boxes, or on a blank square between the don't-come boxes. A player who bets on a numbered square is called a "right bettor"; a player who bets on a blank square is a "wrong bettor." There is also betting on the squares after the come-out roll—that is, after a point. The players' luck will be decided by the dice. Suppose a player bets on the number six. If the player who rolls the dice gets this number before rolling a seven, he wins. If he rolls a seven before rolling a six, he loses his wager. A wrong bettor who, for example, bets a chip

on the blank square under the six, is convinced that the seven will appear before the six. If it does, he wins this bet. If not, his wager disappears into the bank.

Payment of right-bettors' place bets works like this:

- bets on numbers four and ten: nine for five;
- bets on numbers five and nine: seven for five;
- bets on numbers six and eight: seven for six.

For wrong-bettors, the winnings are distributed thus:

- bets on the blank squares below the numbers four and ten: eleven for five;
- bets on the blank squares below the numbers five and nine: eight for five;
- bets on the blank squares below the numbers six and eight: five for four.

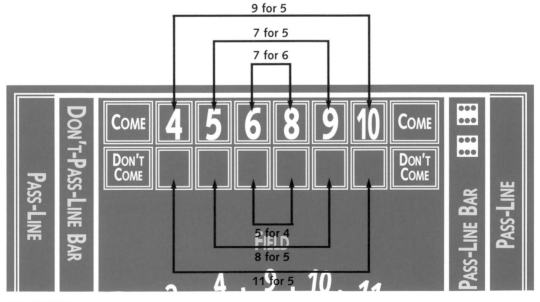

DIAGRAM F:
Place bets. The distribution of winnings and losses tells us that the minimum bet on these squares is four chips.

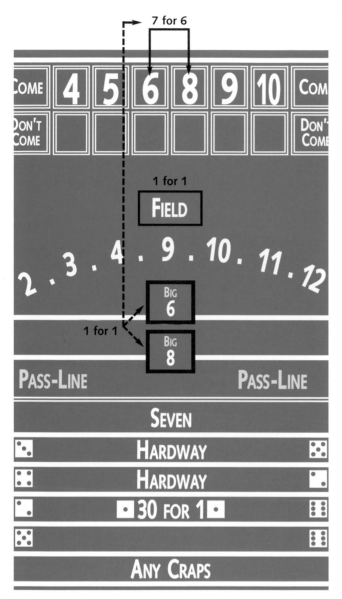

DIAGRAM G:
Field bets and big bets. Winning field bets, big-6 bets, and big-8 bets yield one times the wager. The payout for place bets on six and eight is better, and therefore these squares have preference.

This distribution of winnings and losses tells us that it's impossible to place bets of a single chip. Suppose someone bets on four and the player rolls a four. The winner then gets nine chips from the bank for the five he bets. Thus, a player must bet at least five chips on square four. If he wants to bet more, his wager must always be a multiple of five. In the squares numbered six and eight, the minimum bet is six chips. In the blank squares below the six and eight, the minimum bet is four chips, and in all the other blank squares, the minimum is five (Diagram F).

Field Bets and Big Bets

Field bets are wagers on the "field" square. This square has the numbers two, three, four, nine, ten, eleven, and twelve. If on the roll immediately after the bets are placed the dice show one of these numbers, the player in question gets his wager back. When someone has bet, for example, two chips on this square, and the corresponding player rolls a ten, he gets his two chips back and two more from the bank.

If a player thinks matters through and has enough funds in his reserves, he should never bet on the big-6 or big-8 squares. A chip on big-6 means he is betting that the player rolling the dice will get a six before he gets a seven. A chip on big-8 means he thinks the roller will get an eight before he gets a seven. The payout is one to one. The bets on these squares are exactly the same as the place bets on six and eight, the only difference being that the payout for a place bet is much greater than on the big-6 or big-8 squares. Thus, when a player has sufficient funds, it makes more sense for him to make a place bet than to bet on one of the big squares (Diagram G).

Hardway Bets and Come-Out Bets

Hardway bets are wagers on a double roll, placed on the squares labeled "hardway." The double-three and double-four yield ten times the original wager. With a double-three or a double-four, a player can recoup eight times his original bet. Players must place their bets on the board directly to the side of the dice showing the numbers on which they want to bet—that is, directly to the left or right of the word "hardway." To gain any benefit from these squares, the roller must get the double in question before he rolls a seven, and before the same number is obtained otherwise. For instance, if a player bets on the double-two, he wins if the dice show a double-two before they show a seven *or* a one and a three.

Come-out bets are also known as "one-roll" bets. This means the wager is valid for only one roll. The wager is on a particular combination. In the roll after the bet is placed, if the combination is on the table, the bettor wins. If not, he loses the bet. The squares on which the players place come-out bets occupy the same part of the board as the hardway squares.

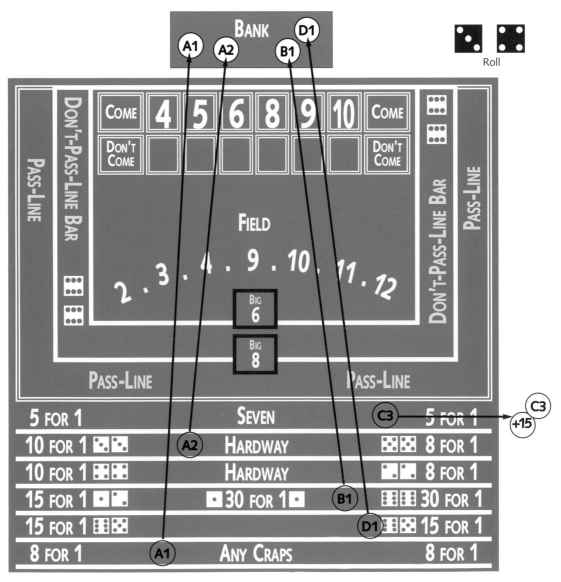

DIAGRAM H:
Hardway bets and one-roll bets. The player rolling the dice gets a three and a four. Player C wins fifteen and the other players lose their wagers.

These are the options for one-roll bets:

1. **Double-Sixes:** If the roll after the bet is placed on this square is a double-six, then the player in question gets thirty chips from the bank for each one wagered. If no double-six comes up, the wager disappears into the bank after one roll.

2. **Double-One:** Also in the case of a double-one, the bank pays the winner thirty times his wager.

3. **Five and Six:** Payout: fifteen times the wager.

4. **One and Two:** Payout: fifteen times the wager.

5. **Seven:** It does not matter how many points are on each die, as long as they add up to seven. Payout: five times the wager.

6. **Craps:** Payout: eight times the wager.

Here's an example of play: Player A bets two chips on the double-three hardway square and one on the craps square. B bets on the double-six, C puts three chips on the seven square, and D puts one chip on the five-and-six square. The dice show a three and a four. The distribution is as follows:

- Player A: loses three chips
- Player B: loses one chip
- Player C: wins fifteen chips
- Player D: loses one chip (Diagram H).

Recouping Chips

Players are not allowed to recoup any chips placed on the come or don't-come boxes once the dice are rolled. Nor can they recover their pass or don't-pass wagers after the come-out roll. Players must wait and let chance decide. In the case of a point, there are often undecided bets on hardway and place-bet squares. Players can withdraw their chips from these squares after the first roll. They can also wait until the next roll.

The Winner

The winner is the one with the most chips at the end of the game. Often, players impose a time limit, such as a half-hour, before the game begins. As an alternative, they can agree that the first player to get a certain number of chips wins. In this case, the other players can keep playing until all win that number of chips.

Tabula
History of the Game

◆ ◆ ◆

Historians agree that the game of Tabula originated with *ludus duodeci scriptorium* (the "game of twelve markings"), which was very popular among the Romans. The Roman game was played on a board with three rows of squares. During the first century, the game's popularity declined significantly. It was replaced by Tabula, which used a board with only two rows of squares, similar to a modern backgammon board. Roman historian Suetonius stated that the emperor Claudius (10 B.C.E.–54 C.E.) loved the game so much that he wrote a book about it. Claudius also had a Tabula board installed in his carriage, so that on long journeys he could enjoy his favorite game.

Four centuries later, the Eastern Roman Emperor Zeno (425–491) was very unlucky in a game of Tabula. Thanks to an unfortunate roll of the dice, he was forced to make three moves that weakened his opening. Eight of his pieces were left in a difficult position. This legendary play situation was described in Asia half a century later by a student named Agathias of Myrine. This epigram was used in the nineteenth century by Louis Becq de Fourquières to reconstruct the precise rules of Tabula.

Etching from a seventeenth-century drawing by David Téniers. Over time, Tabula spread throughout Europe, where it has been enjoyed in taverns since the Middle Ages.

Rules:
Preliminaries

Tabula is played on a board with twenty-four rectangular spaces. Despite their rectangular shape, the spaces on the board are called "points," because each space can be either an exit point, a rest point, or a goal point. At either end of the board are twelve points, side by side. When the board is placed between the two players, each has twelve points in front of him. But this does not mean that the row closest to him is also his finish line. To avoid confusion, the spaces are numbered one through twenty-four. At the start of the game, the board is empty. First the players decide which color each will use; then they distribute the pieces between themselves. Using a die, they decide which player will begin the game. Usually, the player who rolls the higher number is the one to play first.

Positioning the Pieces

In the first stage of a Tabula game, the two players must put all their pieces on the board in the spaces numbered one through twelve. This means that at the start of the game, they can place pieces on only one side of the board. The number of pieces each space can hold is unlimited, so the players can place eight pieces on the same point if they wish.

The first player rolls the three dice. He can add the points of the three dice and put his piece on the point with the number matching his roll. In that case, the rules hold that the number must not be higher than twelve. Players can also make combinations with the numbers they roll. At the start, they can choose after each roll whether they want to put one, two, or three pieces on the board. After the first player moves, it is his opponent's turn. He, too, rolls the three dice and adds one, two, or three pieces to the board.

The German Game of Lange Puff bears a strong resemblance to ancient Tabula. In both games, all pieces enter the board on space number one and move to space 24. Miniature of a medieval manuscript from around 1330 *(Library of the University of Heidelberg).*

Here's an example of play:

White rolls one, two, and four. He can add the points of the dice and put a piece on point 7. He could also put two pieces on the board, in which case the points on one of the dice are counted separately, and the other two are added together. He can choose from the following combinations:

- one piece on point 1, the other on 6;
- one piece on point 2, the other on 5;
- one piece on point 4, the other on 3.

Lastly, White can also add three pieces, one on point 1, one on point 2, and the third on point 4. Player A must put his pieces on the board as soon as possible, so he chooses the third option. Although his intentions are good, the wisdom of putting three

pieces on the table at once depends on other factors, and for several reasons, it might have been better to add up the points on the dice. We will discuss this matter in greater depth in the first match.

Black rolls a three and two fives. Since he, too, wants to put his pieces on the board as soon as possible, he opts for putting down three pieces: one on point 3 and two on point 5 (Diagram A).

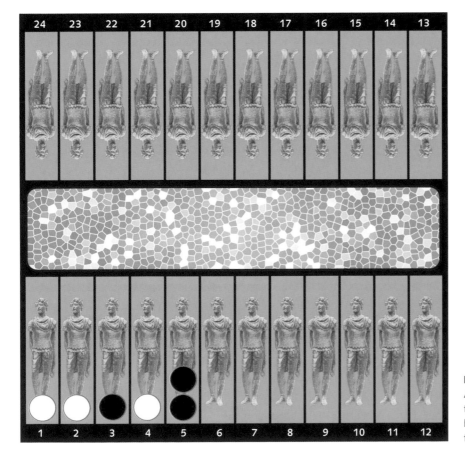

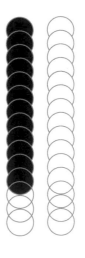

White's roll

Black's roll

DIAGRAM A:
A Tabula board. Setting down the pieces. In the first round, both players added three pieces to the board.

The First Match

As with many other games, the best way to learn how to play Tabula is to practice. The more you practice, the more possibilities you will discover for reaching the goal and for blocking your opponent. You will also develop a greater awareness of potential threats. The following match gives a first impression.

How to Prevent an Attack

1 When a player has two or more pieces on a single point, his opponent cannot add any of his own thereto. Since many pieces are in play, it is possible to place pairs on various points on the board,

making them untouchable to the opponent. Sometimes it may not be prudent to capture an enemy piece, especially if it means weakening your own positions by making them vulnerable to enemy attack (i.e., by leaving single pieces on different points). Several turns may be needed in order to reintroduce a captured piece to the board, and meanwhile the enemy keeps playing. Therefore, it is important from the outset to prevent an attack. In general, it is better to try to protect all your pieces from enemy attacks by not leaving them alone on various points on the board than it is to move several pieces forward at once.

Black's roll

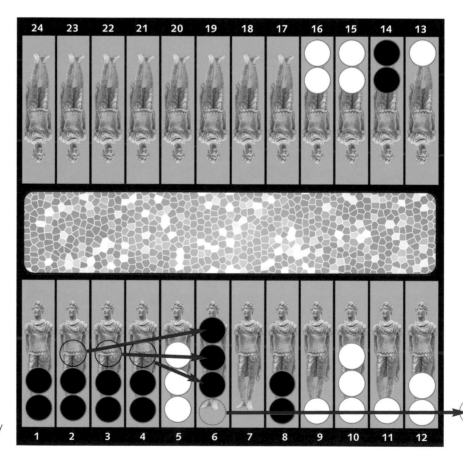

DIAGRAM 1:
Protecting one's pieces. Black captures an enemy piece at point six. White should have foreseen this, because now he has to roll a five to return this piece to the board (since points 1, 2, 3, 4, and 6 are all taken by two or more of Black's pieces).

This is the situation shown in Diagram 1. Black rolls a two, a three, and a four. He captures the white piece on point 6. This way, he doesn't risk being captured. He could have captured the piece at point 9, but in doing so would have left two unguarded pieces on points 6 and 9 (Diagram 1).

An Unfortunate Roll

2 If two pieces are placed on a single point, they can block the opponent, because he cannot use this point as a rest or an endpoint to his roll. Because of the obligation to use all points contained in a roll, a block can be very frustrating. The Emperor Zeno knew this well. The situation shown in Diagram 2 is culled from a game played around 480. White rolled a two, a five, and a six. He couldn't move his pieces

from point 6 because he was blocked by enemy pieces on points 8, 11, and 12. His piece on point 9, meanwhile, is blocked by the black pieces on points 11, 14, and 15. As a result of these obstacles, Zeno was forced to separate the three pairs (at 10, 19, and 20). He moved a piece from 20 to 22—the only possible moves. The result is that, in the end, the eight pieces were left in a weak position (Diagram 2).

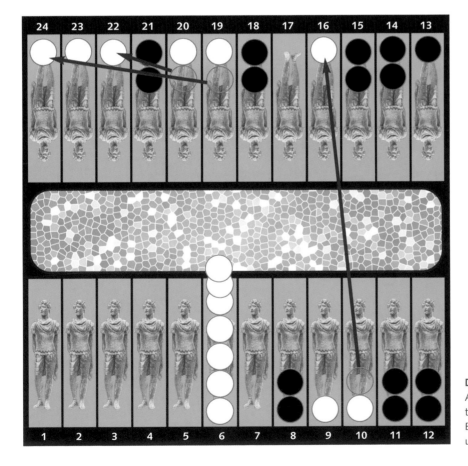

White's roll

DIAGRAM 2:
An unfortunate roll. White rolls two, five, and six. As a result of Black's blockades, his pieces end up in a precarious position.

Etching from the cover of Georg Bauer's book *Arten der Spiele*, Vienna, 1756.

Rules:
Preliminaries

Bashne is played on a grid of eight-by-eight squares. Players put the board between them so that each has a white square on his right-hand corner. During the game, players must sometimes distinguish one piece from the rest. Russian players traditionally marked the piece with chalk. You can also play with pieces already marked on one side, so when the time comes, all you have to do is turn the piece over. Thanks to this trick, salta pieces are well suited to playing this interesting game. Players begin by using the pieces with the unmarked side faceup. When the mark is

---

STRATEGY

When trying to provoke the player into capturing one of your pieces, it's important to keep in mind that he is not obliged to do so. He will capture only if the reward is sufficiently great.

needed, they simply flip the piece over. First they decide who will use which color, and then they divide up the pieces. The pieces are placed on the dark squares on the three lines closest to each player: a player puts his pieces on lines one through three, and his opponent puts his on lines six through eight. The rules of Bashne do not say which player starts, so the players decide this for themselves (Diagram A).

The Movement of the Pieces

By turn, players move their pieces one square forwards or backwards. The pieces may move only through the dark squares, and therefore only diagonally. It is not permitted to jump over one's own pieces. From the movement of the pieces it can be deduced that on the first turn, players may choose among seven different moves.

A piece on a square surrounded by empty squares on all four sides can move in any of four directions (Diagram B).

Capturing Pieces

Bashne differs from most games in regard to how it treats captured pieces. The method of seizure in itself is quite typical: a piece jumps over an enemy piece and into a neighboring empty square. Obviously, the pieces continue moving along the dark squares, so they move and capture only in diagonal lines. Players can capture enemy pieces by jumping either forward or backward and can capture several pieces in a single turn. Capturing pieces is not mandatory, nor is carrying a multiple capture to its end.

When a piece jumps over an enemy piece, the former is called a "capture piece." The piece over which it jumps is an "eliminated piece." The special thing about eliminated pieces in Bashne is that they are not removed from the board; instead, they are placed beneath the capture piece. They become pris-

oners, so to speak, of the capture piece, which now carries them along. The prisoner piece and the capture piece together form a tower. A tower consists of at least two pieces, though in theory, there is no limit to how many pieces can be stacked atop one another. When a single piece captures three enemy pieces in a single turn, for instance, together they become a four-piece tower. Then, the tower can make another multiple capture, rapidly increasing the number of pieces. The capture piece is always on top, and the color of the piece indicates to whom it belongs (Diagram C).

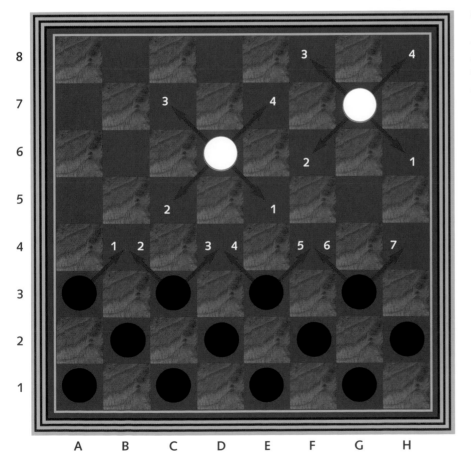

DIAGRAM B:
How the pieces move. In each turn, players move their pieces diagonally either one step forward or one step backward, always along the black squares.

A King

Just as in a game of straight checkers, in Bashne, pieces can also become kings when they reach the opponent's end of the board: Black can earn a king by reaching line 8, and White can earn a king by reaching line 1. A king is distinguished from other pieces by a mark. Suppose one of Black's pieces lands on one of the four dark squares in row 8. The piece isn't crowned by putting another piece on top of it but by flipping the piece over so it shows its mark. A tower is promoted to king in the same fashion, so the top piece in a tower is marked. Kings have greater mobility than ordinary pieces or towers. They move in the same direction, either forward or backward diagonally, but can move across an unlimited number of free spaces. In accordance with their mobility, they can move several spaces in a single turn, and "make a run for it" without having to stop on a square immediately adjacent to a captured piece. A king can also capture towers this way. Of course, a king can also make several captures in a single turn. In this case, the player must remove the mark from the piece at the top of the stack, turning it over and placing it under the capture piece (Diagram E).

DIAGRAM E:
A king. Towers and individual pieces are promoted to kings in the final line of the opponent's half of the board. Kings can move diagonally across an unlimited number of free squares.

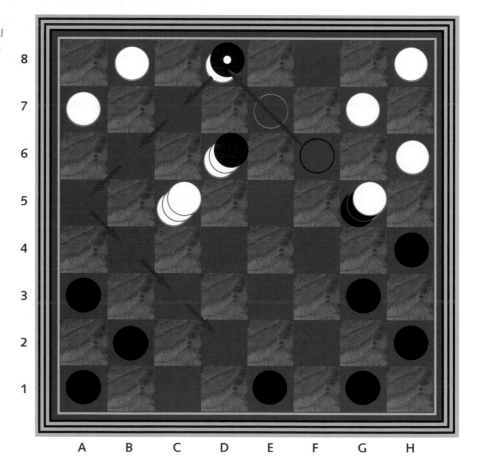

Detail of a 1652 painting by Michael Sweerts (1618–1664). During this era, checkers was a very popular game throughout the European continent.

The Winner

The winner is the player who captures all his opponent's pieces or blocks them so that none can move any further. A combination of these two results is also possible. Often, players decide beforehand that the final result will not be determined until they finish playing ten games. After each game, the winner gets a point for winning the game by forming towers and blocking his opponent's pieces, and two points if he wins exclusively by building towers. The final winner is the player who after ten matches has the most points.

The First Match

Players in a game of Bashne enjoy an unprecedented freedom to move around the board and to plan their attack. For each turn they have many choices, which will undoubtedly prove disconcerting to the beginner. In practice, you see inexperienced players start a match with no clear strategy in mind. This is a way of learning the game through trial and error. After studying the situations described below, a player may begin his first match better prepared. The best way to follow this match is to repeat it step by step on a board from the beginning.

A Cautious Beginning

1 Two beginners are playing a game of Bashne. Black has made the first move, and each player has now made ten. The position of the pieces in Diagram 1 implies that neither player has captured any pieces so far, because twenty-four single pieces remain on the board. This tells us that the players are maneuvering very carefully. In any match, the moment inevitably arrives when one player makes a move that allows him to capture a piece. In this game, that moment has just arrived. It's Black's turn, and any forward move he makes will give White a chance to capture. Black could avoid capture by moving one of his pieces back, a play he could then reverse in his next move, in hopes of forcing White to put one of his pieces in a vulnerable position. But White could also follow the same strategy, which would quickly force the game into a draw. Moving a piece forward and then back in this way rarely makes a match very interesting and should be avoided if at all possible. Therefore, Black decides to

DIAGRAM 1:
A cautious beginning. No pieces are captured until the eleventh round. White captures the black piece on square G5, which was placed there intentionally by Black. Then, the black player liberates his captured piece and captures a white piece.

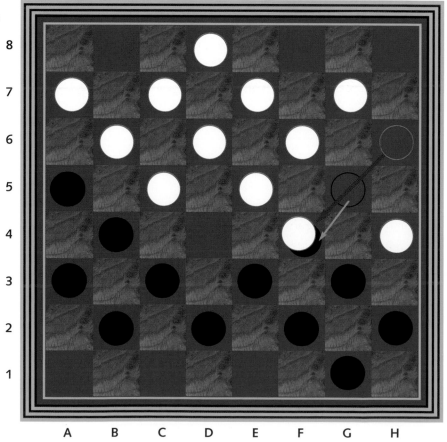

make a move forward and give his opponent the chance to capture. If he can, he will provoke his opponent into making a capture that ultimately benefits only him. When it is time to move forward, Black can choose among these options:

1. C3–D4
2. E3–D4
3. F4–G5

Options 1 and 2 lead to the same situation, and give White an opportunity to make a multiple capture that will result in White getting a king at squares C1 and E1, respectively, without Black being able to capture in return. This is clearly not Black's best move, so Black discards these two possibilities. The third option gives White a chance to capture a black piece, but Black can free that piece immediately by capturing the just-formed white tower. Even though White is under no duty to capture, he does so by moving H6–F4 (White could have moved forward with other pieces). These moves all result in Black forming a tower, but they also offer White the chance to capture the tower that has just been formed.

Instead, Black offers his opponent a piece, which confuses White, who captures the piece immediately. White has not foreseen the consequences of this capture, or at least, has forgotten that capture is not mandatory. As expected, Black liberates his captured piece from F4 in his twelfth move, by capturing squares E3 to G5. After this move by Black, there is a black tower on the board made up of two pieces. By making it appear that he was sacrificing a piece, Black actually gained one (Diagram 1).

Multiple Capture and the Threat of a King

2 From the way the game unfolds, it can be inferred that White is playing rather unimaginatively. So far, he has chosen the most predictable moves, making it easy for Black to set a trap for him. It is also clear that White rarely passes up a chance to capture a piece. An almost inevitable result of playing this way is that in the seventeenth round, White makes an unreflective move that costs him two pieces. He moves his piece from C5 to D4, which gives his opponent the chance to make a multiple capture.

Black takes advantage of this opportunity. He uses his tower to jump over his opponent's pieces in D4 and B6, landing in row 7. After this capture, Black's tower now consists of five pieces. He is also only one space away from row 8, where Black can crown his pieces and turn them into kings. White sees the danger of a black king and moves his piece from C7 to B8, immobilizing the white piece. As soon as White moves it from there a few moves later, Black will move his tower from A7 to B8 and promote it to king. Black can try to reach one of the other squares in row 8 with his tower (Diagram 2).

DIAGRAM 2:

A multiple capture and the threat of a king. White's move from C5 to D4 allows Black to make a multiple capture in his eighteenth move. He ends up with a four-piece tower in a square on row 7, only one space away from the row on which he can crown his piece. White tries to stop Black from gaining a king by moving his piece to B8.

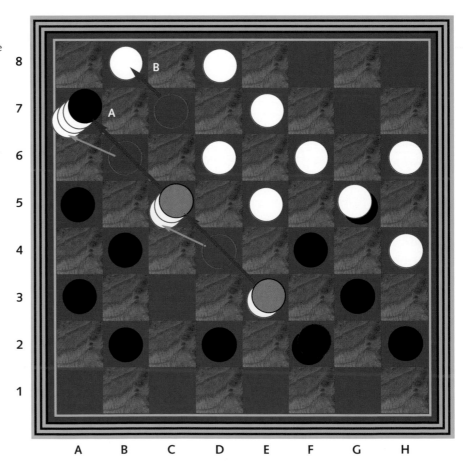

A Black King

3 The previous section described Black trying to gain a king by moving his tower from A7 to a square other than B8. Thanks to an inattentive moment by White, Black sees a chance to promote one of his pieces in another square. In his nineteenth move, Black sets a trap for White by moving his piece from B4 to C5. White doesn't notice this, and takes the black piece on C5 with his piece from D6. By doing this he opens the way for Black, who can now move his piece from F4 to F8, making a double capture. There, he can also promote his tower to a king. He marks the piece on top of the two white pieces by turning it around. The board, meanwhile, is much emptier than before. This is only logical, given that twenty-four of the pieces are scattered over a much smaller number of squares than they were in the opening position. At this stage, the following pieces are on the board: a king with three pieces, a tower with four pieces, two towers with two pieces each, a liberated pair of black pieces, and eleven single pieces (Diagram 3).

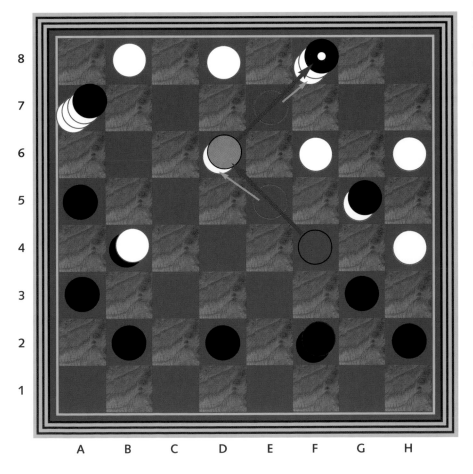

DIAGRAM 3:
Thanks to a moment's distraction by White, Black gains a king, aided by a multiple capture.

In the illustration above, King Francis I of France plays chess with Marguerite of Navarre in 1504. Chess is a war game, and like Rithmomachia, was very popular among gentlemen.

Arno Borst

In the November 1986 edition of the magazine *Faz*, Arno Borst wrote of Rithmomachia: "The war game of numbers taught players a way to treat numbers, people, and things that was described in the medieval philosophy of Boethius. Groups of players were taught by way of Latin manuals with charts and diagrams that the true unity of the quantifiable is never manifested on Earth, and can acquire its form only in conditions of perfect equality. The discussion of equality would prove polemical, and irremediably creates an inequality, but it can give birth to a beautiful symmetry or harmony. Considering that this symmetry does not arise alone, and is never permanent, man must always value inequality anew, according to its inner structure, according to its relationship with the intersection of numbers and its utility in the calculation of long figures. This mathematical game attempted to explain this through the relationship between numbers, natural phenomena, using what Burckhardt called 'symbolic behavior.' Musical intervals and chords were also considered, as were geometric shapes, and all of natural science. Rithmomachia forced its players to be exacting and loyal to the rules, to fantasy and experimentation, to agreement and concentration. Because the law of the logical ordering of numbers and the natural birth and development of combat was nothing more than the development of a blessed life."

Rebirth

Today there is little interest in Rithmomachia, which is played on a sort of double chessboard. But the principles on which it is based undoubtedly make this game of interest to mathematically inclined minds. In Germany, it is understood that this game is well suited to fans of strategy-based board games. In 1987, Detlef Ilmen developed a practicable version of this age-old game, which was marketed by a Munich company.

Playing Rithmomachia

If there is any centuries-old game that has been forgotten and deserves rebirth in the modern age, it is undoubtedly the ingenious game of Rithmomachia, the "battle of numbers." Although it was quite popular during the Middle Ages—especially among rulers, mathematicians, and distinguished intellectuals—the game was reserved for a small elite. Rithmomachia is a great challenge for young and old alike, whether they are beginners or experts. Every piece has a number, which the players use to make their calculations. These are simple operations, but if a person has trouble doing sums in his head, he may use a calculator. The object of this exclusive game is to capture the opponent's pieces. The answers to questions of how many pieces and which pieces to capture depends upon what the players have agreed to at the start of the game. Rithmomachia players may choose among eight possible final goals. The first five are appropriate for beginners and experienced players alike; owing to the gradual increase in the game's difficulty, the final three are reserved for expert players.

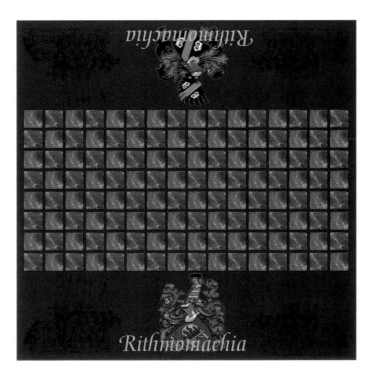

To play the intriguing game of Rithmomachia, all you need is a board and pieces of a single color for each player. The pieces are round, triangular, and square, while Black plays with one piece fewer than his opponent.

Players	Requirements
2	Rithmomachia board
	29 white pieces
Average duration	(10 round, 10 triangular, 9 square)
45 minutes	28 black pieces
	(9 round, 10 triangular, 9 square)
Category	
strategy; war game	

The Objectives of Rithmomachia

Of the eight possible objectives in Rithmomachia, the first five are suited to both beginners and more experienced players. A player who wins a game using one of these first five objectives has won what is called a "common victory." The similarity between the various objectives of the game is that in all of them, the goal is to capture the enemy's pieces using the permitted methods. The object chosen determines which pieces, and how many of them, must be captured, and it decides which strategy must be used by the player in question. These are the (Latin) names of the five objectives which, if attained, constitute a common victory: *corpore*, *bonis*, *lite*, *honore*, and *honore liteque*. A detailed description of each is provided below.

DIAGRAM I:

Capturing a pyramid. The piece at the bottom of the white pyramid has been eliminated. Black attacks, threatening the triangular piece with his number 16 by ambush. White does not want to lose his pyramid, so he offers Black his round number 16 piece. Black accepts the offer.

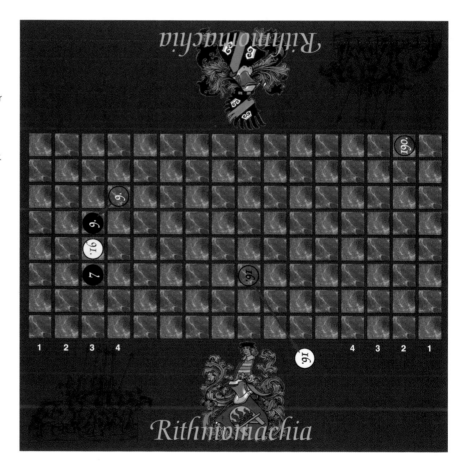

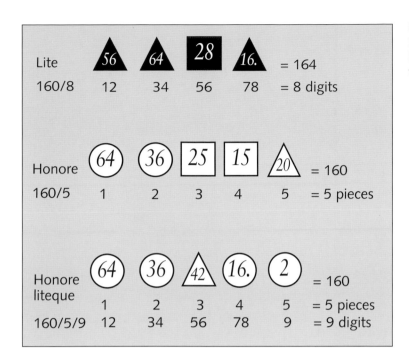

DIAGRAM J:
Lite, honore, and honore
liteque. Examples of common
victories.

Corpore and Bonis

Corpore is the only final objective for which players do not need to keep in mind the numbers marked on the pieces. It is also the ideal object for players who are starting out. Before starting a corpore game, players must agree that victory will go to the first player who eliminates a given number of enemy pieces—twenty, for example. It is important to decide beforehand whether the pyramid will count as a single piece or as the number of pieces it comprises.

If the game is played with the final object of bonis, then one must speak of sums. Players agree that the game will come to an end when the sum of the numbers on one of the player's captured pieces reaches a given total. A common bonis total is 160. It isn't necessary to reach exactly the chosen sum. The first to reach or exceed the agreed-upon total wins.

Lite, Honore, and Honore Liteque

In a game of Rithmomachia where the final goal is lite, players are required to make many calculations

> ### TIP
>
> For the first few games of Rithmomachia, it is advisable to choose the final goal of corpore. You can start thinking about the next challenge, bonis, once you have gained a better understanding of the game.

(feel free to use a calculator!). The chances of reaching this goal depend on the numbers on the captured pieces, as is the case with bonis, and on the total number of digits on the eliminated pieces. Players must agree on both before starting the game. With respect to the sum of the numbers on the eliminated pieces, players can agree that it will be 160 or higher. They also choose a low number, such as 8, to indicate the maximum number of digits that can appear on the group of eliminated pieces with which the players reach their final result. Based on these agreements, the total of 160 can result from a sum of, for example, four numbers with two digits each, or two numbers with three digits and one number with two digits. The number 8 is established as mandatory, so no other number is allowed.

The final object of honore also forces players to make calculations, for it is based on a combination of the number of eliminated pieces and on the numbers engraved on those pieces. Starting, once again, from a final total of 160 points, players agree on the added condition that this sum must be reached with, say, five captured pieces. When one of the players reaches 160 points with the numbers on six of his pieces, he has not earned an honore. In that case, he must keep playing until he has at least 160 points using the numbers on only five captured pieces.

The fifth possible object for a common victory in Rithmomachia is also the most complicated. The final goal of honore liteque combines the three preceding goals. This means that before starting a game of Rithmomachia, players must agree on the following three things:

- the object to be reached;
- the number of pieces with which that object must be reached;
- the maximum number of digits in the eliminated pieces with which the object is to be reached.

Attaining an honore liteque is no mean feat. One possible end to this object is earning 160 points with five captured pieces in which are a total of nine digits (Diagram J).

The Winner

The first player to reach the final agreed-upon goal wins. Rithmomachia is a game that lasts an average of forty-five minutes. During this time, players must be able to maintain their concentration on the game. Therefore, when the game ends, a new one does not start up right away. Two people who play together regularly may decide that the winner receives a point and that the final victory will go to the first player to reach a total of ten points.

Rithmomachia: Part 2

After the preceding description of the rules of the fascinating game of Rithmomachia, and of its five goals, known as "common victories," many readers will already be familiar with its theory, and perhaps have even ventured to play a first match. If these readers now proceed to a second match, it will be clear that this intriguing game has captured their interest. It is fairly certain that, in the months, perhaps even years to come—and possibly for the rest of their lives—these players will often be occupied with the game. Fans of Rithmomachia want as much information as they can get about every facet of the game. Therefore, this chapter is devoted to the in-depth theory of the game, describing ideas and relationships not discussed previously. It also treats of the three final objectives, which have not yet been discussed. If a player reaches one of these, he will have attained a great victory. Attaining such a goal is no "common victory," as evidenced by the lovely names given to these three goals, which each contain the word "victoria," or triumph. Although sometimes the description may seem somewhat mathematical, that does not mean that only a person with solid math skills can attain a glorious victory. The use of a modern device such as a calculator to play this Medieval game is, of course, permitted.

Rithmomachia players in the late fifteenth century. Woodcarving from the book *Récréations et Passe-Temps,* published in 1835 by Librairie Hachette & Cie, Paris.

The Square Pieces in the First Row

The value of the square pieces in the first row are also related to the other pieces. At first glance the relationship may seem hard to find, but if you study the corresponding mathematical formula, you will see that this is not the case:

$$((2n+1) / (n+1)) \, s$$

The letter "n" in the formula stands for the number of the round piece in row 4 as it relates to a square in row 1; for White, this means, for example, that the following pieces are aligned:

A1 and C4

B1 and D4

G1 and E4

H1 and F4

The "s" in the formula represents the value of the piece or the pyramid in the player's second row of the same column (A, B, G, or H) as the square in row 1. You can also see that $s = (2n+1) \times (n+1)$, and that the value of the square pieces in the first row equals the square of $2n + 1$. For example, if one starts with the number 25 on the white square in A1, then "n" is the number 2 on the piece on square C4, and the "s" is the number 15 of the square piece on A2. Observe what happens if these numbers are plugged into the formula: $((2 \times 2)+1 / (2+1)) \times 15 = (5/3) \times 15 = 25$ (Diagram D).

Glorious Victories

Even if the same final goal is always chosen, Rithmomachia remains a fascinating game. Of course, the challenge becomes greater if the player studies the final goal carefully and then moves on to a more difficult one. Each final objective is different and calls for a distinct way of playing, which means a change of strategy for every goal. A player who has sufficiently perfected his common victories can go one step further and try to earn a glorious victory, which comprises three different final goals, of which the last is the hardest. Earning a glorious victory is therefore a milestone in the career of a Rithmomachia

player. The names of the final goals within this category are Victoria Magna, Victoria Mayor, and Victoria Excelentísima. All of them are based on arithmetic, geometry, or a series of harmonious numbers, and require a great deal of calculation. The following is true of all three final goals in this category:

- A winning series must be arranged in a straight line, in rows on your opponent's half of the board; and

- The winning series must contain one of your opponent's pieces.

Regardless of the final goal the players choose, they must imagine which digits will constitute the winning series they will try to form. If a player has a certain series in mind, he must make sure that there are actually pieces with those numbers on the board. Players should not forget that each series must contain one piece from the opponent's set.

A Few Mathematical Concepts

Players who choose a glorious victory as their goal should have a good grasp of mathematics. Since the goal consists of forming a series of numbers that exist in an arithmetical or geometrical relationship, or a harmonic series of a numbers, it is important to have consensus on the definition of these mathematical concepts. The following definitions are offered for those who may need a quick refresher course. An *arithmetical series* is a line of numbers in which exist the same difference between any two consecutive numbers. For example, the series 2, 3, 4 is an arithmetical series because the difference between one and two is the same as the difference between three and four.

A *geometric series* exists when the next number in a series is obtained by multiplying the previous number by another number. For example, the series 2, 4, 8 is a geometric series, because each number in the series is obtained by multiplying the previous number by two.

Finally, a *harmonic series* is a sequence of numbers in which every three consecutive numbers are harmonically proportionate. Thus, if a, b, and c are harmonious, they can be described as the proportion: a/c = (b–a) (c–b). If one substitutes actual numbers for these variables, one gets a series such as: 6/12 = (8–6) / (12–8), or 6/12 = 2/4. The relationship between the two pairs of numbers is equal. Six has the same relationship to twelve as two does to four. The first number in each case equals half the second, so it can be said that there is a harmonic relationship between them (Diagram E).

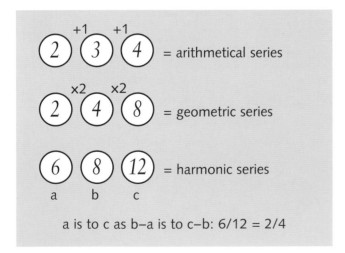

a is to c as b−a is to c−b: 6/12 = 2/4

DIAGRAM E:
A few mathematical concepts. Examples of an arithmetical series, a geometric series, and a harmonic series of numbers.

Victoria Magna

The simplest to attain of the glorious victories is the Victoria Magna. The goal is to place three pieces in a row so that the numbers on the pieces form an arithmetical, geometric, or harmonic series. The pieces in Rithmomachia can form forty-one different arithmetical series, eighteen geometric series, and seventeen harmonic series, but these are not evenly distributed between the two colors. With respect to arithmetical series, White has more possibilities than Black, but the latter has more opportunities to form geometric series. Both players have the same options for forming a harmonic series.

Victoria Mayor

If a player wants to obtain a glorious victory by means of the Victoria Mayor, he must try to get a combination of two of the three series of possible numbers. This means he must form a row of pieces with one of the three possible combinations: arithmetical and geometric, geometric and harmonic, or harmonic and arithmetical. The line must consist of four pieces, which must be situated on squares on the other player's half of the board. Two of the four pieces in the row must belong to a numerical series, and two must belong to the other chosen progression. Altogether there are sixty-one possible ways of obtaining a Victoria Mayor.

For example, White can obtain a Victoria Mayor by putting four pieces with the numbers 2, 3, 4, and 8 in a row in the middle of Black's side of the board. The numbers 2, 3, and 4 form an arithmetical series and 2, 4, and 8 are a geometric progression. The pieces with the numbers 2, 4, and 8 are white. White satisfies the condition that one of the pieces in the series must belong to his opponent, for the number 3 piece is black.

Victoria Excelentísima

Attaining a glorious victory through a Victoria Excelentísima, the most complex victory in the game, is the dream of every Rithmomachia enthusiast. The task of attaining this goal consists of forming a row of four pieces in such a way that the numbers within cover all three possible numerical progressions. This means that the row must consist of a series of numbers that are related to one another arithmetically, geometrically, and harmonically. There are only six possible solutions for a Victoria Excelentísima:

2–3–4–6
4–6–8–12
7–8–9–12
4–6–9–12
3–5–15–25
12–15–16–20

Taking the first combination as an example, the arithmetical series is 2–3–4, where the difference between consecutive numbers in the series is constant. The geometric series begins with the numbers 2 and 4; and the harmonic series is 3–4–6, because 3 is to 6 as 1(4–3) is to 2(6–4).

Evaluation

Each final goal in Rithmomachia is a different challenge and calls for a unique approach. If you choose a more complex goal each time, the goal becomes progressively more difficult, with fewer possible solutions. The winning series in both Victoria Excelentisima and Victoria Mayor consists of a row of four pieces (Diagram F).

A thirteenth-century knight. On their travels to the Middle East, knights would often play Rithmomachia to relax.

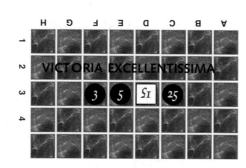

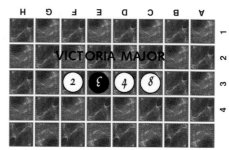

DIAGRAM F:
Victoria Excelentísima and Victoria Mayor.

STRATEGY

It's a good idea to try to figure out what kind of series your opponent is trying to form, and then try to stop him from doing so.

Rithmomachia: Part 3

After the exhaustive theoretical explanation in the previous sections, it is finally time to play a game of Rithmomachia. Up until now, the game has been all about good math skills. But during an actual match, players must also display other skills. Thus, it's advantageous, for instance, to be able to plan ahead and see several moves in advance; an ability to concentrate is also very useful. It may seem that playing Rithmomachia is a very serious, complicated matter. While it's true that the game is more or less complex depending on the final goal, the degree of diffi-culty is closely connected to the experience one acquires in the game. After all, the game develops gradually, starting with the easiest objective and moving toward the most advanced. Thus, everyone plays Rithmomachia with an attain-able goal. Regardless of the end the player aims for, attaining a longed-for victory is always enormously satisfying. Rithmomachia is, first and foremost, a fun and relaxing game, a way to spend a few pleasant hours. The more well-matched the players are, the more enjoyable it will be.

During the age of chivalry, families were distinguished by their coats of arms. Here can be seen the coat of arms of the Marquis of Castilleja del Campo, a knight of the Order of Santiago.

The First Match

The first situations described below are from a game of Rithmomachia played between two opponents. The players are fairly experienced with the goals of corpore and bonis, from the common victories set, so here they opt for the lite goal, which is somewhat more difficult. The task here is to capture the opponent's pieces and then add up the numbers on those pieces. The sum must equal the number agreed upon by the players before starting the game. An added condition is that the captured pieces, whose numbers are added together, must contain a given number of digits.

The players agree that there must be eight digits on the captured pieces, and the numbers on those pieces must add up to at least 160.

Preliminaries

After deciding on an objective, both players draw for the colors, to decide who will make the first move. Finally, they sit across from each other, in front of the narrow sides of the board, and place their pieces on the board in the opening position.

Before making his first move, White asks himself what the quickest way will be to reach the goal of lite. His opponent has five pieces with three-digit numbers. White decides to eliminate one of them. His goal is also to capture two pieces with two-digit numbers and one piece with a single digit. While White thinks this over, Black tries to plan his

> ### STRATEGY
>
> It is smart to try to capture using round pieces with single-digit numbers, using an attack. With this method of capture, a limited move is often sufficient, and it is always gratifying to capture a high-numbered piece with a low-numbered one.

strategy. He realizes that his opponent has only three pieces with three digits, so he decides it's a better idea to capture four pieces with two digits on each. Thus, without realizing it, both players decide to capture four of their opponent's pieces without settling on which ones they prefer.

The Opening Moves

1 In the opening position, White can reach only one black piece with a three-digit number: the 100 piece on square A14. Black's four other three-digit pieces are shielded by other pieces. Moving his number 15 piece from A2 two spaces forward, White captures the enemy piece in question through an encounter. This piece cannot move from its original position, because the adjacent squares are occupied, and it's against the rules to jump over other pieces, whether they are the same color or the opponent's. Therefore, White must start creating a space on the board in which to move, so he moves his triangle piece from A3 in a diagonal line to square D6.

Black is interested in White's double-digit pieces on F3, G3, and H3 but also needs more room to move his pieces freely. He moves out his round piece 3 from F13 in a diagonal line

In his second move, White moves forward with his plan, advancing his square number 15 piece from A2 to A6, while Black tries to gain more mobility for his pieces. In his third move, White moves forward again with number 15. Apparently, Black isn't interested in speculating about the motivation for White's move, because he has either failed to understand that he risks losing his triangular 100 piece—or doesn't care. He is too busy with his own plans and keeps expanding his piece's mobility. In his fourth move, White captures his first piece through an encounter; he does not move piece number 15, but instead removes Black's triangular 100 piece from the board. Black moves his triangular 36 piece, which he hopes to use later on to attack the white pyramid (Diagram 1).

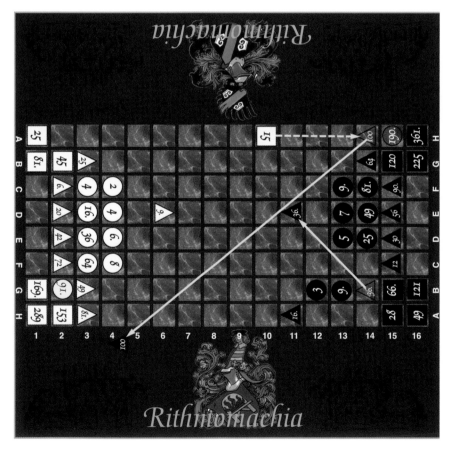

DIAGRAM 1:
Opening moves. White makes the first attack of the game in his fourth move. He captures Black's triangle at A14 through an encounter.

An Attack on a Pyramid

2 Now White must capture two of his opponent's two-digit pieces. He decides to focus on moving some of his pieces toward Black's half of the board, which serves a double purpose. First, he hopes to increase his chances of making an attack. By moving several of his pieces close to Black's, he will be able to capture them by ambush or siege, because these forms of capture require several pieces. Second, by advancing some of his pieces, White hopes to make the rest of his pieces more mobile.

Black has set his sights on the white pyramid. In his last two turns, he moved his number 36 triangle toward the pyramid, reaching White's square G5. Black thinks he will be able to capture the lowest piece in the pyramid, the number 36 square. He is forgetting that the pyramid can move like any one of the pieces it comprises, and since the pyramid has two triangles, it can move three spaces. This is enough for it to capture the black piece. Besides, this piece can also be captured by White's round number 8 piece at White's F4, which can meet Black's piece by moving one space diagonally. Black had good intentions, but they resulted in his capture. With no effort at all, White captures the Black number 36 triangle by means of an encounter. Black should start considering his moves more carefully. For now, he has lost two pieces and has yet to capture any of his own. Like his opponent, Black now decides to move several of his pieces toward the opposite side of the board, beginning with the triangle from F15 to F12 (Diagram 2).

DIAGRAM 2:
An attack on the pyramid. Black wants to capture the lowermost piece in the white pyramid with his triangle at G5. He forgets that the pyramid also contains triangular pieces, which means it is White who will be carrying out this attack. Black decides to move several pieces forward.

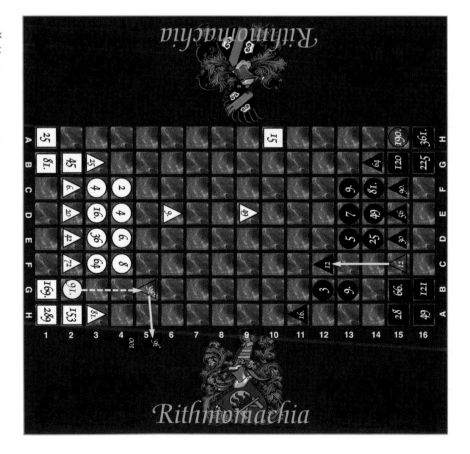

A Belated Encounter and an Attack

3 Both players have been busy for several turns moving their pieces toward their respective adversary's. Since the pieces are now far more spread out over the board, it has become harder to get an overview of the situation. It is of the utmost importance to study the situation on the board carefully before making any moves, because otherwise the players risk missing interesting opportunities. Thus, White realizes he can capture Black's round number 3 piece on G12 by meeting it with his triangle at D9. These two pieces have not moved for a long time and aren't separated by other pieces, but White just realized he can make this attack. Thanks to this belated encounter, he captures a third piece, which brings his total to 139 points and six digits.

STRATEGY

It's interesting to move several pieces toward the center of the board so they can aid one another in attacking the enemy.

Black prepares an attack, moving his piece from E13 one space forward. Thanks to this move, there are now five open squares between his piece and White's number 25 triangle in E6. He wants to capture this piece in his next move. White does not see this threat because he is busy counting points. With one more piece, he will have a double-digit number no lower than 21, and will attain lite. He moves his triangle forward from H3 to H6, and Black is able to make his first capture by attack (Diagram 3).

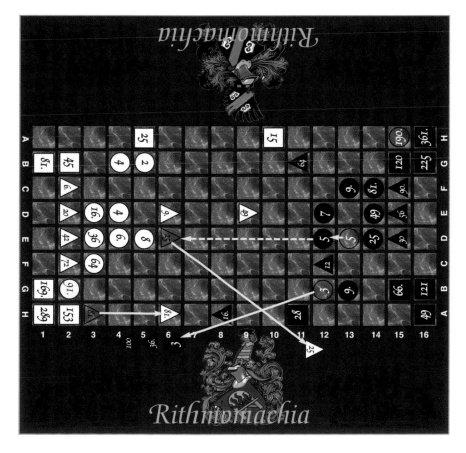

DIAGRAM 3:

A belated encounter and an attack. White realizes he can use his piece at D9 to encounter Black's piece at G12. Black captures his first piece by attacking the white triangle at E6.

black pieces with his own. The ideal setup is one in which a player can make several consecutive multiple attacks. White has made preparations for this, as seen in Diagram 2B. Moving his piece from the left-hand side of the board five spaces to the right, he captures a horizontal line of five black pieces. In his next turn, if he moves his piece four spaces down from the top of the board, he can make another multiple attack—this time on a vertical row of four black pieces. The ultimate success of attacks of this type depends on the opponent's moves (Diagram 2).

The Side Spaces

3 As mentioned, the corner spaces are particularly valuable. The next most important spaces are those along the sides of the board. To capture pieces, they have to be surrounded by one or more pieces on each end. Each piece can capture others either horizontally or vertically. But when a piece is in a space along one side of the board, it can capture in only one direction. It's important that Ming Mang players be aware of this. Diagram 3A shows a white piece on a space along one of the sides of the board with a black piece immediately next to it. It is clear that Black can capture a white piece only in a vertical line.

The importance of the spaces along the board's sides increases when, instead of a single piece, there is a whole row of them. The more pieces there are in that row, the more important the piece in the side space becomes, because the opponent simply cannot capture one of these lines. To do so, he would have to surround the row vertically, and this is impossible. Likewise, Black cannot capture the white row in Diagram 3C. In conclusion, players must always keep in mind the spaces along the sides of the board and make good use of them whenever possible.

DIAGRAM 3:
The spaces along the sides.

3A: Black can capture the white piece only by surrounding it vertically.

3B: White cannot surround this line because Black's end piece is on the margin of the board.

3C: Black cannot eliminate White's horizontal line.

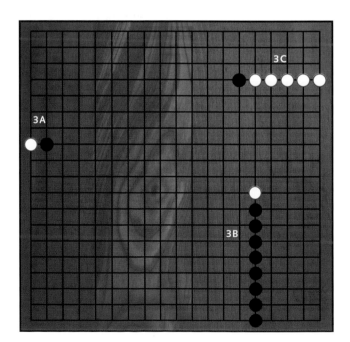

Tangram
History of the Game

◆ ◆ ◆

The game of Tangram, whose Chinese name is *qi qiao ban*, may have originated during the Eastern Zhou period (770–221 B.C.E.). The words *qi qiao* refer to the custom of passing a wire through a seven-eyed needle on the seventh day of the seventh month, in an effort to bring good fortune. The first books on Tangram were printed under the Jiaqing emperor (1796–1820). The first European publications are dated from 1805. Around 1900, puzzle fanatics Sam Loyd and Henry Dudeney unleashed a new Tangram craze with their series of books; in *The Eighth Book of Tan*, Loyd wrote that Li Hung Chan had demonstrated the Pythagorean theorem thousands of years earlier with the help of Tangrams.

In 1837, the educator Friedrich Fröebel (1782–1852) was the first to use wooden blocks in a children's game. He was in contact with the brothers Otto and Gustav Lilienthal when a certain Jan Daniël Georgens asked Gustav to illustrate books. A partnership was forged among these four men which culminated in their own issue of "Fröebel Toys." The Lilienthal brothers found the wooden blocks awkward and devised a more appropriate material in a mixture of clay, sand, and linseed oil. The first nine-piece set made from the new material appeared on the market under the name *Georgens*, accompanied by a pamphlet with examples.

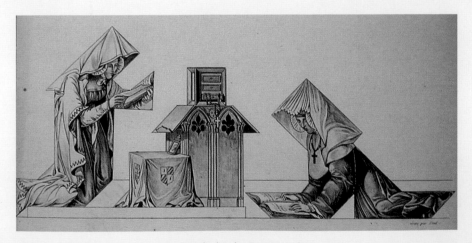

The art of designing without having studied it, by Eugene Isabey, 1818.

From Jerry Slocum's puzzle collection, a Hongmu ("sourwood") Tangram table from the mid-to-late Qing period.

Anker Blocks

Because of their high price, the Georgens blocks were not moving well. Desperate, Gustav Lilienthal and Jan Daniël Georgens asked that the German publisher F.A. Richter launch a great advertising campaign in his world-famous magazine, *Anker*. The shrewd Richter carried out the task, and at the same time made a bid for the company, which was drowning in debt. Upon taking ownership of the company, he changed the name of the blocks to Anker Blocks. He sent a number of them to a team of artists who came up with wonderful constructions using them.

Fined

Richter filed a claim against the toys' original inventors when they tried to reintroduce them into the market under a new name. Richter won the suit, and Gustav Lilienthal and Jan Daniël Georgens were fined 10,000 marks—an astronomical sum at the time. The first artificial stone Tangram puzzle, issued by Richter & Cie A.G. Rudolstadt, appeared in May of 1891 under the name "Anker Puzzle"; sixteen

other puzzles quickly followed. Under the inspired direction of Richter, Anker building blocks and Tangram puzzles spread rapidly throughout the world.

Famous Fans

Famous authors such as Lewis Carroll and Edgar Allan Poe enjoyed the game of Tangram, and tradition has it that during his exile, Napoleon, too, was an avid Tangram player. In nineteenth-century China, the game was so popular that the shape of the pieces was integrated into ordinary designs such as those adorning fountains, decorative lacquer boxes, and tables.

Jerry Slocum

Many puzzle collectors in the past have been fascinated by the Tangram phenomenon—when were the first puzzles made, by whom, and why? One of these staunch collectors is the puzzle historian, collector, and author, Jerry Slocum. Among the 25,000 puzzles in the collection in Slocum's Beverly Hills puzzle museum are a unique series of Tangrams: specimens from 1813 onward, with various different finishes, including ivory, mother of pearl, ceramic, and porcelain, alongside dozens of wood and plastic sets. In his collection, the best piece is considered to be a Hongmu Tangram table from the mid-to-late Qing period (1644–1911), of which there are probably only two in existence.

The Richter company's Kreuzzerbrecher, one of thirty-six designs the company issued alongside Tangram.

Playing Tangram

The centuries-old Chinese game of Tangram is also known as the "board of wisdom," "board of seven sages," or "game of shapes." The word tan means "seven" and refers to the seven pieces in the game. The words "sage" and "wisdom" connote a game for bright people. To know if one is a member of this group, he must accept the challenge of Tangram. This game is a challenge to the imagination and creativity of one or more players, who try to arrange the pieces so they reproduce certain shapes. After the explanation below, you may see why the name "game of shapes" points to the object of this game.

Tangram resembles Western puzzles in a way. The main difference is that Tangram offers players countless possibilities. Owing to the enormous popularity of this game, there have been many attempts to market similar puzzles, but none has matched the elegance and simplicity of Tangram. Tangram is not only a delightful children's game but also a surprising mental exercise, a relaxing pastime as well as a complex test of a player's creativity.

A Tangram booklet from 1814 with an ivory cover and silk pages.

Players	Requirements
unlimited	one or more Tangram sets
Average duration	
variable	
Category	
skill; dissection puzzle	

Rules:
Preliminaries

Tangram can be played in one of two ways. The first consists of forming existing shapes. More than 2,000 kinds of puzzles have been published, and there must be thousands more that have never been recorded. With a bit of fantasy, humor, and determination, players can reproduce countless patterns and shapes, such as animal silhouettes, objects, dolls, caricatures, etc. The pages that follow show only a few of these. If you are unable to replicate any of these, the solutions are included at the end.

The other possibility is to design figures of one's own. If you let your imagination run wild, you are sure to come up with some interesting new shapes. One way to record puzzles you yourself have discovered is to trace them with a pencil.

TIP

You can share your most interesting shapes with Tangram-loving friends and acquaintances around the world by fax.

Tangram can be played in solitaire, but one can also introduce a competitive element to the game, whereby several players try to construct certain shapes as quickly as possible. The first player to solve a given puzzle wins.

The Bases of Tangram

It does not matter whether you make up your own designs or try to reproduce existing forms, whether you play alone or with a friend—the rules are always the same. A Tangram set consists of seven pieces, or *tans*. The square can be thought of as the basic shape among the seven pieces. The pieces are usually put away arranged in a square.

When assembling figures, you must always remember the following rules: each figure must consist of seven *tans* laid flat. The *tans* must be placed side by side and must never overlap (Diagram A).

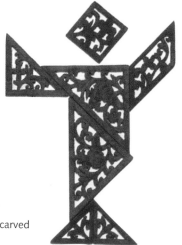

A figure assembled from a carved wooden Tangram set.

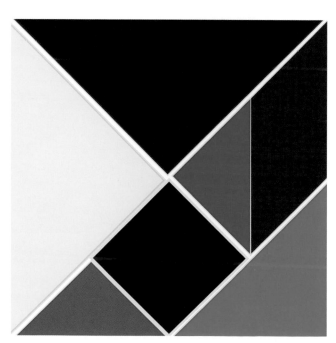

DIAGRAM A:
The basic configuration of Tangram.

Puzzles

The following pages are full of puzzles. If you are the sporting kind, try not to look at the solutions on the last two pages.

Chinese Tangram characters
qi qiao ban (*ch'i ch'io pan*).

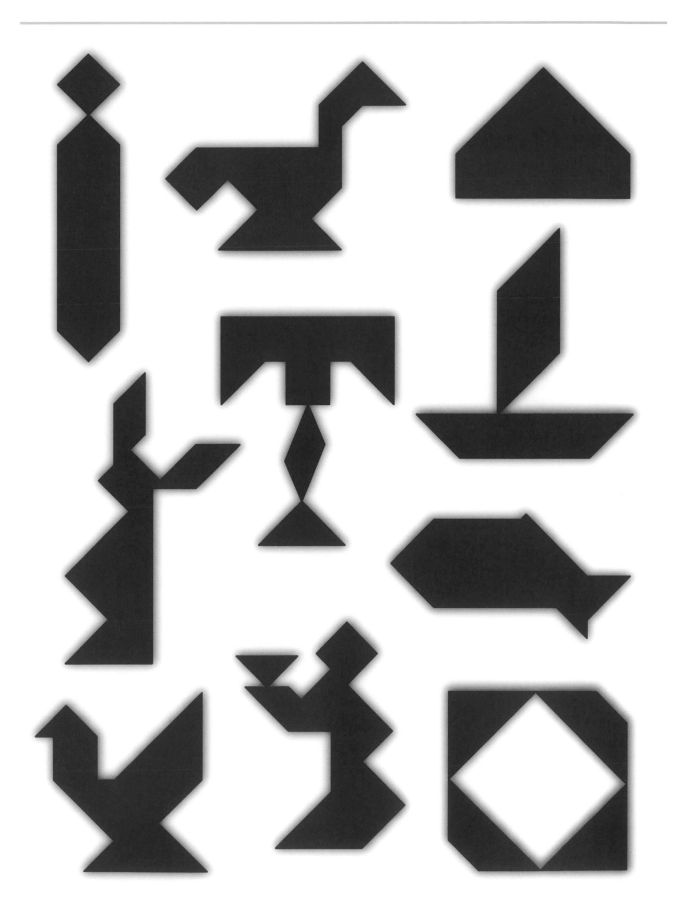

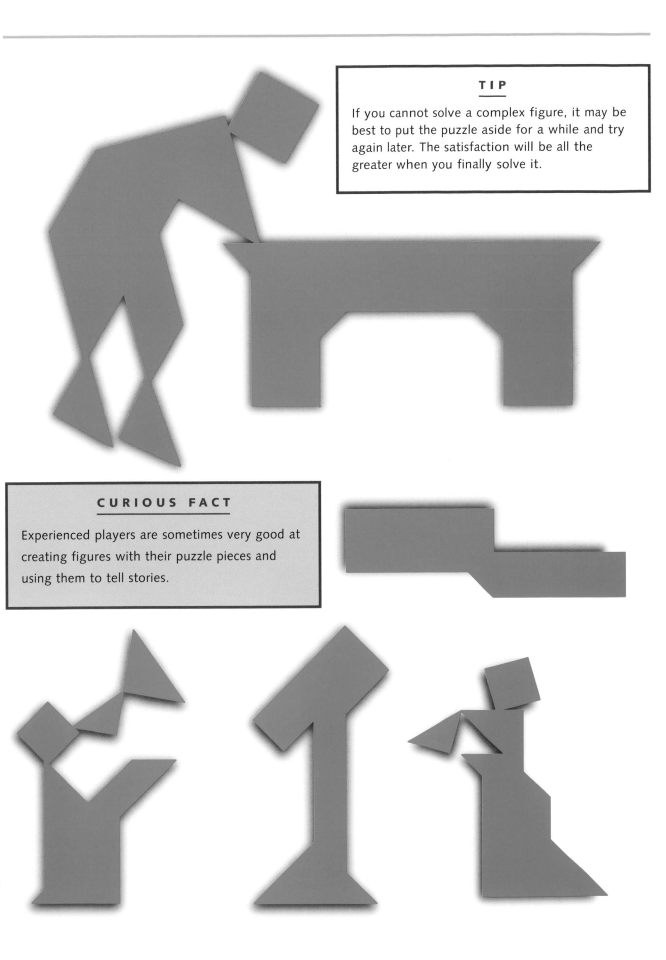

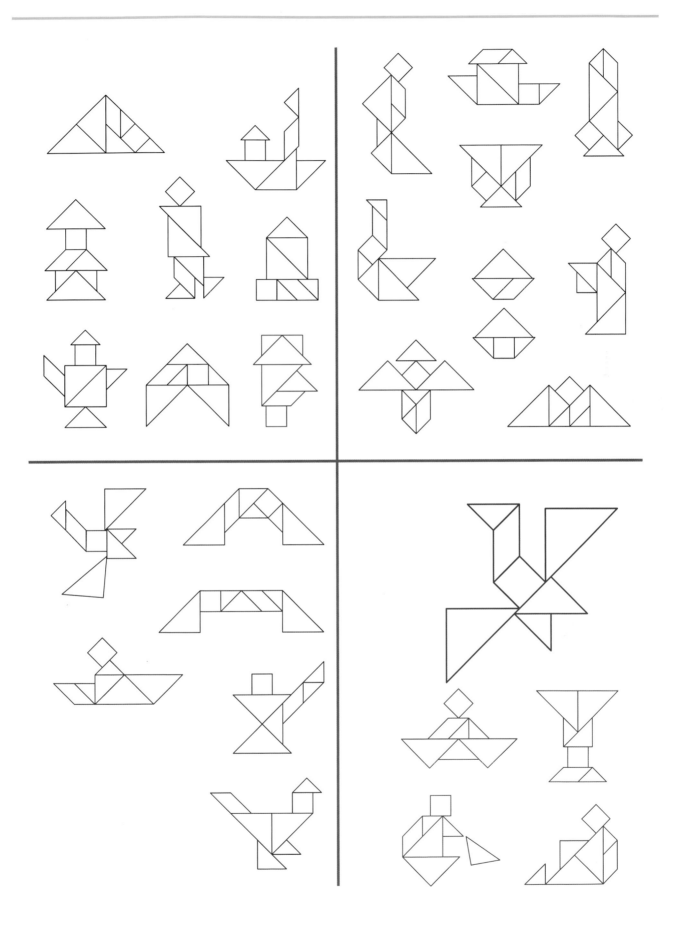

Yut
History of the Game
◆ ◆ ◆

Historians and games experts alike agree that Yut, also romanized as *nyout*, originated in Korea. There is no consensus, however, as to when this racing game originated. R.C. Bell, Giampaolo Dossena, and Stewart Culin claim that Yut has been played since the very foundation of the Korean kingdom in 1122 B.C.E. If so, Yut would be an ancestor of many board games, including pachisi, patolli, and even chess. Harold Murray believed this claim to be unfounded, and that no one knows for sure how old this game is. It is true that no ancient sources remain, and the first traces of this game date from the nineteenth century. However, according to Culin, some of the similarities between Yut and a third-century Chinese game of prophecy suggest that the Korean game is roughly the same age.

In Korea, Yut was actually used for several centuries for divination. The spaces on the board were marked with special symbols. Boards have also been found with symbols that tell stories from the Chinese Han dynasty (202 B.C.E. to 220 C.E.). Even in contemporary South Korea, Yut sticks are tossed once a year to attain a glimpse into the future. In Seoul, you can find books describing all the possible combinations and their meanings.

Yut players in Korea
(*Culin, 1898*).

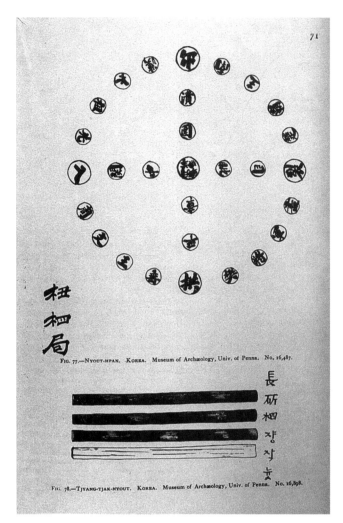

A page from the book *Chess and Playing Cards* by Stewart Culin, 1898. Culin was the first researcher to write about Yut.

The Throwing Sticks

The word *Yut* refers to wood shaped like a spoon—the tossing sticks that are part of the game. The Yut sticks are flat and white on one side, rounded and black on the other. Because players of old made their own sticks (of several types of wood), the sticks were often slightly different sizes. They were always tossed together in the same manner to prevent the players from influencing the results. Yut sticks typically measured about 2 inches (5 cm) in diameter and were about 12 inches (30 cm) long.

From Korea to North America

The most remarkable feature of Yut is the shape of the board: a series of circles along the outside forming a circle, with a cross inside it. This kind of game board is very unusual, and is found elsewhere only in Mexico and Guatemala. For some researchers, findings from the Aztec and Mayan eras prove that this type of game traveled from northeast Asia to North America. One example found in North America is a Mayan game from the seventh century C.E. Inside a temple in the city of Palenque, the Mexican archeologist Alberto Ruiz found a flat stone engraved with the original Mayan game. The stone is dated from the year 800. In Chichen Itza, Yucatán, a game board was found scratched into the lime on an embankment in a marketplace, bearing an undeniable resemblance to the Yut board. In the sixteenth century, the Spaniards made reference to a game called *patolli*. The board for this game also bears a remarkable resemblance to that of Yut.

Playing Yut

The kingdom of Korea was founded in the year 1122 B.C.E., by which time Korean civilization was already well developed. One of its fruits is the game Yut, which is especially popular in modern-day South Korea, and is also known as *cheok-sa* or *sa-hee*. This fascinating racing game belongs to the "cross and circle" family of games, which has existed over many centuries with little change. The object of the game is to move pieces through the entire course marked on the board; the first player to do so is the winner. The throwing sticks decide how many spaces a player may move his piece. But Yut is not merely a game of chance, for it also appeals to the player's strategic ability and creativity.

This game calls for a Yut board and up to sixteen pieces of four different colors.

Players	Requirements
2 or 3	Yut board
	4 each, white, black, red,
Average duration	green pieces
20 minutes	4 throwing sticks
Category	
racing; cross and circle	

Rules:
Preliminaries

The Dablot Prejjesne board is a grid of five-by-six squares. Each of these thirty squares is crisscrossed by two diagonal lines, forming seventy-two points of intersection. The pieces sit on these points, which from now on will be referred to as "spaces." The white army consists of twenty-eight Laplanders, one Lapp prince, and one Lapp king. White go pieces are recommended to represent the Laplanders. The Lapp prince is larger than the other pieces. The best way to represent the prince is with a white poker chip. For the Lapp king, a yellow pawn is recommended. The other player controls twenty-eight peasants, one landowner, and the landowner's son. The twenty-eight peasants are represented by black go pieces; a black poker chip stands for the landowner's son, and the red pawn represents the landowner. You can also use pieces from other games as long as the different types are clearly distinguishable. After deciding which

player will be on which side, players divide up the pieces and sit before the board. For greater clarity, the spaces in the diagrams to follow are numbered from 1 to 72, starting at the bottom right-hand corner and ending on the upper left. In the opening position, the Laplanders fill the spaces numbered 1 through 28; the Lapp prince is in space 33 and the king is in 39. The peasants fill the spaces numbered 45 to 72; the landowner is on 34; and the landowner's son is on 40. Players draw for the first move, then take their respective turns (Diagram A).

VARIATION

Dablot Prejjesne can be timed. Players agree that the winner will be the player who has captured or blocked the most enemy pieces within, say, fifteen minutes.

DIAGRAM A:
A Dablot Prejjesne board with the pieces in the opening position.

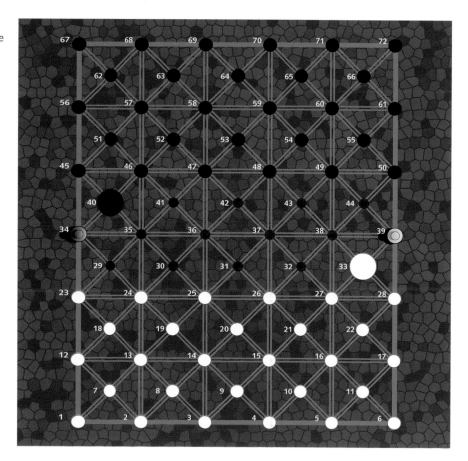

How the Pieces Move

Each piece has exactly the same mobility as every other. That is, there is no difference between how a Laplander moves and how the landowner's son or the king moves. The pieces move along the lines on the board. Players take turns moving one of their pieces horizontally, vertically, or diagonally. All the pieces can move backward as well as forward. One condition, however, is that they must always land on an empty space, because there can never be more than one piece on a single space. The number of possible options for moving a piece therefore depends on its position on the board. If you look at the possible moves for a piece from different positions on the board, you will see that the maximum number of possible moves is eight and the minimum is three (Diagram B).

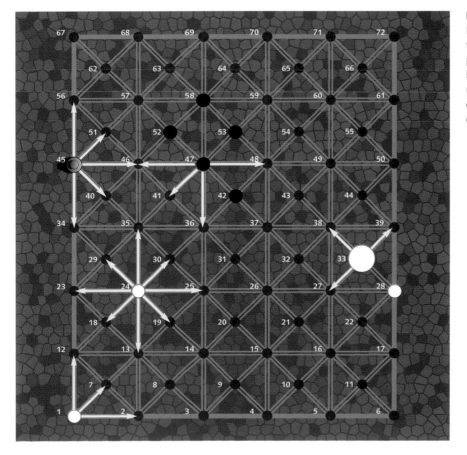

DIAGRAM B:
How the pieces move. Players take turns moving one of their pieces along the lines on the board and into a free space. The number of possible moves depends on the piece's position on the board.

A group of people play a game of Chinese dominoes somewhere in China. They are using "money cards," a precursor to paper money. The dots on the cards match the dots in Chinese dominoes *(Photo: Pim Smit, Amsterdam)*.

The Winner

The winner is the player who finishes with the highest number of points. The game ends when the player whose turn it is cannot add any dominoes to the table because he has none left. At this juncture, players count up the total value of their respective winning combinations. Usually the players agree that the winner in the first match makes the first move in the next. Often, players have agreed beforehand to play a given number of matches (five, for example). The winner is the player with the most points at the end of the last match.

The First Match

After reading the rules of the fascinating game named Tsung Shap, it becomes clear that this game offers an interesting combination of calculation, concentration, and luck. With each move, players consider how many dots there are on the domino just pulled from the stack and what possibilities it has to offer when combined with the tiles already on the table. The sample situations described below are from a game between two beginning Tsung Shap players. To avoid confusion, they are referred to in the description as Players A and B.

The Opening Moves

1 The players have formed their stacks and then chosen four, for a total of sixteen dominoes each. The coin toss has decided that Player A will start the game. He takes the tile from the top of the stack to

his right and puts it down in the middle of the table. The tile is 5–1. Then it's Player B's turn. Since he can form a winning combination only if there are at least two tiles on the table, he can add the tile he just pulled, the 6–3, without giving it any further thought.

Now Player A takes a double-one. This does not count as a pair, a triple, or a sweep because the total number of dots on the three tiles adds up to seventeen. Player B turns over another tile: the 4–2. Meanwhile, there are now three tiles on the table,

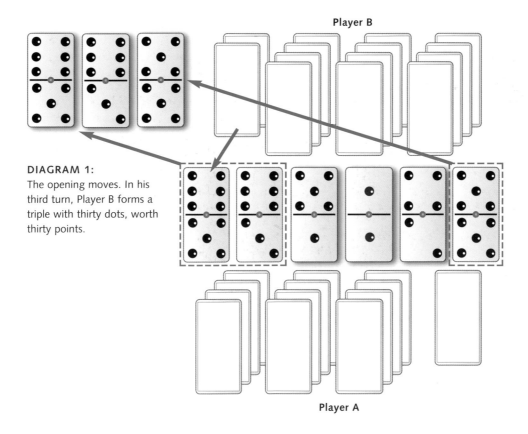

Player B

DIAGRAM 1:
The opening moves. In his third turn, Player B forms a triple with thirty dots, worth thirty points.

Player A

making a sweep impossible. The other two possibilities don't apply here, either. The first to form a winning combination is Player B. In his third turn, he takes a 6–5. The number of dots on the tiles at each end of the line adds up to nineteen, so this player has a thirty-point triple. He takes the three tiles and puts them aside in a stack. Then it's Player A's turn again (Diagram 1).

A Wasted Opportunity

2 In his seventh turn, Player B turns over a tile from the stack. It's the 5–1 tile. The same exact tile is on the line, but since it isn't on either end of the line, there is no pair.

A FIRST MATCH

Below is a transcription of every play in the game, from which were culled the opening situations described in these pages. The letters "L" and "R" indicate which side of the line a tile has been added to. To repeat the match play by play, arrange all the dominoes on the table faceup, to make it easy to pick the right tiles.

1. **A: 5–1, B: 6–3L;** 2. **A: 1–1R, B: 4–2R;** 3. **A: 5–5R, B: 6–5L (trio);** 4. **A: 2–2L, B: 6–4R (trio);** 5. **A: 2–1R, B: 4–1L;** 6. **A: 6–6L (trio), B: 3–3R;** 7. **A: 6–1L, B: 5–1R;** 8. **A: 4–3L, B: (trio of A) 5–2L;** 9. **A: 2–2L, B: 1–1R;** 10. **A: 3–3L, B: 6–1L;** 11. **A: 5–3R, B: 6–2R;** 12. **A: 3–2L, B: 5–4L;** 13. **A: 6–6L, B: 6–5R;** 14. **A: 5–5L, B: 4–4L (trio);** 15. **A: 6–4L (trio), B: 3–1R (trio);** 16. **A: 3–1L, B: 4–4R.**

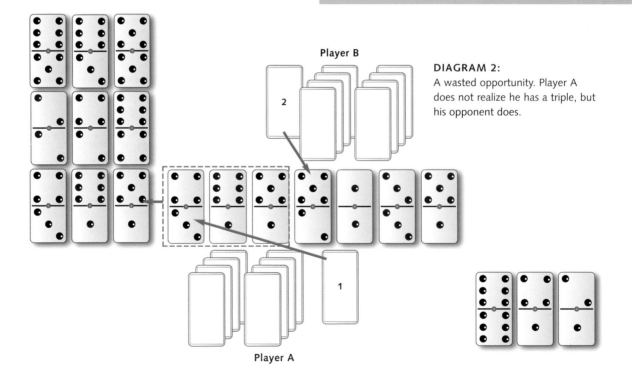

Player B

DIAGRAM 2:
A wasted opportunity. Player A does not realize he has a triple, but his opponent does.

Player A

In his eighth turn, Player A turns over the 4–3 tile. He adds it to the left side of the line and passes the turn on to his opponent. He has completely overlooked the fact that he has a triple. The number of dots on the last two tiles on the left end of the line add up to thirteen, which equals the number of points on the tiles at each end. If you add to these the seven points from the tile he just turned over, they form a triple worth twenty points. His opponent, on the other hand, does notice this winning combination, and takes the three tiles from the table. He then takes the 5–2 piece, which yields nothing. Thanks to his opponent's carelessness, Player B has won some points in his eighth turn (Diagram 2).

The Final Triple

3 After the last move by Player B, both players have put down half their tiles on the table. The struggle continues, and for the next few plays, neither opponent is able to form a winning combination. At one point, the line of dominoes on the table is fifteen tiles long. In his fourteenth move, Player B is able to cut this number down to thirteen by forming

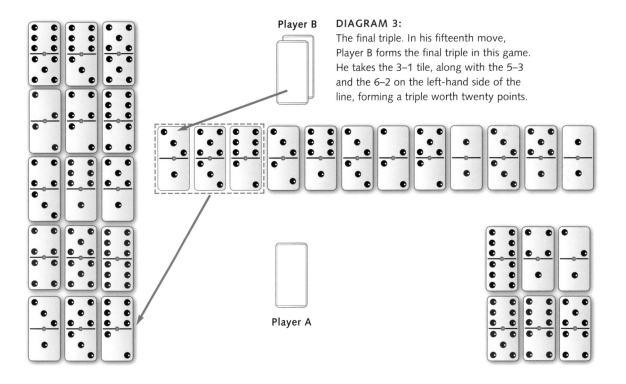

Player B

DIAGRAM 3:
The final triple. In his fifteenth move, Player B forms the final triple in this game. He takes the 3–1 tile, along with the 5–3 and the 6–2 on the left-hand side of the line, forming a triple worth twenty points.

Player A

Player A   **Player B**

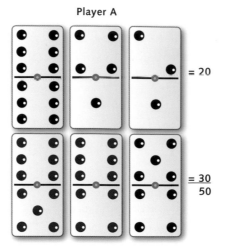

= 20

= 30
50

= 30

= 20

= 20

= 30

= 20
120

a triple. Immediately thereafter, Player A forms a triple of his own, so the line is cut even shorter. His opponent's response is to form yet another triple, but after this winning streak, the game of Tsung Shap has come to an end (Diagram 3).

Tallying the Points

4 At the end of this match, both players have put down all their tiles on the table and proceed to count up their points. Player A has two triples worth a total of fifty points. His opponent, Player B, has five triples, worth a total of 120 points. These seven triples comprise twenty-one of the dominoes, so there is still a line of eleven dominoes on the table.

Player B is the clear and uncontested winner in this game of Tsung Shap. Other than Player A's missed opportunity, you couldn't really say that one of them played better than the other. It's worth noticing that in this match, players formed only triples and no pairs or sweeps (Diagram 4).

V A R I A T I O N

The most important difference between "regular" Tsung Shap and an interesting variation is that in the variation, players can look at their tiles and decide which ones to play for each turn. Therefore, the final score tends to be much higher.

Coan Ki
History of the Game

◆ ◆ ◆

Coan Ki is part of the tables, or backgammon, family of games. This word, in fact, is simply the Western name for this type of game. In all likelihood, this family of games, which is quite broad today, is descended from Egyptian Senat (see page 163). During the Roman era, a board game developed from Senat, which was played on a twelve-line grid. The first precursor to backgammon was known much before the Common Era. But this twelve-line game was not restricted to the West or to the Roman sphere of influence. It went as far as Asia, where the boards (and as a result, the rules of the game) acquired a character of their own.

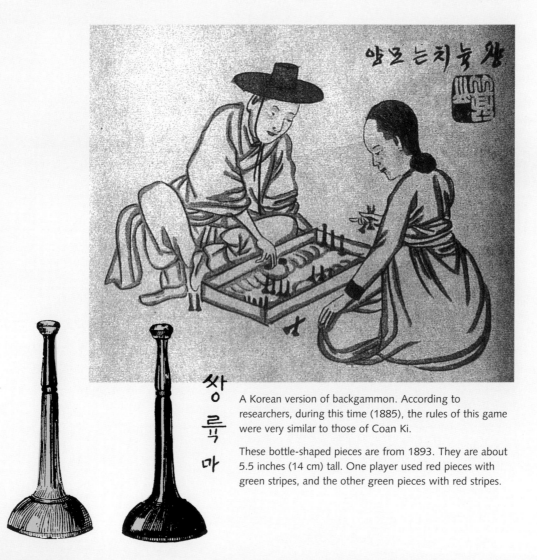

A Korean version of backgammon. According to researchers, during this time (1885), the rules of this game were very similar to those of Coan Ki.

These bottle-shaped pieces are from 1893. They are about 5.5 inches (14 cm) tall. One player used red pieces with green stripes, and the other green pieces with red stripes.

Two geishas play a Japanese variation of Coan Ki called *sunoruku*.

While most board games in Asia were played exclusively by men or by women, the backgammon variations found many enthusiasts among both sexes. A game of Coan Ki is made more enjoyable among friends or family members.

The Game Board and Pieces

The Asian variations on backgammon, unlike their ancient twelve-line ancestor, have a different number of squares. Coan Ki is played on a board with two sets of eight squares. It's also worth noting that the traditional Coan Ki board has no demarcation in the center. If the players sit on the short ends of the board, each of them has his eight squares in front of him, although in practice the players often sit facing the long ends of the board. But this can be confusing, so it is recommended only for experienced players. The original Coan Ki pieces were bottle-shaped. When a piece reached its goal, it was placed on its side on the final square to make clear to both players that it was no longer in play.

One of the few images extant of an original Chinese Coan Ki board, from 1882.

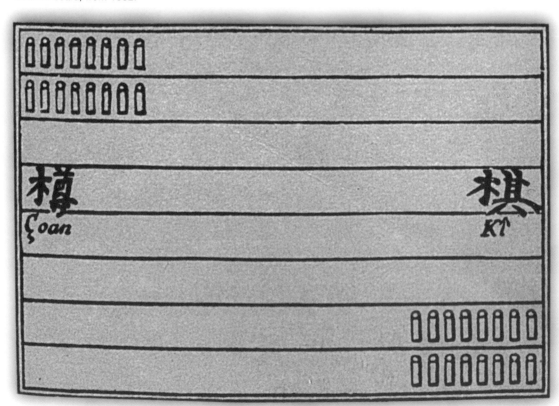

Playing Coan Ki

The English name for this fascinating Chinese diversion is "The Bottle Game." The name refers to the pieces, which originally were shaped like bottles or vases. The first mention of this game in the West appeared in the two-volume collection *De Ludis Orientalibus*, by the scholar Dr. Thomas Hyde. This groundbreaking book about board games was published in 1694 by Oxford University Press. Hyde's description of the game is not quite complete. Thanks to the efforts of various experts, a playable version of the game was reconstructed which offers a great challenge to both players and a wide variety of permutations. The winner is the first player to run the course around the board with all his pieces and return them to their opening positions. He is rewarded with the honor of being the first to finish as well as with the contents of the pot.

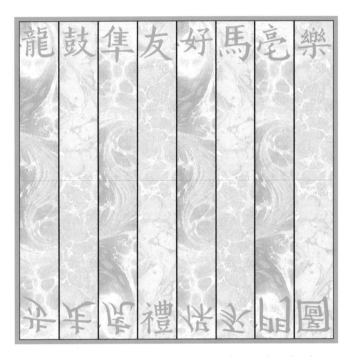

Coan Ki, or the Bottle Game, is played on a stark game board with two sets of sixteen pieces of two different colors. It's important that the sides of the pieces be distinguished with a different mark or color.

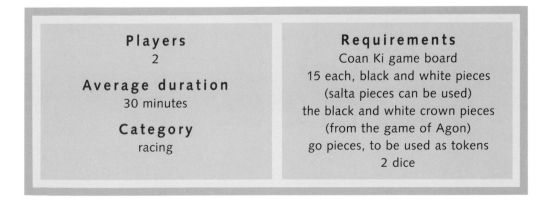

Players
2

Average duration
30 minutes

Category
racing

Requirements
Coan Ki game board
15 each, black and white pieces
(salta pieces can be used)
the black and white crown pieces
(from the game of Agon)
go pieces, to be used as tokens
2 dice

Rules:
Preliminaries

The Coan Ki board is as simple as this ingenious game is complex. The board is a rectangle divided by seven vertical lines into eight long tracks, with no other symbols. An imaginary horizontal line through the center of the board divides it into the White and Black players' respective halves. Each player puts his pieces on the tracks on his own side of the board. (From now on, these tracks are referred to as "squares.") The players sit across from one another on either end of the tracks, with the board on a table between them. They each get sixteen pieces, white or black. It's important that one of the sides of each piece be blank and the other

be marked with a sign. It is advisable for Coan Ki players to use fifteen salta pieces each as well as the crown pieces from the game of Agon.

After deciding who will play which color, the pieces are divided up and placed on the board in the opening position. Each player arranges the pieces regularly along the two squares to his left. This means that each puts down eight pieces in square 1 and eight in square 2. The pieces should be as close together as possible so that each player takes up only half the board. Once this is taken care of, players must still agree on what they will wager. Candies or matches are often used, but it is more preferable to use go pieces as tokens. The final decision to make before starting is how many tokens to put in

DIAGRAM A:
A Coan Ki board with the pieces in the starting position.

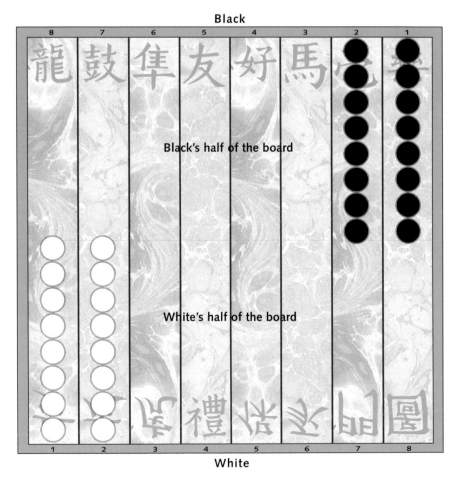

the pot at the start of the game. Usually each player puts in ten tokens. It's important to plan on a plentiful reserve, because players may have to pay into the pot throughout the game without getting any tokens back. Finally, players roll the two dice at once. The player with the higher roll uses that roll to start the game (Diagram A).

How the Pieces Move

A roll of the dice determines how many squares a player can move his piece or pieces. The four types of rolls are explained below. The pieces move across the board counterclockwise, going through the following phases:

- From square 1 or 2, the pieces move through the other squares on the player's own half of the board, to square 8;
- From square 8, the pieces cross over to the opponent's square 1;
- The pieces then move through all the squares on the opponent's side;

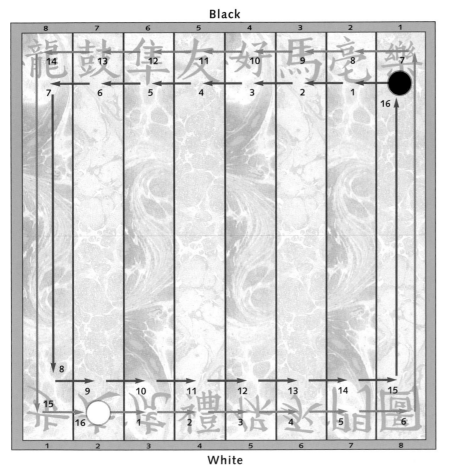

DIAGRAM B:
How the pieces move. Each player moves his sixteen pieces counterclockwise around the board. The final position is the same as the opening position.

• From the opponent's square 8, the pieces cross back over to square 1 on their own side of the board.

The object is to move all the pieces through the board and return them to their original squares. When moving a piece, a player can pass it through squares occupied by some of his own or his opponent's pieces. A piece whose goal is square 2 must always pass through square 1 first. That is, a player cannot move a piece from square 8 on his opponent's side directly into his own square 2. Thus, a complete run around the board comprises sixteen squares. Each time a piece reaches its goal, it is turned over and stays there, showing the marking underneath, so the players know exactly how many pieces have completed the course and which pieces still need to start out (Diagram B).

A Double and a Line

After each roll, players can choose the piece or pieces they want to move. A player can move either the pieces he has already moved before or a piece that has yet to start the course. This means he need

Two Japanese women play *sunoruku,* a game from the same family as Coan Ki.

not move a piece from square 2 before moving a piece from square 1. Below are described two types of roll and the possibilities they offer:

1. A double

When a player rolls a double, he has two options. He can move two pieces the total number of points, or move one piece half that number. For example, if a player rolls double-threes, he can move two pieces six squares each, or one piece three squares.

2. A line

A line consists of two consecutive numbers, as when one die shows three points and the other shows four. If a player rolls a line, he can choose between two possibilities, but must always move two pieces. One piece can move as many squares as the lowest number on the dice, and the other moves the sum of the numbers on both dice. The other option is to move two pieces the lower of the two numbers, and move the other piece one more square. The latter will then have moved the total number of points rolled. For example, a three-four roll offers the following options:

• Move one piece three squares and the other seven;
• Move two pieces six squares and one of them an additional square. This piece will have moved a total of seven spaces (Diagram C).

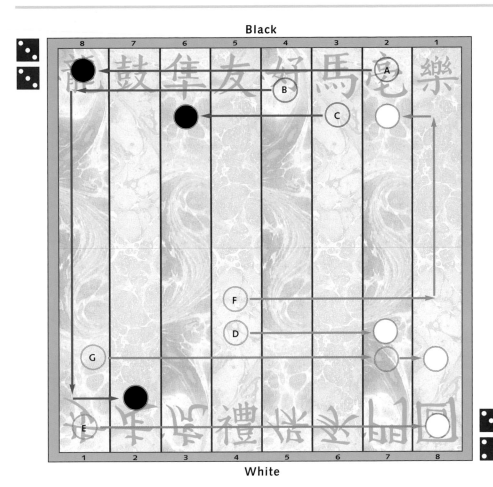

Black

White

DIAGRAM C:
A double and a line. If a player rolls a double, he can move two pieces the total number of points rolled (A + B), or move one piece half that number of squares (C). In the case of a line, the player moves one piece the lower number of points on the dice, and moves another the total number of points (D + E); alternatively, he can move one piece twice the number of points and move the other one an additional space beyond that number (F and G).

A Penalty Roll and the Scaled Fine System

There is one penalty roll in Coan Ki which the players will try their hardest to avoid: the double-one. If a player has the bad luck of rolling this combination, he gets a penalty of ten percent of the pot. He must take this sum from his reserves and pay it into the pot. But that's not all: he also loses one piece. This is the only way a player can lose a piece, because there is no capturing in Coan Ki. The silver lining is that the rules of the game are silent as to which piece must be removed from the board. Therefore, the player will choose a piece that has not yet started its course along the board, or which has made the least progress of all his pieces. Before the player can move

> ### CURIOUS FACT
>
> Coan Ki bears a resemblance to backgammon, but experts believe the former to be more complex and more demanding of its players.

another piece, he must reintroduce this piece on square 1. To do this the player must roll a one. This can take a long time. While he tries to do so, his opponent may reach the goal. To avoid wasting time, he can avail himself of the escape clause: if the player is willing to pay a fine of 20 percent of the pot, he can leave all his pieces on the board.

At the start of the game, when each player has bet ten tokens, there are twenty tokens in the pot. After a player pays a ten-percent penalty, the pot will grow to twenty-two tokens. The next time a player rolls a double-one, ten percent and twenty percent of the pot will equal a fraction. The rules of Coan Ki say to round up, so fines can increase very rapidly. Of course, the progressive increase in fines, and the rounding-up rule, increase the tension in the game considerably and ultimately reward the winner (Diagram D).

The Other Rolls

After explaining the double, the line, and the penalty roll, there is one other roll to cover. This roll comprises all other combinations, and lets the players choose between moving one or two pieces. In the former case, the piece moves as many squares as the total number the player rolled; in the latter, one piece moves the number of squares on one of the die and the other moves the number on the other die. For example, if the player rolls a one-three, he can move one of his pieces four squares, or move one piece one square and the other piece three squares.

Blocking

Blocking is an important weapon on the road to victory, because it can significantly restrict your opponent's mobility. Pieces can jump over a block of the same color, but the opponent's pieces will be stopped. A block consists of eight pieces in a single square between 3 and 8. Players can construct a block in any square except the opening ones. Eight pieces on the opening squares are not considered a block, and can be jumped over by the opponent's pieces. However, eight is the maximum number of pieces allowed per square. A block is eliminated if one of the pieces is moved from the blocking square. Then, either player can put one of his pieces in that square, or jump over it (Diagram E).

			= penalty roll
start			20
penalty roll 1.	10%		2
			22
penalty roll 2.	20%	4.4 =	5
			27
penalty roll 3.	10%	2.7 =	3
			30

DIAGRAM D:
A penalty roll and the scaled fine system. A first penalty roll results in a fine of ten percent of the pot and the loss of one piece. As an alternative, the player can pay a fine of twenty percent of the pot and keep all his pieces. The diagram reflects the progressive increase in fines in the penalty system.

Finishing

Every piece must end up in the same square where it started—eight pieces in square 1 and eight in square 2. To accomplish this, a player must roll the exact number of points needed to land on that square, because players must use every point rolled and may not move a piece backward. Players must turn over a piece as soon as it arrives at its final destination.

The Winner

The winner is the player who finishes the course around the board with all his pieces and returns them to their opening position. The winner gets the entire pot. Sometimes the players decide before beginning that the winner will be the first player to earn a given number of tokens. If so, players must bet the same number of tokens at the start of each round.

STRATEGY

You should try to build a block in the most strategic place possible. If you build it in your opponent's square 3, for example, his mobility is seriously limited, but your own pieces continue to move optimally.

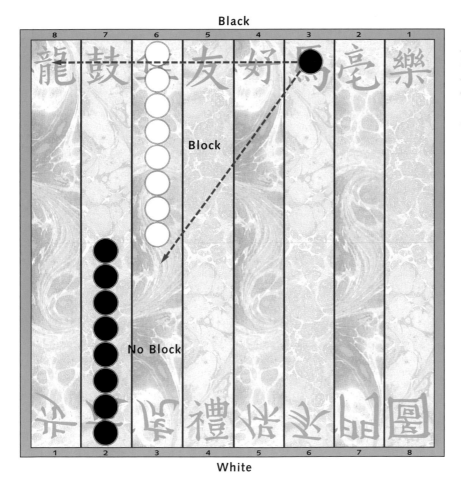

Black

White

DIAGRAM E:
A block consists of eight pieces in any single square between 3 and 8. A player may not jump over his opponent's block, and neither player may add any more pieces to this square.

After each roll, players must determine which of their pieces they can move. Often, a roll cannot be used in its totality, or is of no use at all. When this happens, the total is lost and the dice pass to the other player, because a player must use a roll even if he would rather not do so. For instance, a particular move can force a player to take apart a block.

The First Match

The time has come to play a first game of Coan Ki. For a beginner, it's important to remain calm. There are many pieces in play, and each roll offers a wide array of possibilities. It is critical that you weigh each of these options every time, and make a well-considered choice. As can be seen, if a player takes time familiarizing himself with the game, then it becomes easier to understand. The following situations have been chosen to help the new player find his way.

Wide Distribution of Pieces

1 The only roll that can always be "used" is the penalty roll—the double-one. After all, this roll does not require the players to move any pieces, but to pay a fine. It often happens that a player cannot use the number he rolled. This tends to occur especially when many pieces are close to the last square.

To reduce the chances of wasting a roll, one should spread the pieces more or less evenly throughout the board. A second argument for a wide distribution of the pieces is that it maximizes the number of pieces you can use to make a move. This theory is borne out in the game situation illustrated in Diagram 1.

The black pieces are spread out between four squares, and the white pieces take up ten squares. It should be clear now that the odds of not being able to use a roll are much higher for Black. Suppose Black rolls a six-five line. It does not matter which option he chooses, because he will always have to move one of his pieces the total number of points rolled. This means Black cannot use this roll. Even the black piece farthest from the goal would overshoot it if it were to move eleven squares. For White, the same roll would not pose a problem. If he has to move eleven squares, White can choose between his piece on his own square 6 and the one in square 7 (Diagram 1).

TIP

To increase the game's tension, players can agree that when one of them incurs a penalty roll, the other player gets to decide which piece to remove from the board.

A Well-Considered Choice

2 Experience has shown that many beginners tend to opt for moving along as many squares as possible. For example, they usually prefer to use a double-five to move two pieces ten squares instead of five. But experienced Coan Ki players exhibit a very different pattern of play. They tend to base their choices on something other than the desire to run through the course as quickly as possible with all their pieces. And they have good reasons for doing so. One of these reasons is the need, mentioned earlier, for a wide distribution of the pieces among the squares. The second reason has to do with constructing a block.

In Diagram 2, it is Black's turn. He rolls double-threes, so he can move two of his pieces six squares each. This means he can move two pieces from White's square 3 to his own square 1, where he can

VARIATION

Sometimes players agree that a piece can finish in a square beyond the goal. The pieces must then fulfill the condition of completing another lap around the course.

then turn them over. Attractive as this option is, Black chooses the second option. He moves his piece from square 8 three spaces, and forms a block in White's square 3. White still has seven of his pieces in squares 1 and 2, and they are all immobilized now (Diagram 2).

Black

White

DIAGRAM 1:
Optimal distribution of pieces. Black will have to pass on his turn because he cannot move any of his pieces. Thanks to a better piece distribution, White has no problem making use of the same roll.

Rules:
Preliminaries

The board, as well as each of its halves, is divided in two. Each player has twelve spaces, which are divided into six outer and six inner spaces, which will be referred to as "squares." Squares B1 to B6 are Black's inner squares, and his outer squares are labeled B7 through B12. Squares W1 through W6 are White's inner squares, and W7 through W12 are his outer squares. After deciding which color each player will use, players divide up the pieces. They each put their pieces in three stacks of five on their respective opponents' square (B1 or W1). At the start of a game

of Nardshir, all the pieces are placed on the board. Next, players take turns rolling a die to decide who will begin. If both players roll the same number, each rolls again (Diagram A).

DIAGRAM A:
A Nardshir board with the pieces in the starting position.

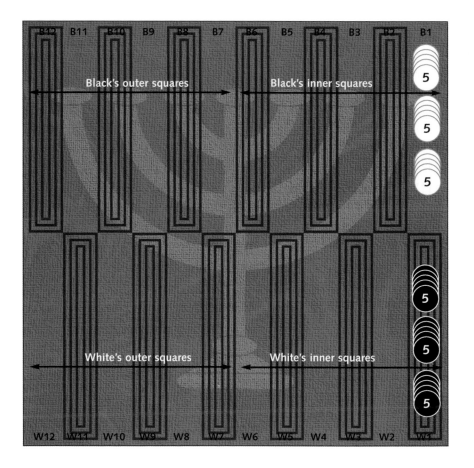

How the Pieces Move

The white pieces move counterclockwise (Diagram B). They start out at square B1 and move from right to left toward square B12, from which they then cross the board perpendicularly to square W12. From this square they then move from left to right, on their way ultimately to leaving the board through W1. The black pieces move in the opposite direction, running clockwise around the board. They start at W1 and move from right to left toward W12. Once they reach this square, they cross the board to their own outer square, B12, where they then move into their own inner squares. Finally, they leave the board through square B1. Since the pieces move in opposite directions, they are bound to run into one another along the way. A roll of the dice determines how many squares each piece moves per turn.

Capturing Pieces

In Nardshir, pieces are captured in a very unusual fashion. In fact, "capturing" is precisely the word for it, because instead of removing the pieces from the board, they are imprisoned in the square where they are captured. Pieces can be eliminated only when they sit alone on a square. When a piece lands

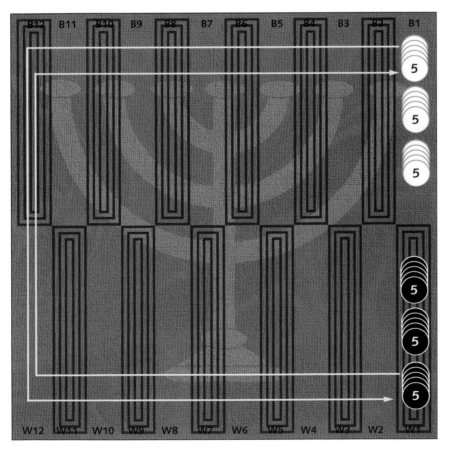

DIAGRAM B:
How the pieces move. The white pieces move counterclockwise, the black pieces clockwise. Each piece starts in the opponent's square 1 and exits the board through its own inner square 1.

Players must pay attention to the closed squares. The movement of a piece must always end in an open square. This rule also applies to the squares in between when a piece moves the total number of points rolled. Take, for instance, a case in which the player rolls a three-five and then decides to move one piece eight spaces. The last square from his starting point must be open, and so must the third or fifth squares, also counting from the starting square. Players must use all the points in a roll; if they cannot, they lose their turn (Diagram D).

Removing Pieces

Players can start removing their pieces from the board once they are all in their inner squares. At this stage, players must also use the points they roll in their entirety, and can choose to move one, two, or four pieces. Suppose Black rolls a two-three: he can choose between removing one piece from B5, or removing two pieces from B2 and B3.

A player may not remove a piece from a square whose number does not match the numbers he rolled. There is one exception to this rule. When there are no pieces in the square with either the exact number rolled or the higher of the two numbers rolled, a piece can be removed from another square. In the example above, where the player rolled five points, squares 5 and 6 are free, so Black can remove a piece from any other inner square. At this stage, it is sometimes permitted to use only part of the points rolled (Diagram E).

Tallying the Points

At the end of each game, the players count up their points. At this juncture, only one player has pieces on the board.

Games in the backgammon family have disseminated throughout the world, and can be found most anywhere with both rural and urban features. The Japanese players in the image above are playing the variant *sunoruku*, native to their culture.

The winner gets one point for every piece on his opponent's inner squares and two points for every piece on the opponent's outer squares. Each enemy piece on the player's own outer squares earns him three points; and the greatest reward, four points, is given for every enemy piece on the player's own inner squares.

The Winner

The winner is the first player to complete the course around the board with all his pieces and to withdraw them all from the board. The tallying method just described is appealing only when the challengers have agreed to play a series of games. In that case, the winner is the first player to reach a predetermined number of points. This multigame system is also well suited to games played among four players.

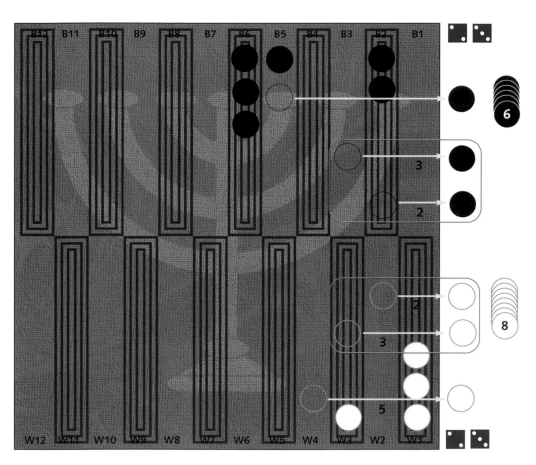

DIAGRAM E:
Removing the pieces. Players can start to remove their pieces once all their pieces are in their inner squares. At this phase, players are sometimes permitted to forgo using every point they rolled.

The Final Moves

3 White keeps the black piece on W3 imprisoned as long as possible, which proves a considerable obstacle for Black. Diagram 3 shows how the remaining fourteen black pieces are distributed among the inner squares from B1 to B4, while White has already removed eight of his pieces from the board. Then White rolls a double-three. He can no longer move any pieces, but must use the points he rolls in any way possible, and so removes the two pieces from W3, and the black piece finally regains its liberty. White continues, taking two pieces from W2 off the board. It's clear that Black wants to put his newly freed piece on one of his inner squares as soon as possible, and hopes to do so by rolling some high points (Diagram 3).

The Final Position and Tally

4 The difference between the motives of the two players is so great that this is hardly an exciting finish. For his final turns, Black rolls a five and then a three, so his liberated piece immediately goes to square W11. He cannot stop White from shortly taking his last pieces off the board. White has won the game. For each of Black's fourteen pieces in White's inner squares, White gets one point. The black piece on square W11 earns White three points. All told, White earns seventeen points in this match (Diagram 4).

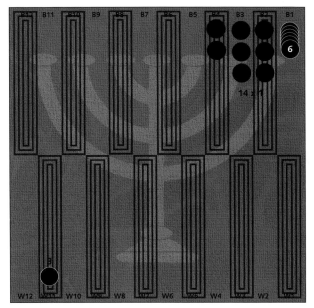

DIAGRAM 4:
The final position and tally. Black is unable to put all his pieces in his inner squares before White finishes the game. White scores seventeen points.

Mastermind®
History of the Game

◆ ◆ ◆

The history of this intriguing game is short but interesting. The game was designed in 1971 by Mordecai Meirowitz, who took his inspiration from the old English game of Bulls and Cows. This game for two players was especially popular among English children. One of the players would establish a code which the other player had to crack. Meirowitz replaced the written code of the children's game with colored game pieces, and substituted a game board for pencil and paper. And so was born Mastermind®, a game which quickly spread throughout the world and has sold millions of copies. Mastermind is a registered trademark of Invicta Toys and Games, Ltd (licensed to Pressman Toy Company for the U.S., Orda Industries for Israel, and Hasbro International for all other countries).

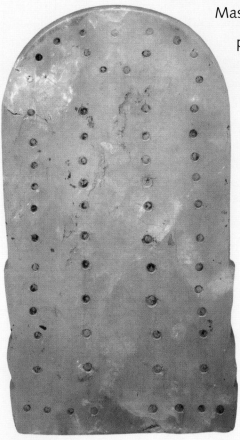

Many countries hold a competition for the title of National Mastermind Champion. To qualify for the nationals, players must first win enough mandatory qualifying tournaments. An indicator of the speed with which Mastermind's popularity grew is that by 1975, Britain was already holding its national championship. Today, there are even international Mastermind tournaments.

A slate from 900 to 800 B.C.E., from Sam'al in the Assyrian Empire. It may have been used for playing games similar to Mastermind as well as Dogs and Jackals and other racing games.

A 1994 variation on the code-breaking game by Hasbro International. With this variation, the pieces can be stored in the lid during the game and the code is placed at one end, hidden below the board.

The Future

Though this game's history may be short, its future will no doubt be long and ingenious. For one thing, a good Mastermind player is distinguished by a combination of reason and intuition. A game of Mastermind can be thought of as an exercise in deductive reasoning. Beyond the rational aspect of the game, however, its psychological factors are intimately connected with intuition and feeling. If you know your adversary well, you may be able to guess which combinations of colors he will choose. Further, the many possibilities for variation, and consequently different levels of difficulty, make Mastermind a game certain to keep its appeal from one generation to the next.

Variations

One of the most sublime traits of Mastermind is its flexibility. By changing the rules, you can create more challenges and variations, and thus lower or raise the level of difficulty. For example, sometimes the game is played with eight colors instead of six, while the rules remain the same. Other variations apply different methods for creating the code. The game becomes harder if the players leave one or more of the spaces in the code empty. The same occurs when the secret code can be used for more than one color. Thus, the number of permutations rises to 1,296 (6^4). The game is even more complex if the code maker, besides using two pieces of the same color, also leaves one or two open spaces. In that case, the code maker can choose from 6,561 possible combinations. Sometimes the game is played on a board in which each of the code breaker's rows contains five spaces. In this so-called super-variation on the game, players use pieces of eight different colors in five spaces. The total number of permutations in this case is 32,768 (8^5), of which 6,720 consist of the same colors.

Playing Mastermind

A player is likely to get hooked on Mastermind after just one game, and want to play again and again. It's the perfect game for those analytic spirits who enjoy a challenge. In this game, chance plays a much smaller part than logical understanding, so winning depends largely on each player's mental gymnastics. Though that might make the game sound very serious, Mastermind is first and foremost a game for playing at home, designed for players ages eight and up. It's very easy to explain the object of the game, but quite hard to actually attain it. A game of Mastermind is played by two people, each of whom has a very clear goal. One player creates a code, which the other player must try to decipher. Once he does, players switch roles. The player who cracks a code in the fewest turns wins.

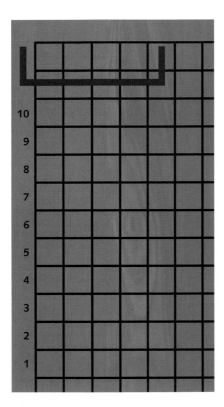

Mastermind is played on a long, rectangular board with a large array of pieces. At first, fifteen pieces of six different colors are enough. Points are scored with other pieces of two colors, such as black and white, which go into squares used for keeping score.

TIP

You can learn a great deal by analyzing this game using only three colors and two squares for each row where the code breaker must decipher the code. In this setup, the number of possible codes is the square of three (nine). Six of these possibilities are combinations of different colors, and the other three use the same ones but are found in different positions.

Players
2

Average duration
30 minutes

Category
logic; code breaking

Requirements
game board that can be adapted to Mastermind
a cover for the code pieces
15 pieces each, in six colors
(e.g., red, yellow, green, blue, white, black)
30 smaller pieces of two colors
(e.g., black and white)

Rules:
Preliminaries

The two players in a game of Mastermind assume very different roles. One is called the code breaker, the other the code maker. The code maker acts as a teacher of sorts, as he must provide feedback on each of his opponent's attempts to crack the code. These three tasks each require different sections on the board, so the board is divided into three parts. The first part is a horizontal row of four squares, where the pieces that form the code are located. The coding squares must be well protected to ensure that the code breaker cannot see them, so they are placed under a special cover that allows only the code maker to see them.

The second part of the board is for the code breaker. It consists of ten horizontal rows with four squares in each; thus, the code breaker can make a maximum of four attempts per turn at cracking the code. These squares are located opposite the squares that contain the code.

The third part of the board is a vertical row of ten spaces located to the side of the code breaker's squares. These are the scoring spaces, where the code maker indicates the results of the code breaker's attempt to crack the code. Note: a go board has enough room for all these spaces, and is therefore an adequate substitute for a Mastermind board.

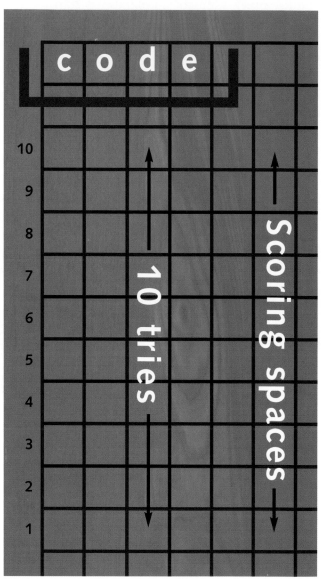

DIAGRAM A:
A Mastermind board and the starting position for the game accessories. The ten rows with four squares apiece belong to the code breaker; the others are used by the code maker.

VARIATION

During the first few turns, the pieces can be arranged according to a predetermined system, to gather as much information as possible. In this case, each color is assigned a number and played as follows:

1. **1–2–3–4**
2. **5–1–2–3**
3. **6–5–1–2**

Go pieces can also be used in Mastermind as score pegs. There is no definite number of score pegs, but thirty black and thirty white pieces are generally enough. Before starting the game, players must decide who will play what role. Next, players take their seats opposite the narrow ends of the board. The code maker sits on the side with the encoding pieces. He gets one piece of each color and makes sure that all the scoring spaces are within his reach; the code breaker gets all the remaining pieces (Diagram A).

The Code

The code maker arranges the combination, putting one piece on each empty space earmarked for this purpose. A valid Mastermind code must fulfill two conditions. First, there must be only one piece on each encoding square. This means that a code will always consist of four pieces. These pieces should each be a different color, because more than one piece of any color is not allowed on the encoding squares in the standard rules. As long as the players observe these two rules, they can choose any combination of colors they please. Of course, they may also decide for themselves their rule for multiple colors of encoding pieces. With six different colors and four squares, there are a total of 1,296 possible permutations. This number is reduced to 360 if the combinations also fulfill the condition of being made up of four different colors. (There are fifteen possibilities for choosing four colors out of six; each of these in turn allows for twenty-four orders of position in the four squares. Thus, the total number of combinations is 360, because 24 x 15 = 360.)

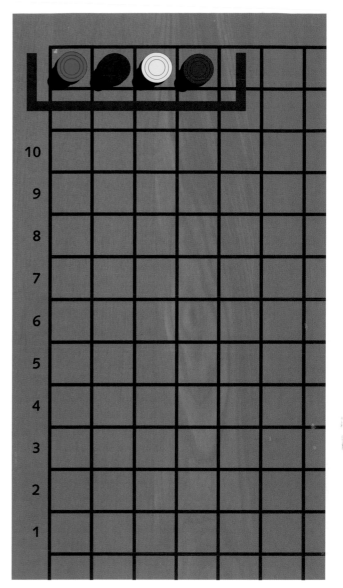

DIAGRAM B:
The code. The code must consist of four pieces, each of a different color. This is one of 360 possible permutations.

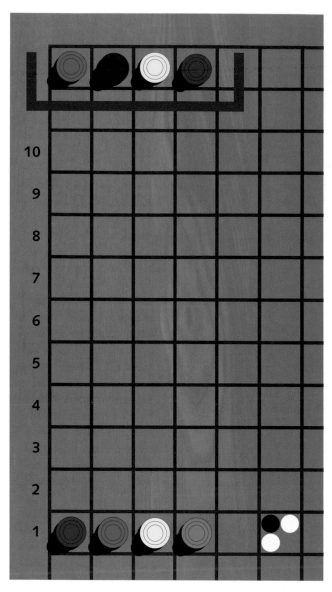

DIAGRAM C:
Encoding pieces and scoring pegs. The code breaker puts four pieces of different colors in the first row. The code maker puts one white scoring peg in the corresponding box for each color the code breaker got right, and one black scoring peg for each piece whose color and position are both right.

When the code maker chooses one of them, he must make sure his opponent cannot see what he is doing (Diagram B).

Coding Pieces and Scoring Pegs

Once the code maker forms his code, the code breaker can make his first attempt at cracking it. This means guessing which colors are in the four squares of the code, and in which order they are arranged. To do this, the code breaker puts any four pieces in his first row. The only condition here is that he must use four different colors. Then, the code maker reveals the result of this first move by putting one or more scoring pegs in the spaces beside the first row of squares. For each piece that is the right color but in the wrong place, the code maker puts one white piece in the corresponding scoring square. When the color and position of a piece are both correct, the code maker adds one black piece. But the code maker does not reveal which pieces the scoring pegs refer to. For instance, if the code maker adds two white pieces and one black piece, the code breaker can infer that: two of the colors are correct, but are not in the right spaces; one color is correct and in the right position; and one of the colors in the first row is not a part of the code.

Example:

The hidden code is red, yellow, black, and green, and the code breaker opens with the combination blue, yellow, green, red. The code maker puts two white pieces in the scoring area beside row one (one for the green piece and one for the red). Next to these he adds a black scoring peg to denote that both the color and the position of the yellow piece are correct (Diagram C).

Dénouement

With the help of this information, the code breaker then places four pieces in the second row. Then, this second attempt is evaluated by the code maker. The game continues until the code breaker has cracked the code and received four black scoring pegs (Diagram D). At that point, the code maker removes the cover, revealing the code pieces, and the players count how many turns it took the code breaker to crack it. Then the player who just played the code breaker now plays the role of code maker, and vice versa. After each game, players count the number of turns the respective code breaker took to crack the code. If after his tenth turn a player still does not know the code, he must give up.

The Winner

The winner is the player who cracks the code in the fewest moves. Sometimes both players crack their codes in the same number of tries. If so, they each receive a point. If there is a winner and a loser, then only the winner receives a point. Often the players agree that the final winner will be the first player to score ten points. It may happen, too, that the code maker makes a mistake when giving out the scoring pegs, making it impossible for the code breaker to find the solution. It is advisable to agree beforehand on how to handle a situation like this. Players might, for example, agree to declare the game void, start over, and take a point away from the errant code maker as a penalty. If the code maker has yet to score any points, his mistake will give him a balance of –1 point. Sometimes a penalty point is also subtracted from a player who is unable to crack the code after ten tries.

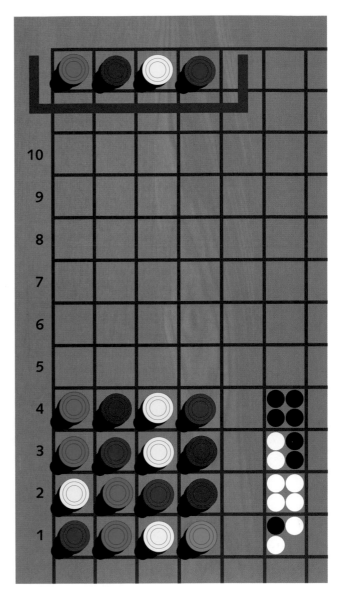

DIAGRAM D:
A final position. The code maker puts four black pegs in the scoring area. The code breaker has taken four turns to find the solution.

The First Match

From the preceding description of the rules, the reader may have discerned that Mastermind is a game that requires a great deal of concentration from both players. The code maker must not make any mistakes when evaluating his opponent's moves, because it will cost him a penalty point. On the other hand, if the code breaker loses focus for a moment, he may have to make an unnecessary extra move. A single move can make the difference between winning and losing. A player will go nowhere without a little bit of luck, and Mastermind has allotted a minor role to chance. Still, players must depend mainly on their logical reasoning abilities. The following pages are an attempt to show the beginner how certain combinations are chosen. The examples are based on a game of Mastermind between two beginners.

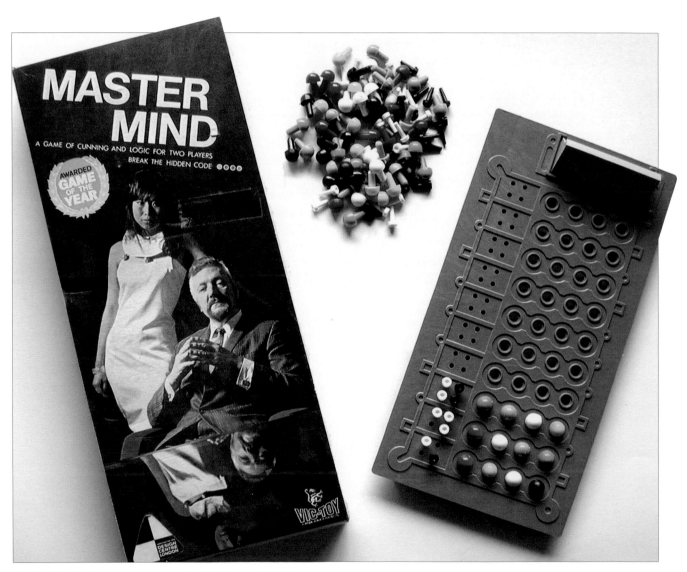

The first Mastermind set was released in 1971 by Invicta Plastics, Ltd., England. It was named "Game of the Year" by the Design Center of London.

Strategies

In theory, each Mastermind player has two strategies to choose from: defensive or offensive. If he chooses an offensive strategy, he will try to crack the code using the smallest number of moves. A defensive strategy means the player will try not to take more than a certain number of turns. The disadvantage to the defensive strategy is that the player runs the risk of making more moves than with an offensive strategy. In any case, it is an advantage to play the code maker in the first round. If you then play the part of code breaker, you will at least know how many moves your opponent took to break the code, so you know the number you need in order to win. The code breaker in the second round, therefore, can adjust his strategy accordingly.

The Second Try

1 Two players have just started a game of Mastermind. The code is now formed and hidden, and the code breaker has chosen an offensive strategy. He has put four random pieces in the first row, which yield two white scoring pegs. This says that he has not put any of the pieces in the right squares but did get two of the colors right. Now he must fill the squares in the second row. Of course, it makes no sense to put any of the pieces in the same positions as before. When you get two colors right, it means you also got two colors wrong. The code breaker decides to take white and red as the correct colors. He puts two pieces of these colors in the second row and switches the yellow and black pieces for blue and green, which were not used before. As a result, he gets two more white scoring pegs (Diagram 1).

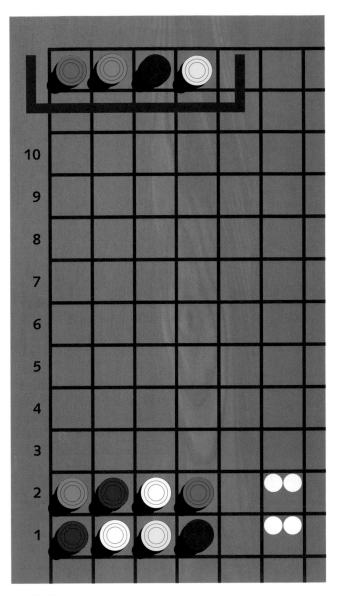

DIAGRAM 1:
The second try. The code breaker assumes that the red and white colors are correct, and so trades the black and yellow pieces for blue and green. As a result, he scores two more white pegs.

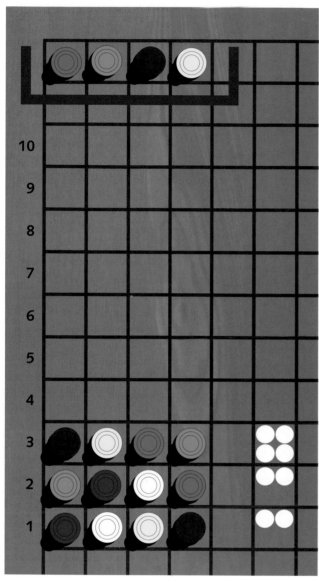

DIAGRAM 2:
The third try. The two scoring pieces in row 2 tell us that the colors white and red are not part of the code. The code breaker has now found the right colors.

The Third Try

2 The code breaker has to place a combination of pieces in the third row. He has yet to receive a black scoring piece, which means he has not yet put any of the pieces in the right squares. So on the third try, he knows not to leave any of the pieces in the

same positions as before. A moment ago, the code breaker started from the assumption that white and red were the correct colors. If this were right, then the yellow and black pieces in the first row would be wrong, so he traded them for blue and green. According to the code maker's evaluation, the choice of pieces in the second row should have earned four scoring pegs, but this time he also gets only two. Therefore, yellow and black were the right colors, after all, and blue and green must be part of the code as well. After some reflection, the code breaker puts blue, green, yellow, and black pieces in the third row. And, sure enough, the code maker puts four white scoring pegs in the corresponding square. The code breaker has found the right color combination, though none of his pieces are in the right square (Diagram 2).

The Fourth Try

3 The code breaker is about to make his fourth move. He knows which colors he must put in the fourth row and that none of the pieces have been in the right squares so far. He starts with a black piece. This color has already been in the outer squares, so now it must be put in one of the two middle squares. The same goes for the blue piece, which he also places in one of the middle squares. Since the black and blue pieces can be in only one or another of the middle squares, the green piece must belong in one of the other squares. The right-hand square was incorrect, so the code breaker can be certain that it belongs on the left-hand square. Thus, the code breaker also knows for sure that the yellow piece belongs on the outer right-hand square. He puts his pieces in place and anxiously waits for his opponent to uncover the code. It does not happen. Instead, the code breaker's fourth try is evaluated, as expected, with two white and two black scoring pegs (Diagram 3).

The Fifth Try

4 With the information gathered so far, the code breaker's fifth try will be a piece of cake. All the colors are clearly correct. Two of the pieces in the fourth row are in the right place. Therefore, in the fifth try, the code breaker has to leave two pieces in the same place. He knows for certain that the green and yellow pieces are in the right positions, so it's only logical to assume that the two black scoring pieces refer to these two, and to leave them in the outer squares. Based on this assumption, the only logical move is for the blue and black pieces to switch places, which is exactly what the code breaker does. He earns the four coveted black scoring pegs, having cracked the code in five turns (Diagram 4).

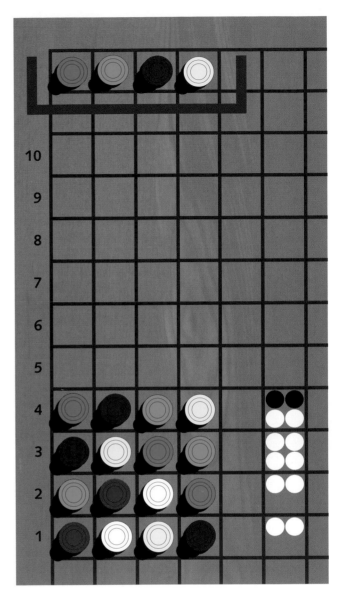

DIAGRAM 3:
The fourth try. Now all the colors are right, but the scoring pegs indicate that they are still not in the right squares.

An Odd Number of Scoring Pieces

5 In this first game you can appreciate where luck enters the picture. Since the code breaker had the luck of getting two score pieces instead of three in both the first and second turns, by the third turn he had figured out the right color combination. In Diagram 5, the code breaker has received three white scoring pieces after his first turn, signifying that one of his colors is wrong. He decides to replace the white piece with a red piece, and again gets three white score pieces. It's very likely this player will need a few more tries to figure out the right color combination. If you put this idea to the test, you will find that in the first and second turns, it is actually better to get two points instead of three.

In the model game in Diagram 4, the code breaker was less fortunate in the fourth try. He had found the right color combination, and with a bit of luck could have put all the pieces in their right positions. But intuition failed him, so he had to take another turn.

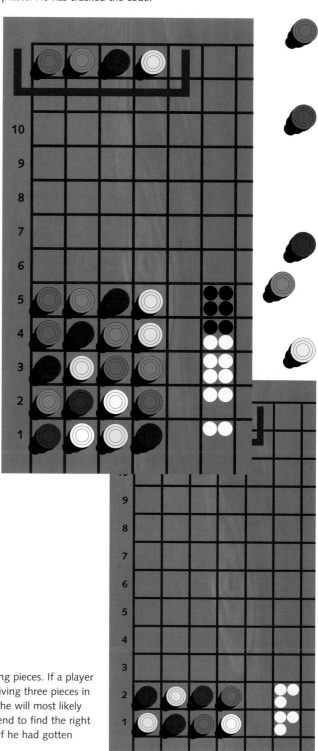

DIAGRAM 4:
The fifth try. After carefully weighing the options, the code breaker decides to have blue and green switch places. He has cracked the code.

DIAGRAM 5:
An odd number of scoring pieces. If a player has the bad luck of receiving three pieces in his first couple of turns, he will most likely need more turns in the end to find the right color combination than if he had gotten only two scoring pieces.

The Royal Game of Ur
History of the Game

◆ ◆ ◆

Around 1925, archeologists uncovered some of the greatest treasures found in Mesopotamia (present-day Iraq and eastern Syria). It happened during an excavation sponsored by the University of Pennsylvania and the British Museum, led by Sir Charles Leonard Woolley. The archeologist uncovered tombs near the Sumerian city of Ur, the biblical "Ur of the Chaldees." The tombs were the mysterious collective sepulchers of priests who had been sacrificed to the gods, or perhaps the tombs of royalty. Among the many treasures Sir Woolley discovered were some interesting game boards. It was quickly established that these specimens dated to some 3000 years B.C.E., making them without a doubt the oldest games found. It is believed they were gifts to deceased Sumerian royalty or to the very rich, to keep them company as they made their journey to the afterlife.

This board, discovered by Sir Charles Leonard Woolley, is a beautifully decorated specimen of one of the oldest game boards ever found (*Photo: The British Museum, London*).

A Royal Game

The game that was played on these boards has come to be known throughout the world as the Royal Game of Ur. The archeological data indicate that the game was played with two sets of seven pieces. One of the pieces was of a light color and bore five dark dots, while the other was dark with light dots. Researchers have found splendid pieces made of white conch shell embedded with lapis lazuli dots, as well as specimens in black slate with the dots made of conch shell. Further excavations have uncovered six pyramid-shaped dice with two blank corners and two marked corners. The five boards found by British archeologist Woolley were all of the same type, the only difference being their decorations and the materials from which they were made. In Woolley's 1946 book, *The First Phases*, he reproduces two examples of these boards. One is a simple conch shell board. The other is covered with a layer of conch shell plates encrusted with lapis lazuli and red sandstone. This board is one of the great treasures of the British Museum. Other boards feature conch shell plates engraved with images of animals. All of them have a colorful rosette in the center row on the widest part of the board.

An Ancestral Game

The original rules of the royal game of Ur are lost to the ages. The shape of the board, however, and cuneiform tablets with rules of the game at a much later time (200 B.C.E.), have supplied researchers with sufficient clues for reconstructing it. In all likelihood, the game is an ancestor of the tables, or backgammon, family of games. The Royal Game of Ur is probably 200 to 300 years older than the oldest known Senat board from Egypt. In 1922, Howard Carter opened the tomb of the pharaoh Tutankhamen, who died in 1352 B.C.E. Among the fabulous treasures and riches found in the funeral chamber of this ancient Egyptian king were four game boards. These boards bear such a strong resemblance to the Royal Game of Ur that it is safe to assume that Ur was the birthplace of those games. The Egyptian specimens usually came with a small box for storing the dice and game pieces. The boards were used for playing a game called *tau*. Many of these boards were made so that the bottom of the board could be used to play Senat.

A later variation of the Royal Game of Ur.

Playing The Royal Game of Ur

The Royal Game of Ur can keep the minds of players and spectators alike busy for a good half hour at a time. The idea that this game was played some 3000 years B.C.E., in what was then Mesopotamia, makes it especially interesting. In the course of archeological digs, twenty-one little white balls were found alongside an Ur board. It is believed that our ancestors used these for wagering. Present-day players can follow their example, but this game can also be a great challenge, and very tense, even without wagering.

The Royal Game of Ur calls for special, pyramid-shaped dice. But luck is not the only factor that decides whether a player wins or loses, for the game also demands a good strategic mind on the part of the players, giving them cause to reflect. The object of this dynamic game is to place all the pieces on the board, only to remove them again as quickly as possible after they have run their course. The winner is the first player to do so.

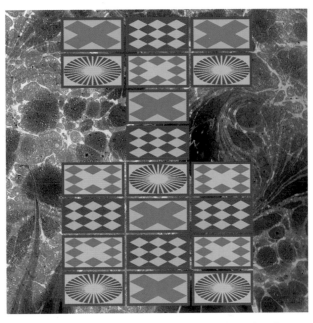

The Royal Game of Ur requires a special board. The order of events in this ancient game is decided in part by rolling the six pyramid-shaped dice. The other accessories required are seven game pieces for each player, and plenty of go pieces to use as betting tokens.

Players	Requirements
2	special game board
	7 each, red and blue game pieces
Average duration	6 pyramid-shaped, four-sided dice
30 minutes	(or 3, to be shared)
	50 go pieces to use as
Category	betting tokens
racing	

Rules:
Preliminaries

The board in the Royal Game of Ur is divided into three sections. The first is used exclusively by the owner of the red pieces, and the squares on the second are for the blue pieces. There are six squares on each of the two long sides of the board. The third is the middle column of the board, which consists of eight squares. This part is used by both players. Of the total of twenty squares, sets of five are marked and colored differently.

The six four-sided dice each have two marked corners. Each player gets three dice at the start of the game (or three can be shared by the two players). One player throws his dice up in the air, and the other player must guess how they will land—whether

with a marked or a blank corner on top. If he guesses right, he can choose the color of pieces and which side of the board he wants to use. He also gets to make the first move. Of course, if he guesses wrong, he gets none of these things. After this step, players divide up the pieces and take a seat at one of the long sides of the board. Before starting, they must decide what the wager will be. In this case, players use go pieces. In lieu of a set of go pieces, players

DIAGRAM A:
A board for the Royal Game of Ur with the accessories for the game.

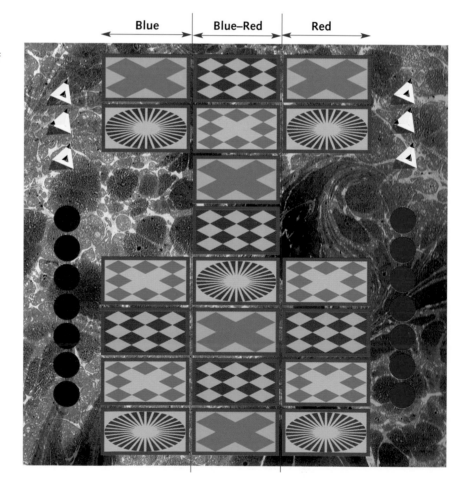

Blue   Blue–Red   Red

can use matches or any other chips or tokens they please. Other possible tokens include candy, pearls, beans, or change. In any case, one should have plenty of tokens on hand. Twenty-five is a common number. Finally, players decide how many of these to bet, and how many they must pay per turn throughout the game. Once these matters are decided, the first player can roll the dice (Diagram A).

Rolling the Dice

From the foregoing, it is clear that the squares on the board are all free at the start of the game. A roll of the dice decides whether a player can add a piece or not, and later, how many spaces the piece can move. The player whose turn it is rolls three dice on the table at once. To evaluate the roll, you look at the points on the tops of the pyramids. There are four possible combinations, each of which yields a different result:

- Three marked points: move five spaces or add a piece and roll again.
- Three unmarked points: move four spaces and roll again.
- Two unmarked points and one marked point: move no spaces and pass the dice.
- One unmarked point and two marked points: move one space and roll again.

A piece can be added only if the roll yields three marked points. Players often get more than one roll per turn (Diagram B).

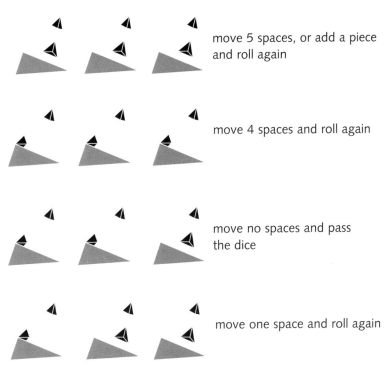

move 5 spaces, or add a piece and roll again

move 4 spaces and roll again

move no spaces and pass the dice

move one space and roll again

DIAGRAM B:
Rolling the dice. These are the four possible permutations, each offering different results.

Capturing Pieces

How the pieces move is shown in Diagram C. Every piece is shielded from enemy attacks as long as it sits in one of its own squares, because these squares are off-limits to the other player. As soon as a piece moves to the center of the board, it can encounter enemy pieces. In these eight center squares, the pieces can capture one another. This means that each player has eight "combat squares" and six "safe squares." When a piece lands on a square in the middle of the board that has already been taken by an enemy piece, it eliminates the piece on that square. The piece is removed from the board and returned to its keeper. This player will have to roll three marked points in order to put the captured piece back on the board. Players need not capture

pieces every time they have the chance, but doing so stops the enemy from reaching his goal, so it is a good idea to capture if the opportunity arises (Diagram D).

DIAGRAM C:
How the pieces move. This is the course the pieces must complete around the board. There cannot be more than one piece on any square.

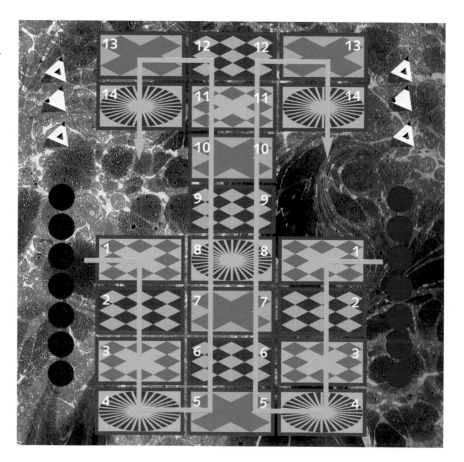

The Wager

At the start of the game, players bet a certain number, say, two tokens (e.g., go pieces) per player, for a total pot of four tokens. Over the course of the game, the pot will grow larger. This has to do with the five circular spaces on the board. Each player has two of these, and the fifth space in the middle of the board is used by both. Every time a player puts a piece on one of these spaces, his opponent is assessed a penalty point and pays a fine of one or more tokens into the pot. The fine can be whatever the players decide at the start of the game, but it is usually one token.

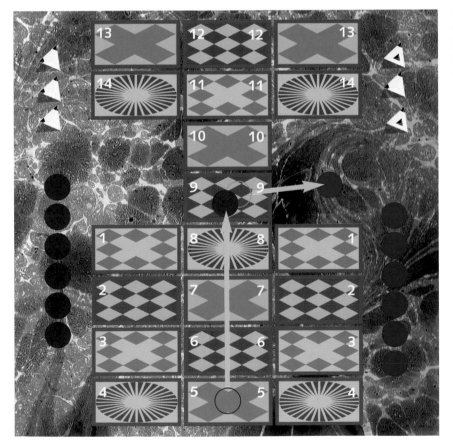

DIAGRAM D:
Capturing pieces. When a piece lands on a square in the middle section of the board that is already taken by an enemy piece, the enemy piece is captured.

Removing the Pieces

The object of the game is for all a player's pieces to run their course and then leave the board. To remove a piece from the board, its player must roll exactly the right number of points needed to move it out. This means, for example, that to remove a piece from square 14, the player must roll a one (one unmarked point and two marked points on the dice). If a piece is on square 11 and the player rolls a four (three unmarked points), he can take the piece off the board. But if he rolls a five (three marked points), the piece must stay in square 11. Players would do well to separate the pieces they remove from the others, to avoid mixing them up with captured pieces that have yet to re-enter the board and run their course (Diagram E).

VARIATION

Players can also play under a "penalty point" system in which the loser gets a penalty point for every piece remaining on the board. The final loser is the first player to receive ten or more penalty points.

VARIATION

To change the rules of the game, sometimes players agree to be able to put several pieces of the same color in a single square. The circular spaces, however, are always excluded from this rule.

Finishing

Players in a game of Ur have a lot freedom of choice. If a player rolls a five, he can make the choice of moving a piece already on the board or of adding a new piece. Also, a player does not have to capture a piece every time he gets the chance; players can decide for themselves which piece they will move in any given turn. There is one important condition, however, that players must always respect: they must use a roll whenever possible, even if it results in an unfavorable move.

The Winner

The winner is the first player to take all seven of his pieces off the board. The winner is compensated with the contents of the pot.

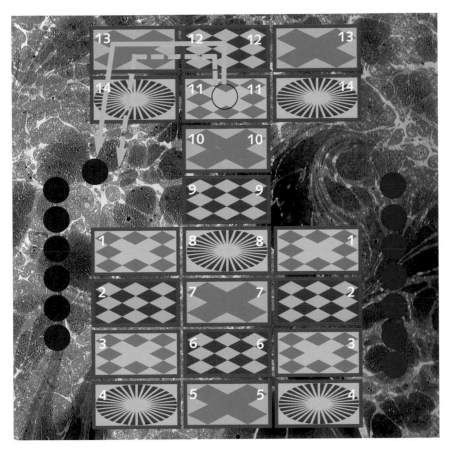

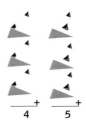

DIAGRAM E:
Removing pieces. A piece can be removed from the board only when the player rolls the exact number of points needed to move it past the final square.

When playing in a competition, there are several ways to decide the final winner. The winner can be the player who has won the most matches of a predetermined number. It can also be fun to agree that the winner will be the player who earns the most tokens after a given number of matches. In this case, players jot down the number of tokens won after each match. In the latter scheme, it is possible to win the competition without having won the most matches.

The First Match

At this point, the reader understands enough theory to begin a first game of Ur. In practice, it's been found that beginners play very differently from experienced players. A player's approach to the game evolves over time, and it's important to develop personal strategies and become aware of the opportunities and the risks that you can expect in every match. The following opening game situations are designed to give beginners the lay of the land.

The Right Balance

1 The more pieces a player has on the board, the more chances he has of impeding his own mobility. Since there can never be more than one piece on a single square, it is quite likely that any given roll will be useless because it would result in moving a piece into an occupied square. This risk also exists for pieces in the eight squares in the middle of the board, where they are unprotected from enemy attack. Thus, it's important to leave this section of the board as soon as possible.

DIAGRAM 1:
The right balance. Red has four pieces in a vulnerable position, and hampers his own mobility with several others. Blue's position is more balanced and offers more options.

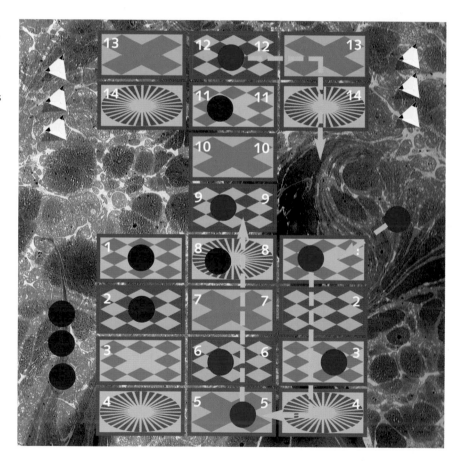

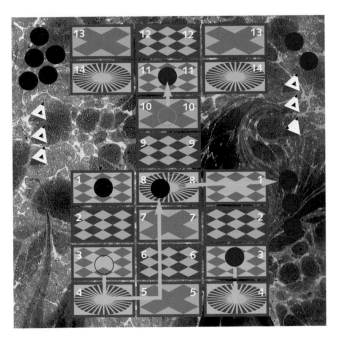

DIAGRAM 2:
The squares decorated with circular patterns. Blue kills two birds with one stone by eliminating an enemy piece and forcing him to pay a fine. Red is afraid of losing, so he does not put any pieces in his circle-squares.

If you keep these factors in mind, you will probably reach the conclusion that it's better not to put too many pieces on the board all at once. But not having enough pieces is also a problem, because then it's likely you will not be able to use a roll because none of your pieces can move the number of points rolled. Your goal should be to find the right balance between the pieces you have both on and off the board. In any event, it's always a good idea to leave one piece in your own section. Then, when you remove a piece from the board, you can still keep moving with a piece from your own section. If you do not, you risk having to pass up several turns before rolling a five and being able to add a new piece.

The foregoing principle is demonstrated in Diagram 1. There are six red pieces on the board, four of which are in the middle section of the board.

Red rolls a four. He cannot add his final piece to the board, and cannot remove his piece from square 12. Red can move the piece on square 3, but doing so would put it in a vulnerable position. The best option seems to be to move the piece on square 9. He could also move his piece on square 6. Red cannot move any other pieces because they are all blocked by one of his own. The next roll could yield some interesting options. Blue has arranged his pieces very differently: two in the middle squares, two in his own section, and three off the board. If he rolls a four, he can capture an enemy piece with three of his pieces, or remove the piece on square 11 from the board. It's clear that Blue's more balanced position offers more options and greater protection (Diagram 1).

The Squares with Circular Patterns

2 When the players agree that the player with the most tokens wins the game, it is undoubtedly good strategy to control the squares with circular patterns. The more often you put a piece on one of these squares, the more the pot will grow. In theory, the ideal move would be to put a piece on square 8, when that square is occupied by an opponent's piece. Capturing on this square means killing two birds with one stone: the enemy loses a piece and has to pay a fine. It's a good idea not to leave pieces in these circle-squares for very long. After all, it gives your other pieces the opportunity to land on one of these squares and add up more tokens. But sometimes it's better to avoid these special squares altogether, if you think you might lose the game. That way, you can try to keep the pot from growing.

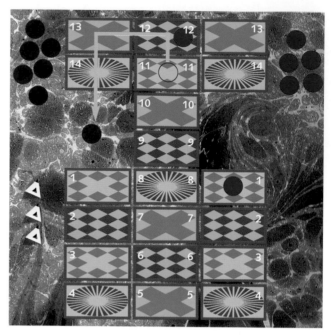

DIAGRAM 3:
The final position. Red has to roll three ones before he can remove the piece on square 12 from the board. Blue wins by rolling a four and removing his final piece.

In Diagram 2, Blue has taken five of his pieces off the board. On his turn, he rolls a five and captures the red piece on square 8. Now red has to put that piece back on the board, and must add a token to the pot. So far, Red has taken only two pieces off the board and is worried he might lose. Thus, when he rolls a one, he does not move his piece from square 3 into the nearest circle-square but instead moves his piece from square 10 to 11 (Diagram 2).

The Final Position

3 Often after a roll, players can choose to move any of several pieces. When choosing a piece, they should keep a few things in mind, such as the possibility of capturing, or of putting a piece on a circle-square. It's also useful to make a few calculations, which can save you a lot of time. A roll of the dice can result in moving a piece one, four, or five spaces. If a piece is on square 12, it means that before its owner can remove it from the board, he will have to roll three ones to reach the end. If you are aware of this, you will naturally try to keep your pieces out of such disadvantageous positions. In Diagram 3 you can see that Red still hasn't realized this. He still has to remove two pieces from the board, one of which is in square 12. Blue has made better calculations. He rolls a four and takes the last of his pieces off the board. He wins the game, and takes the pot (Diagram 3).

Thaayam
Nature of the Game

◆ ◆ ◆

Thaayam is a special kind of board game. It originated in southern India, where it was originally played only by women and girls. This was a result of the division of labor between men and women, and not to a lack of interest on the part of men. When it was almost time to harvest the rice, the women had to spend many days in the rice fields, scaring away birds, and passed the time playing all kinds of games. Thaayam appears to have been their favorite. This fascinating game is played on a square board with four unusual, blank dice that have three black sides and three white. In very remote times, Thaayam players made their own dice using cubical tamarind seeds, which are chocolate colored. Three of their sides were whitened by sanding them down with a stone, so that the shell disappeared, leaving the tiny pit exposed. The winner of this game is the first player to take four of his own pieces off the board.

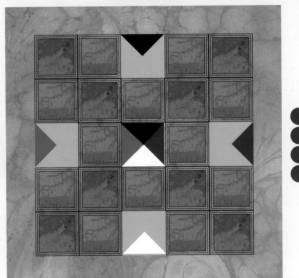

DIAGRAM A:
The Thaayam board and other accessories.

Players	Requirements
2, 3, or 4	five-by-five game board with special markings
Average duration	4 each, red, blue, green, and white pieces
30 minutes	4 special dice
Category	
racing (spiral)	

Rules:
Preliminaries

The Thaayam board is made up of a grid of five-by-five squares. The center square is specially marked and is known as "the castle." The middle square on each side is also marked. These are the "palaces," of which each player has one. Each player gets four pieces, and they must use pieces of a different color, which should be stackable. Stackable pawns or poker chips are ideal for playing Thaayam (Diagram A).

Players put the board on the middle of the table, and each sits at one side. They leave their pieces beside the board, in front of their respective palaces. There are several ways to decide who begins. Players often roll a conventional die, and the high roller makes the first move. When two or more players roll the same number, they must roll again. They can also decide using the Thaayam dice. The following section discusses the value of the possible rolls of the Thaayam dice. At the end of his turn, the first player passes the dice to the player to his right (the players take turns counterclockwise).

Rolling the Dice

As with normal dice, the result of a roll is decided according to the points on the top of each die. The four Thaayam dice are blank, but each has three dark sides and three light sides. What counts is how many dice land with a light side up. Since the four dice are rolled all at once, the number of possibilities ranges from zero to four. These are the possible permutations and their respective point values:

- one light side: one point;
- two light sides: two points, and the turn is over;
- three light sides: two points, and the turn is over;
- four light sides: four points;
- no light sides: eight points.

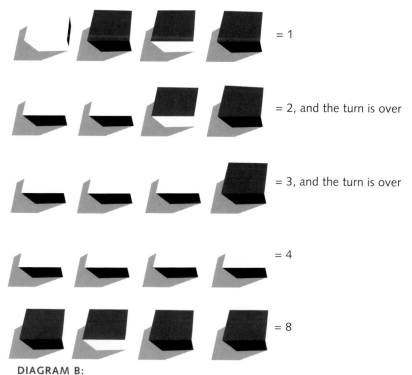

DIAGRAM B:
Rolling the dice. The five possible rolls and their point values.

Each player rolls the dice until obtaining a two or a three; only then can he move one or more of his pieces. Thus, players do not necessarily move after every roll, but perhaps only after they have completed all their rolls. Players note down what they rolled so as not to forget (Diagram B).

How the Pieces Move

The game begins with an empty board. Players must roll a one before they can put a piece on the board. Every piece enters the board through the players' respective palaces, and then moves counterclockwise around the board through the squares along the sides. When they reach the square to the left of the palace, the pieces change direction. From this point on, they move clockwise through the inner squares. Finally, they enter the castle, passing through the

square immediately above the palace. The final goal of each piece is to leave the board, so the players remove the pieces after they reach the castle (Diagram C). They must roll a one, and can remove a piece only if they do so. In addition, they can put more than one of their own pieces in a single square. Finally, pieces may not move backward.

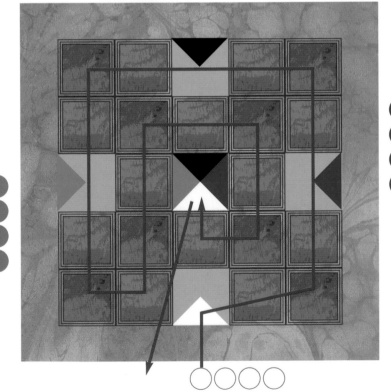

DIAGRAM C:
How the pieces move. Every piece enters the board through its palace and exits the board through the castle in the center of the board. The pieces may not move backward.

Combinations

A piece moves the number of spaces the player rolled on the dice, and a turn consists of several rolls. Players can move a different piece with each roll, and can use their rolls in any order. Suppose a player rolls the following series: one, four, one, four, two. His turn is over after the last roll, because it's a two. He can now use the ones to put two new pieces on the board, but he could also move one piece two spaces, or move two pieces one space. Another option would be to put a piece in the palace and move this piece or another one space. He could also add up the two fours and the two from the other rolls and move a single piece ten squares, or he could use these rolls to move two or three different pieces. Obviously, the player could also move one piece a grand total of twelve squares. This example shows that in Thaayam, players have a great deal of freedom to choose how they move their pieces (Diagram D).

TIP

It's a good idea to put away the pieces you remove from the board so they will not be mistaken for captured pieces.

Players must use every roll in a given turn, unless it's absolutely impossible to do so. This happens, for instance, when a player has not yet put any pieces on the board. Suppose a player in this situation rolls eight, four, one, four, then three points. The first rolls, the eight and the four, are lost, because he cannot move any of his pieces. With the one, he puts his first piece on the board, and then moves four and three, or three and four spaces, for a total of seven spaces. As mentioned above, players can use their rolls in any order. If a player still has no pieces on the board, this holds for every roll after the one, because this is the roll he must get to put a

DIAGRAM D:
Combinations. Players must use every one of their rolls if possible. They can move a different piece for each roll, or form any combination they wish.

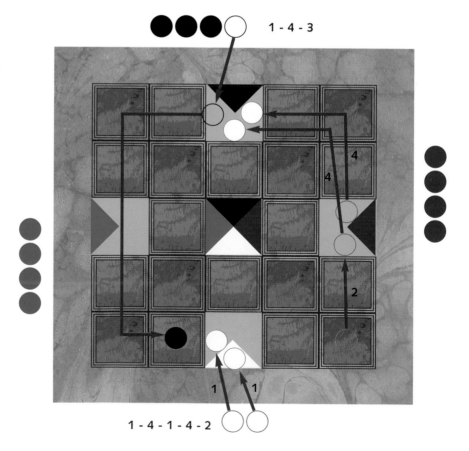

piece on the board. Any roll before the one is lost; nor can the player split a roll between two pieces. If, for instance, he rolls an eight, he must move one piece eight spaces.

Capturing Pieces

Pieces are captured in the usual manner in Thaayam. When a piece lands on a square already occupied by the other player's piece, the latter is eliminated and removed from the board. This holds true when a player combines two rolls. If a player adds, for instance, the three and four rolls, he can also capture enemy pieces in the third or fourth square. Captured pieces are returned to their owner, who must then roll another one before returning them to the board, through their respective palaces. More than one piece of the same color can coexist

in a single square, but the player risks having these pieces captured all at once. When a piece lands on a square occupied by two or more enemy pieces, the enemy pieces are captured all at once. These pieces must also be reintroduced, one by one, through their owner's palace. When a player captures an enemy piece, he gets an additional turn. Note, however, that players are not forced to capture pieces every time they have the chance to do so.

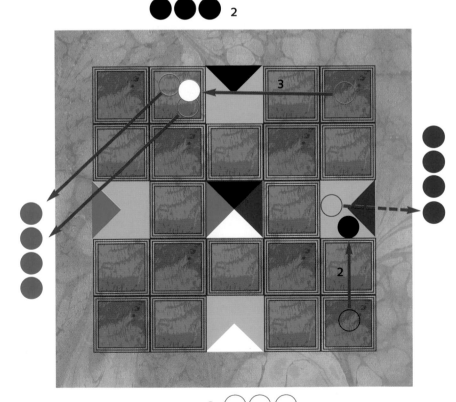

DIAGRAM E:
Capturing pieces. When a piece lands on a square occupied by one or more enemy pieces, the enemy pieces are captured. Pieces inside a palace or inside the castle are shielded from attack.

There are squares on which pieces may not capture one another; on these squares, they are shielded from attack. These are the five marked spaces on the board—the four palaces and the castle. These are safe ports, which symbolize the sacred status of a guest. When a piece takes lodging in an enemy palace, he may not be attacked. Thus, there can be any number of pieces belonging to any player seeking asylum on these special squares at one time (Diagram E).

Twins

The "twins" variation guarantees excitement, as well as an additional challenge. Twins are two stacked pieces of the same color. When a player puts two of his pieces in the palace across from his own, he can decide to have these pieces carry on as twins. If he does not, they will continue as individual pieces, and the same rules apply as before. In the latter case, the pieces are not stacked, but placed side by side.

The most important rule with respect to twins is that only a twin can capture another twin. Conversely, a twin can be captured only by an enemy twin. An individual piece can move into a square occupied by a twin without fear of capture. The movement of twins can also end in a space occupied by an enemy, but the twins may not capture that

piece. Twins may not capture single pieces, nor can they be captured by single pieces. Like individual pieces, twins are shielded from attack inside the marked spaces.

Twins move half the number of squares the player rolled on the dice. Odd numbers are "corrected" by subtracting a one. Suppose a player rolls the series four, one, four, two. If he subtracts a one from this total, he gets ten points. Since the twins move half the total spaces of any given roll, here they will move five squares. Also, when a player has twins, he may combine moves. In this example, he can decide to move his twins four spaces, or half of the two eight rolls, and then move a single piece three spaces. This means that twins arriving at the castle immediately revert to two single pieces. First, the pieces' owner must immediately break the stack up and separate the two pieces. But there might be so many pieces in this square that there is not enough room to do this, so it makes sense to stack pieces on this square. The important thing is that the players all remember there can be no twins in this square (Diagram F).

TIP

If you lose a Thaayam die, you can replace it with a Senat die. The flat side corresponds to the white side, and the rounded side stands for the black.

Dead Twins

Thaayam provides two ways to reintroduce captured twins:

1. Taking the captured twins as two individual pieces. In this case, the owner must roll a one for each piece to return it to its palace.

2. Players agree that when twins are captured, they may return to the board only as such—in other words, once a twin, always a twin, until it reaches the castle. When applying this rule, players must roll two ones in a single turn in order to return a set of twins to the board. Say one of the players rolls the series four, one, eight, four, one, two. He can use the first four to move a piece four spaces, and thanks to the two ones, he can also return his twin to the palace. If he then adds the rolls eight and two, the twins can move five spaces. This player can also move another piece ten spaces, or even fourteen, if he adds the remaining four to his total roll.

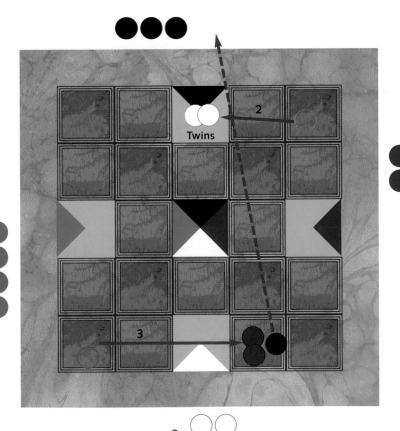

DIAGRAM F:
Twins. A player can form a set of twins with two pieces that are in the palace across from his own. Twins move half the usual number of squares (half of the points rolled) and can only capture or be captured by other twins.

It is recommended that players decide before starting a game which rule they will apply for reintroducing a set of twins to the board.

Removing Pieces

Finally, players must remove their pieces from the board. They can do so only after they get all four of their pieces into the safety of the castle. Once they start this final phase, they can continue unmolested until all their pieces have been taken off the board. Here, rolling the dice plays a very important part, because the players can remove a piece each time they roll a one. As when introducing pieces to the board, it often happens in this final stage that a player cannot use every roll. When someone rolls, for instance, the series eight, four, one, one, two, the first two rolls are lost and the player can remove just two pieces from the board. He also loses the final roll, because he can no longer remove any pieces.

The Winner

The winner is the first player to take four of his own pieces off the board. If there are more than two players, the others continue playing to decide who finishes in second, third, or fourth place. Players often use a point system, according to which the winner receives one point for each player, and each subsequent player to finish gets one point less than this. So when a game is played among four people, the winner gets four points, the player in second place gets three, the next player gets two, and the loser gets one. In this case, the final winner will be the first player to reach a predetermined number of points, such as ten.

The First Match

The time has come to play your first game of Thaayam. It's clear that luck plays an important part, since after all, a good part of the game is about rolling the dice. Since there are so many choices with regard to moving pieces, the player's concentration and strategic understanding are also very important. If you keep in mind the following tips and arguments, you may consider yourself well prepared.

Loss of Momentum

1 Thaayam is usually played by four people, each of whom generally roll the dice several times in one turn. Therefore, when a player finishes his turn, it will be a while before he goes again. The situation on the board can change considerably in the intervening period. When a player cannot use one or more of his rolls, he loses momentum. This happens regularly when there are no pieces yet on the board, and the player must wait to roll a one. But sometimes a player puts a piece in the castle only to realize that his other pieces are still off the board. This player could have avoided losing momentum if he had added another piece to his palace in time. When a player rolls a one, he must always weigh the pros and cons of adding a new piece to the board. Another advantage of having more than one piece on the board is that it increases the player's options for moving pieces, which also reduces the risk of a slowdown. Of course, players should use the marked spaces whenever possible, where the pieces are protected from enemy attacks.

Diagram 1 shows that Green has not taken into account the risk of a slowdown. He rolls four, eight, four, and two. He uses the first roll to put his only piece on the board in the castle. This means he now has to roll a one, so he loses his other three rolls. Red should put a piece in his own palace to prevent the same thing from happening. Black and White have all their pieces on the board, so for the moment, they are not at risk of losing speed (Diagram 1).

Twin Sense and Nonsense

2 Players would do well to weigh the pros and cons of twins before playing the game. Here, too, they must consider what agreement they reached with regard to reintroducing eliminated twins into play. Starting from the principle, "once a twin, always a twin," it can be very disadvantageous to have one of these duos. Suppose Red has two pieces in the castle and also has a set of twins. If the twins are captured, it can be a long time before he can reintroduce them into his palace.

Twins do not move as quickly as individual pieces, which can be a drawback. They tend to be useful when one or more players already have one, because a twin can be captured only by another twin. It makes sense, then, to form a set of twins as soon as one of the other players has one. If not, the player with the only twins has a valuable monopoly position.

In Diagram 2, it is Black's turn. He rolls an eight and a two. He uses the second roll to move his twins one space. Thus, he captures the red twins and gets an extra turn. Now Red must roll two ones in one turn if he wants to put his twins back on the board. Black uses his eight to move a single piece from one safe square to another (Diagram 2).

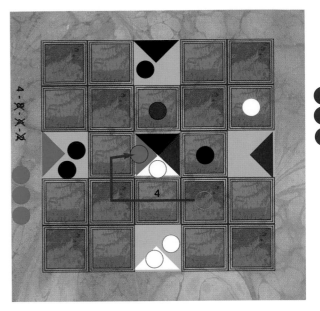

DIAGRAM 1:
A slowdown. The more pieces there are on the board, the harder it is to suffer a slowdown. Green hasn't taken this into account, so he loses three rolls. Red also risks suffering a loss of speed very soon. Black and White have more freedom of movement, since they have already put all their pieces on the board.

8 - 2

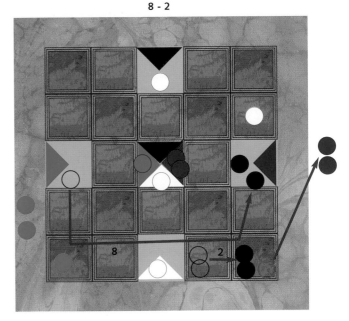

DIAGRAM 2:
Twin sense and nonsense. Twins are appealing, especially when every player has one, because only a twin can capture another twin.

Blocking the Opponent

3 Players are often so obsessed with reaching their goal that they lose sight of their opponents. Even so, it's important for them to exercise self-control and eventually join forces with one or two of them against the other(s). Once an opponent has all his pieces in the castle, it is not longer possible to block them. Thus, you must be especially careful once an opponent has three of his pieces in the castle. It is more important at this point to invest your energy in capturing the fourth piece than it is to reach your own goal. This theory also holds when the opponent has two pieces in the castle but still has a set of twins roaming around the board.

The foregoing is illustrated by Diagram 3. It's Green's turn, and he rolls four and three. He has put one piece in the castle and can add another by moving four spaces. There are two red pieces on the board, and the red twin is also near this central square. Green decides to avoid the danger of a red victory, and to wait until later to add his own piece to the castle. Instead, he captures the red twin (Diagram 3).

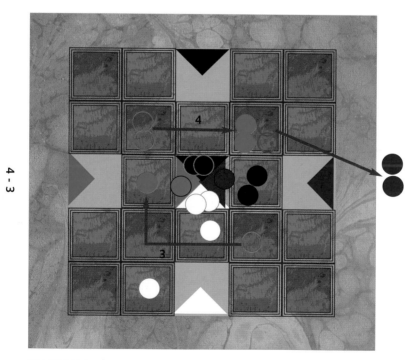

DIAGRAM 3:
Blocking the opponent. When all a player's pieces are in the castle, he can no longer be blocked. Green can put a piece in the castle or capture the red twin. He chooses the latter, because Red is dangerously close to winning.

Index

Agon, 277–286
  basics (players, duration,
    materials, category), 277
  blocking, 285
  board, 277
  capturing pieces, 279–280, 284
  evaluating game, 286
  loss by speed, 283
  match example, 282–286
  moving pieces, 278–279
  nature of, 277
  opening moves, 281, 282
  piece names, 277
  preliminaries, 278
  winning, 279–280, 286
Alquerque, 199–210
  Base variation, 210
  basics (players, duration,
    materials, category), 201
  boards, 201, 209
  capturing pieces, 202–203,
    206
  checkers and, 380
  counterattack, 205
  difficult case, 208
  final struggle, 207–208
  game example, 204–208
  history of, 199–200
  moving pieces, 202
  object of, 201
  opening moves, 204
  preliminaries, 202
  pursuit, 205
  repelling attack, 206
  variations, 209–210
  winning, 203
Alsa, 151–152
Assault, 235–250
  advance example, 247
  basics (players, duration,
    materials, category), 237
  boards, 237, 240, 241
  capturing pieces, 239, 241,
    248
  entrapment, 244–245
  escaping siege, 248
  finishing game, 249
  Frenchmen, 238–239
  German in fortress, 246
  Germans, 238–239
  history of, 235–236
  manipulations, 246
  match example, 243–249
  moving pieces, 238–239
  object of, 237
  opening moves, 243
  playing with space, 244
  winning, 242, 249–250

Backgammon, 7–18
  automatic raising, 17
  basics (players, duration,
    materials, category), 9
  bearing off, 15
  blocking, 11

board, 9
  capturing pieces, 14
  doubling cube, 16–17
  gammon and backgammon
    defined, 18
  history of, 7–8
  meaning and evolution, 8
  moving pieces, 12
  object of, 9
  preliminaries, 10
  rolling dice, 10–11
  rolling doubles, 12–13
  rules, 10–18
  tabula and, 7, 559
  winning, 18
Bashne, 571–584
  basics (players, duration,
    materials, category), 571
  beginning game, 578–579
  board, 571
  capturing pieces, 573–575,
    580
  final position, 583, 584
  history of, 569–570
  kings, 576, 580, 581
  match example, 578–584
  moving pieces, 572, 573
  multiple capture/threat of
    king, 580
  object of, 571
  preliminaries, 572
  Shashki and, 569
  towers, capturing, 574–575
  weighing every move,
    582–583
  winning, 577
Belgian checkers, 162
Bergen (dominoes), 77–78
Bidou, 337–348
  basics (players, duration,
    materials, category), 337
  betting, raising, folding,
    340–341, 344–345
  continuation, 342
  dice vocabulary, 337, 348
  final chips, 347
  first round, 339–340
  history of dice games and,
    335–336
  match example, 346–348
  for more than two players,
    343–345
  penalties, 346
  possible combinations, 338
  preliminaries, 338
  rolling dice, 339–340
  second/third rounds, 342
  ties, 348
  for two players, 339–343
  winning, 342
Bonzo the Dog, 30
Brepols' Goose, 147, 148–149

Cat and Birds checkers, 161
Checkers. See Bashne; Chinese
    checkers; English checkers;
    Polish checkers
Chimera of Gold, 393–402
  backward moves, 400, 401

basics (players, duration,
    materials, category), 393
  board, 393
  calculating path, 398
  capturing pawns, 395, 396
  evaluating game, 402
  finishing game, 397, 401, 402
  history of, 393
  match example, 398–402
  moving pawns, 394–395
  object of, 393
  obstacles, 396, 399–400
  preliminaries, 394
  variation, 397
  winning, 397
Chinese checkers, 475–484
  basics (players, duration,
    materials, category), 477
  boards, 476, 477, 482
  closed formations, 484
  evaluating game, 484
  history of, 475–476
  ladders, 483
  levels of play, 477, 482
  match example, 482–484
  moving pieces, 479–480, 481
  number of players/placement
    of pieces, 478
  preliminaries, 478
  winning, 481
Chinese chess, 211–234
  basics (players, duration,
    materials, category), 213
  bifurcated attacks, 224
  blocking, 231
  boards, 212, 213
  cannons, 214, 216, 219, 223,
    227–229
  capturing pieces, 218
  chariots, 214, 216, 219, 227
  checkmate, 218, 233–234
  Chinese names for, 211
  elephants, 214, 217, 219, 221
  emperors, 214, 215, 219, 221,
    230
  in fortress, 230
  history of, 211–212
  horses, 214, 216, 217, 219,
    222, 229–230
  ideal situation, 231–232
  mandarins, 214, 215, 219
  match example, 226–234
  moving pieces, 215–217, 219,
    221–224, 226–234
  object of, 213
  opening moves, 226, 232–233
  piece names/symbols, 214,
    215–217
  piece values, 219
  preliminaries, 214–215
  protecting emperor, 230
  soldiers, 214, 217, 218, 219,
    222, 230
  stalemate, 218, 235
  starting game, 215
  time limits, 220
  winning, 220
Chinese dominoes, 105–106
Coan Ki, 677–688

basics (players, duration,
    materials, category), 679
  blocking, 684, 685
  board, 678, 679
  distribution of pieces, 686
  doubles, 682, 683
  finishing game, 685, 688
  history of, 677–678
  lines, 682–683
  match example, 686–688
  moving pieces, 681–682
  penalty roll/fine system,
    683–684
  pieces, 678
  preliminaries, 680–681
  rolls explained, 682–684
  winning, 679, 685–686
Craps, 541–556
  basics (players, duration,
    materials, category), 543
  bets, 548, 549–556
  big bets, 554
  board (table), 543, 547, 548
  calculating probabilities,
    548–549
  come/don't-come bets,
    550–552
  come-out bets, 555–556
  craps defined, 545
  dice, 542
  example of play, 546–547
  field bets, 554
  hardway bets, 555–556
  history of, 541–542
  initial rolls, 545–546
  naturals defined, 545
  one-roll bet options, 555–556
  overview, 543
  pass line/don't-pass line bets,
    549
  place bets, 553–554
  point defined, 545
  preliminaries, 544
  recouping chips, 556
  rolling dice, 544
  winning, 556

Dablot Prejjesne, 655–666
  basics (players, duration,
    materials, category), 657
  blocks, 665–666
  board, 656, 657
  capturing pieces, 660–661,
    664–665
  history of, 655–656
  match example, 663–666
  moving pieces, 659
  multiple captures, 664–665
  object of, 657
  one-on-one combat, 661–662
  opening moves, 663–664
  pieces, 656
  preliminaries, 658
  winning, 662, 663
Diagonal checkers, 162
Dice games. See also specific
    games
  history of, 335–336
  slang vocabulary, 337, 348

Dice poker, 173–186
basics (players, duration, materials, category), 175
betting on, 178
building variation, 184–185
calling and covered calling, 180–181
flow of game, 177
game example, 179
Golden Rules, 185
history of poker and, 173–174
liar variation, 182–183
by numbers, variation, 185–186
object of, 175
with penalty points, 178
possible combinations, 176
preliminaries, 176
undercalling, 182
values, 177
variations, 180–186
winning, 177
Dominoes. See also Tsung Shap
advanced players, 73
alphabetical, example, 87
basics (players, duration, materials, category), 71
blocked matches, 74, 78
block game, 73–74
distributing tiles, 72
"draw" vs. "block," 72
history of, 69–70
making first move, 73
match example, 75–76
placing tiles, 72
preliminaries, 72
rounds, 74, 75–76
rules, 72–73, 74. See also Dominoes variations
winning, 74, 78
Dominoes variations. See also Forty-Two (dominoes); Solo dominoes
Bergen, 77–78
Chinese dominoes, 105–106
Fools, 79–80
Tien Gow, 99–104
Duodecim Scripta, 287–298
basics (players, duration, materials, category), 289
blocked pieces, 294, 297
boards, 288, 289
capturing pieces, 293–294
evaluating game, 298
final phase, 294–295, 298
fritilus (dice cup), 288
grave error, 297, 298
history of, 287–288
match example, 296–298
moving pieces, 292–293
object of, 289
preliminaries, 290
putting pieces on board, 291
rolling dice, 290–291
winning, 295

English checkers, 153–162
basics (players, duration, materials, category), 155

Belgian checkers variation, 162
blocking to win, 160
board, 155
capturing pieces, 156–157
capturing to win, 160
Cat and Birds variation, 161
classic traps, 159
crowning, 157–158
diagonal checkers variation, 162
history of, 153–154
match example, 158–160
moving pieces, 156
preliminaries, 156
variations, 161
winning, 158, 160

Fools (dominoes), 79–80
Forty-Two (dominoes), 81–94
basics (players, duration, materials, category), 81
bidding and raising, 84–85
considerations, 89
distributing tiles, 83
finishing game, 86, 94
match example, 87–97
point values and scoring, 82–83, 94
preliminaries, 82
preparation, 88–89
tricks, 85, 89–93
trumps, 83
winning, 86

Go, 299–334
atsumi, 323–324
basics (players, duration, materials, category), 301
black's sphere of influence, 327
board, 301
capture go version, 304–305
capturing pieces, 304
chains, 303
counting points, 310–312, 313
dividing and conquering, 322
double atari, 308, 310
draw (jigo), 313
exception to "less groups" rule, 321
excessive groups, 320, 321
eyes (true and false), 307–308
fill-in method, 313, 314
flexible arrangement, 319–320
groups (living and dead), 306–307
history of, 299–300
importance of corners, 317, 318
kakari, 318–319
ko rule, 305
ladders, 316
liberties, 303
match example, 326–334
Ming Mang on go board. See Ming Mang

object of, 301
opening moves, 326
optical illusions, 317
preliminaries, 302, 326
putting pieces on board, 302–303
seki, 308
serial atari, 309, 311
shimari, 318
strategies, 316–323
suicide, 304
tallying points, 334
terminology, 314
territorial, 306
virtues and, 300
webs, 316–317
winning, 313
Goose, 141–152
Alsa variation, 151–152
basics (players, duration, materials, category), 143
boards, 142, 143, 147, 151
Brepols' variation, 147, 148–149
end of run, 146–147
history of, 141–142
human life cycle and, 142
match example, 144–147
monkey variation, 149–150
moving/capturing pawns, 145, 146
norms and values, 142
numerical symbols, 142, 146
object of, 143
preliminaries, 144
variations, 148–152
winning, 147

Hasami Shogi, 513–522
basics (players, duration, materials, category), 513
beginner variation, 522
behind lines, 521
board, 513
capturing pieces, 515, 516
changing plans, 519, 520
evaluating game, 522
finishing game, 516, 517, 522
match example, 518–522
moving pieces, 514–515
open end danger, 520
opening moves, 519
preliminaries, 514
winning, 517
Hasami Shogi (war game), 513, 523–526
basics (players, duration, materials, category), 523
board, 523
capturing pieces, 525
finishing game, 526
moving pieces, 524
preliminaries, 524
winning, 526
Hex, 449–460
alternate games on board, 459–460
basics (players, duration, materials, category), 449

board, 449
corner cells, 451, 452
evaluating game, 457–458
final moves, 456
good lines, 453
intermediate moves, 455–456
match example, 454–458
nature/history of, 449
opening moves, 454
positioning pieces, 451
preliminaries, 450
Who's Got the Loot? game, 459–460
winning, 453
Horse races, 251–264
basics (players, duration, materials, category), 253
betting on, 263
boards, 253, 256, 261, 262, 264
capturing pieces, 255
Clingendaels variation, 263–264
example of play, 256
game example, 259–260
history of, 251–252
Jockey variation, 262–263
Lucky Race Game, 261–262
moving pieces, 254–255
object of, 253
preliminaries, 254
special squares, 256–258
variations, 261–264
winning, 258, 259, 260

Jinx, 425–434
basics (players, duration, materials, category), 425
capturing and jinxing, 428, 432–433
finishing game, 429, 433–434
for four, 425, 429–430
match example, 431–434
moving pieces, 427
nature of, 425
opening moves, 431–432
preliminaries, 426
strategic positions, 432–433
for three, 425, 430
winning, 429
Jungle, 265–276
basics (players, duration, materials, category), 265
blocking, 274
boards, 265, 274
capturing pieces, 267, 268
double threats, 275
ending game, 275
evaluating game, 276
importance of teamwork, 272
match example, 271–276
moving pieces, 267, 268–269, 271–276
nature of, 265
opening moves, 271
preliminaries, 266
special squares, 269–270
tiger moves, 273
winning, 270, 275

Mancala (Wari), 349–364
  attacks, 360–362
  basics (players, duration, materials, category), 351
  boards, 355, 362
  buffers, 354, 363
  capturing pieces, 353–354
  evaluating game, 362, 363
  finishing game, 356, 364
  history of, 349–350
  match example, 356–364
  midgame tactics, 359–363
  moving pieces, 353
  object of, 351
  opening moves, 357–358
  preliminaries, 352
  prohibitions, 355
  sacrificing pieces, 358
  symbolism and religious significance, 350
  twelve plus pieces in pit, 354
  winning, 356
Mastermind®, 699–710
  basics (players, duration, materials, category), 701
  board, 700, 701
  code, 703–704
  coding pieces, 704
  dénouement, 705
  history of, 699–700
  match example, 706–710
  object of, 701
  preliminaries, 702–703
  variations, 700
  winning, 705
Mikado, 403–414
  alternate names for, 404
  basics (players, duration, materials, category), 405
  drawing sticks, 407–408
  finger technique, 411
  history of, 403–404
  match example, 411–414
  Mikado (stick), 406, 408, 409
  Mikado technique, 411, 412
  object of, 405
  pile, 406–407
  preliminaries, 406
  sets, examples, 404, 410, 412, 413
  sticks and point values, 406
  tallying points, 409, 412, 414
  variation, 410
  winning, 409
Ming Mang, 619–626
  basics (players, duration, materials, category), 619
  board, 619
  capturing pieces, 621–622
  corner spaces, 624–625
  match example, 624–626
  moving pieces, 620–621
  multiple attacks, 625–626
  nature/history of, 619
  object of, 619
  preliminaries, 620
  side spaces, 626
  winning, 622–623

Nardshir (nard), 7, 689–698
  basics (players, duration, materials, category), 689
  board, 689
  capturing pieces, 691–692
  final moves/position, 698
  history of, 689
  match example, 696–698
  moving pieces, 691
  open and closed squares, 692
  opening moves, 696–697
  preliminaries, 690
  removing pieces, 694, 695
  rolling dice, 693–694
  symbolic meaning, 689
  tallying points, 694, 698
  winning, 695
Nine Men's Morris, 60, 69

Othello, 527–540
  basics (players, duration, materials, category), 529
  board, 528, 529
  capturing pieces, 531, 532–533, 539
  history of, 527–528
  match examples, 535–540
  moving pieces, 531
  multiple attacks, 533
  object of, 529
  opening moves, 530–531
  preliminaries, 530
  short game, 536
  tournaments, 528, 539–540
  unequal-strength players, 537
  value of squares, 538
  winning, 534

Pachisi, 187–198
  barriers, 192
  basics (players, duration, materials, category), 189
  boards, 188, 189, 190
  capturing pawns, 192
  charkoni, 190, 191, 193, 194
  game example, 195–198
  history of, 187–188
  moving pawns, 191
  object of, 189
  passing turn, 194
  preliminaries, 190
  reincarnation and, 188
Pick-up sticks. See Mikado
Poker. See Dice poker
Polish checkers, 379–392
  basics (players, duration, materials, category), 379–380
  board, 381
  capturing pieces, 382–383
  crowning, 383–384
  ending game, 390–392
  history of, 379–380
  match example, 385–392
  midgame combinations, 389–390
  moving pieces, 382
  object of, 381
  opening moves, 385–388
  playing positions, 388

  preliminaries, 382
  winning, 384

Queen's Guard. See Agon

Renju, 415–424
  basics (players, duration, materials, category), 415
  black and white, 419–420
  evaluating game, 424
  finishing game, 420, 424
  forbidden for black, 418
  halfway point, 422–423
  match example, 421–424
  multiple sets of rules, 415
  nature/history of, 415
  opening moves, 421–422
  open threes, 416
  placing pieces, 416
  preliminaries, 416
  two open threes, 417
  winning, 420
Rithmomachia, 585–618
  ambush captures, 593, 594
  attack captures, 592, 593
  basics (players, duration, materials, category), 587
  belated encounter/attack, 613
  board, 587
  bonis, 599
  capturing pieces, 591–594
  capturing pyramids, 595–597, 598, 612
  common objectives, 598–600, 601
  corpore, 599
  encounter captures, 591, 592
  evaluating game, 608, 618
  final position, 616–617
  glorious victories (Victoria Magna/Mayor/Excelentísim, 601, 606, 607–608
  history of, 585–586
  lite, honore, honore liteque, 599–600
  match example, 610–618
  mathematical concepts, 606
  moving pieces, 589–590
  numbering principles, 602–607
  object of, 587
  opening moves, 610–611
  opening position, 588, 589, 602–604
  preliminaries, 588–589, 610
  pyramid composition and captures, 595–597, 598, 612
  round pieces, 602
  siege captures, 594, 595
  square pieces, 604, 605–606
  triangular pieces, 603–604
  winning, 600, 601, 606, 607–608
Royal Game of Ur, 711–722
  balancing pieces on/off board, 720–721
  basics (players, duration, materials, category), 713
  boards, 711, 713

  capturing pieces, 716, 717
  final position, 722
  finishing game, 718
  history of, 711–712, 713
  match example, 720–722
  object of, 713
  preliminaries, 714–715
  removing pieces, 718, 719
  rolling dice, 715
  squares with circular patterns, 721–722
  wagers, 717
  winning, 718–719
Russian checkers. See Bashne

Salta, 33–44
  basics (players, duration, materials, category), 35
  boards, 35, 38
  history of, 33–34, 44
  jumping, 37–38
  match example, 40–43
  moving pieces, 37
  object of, 35, 38
  preliminaries, 36
  solo game, 44
  winning, 39
Saxon Hnefatafl, 485–496
  basics (players, duration, materials, category), 487
  board, 488
  capturing pieces, 490, 491
  history of, 485–486, 487
  imperiled king, 495
  king, 491, 492, 495
  match example, 493–496
  moving pieces, 489, 490, 491
  opening position, 493
  preliminaries, 488–489
  strategies for white and black, 493–494
  winning, 492, 496
Senat (senet or s'ent), 163–172
  basics (players, duration, materials, category), 165
  blocking, 167
  board, 165
  capturing pieces, 167
  ending game, 171
  history of, 163–164
  marked houses, 168
  match example, 169–171
  moving past blocks, 170
  moving pieces, 166–167
  object of, 165
  preliminaries, 166
  removing pieces from board, 168
  symbolic meaning, 164, 165
  variations, 172
  winning, 168
Shashki, history of, 570. See also Bashne
Shaturnanga, 107. See also Shogi
Shogi. See also Hasami Shogi; Hasami Shogi (war game); Shogi (match example)
  about, 117